LUTHER'S WORKS

American Edition

VOLUME 44

Published by Concordia Publishing House

and Fortress Press in 55 volumes.

General Editors are Jaroslav Pelikan (for vols. 1-30)

and Helmut T. Lehmann (for vols. 31-55)

LUTHER'S WORKS

VOLUME 44

The Christian in Society

I

EDITED BY

JAMES ATKINSON

GENERAL EDITOR

HELMUT T. LEHMANN

FORTRESS PRESS / PHILADELPHIA

Library of Congress Catalog Card Number 55-9893
ISBN 0-8006-0344-3

Printed in the United States of America 1-344

GENERAL EDITORS' PREFACE

The first editions of Luther's collected works appeared in the sixteenth century, and so did the first efforts to make him "speak English." In America serious attempts in these directions were made for the first time in the nineteenth century. The Saint Louis edition of Luther was the first endeavor on American soil to publish a collected edition of his works, and the Henkel Press in Newmarket, Virginia, was the first to publish some of Luther's writings in an English translation. During the first decade of the twentieth century, J. N. Lenker produced translations of Luther's sermons and commentaries in thirteen volumes. A few years later the first of the six volumes in the Philadelphia (or Holman) edition of the *Works of Martin Luther* appeared. But a growing recognition of the need for more of Luther's works in English has resulted in this American edition of Luther's works.

The edition is intended primarily for the reader whose knowledge of late medieval Latin and sixteenth-century German is too small to permit him to work with Luther in the original languages. Those who can will continue to read Luther in his original words as these have been assembled in the monumental Weimar edition (*D. Martin Luthers Werke*. Kritische Gesamtausgabe, Weimar, 1883-). Its texts and helps have formed a basis for this edition, though in certain places we have felt constrained to depart from its readings and findings. We have tried throughout to translate Luther as he thought translating should be done. That is, we have striven for faithfulness on the basis of the best lexicographical materials available. But where literal accuracy and clarity have conflicted, it is clarity that we have preferred, so that sometimes paraphrase seemed more faithful than literal fidelity. We have proceeded in a similar way in the matter of Bible versions, translating Luther's translations. Where this could be done by the use of an existing English version—King James, Douay, or Revised Standard—we have done so. Where it could not, we have supplied our own. To indicate this in each specific instance would have been pedantic; to adopt a uniform procedure would have been artificial—especially in view of Luther's own inconsistency in this regard. In each volume the translator will be responsible primarily for matters of text and language, while the responsibility of the editor will extend principally to the historical and theological matters reflected in the introductions and notes.

Although the edition as planned will include fifty-five volumes, Luther's writings are not being translated in their entirety. Nor should they be. As he was the first to insist, much of what he wrote and said was not that important. Thus the edition is a selection of works that have proved their importance for the faith, life, and history of the Christian church. The first thirty volumes contain Luther's expositions of various biblical books, while the remaining volumes include what are usually called his "Reformation writings" and other occasional pieces. The final volume of the set will be an index volume; in addition to an index of quotations, proper names, and topics, and a list of corrections and changes, it will contain a glossary of many of the technical terms that recur in Luther's works and that cannot be defined each time they appear. Obviously Luther cannot be forced into any neat set of rubrics. He can provide his reader with bits of autobiography or with political observations as he expounds a psalm, and he can speak tenderly about the meaning of the faith in the midst of polemics against his opponents. It is the hope of publishers, editors, and translators that through this edition the message of Luther's faith will speak more clearly to the modern church.

J. P.
H. T. L.

CONTENTS

ABBREVIATIONS

CIC — *Corpus Iuris Canonici,* edited by E. Friedberg (Graz, 1955).

CL — *Luthers Werke in Auswahl,* edited by Otto Clemen, *et al.* (Bonn, 1912-1933; Berlin, 1955-1956).

C. R. — *Corpus Reformatorum,* edited by C. G. Bretschneider and H. E. Bindseil (Halle/Saale, 1834-1860).

EA Var. arg. — *D. Martin Luthers Sämmtliche Werke.* Erlanger Ausgabe: Opera latina varii argumenti ad reformationis historiam imprimis pertinentia (Frankfurt/Erlangen, 1865-1873).

LCC — *Library of Christian Classics.* John T. McNeill and Henry P. van Dusen, General Editors (Philadelphia, 1953-).

LW — American Edition of *Luther's Works* (Philadelphia and St. Louis, 1955-).

MA^3 — *Martin Luther.* Ausgewählte Werke, 3rd edition (München, 1948-).

MPL — *Patrologia, Series Latina,* 221 vols. in 222, edited by J. P. Migne (Paris, 1844-1904).

O.D.C.C. — *The Oxford Dictionary of the Christian Church,* edited by F. L. Cross (2nd ed., Oxford University Press, 1958).

PE — *Works of Martin Luther.* Philadelphia Edition (Philadelphia, 1915-1943).

PNF — *The Nicene and Post-Nicene Fathers of the Christian Church.* First Series: edited by Philip Schaff. Second Series: edited by Philip Schaff and H. Wace (New York, 1886-1900).

St. L.	– *D. Martin Luthers sämmtliche Schriften,* edited by Johann Georg Walch. Edited and published in modern German, 23 vols. in 25 (2nd ed., St. Louis, 1880-1910).
WA	– *D. Martin Luthers Werke.* Kritische Gesamtausgabe (Weimar, 1883-).
WA, Br	– *D. Martin Luthers Werke.* Briefwechsel (Weimar, 1930-).
WA, DB	– *D. Martin Luthers Werke.* Deutsche Bibel (Weimar, 1906-1961).
WA, TR	– *D. Martin Luthers Werke.* Tischreden (Weimar, 1912-1921).

INTRODUCTION TO
The Christian in Society

"Good Heavens! Spalatin, how excited you are! More than I or anyone else. I wrote you before not to assume that this affair was begun or is carried on by your judgment or mine or that of any man. If it [the Reformation] is of God, it will be completed contrary to, outside of, above, and below, either your or my understanding. . . . Let God see to it, for he acts through me, since I am certain that none of these things have been sought by me, but they were all drawn from me, one and all, by a fury not my own."[1]

"All that I have done is to further, preach and teach God's Word; otherwise I have done nothing. So it happened that while I slept or while I drank a glass of Wittenberg beer with my friend Philip [Melanchthon] and with Amsdorf, the papacy was weakened as it never was before by the action of any prince or emperor. I have done nothing; the Word has done and accomplished everything. . . . I let the Word do its work!"[2]

These statements reflect the confident spirit that distinguishes Luther's ethic: "He acts through me. . . . I let the Word do its work!" How men live, like what they believe, depends wholly on their response to the unceasing activity of the living God in their midst. Whether as revealed in his Word or as hidden in his world, it is ultimately God alone who reigns over the whole creation.

For Luther, this means that Christian ethics, like Christian dogmatics, must be at once eschatological, existential and evangelical. It must be eschatological because the eternal God and the Evil One are ultimately the chief actors at work in human history. It must be

[1] Preserved Smith (ed.), *Luther's Correspondence and Other Contemporary Letters* (Philadelphia: The Lutheran Publication Society, 1913), I, 286-287. Cf. also *WA*, Br 2, 43.

[2] *The Second Sermon, March 10, 1522, Monday after Invocavit. LW* 51, 77 (WA 10^{III}, 18-19).

existential because it is decision-making men and women whom God and the Adversary employ as the willing instruments of their rule. Finally it must be evangelical because only the gospel of Jesus Christ can truly reveal the nature of God and the meaning of human existence.

Luther's social and political thought has often been attacked by critics who have either rejected or misunderstood these biblical and theological presuppositions. For example, some sociologists of religion (Max Weber, R. H. Tawney) have shown no appreciation for the demonic dimension of Luther's eschatological ethic. Other moral philosophers (Jacques Maritain, Eduard Heimann) have been alienated by the contextual flexibility of Luther's existential ethic. Following the abortive attempt of some German Lutheran theologians (Paul Althaus, Friedrich Gogarten, Emmanuel Hirsch) to baptize the ideology of Nazism in the name of Luther's political thought, other contemporary Reformed theologians (Karl Barth, Emil Brunner, Reinhold Niebuhr) have likewise objected strongly to the dialectical opposition between the realms of law and gospel in Luther's evangelical ethic.

Our limited task here is to demonstrate the unity, not argue the validity, of Luther's ethic. We shall first outline the theological foundations of his Christian ethic of "faith active in love" and his closely interrelated social ethic of "love seeking justice" in God's interacting "two kingdoms" of redemption and creation. Then we will illustrate the important role of Christian social action in Luther's own life and thought.

For Luther the biblical message of salvation is a tension-filled unity which can be viewed from the perspective of any of its constitutive elements. He can speak of "grace alone," "Christ alone," "Scripture alone," or "faith alone," and mean thereby the same saving Event in terms of its eternal source, historical expression, apostolic witness, or personal appropriation. In fidelity to this Christ-centered faith, Luther roundly condemns the moral and rational work-righteousness inherent in the philosophical theology of Rome in his day. Reason must submit to Scripture and works must bow to faith. In an evangelical "theology of the cross," man humbly confesses that "the righteous shall live by faith" (Rom. 1:17).

With their salvation thus assured in the unmerited forgiveness of Christ, grateful Christians are free to redirect their reason and good works toward serving their neighbors' welfare. Luther grounds his ethic in the paradoxical nature of Christian freedom which accepts liberation from satanic bondage as God's invitation for human service. All men act as their brother's keeper: willingly in faith, begrudgingly in rebellion. Since the Christian is at once righteous and sinful, his enforced service aids his self-discipline while his voluntary service meets his neighbors' needs. Against the presumption of Roman clericalism, Luther insists that all baptized Christians be permitted the beneficial exercise of their royal priesthood in loving service to their God-given neighbors.

In opposition to all unevangelical ethics of principles, "blue laws," ideals, or rules and regulations, Luther portrays the biblical pattern of a life of "faith working through love" (Gal. 5:6). A Christian ethic based on the "divine indicative" of God's grace (rather than the "divine imperative" of God's law) preserves the freedom of the believer under the guidance of the Holy Spirit through the Bible, the church, and prayer, to discover anew in each concrete situation what the will of God permits or requires of him then and there.

For the biblical foundation of his social ethic, Luther rooted his doctrine of the "two kingdoms" of creation and redemption in the Pauline eschatology of the "two ages" (*aeons*), in Adam and in Christ (Romans 5). In the kingdom of God, the Redeemer rules all regenerate believers through Christ and the gospel in personal faith and love. In the kingdom of men, the Creator rules all sinful but rational creatures through Caesar and the law in civil justice and order. As both Redeemer and Creator, God is at once the Lord of both kingdoms; as both righteous and sinful, the Christian is at once a subject of both kingdoms. Hence for an evangelical theology of society, the two kingdoms must always be properly distinguished, but never separated in secularism or equated in clericalism.

By this doctrine of the "two kingdoms" of creation and redemption, Luther reaffirmed the "sacred secularity" of the ordinary tasks of the common life as those which best serve our neighbors' needs to God's glory. Whether empowered by Christ in faith-activated

love (Christian righteousness) or compelled by Caesar in law-abiding reason (civil righteousness), the Christian citizen lives not for himself but for the benefit of others.

Christian social action was clearly a major concern in Luther's life and thought. It is therefore highly appropriate that Volumes 44 to 47 of the American Edition of Luther's Works should be devoted to sermons and treatises dealing with the general theme of "The Christian in Society." The profound effects of the Reformation in the area of religion is common knowledge to all. What is not so well known—or, at least, not so commonly acknowledged—is the impressive social reformation which Luther's theology envisioned and partially brought about in the broad and inclusive expanse of the common life.

Luther's emancipation of the common life was not so popular a crusade as it might at first appear. His understanding of the Christian life compelled him to combat both unevangelical extremes of clericalism and secularism (*To the Christian Nobility*).[3] Opposing the enthusiasts, he had to fight for the preservation of music, art, and sculpture in the worship life of the church (*Against the Heavenly Prophets*).[4] Against Roman Catholics, he had to struggle for the opening of the monasteries and the freedom of all Christians to marry and to engage in secular pursuits without endangering their salvation (*The Judgment of Martin Luther on Monastic Vows,* 1521;[5] *The Estate of Marriage,* 1522;[6] *Whether Soldiers, too, Can Be Saved,* 1526).[7]

Against selfish parents and lax public officials, he also fought for educational reforms and the establishment of community chests to replace the illiteracy and begging so prevalent in his day (*A Sermon on Keeping Children in School,* 1530;[8] *Ordinance of a Common Chest, Preface,* 1523).[9] Against irresponsible merchants, he attacked economic injustice and proposed government controls to halt unfair commercial and labor practices (*Trade and Usury,* 1524).[10] Against

[3] Cf. in this volume, pp. 115-217.
[4] Cf. *LW* 40, 73-223 (*WA* 18, 62-125, 134-214).
[5] Cf. in this volume, pp. 243-400.
[6] Cf. *LW* 45, 11-49 (*WA* 10^{II}, 275-304).
[7] Cf. *PE* 5, 29-74 (*WA* 19, 623-662).
[8] Cf. *PE* 5, 133-178 (*WA* 30^{II}, 517).
[9] Cf. *LW* 45, 159-194 (*WA* 12, 11-30).
[10] Cf. *LW* 45, 231-310 (*WA* 15, 279-313, 321-322; *WA* 6, 36-60).

both the reckless mobs which confused their Christian freedom with their civil rights, and the cruel rulers who disregarded their responsibility to God for their subjects' economic and social welfare, Luther appealed for both civil obedience and—less strongly!—political justice in a community of law and order (*Psalm 82*, 1530).[11]

It is true, however, that Luther did not normally conceive of the Christian's social responsibility as transforming the existing structures of society. While persons can be transformed by the gospel in the kingdom of God, institutions can only be reformed by the law in the kingdom of men. As long as men are not required to sin against God and conscience, they care to accept the social structures for what they are (the Creator's dikes against sin), and try to act like responsible Christian citizens within these structures (as the Redeemer's channels of serving love). When our secular occupations among men are faithfully acknowledged to be part of our religious vocation under God, then love provides law with its ethical content and law provides love with its social form.

For example, against those who would spiritualize marriage into a Christian sacrament, Luther protests that marriage belongs essentially to the realm of creation and not redemption. It is therefore ruled by God's law and not his gospel, and, as such, is one of God's temporal remedies against sin and not a sanctifying means of grace.

On the other hand, against those who might misinterpret this liberating message as justification for carnal lust and license, Luther is equally insistent that marriage is rooted firmly in the creative will of God as one of his own divine ordinances. Although it is not a sacrament of the church, there is nevertheless no higher social calling in which a Christian can exercise his faith in deeds of serving love for his family and neighbors. Hence, the ex-monk Luther eventually married an ex-nun as a public testimony of faith in witness to his restoration of the evangelical view of marriage and home life under God.

For Luther's social ethic, all offices and stations of life—ecclesiastical, domestic, economic, political—embody in institutional form a particular command of God's law. They are all integrated within

[11] Cf. *LW* 13, 39-72 (WA 30^{I}, 189-218).

the earthly kingdom of men as the Creator's divinely-ordained bulwarks in his ongoing struggles against Satan.[12] There is no particularly "Christian" form of these nonredemptive "orders." Though corrupted by sin themselves, the natural "orders" are still the means by which the Creator graciously preserves his fallen world from even greater chaos, injustice, and suffering.

This is why the church can "Christianize" politicians and economists but not politics and economics. These "orders" are ordained by God to remain secular, enjoying a relative (never absolute) autonomy of their own under the sovereign law of the Creator. Hence not faith and love but reason and justice are regulative for the temporal realm of life. At the same time, however, it cannot be emphasized too strongly that faith can illumine reason and love—can temper justice whenever Christians meet their civil responsibilities as part of their religious discipleship. We need to learn anew from Luther that it is only through both the priestly service of Christian citizens and the prophetic judgment of Christian churches that society's "sacred secularity" is saved from godless secularism.

WILLIAM H. LAZARETH

[12] Cf. Lazareth, *Luther on the Christian Home* (Philadelphia, Muhlenberg Press, 1960), pp. 137-138.

INTRODUCTION TO VOLUME 44

The six works of Luther presented in this volume were written between two highly significant events. The first of these events was the debate at Leipzig in 1519 with the formidable John Eck. It was there that Luther not only challenged the inerrancy of church and councils, but went on to deny papal authority because it was contrary to Scripture, and to affirm that in matters of faith his sole authority was the Word of God.[1] The second event was the Diet of Worms in 1521, perhaps the most dramatic public event in Luther's entire career.[2]

Between these two landmarks of history Luther faced a colossal task. It became increasingly clear to all that the movement which centered about him was infinitely more than a "monkish quarrel." Luther was forced to defend the emerging Reformation against manifold attacks and to clarify his own position. At one and the same time he had to address himself to the theologians and scholars who differed from him on a wide variety of grounds (e.g., John Eck, Hieronymous Emser, Thomas Murner, Jerome Aleander, and Johann Cochlaeus), as well as those who generally agreed with him, but were apprehensive about where his theology would lead (e.g., Erasmus, Johannes von Staupitz, and, in the early stages, even George Spalatin); to Emperor Charles V, whose concept of reformation was a purified medievalism;[3] to the responsible laity, i.e., the

[1] Cf. *The Leipzig Debate*. *LW* 31, 307-325.

[2] Cf. *Luther at the Diet of Worms*. *LW* 32, 101-131.

[3] Charles stressed the unity of the medieval Catholic church, its liturgical and spiritual continuity and universality, and also its authority. Nevertheless, his support of the pope and the curia had certain reservations, and for him authority lay more in a general council than in the pope himself. Charles was disquieted, however, by the thoroughness of Luther's attack on the papacy and by Luther's shifting of authority away from the papacy, for he sensed in this a threat to secular as well as to spiritual authority. He preferred a reformation along the lines of that evolving in Spain. This, however, was not reformation as Luther conceived it, but rather a restoration of medieval piety stripped of its gross abuses. Cf. Thomas M. Lindsay, *A History of the Reformation*, Vol. I (New York: Charles Scribner's Sons, 1916), p. 264, n. 2; cf. also C. V. Wedgwood (trans.), Karl Brandi's *The Emperor Charles V* (New York: Adolf A. Knopf, 1939), pp. 124 ff., and Edward Armstrong, *The Emperor Charles V*, Vol. I (London: Macmillan Co., 1910), chaps. 1-4.

nobility; and to the common man. In the six writings presented here the reader will find Luther defending, clarifying, and expounding his views on the role of the Christian in society as he treats the problems of marriage and parenthood, works and faith, the responsibility of the Christian to church and state, vows and monasticism, confession and conscience, and the kind of life which is really good.

The first of these works is *A Sermon on the Estate of Marriage* (1519). Preached in the church in Wittenberg, this sermon extolled marriage and the godly rearing of children in an age long conditioned to the idea of celibacy as the ideal vocation.

The second writing, *Treatise on Good Works* (1520), was Luther's response to the charge of his enemies and the fears of his friends that he denied and even forbade such works. To be sure, Luther did deny the medieval scheme of salvation which held that a man's own works and efforts made him acceptable in God's sight. The gospel spoke otherwise to Luther. For him genuinely good works can issue only from faith in God. Furthermore, God provides the occasion and opportunity to do such works in the circumstances in which the Christian lives. Luther thus demolishes the false and human distinctions which designate some works as "religious" and others as "secular."

To the Christian Nobility of the German Nation Concerning the Reform of the Christian Estate (1520) is a devastating indictment of ecclesiastical corruption and social decay, accompanied by specific proposals for reform. The document reflects the hope Luther once cherished that an ecumenical council would be able to effect a reformation.[4] Such a council, he insisted, must not be controlled by Rome, for then the council would be but a farce. Luther insisted that it was the duty of the emperor and of the nobility as the chief laymen of Christendom to summon a council and to enforce its decisions. This procedure, Luther emphasized, had sound historical precedent, for it was Emperor Constantine who had convened the first ecumenical council at Nicaea. In his *To the Christian Nobility* Luther's critique and specific proposals for reform reveal the wide range of his Christian concern: from simony to pil-

[4] Cf. *On the Councils and Church* (1539). *LW* 41, 3-178.

grimages; from the curricula of the schools and universities to trade and commerce; from eating and drinking to public morals and finery.

An Instruction to Penitents Concerning the Forbidden Books of Dr. M. Luther (1521) sought to give comfort and reassurance as well as a means of defense to those to whom the sacraments were denied because they possessed or read books by Luther. At the same time this *Instruction* very clearly states what a Christian pastor's duty is toward penitents who seek release from and pardon for their sin.

In *A Sermon on the Three Kinds of Good Life for the Instruction of Consciences* (1521) Luther the pastor and preacher speaks in a forthright and direct fashion to his people about what really fulfils the will of God: cheerful and willing service issuing from faith in him who has redeemed us in Christ Jesus our Lord.

The Judgment of Martin Luther on Monastic Vows, written in 1521, is a refutation of the teaching and popular belief that there are two kinds of morality: a higher or spiritual type manifested in the taking of the vows of poverty, chastity, and obedience, and withdrawal from the world into the "religious" life; and a lower or secular morality outside of cloister walls. This lengthy but gripping treatise is both an affirmation and a confession that the life of Christian service and obedience cannot and must not be lived shut up within monastery and convent or covered with a garb, but must be lived by God's people among God's people in God's world.

I wish to express my sincere thanks to Mr. Bernard Lane, veteran of the Royal Air Force, for his assistance in the preparation of the manuscript.

J. A.

LUTHER'S WORKS

VOLUME 44

A SERMON ON THE ESTATE OF MARRIAGE

1519

Translated by James Atkinson

INTRODUCTION

In 1519 on the second Sunday after Epiphany (January 16), for which the Gospel lesson is John 2:1-11, the wedding at Cana, Luther preached on the subject of marriage. The sermon was written down by a hearer while Luther preached it, and this version was published almost immediately and without Luther's knowledge.[1] Luther was not satisfied with that version and undertook a revision, which he published in May of the same year.

In this brief sermon Luther speaks of marriage as God's gracious gift to men and women. It is God who gives a man and woman to each other; therefore, those who wish to marry should seek God's guidance in finding a spouse. Marriage, then, is far more than mating. It is a matter of choosing and accepting the spouse God gives just as Adam chose and accepted Eve as his wife.

Luther goes on to discuss the problem of lust and the desire for self-gratification which has contaminated human nature since the fall and is present even within the marital estate. This leads him to speak of marriage as a God-given hospital in which incurables are preserved from falling into graver sin. In developing his theme Luther describes marriage as a covenant of physical and spiritual fidelity. This covenant of fidelity consists of a man and a woman giving and surrendering themselves to each other not for their own desire or gratification, but for each other's need and welfare. This, Luther says, is the right kind of love.

But marriage is more than a relationship of physical and spiritual fidelity between a man and a woman, more than a hospital to contain and circumscribe physical lust and desire. Its chief end and purpose is to bear and rear children. There is no shorter road to heaven, Luther says, than to rear children in the love of God and for his service. By the same token, "Hell is no more easily earned than with respect to one's own children."[2] The greatest mistake parents can make is to indulge their children and make every kind of

[1] The text of this sermon is given in *WA* 9, 213-219.
[2] Cf. pp. 12-13.

provision for their physical wants and temporal needs while neglecting to provide for their souls. If parents cannot or will not make such provision, they should seek out those who will.

The translation of this sermon is based on the German text, *Ein Sermon von dem ehelichen Stand,* in *WA* 2, (162) 166-171.

A SERMON ON THE ESTATE OF MARRIAGE

Preface

A sermon on the estate of marriage has already been published in my name, but I would much rather it had not. I know perfectly well that I have preached on the subject, but it has never been put into writing yet, as I am about to do at this moment. For this reason I determined to revise this same sermon, and improve it as much as possible. I ask every good soul to disregard the first sermon published and discard it. Further, if anybody wants to start writing my sermons for me, let him restrain himself, and let me have a say in the publication of my words as well. There is a vast difference between using the spoken word to make something clear and having to use the written word.

A Sermon on the Estate of Marriage Revised and Corrected by Dr. Martin Luther Augustinian at Wittenberg

1. God created Adam and brought all the animals before him. Adam did not find a proper companion among them suitable for marriage, so God then said, "It is not good that Adam should be alone. I will create a helpmeet for him to be with him always." And he sent a deep sleep upon Adam, and took a rib from him, and closed his side up again. And out of this very rib taken from Adam, God created a woman and brought her to him. Then Adam said, "This is bone of my bone, and flesh of my flesh. She shall be called a woman, because she was taken from her man. This is why a man shall leave his father and mother and cleave to his wife, and the two shall be one flesh" [Gen. 2:18-24].

All of this is from God's word. These words teach us where man and woman come from, how they were given to one another, for what purpose a wife was created, and what kind of love there should be in the estate of marriage.

2. If God himself does not give the wife or the husband, anything can happen. For the truth indicated here is that Adam found no marriageable partner for himself, but as soon as God had created Eve and brought her to him, he felt a real married love toward her, and recognized that she was his wife. Those who want to enter into the estate of marriage should learn from this that they should earnestly pray to God for a spouse. For the sage says that parents provide goods and houses for their children, but a wife is given by God alone [Prov. 19:14], everyone according to his need, just as Eve was given to Adam by God alone. And true though it is that because of excessive lust of the flesh lighthearted youth pays scant attention to these matters, marriage is nevertheless a weighty matter in the sight of God. For it was not by accident that Almighty God instituted the estate of matrimony only for man and above all animals, and gave such forethought and consideration to marriage. To the other animals God says quite simply, "Be fruitful and multiply" [Gen. 1:22]. It is not written that he brings the female to the male. Therefore, there is no such thing as marriage among animals. But in the case of Adam, God creates for him a unique, special kind of wife out of his own flesh. He brings her to him, he gives her to him, and Adam agrees to accept her. Therefore, that is what marriage is.

3. A woman is created to be a companionable helpmeet to the man in everything, particularly to bear children. And that still holds good, except that since the fall marriage has been adulterated with wicked lust. And now [i.e., after the fall] the desire of the man for the woman, and vice versa, is sought after not only for companionship and children, for which purposes alone marriage was instituted, but also for the pursuance of wicked lust, which is almost as strong a motive.

4. God makes distinctions between the different kinds of love, and shows that the love of a man and woman is (or should be) the greatest and purest of all loves. For he says, "A man shall leave his

father and mother and cleave to his wife" [Gen. 2:24], and the wife does the same, as we see happening around us every day. Now there are three kinds of love: false love, natural love, and married love. False love is that which seeks its own, as a man loves money, possessions, honor, and women taken outside of marriage and against God's command. Natural love is that between father and child, brother and sister, friend and relative, and similar relationships. But over and above all these is married love, that is, a bride's love, which glows like a fire and desires nothing but the husband. She says, "It is you I want, not what is yours: I want neither your silver nor your gold; I want neither. I want only you. I want you in your entirety, or not at all." All other kinds of love seek something other than the loved one: this kind wants only to have the beloved's own self completely. If Adam had not fallen, the love of bride and groom would have been the loveliest thing. Now this love is not pure either, for admittedly a married partner desires to have the other, yet each seeks to satisfy his desire with the other, and it is this desire which corrupts this kind of love. Therefore, the married state is now no longer pure and free from sin. The temptation of the flesh has become so strong and consuming that marriage may be likened to a hospital for incurables which prevents inmates from falling into graver sin.[1] Before Adam fell it was a simple matter to remain virgin and chaste, but now it is hardly possible, and without special grace from God, quite impossible. For this very reason neither Christ nor the apostles sought to make chastity a matter of obligation. It is true that Christ counseled chastity,[2] and he left it up to each one to test himself, so that if he could not be continent he was free to marry, but if by the grace of God he could be continent, then chastity is better.[3]

Thus the doctors[4] have found three good and useful things about the married estate, by means of which the sin of lust, which flows beneath the surface, is counteracted and ceases to be a cause of damnation.

---

[1] It was not until 1523 that Luther complemented his view of marriage as a "remedy against sin" with that of marriage as an "estate of faith." Cf. Lazareth, *Luther on the Christian Home*, pp. 233-234.
[2] Cf. Matt. 19:10-12.
[3] Cf. I Cor. 7:8-10.
[4] Luther means the church's theologians.

First, [the doctors say] that it is a sacrament. A sacrament is a sacred sign of something spiritual, holy, heavenly, and eternal, just as the water of baptism, when the priest pours it over the child, means that the holy, divine, eternal grace is poured into the soul and body of that child at the same time, and cleanses him from his original sin. This also means that the kingdom of God, which is an inestimable benefit, in fact immeasurably greater than the water which conveys this meaning, is within him. In the same way the estate of marriage is a sacrament. It is an outward and spiritual sign of the greatest, holiest, worthiest, and noblest thing that has ever existed or ever will exist: the union of the divine and human natures in Christ. The holy apostle Paul says that as man and wife united in the estate of matrimony are two in one flesh, so God and man are united in the one person Christ, and so Christ and Christendom are one body. It is indeed a wonderful sacrament, as Paul says [Eph. 5:32], that the estate of marriage truly signifies such a great reality. Is it not a wonderful thing that God is man and that he gives himself to man and will be his, just as the husband gives himself to his wife and is hers? But if God is ours, then everything is ours.[5]

Consider this matter with the respect it deserves. Because the union of man and woman signifies such a great mystery, the estate of marriage has to have this special significance. This means that the wicked lust of the flesh, which nobody is without, is a conjugal obligation and is not reprehensible when expressed within marriage, but in all other cases outside the bond of marriage, it is mortal sin. In a parallel way the holy manhood of God covers[6] the shame of the wicked lust of the flesh. Therefore, a married man should have regard for such a sacrament, honor it as sacred, and behave properly in marital obligations, so that those things which originate in the lust of the flesh do not occur [among us] as they do in the world of brute beasts.

Second, [the doctors say] that marriage is a covenant of fidelity. The whole basis and essence of marriage is that each gives himself or herself to the other, and they promise to remain faithful to each

[5] Cf. I Cor. 3:21-23.
[6] Cf. Ps. 32:1; Rom. 4:7.

other and not give themselves to any other. By binding themselves to each other, and surrendering themselves to each other, the way is barred to the body of anyone else, and they content themselves in the marriage bed with their one companion. In this way God sees to it that the flesh is subdued so as not to rage wherever and however it pleases, and, within this plighted troth, permits even more occasion than is necessary for the begetting of children. But, of course, a man has to control himself and not make a filthy sow's sty of his marriage.

At this point I want to say what kind of words[7] should be used when two people are betrothed[8] to each other. The matter has been dealt with at such length, in such depth, and in such concise fashion that I myself am much too inadequate to understand it all, but I am afraid that there are many who are as married people, whom before now we thought unmarried. But because the estate of marriage consists essentially in consent having been freely and previously given one to another, and also because God is wonderfully merciful in all his judgments, I will leave it all to his care. The generally accepted formula is "I am thine, thou art mine," and though some intended it most strictly, it is not enough when they say, "I will take thee" or "I am willing to take thee" or when they use some other form of words. Nevertheless I would still prefer to consider the words in the sense in which they have been understood up to the present.

Similarly, when someone has made a clandestine betrothal, and subsequently takes another, either clandestinely or publicly, I am still not sure whether what we write about it or the judgment we make on it is altogether right. My advice is that parents persuade their children not to be ashamed to ask their parents to find a marriage partner for them. Parents should make it clear from the start that they want to advise their children so that they in their turn may remain chaste and persevere in expectation of marriage.

[7] In the earlier sermon Luther mentioned briefly the significance of the words used in betrothal. Cf. *WA* 9, 216-217.

[8] Luther generally regarded betrothal (engagement) as equivalent to marriage. Opposed to long engagements, he expressed the opinion that it would be best if engagement, marriage, and consummation took place on the same night. *WA*, TR 3, No. 3179. Cf. Olavi Lähteenmaki, *Sexus und Ehe bei Luther* ("Schriften der Luther-Agricola Gesellschaft," No. 10 [Turku, 1955]), pp. 99-128.

In return, children should not become engaged without the knowledge of their parents. You are not ashamed, are you, to ask your parents for a coat or a house? Why be foolish then, and not ask for what is far greater, a partner in marriage? Samson did it. He entered a city and saw a young maiden who pleased him. Thereupon he immediately goes back home and says to his father and mother, "I have seen a young maiden whom I love. Dear parents, get me this girl for a wife" [Judg. 14:1-2].

Third, [the doctors say] that marriage produces offspring, for that is the end and chief purpose of marriage. It is not enough, however, merely for children to be born, and so what they say about marriage excusing sin does not apply in this case. Heathen, too, bear offspring. But unfortunately it seldom happens that we bring up children to serve God, to praise and honor him, and want nothing else of them. People seek only heirs in their children, or pleasure in them; the serving of God finds what place it can. You also see people rush into marriage and become mothers and fathers before they know what the commandments are or can pray.

But this at least all married people should know. They can do no better work and do nothing more valuable either for God, for Christendom, for all the world, for themselves, and for their children than to bring up their children well. In comparison with this one work, that married people should bring up their children properly, there is nothing at all in pilgrimages to Rome, Jerusalem, or Compostella,[9] nothing at all in building churches, endowing masses, or whatever good works could be named. For bringing up their children properly is their shortest road to heaven. In fact, heaven itself could not be made nearer or achieved more easily than by doing this work. It is also their appointed work. Where parents are not conscientious about this, it is as if everything were the wrong way around, like fire that will not burn or water that is not wet.

By the same token, hell is no more easily earned than with

[9] Compostella, a Spanish town, was a famous and popular shrine. According to Spanish tradition, James the son of Zebedee was martyred there (see Acts 12:2). The name Compostella is a corruption of Giacomo Postolo, i.e., James the Apostle. Luther mentions this shrine frequently. Cf. pp. 27, 68, 70.

respect to one's own children. You could do no more disastrous work than to spoil the children, let them curse and swear, let them learn profane words and vulgar songs, and just let them do as they please. What is more, some parents use enticements to be more alluring to meet the dictates of the world of fashion, so that they may please only the world, get ahead, and become rich, all the time giving more attention to the care of the body than to the due care of the soul. There is no greater tragedy in Christendom than spoiling children. If we want to help Christendom, we most certainly have to start with the children, as happened in earlier times.

This third point seems to me to be the most important of all, as well as being the most useful. For without a shadow of doubt it is not only a matter of marital obligation, but can completely eclipse all other sins. False natural love blinds parents so that they have more regard for the bodies of their children than they have for their souls. It was because of this that the sage said, "He who spares the rod hates his son, but he who loves him is diligent to discipline him" [Prov. 13:24]. Again, "Folly is bound up in the heart of a child, but the rod of discipline drives it far from him" [Prov. 22:15]. Or again, "If you beat him with the rod you will save his life from hell" [Prov. 23:14]. Therefore, it is of the greatest importance for every married man to pay closer, more thorough, and continuous attention to the health of his child's soul than to the body which he has begotten, and to regard his child as nothing else but an eternal treasure God has commanded him to protect, and so prevent the world, the flesh, and the devil from stealing the child away and bringing him to destruction. For at his death and on the day of judgment he will be asked about his child and will have to give a most solemn account. For what do you think is the cause of the horrible wailing and howling of those who will cry, "O blessed are the wombs which have not bore children, and the breasts which have never suckled" [Luke 23:29]? There is not the slightest doubt that it is because they have failed to restore their children to God, from whom they received them to take care of them.

O what a truly noble, important, and blessed condition the estate of marriage is if it is properly regarded! O what a truly pitiable, horrible, and dangerous condition it is if it is not properly regarded! And to him who bears these things in mind the desire of the flesh may well pass away, and perhaps he could just as well take on chastity as the married state. The young people take a poor view of this and follow only their desires, but God will consider it important and wait on him who is in the right.

Finally, if you really want to atone for all your sins, if you want to obtain the fullest remission[10] of them on earth as well as in heaven, if you want to see many generations of your children, then look but at this third point with all the seriousness you can muster and bring up your children properly. If you cannot do so, seek out other people who can and ask them to do it. Spare yourself neither money nor expense, neither trouble nor effort, for your children are the churches, the altar, the testament, the vigils and masses for the dead for which you make provision in your will.[11] It is they who will lighten you in your hour of death, and to your journey's end.

---

[10] Luther uses the word *ablasz*, which also means "indulgence."

[11] Testamentary bequests endowing masses to be said in one's behalf after death were not uncommon in Luther's day. He treats this practice at some length in *To the Christian Nobility*, pp. 180-181.

TREATISE ON GOOD WORKS

1520

Translated by W. A. Lambert

Revised by James Atkinson

INTRODUCTION

In 1515 Luther was called to the pastorate of the town church of Wittenberg. To his academic responsibilities then were added those of a parish pastor, and the exercise of these pastoral duties provided the occasion for his first published works. In 1517 he published *Seven Penitential Psalms.*[1] In October of that same year, certainly with his congregation in mind, he addressed the *Ninety-five Theses* to his academic colleagues and his students.[2] The following year his *Sermon on Indulgences and Grace*[3] and that *Concerning Penitence*[4] were published for the benefit of his congregation. During the fall and winter of 1517-1518 he delivered before the Wittenberg congregation two series of sermons, one on the Ten Commandments and the other on the Lord's Prayer. These sermons were published in 1518.[5] Despite his involvement with the growing theological controversy and negotiations occasioned by the *Ninety-five Theses,* Luther continued to write and publish prolifically for the benefit of his congregation.[6]

The present *Treatise on Good Works* belongs to this body of essentially pastoral writings. In February of 1520 Luther's old friend Spalatin, private secretary to the elector, reminded him of his promise to prepare a sermon on the subject of good works and urged him to set about it.[7] The reason behind Spalatin's urging is not at all obscure. Luther had been accused by his enemies that his stress on justification by faith alone had led—and indeed would increasingly lead—to a total neglect of good works and a concomitant rise of lawlessness, license, and immorality. This accusation was a concern shared even by those who were favorably inclined

[1] Cf. *LW* 14, 137 ff.
[2] *LW* 31, 17-33.
[3] *WA* 1, 243-246.
[4] *WA* 1, 319-324.
[5] *WA* 1, 250-256; *WA* 2, 80-130.
[6] Among these writings are his *Sermon on the Estate of Marriage* (1519), in this volume, pp, 3-14, and *Fourteen of Consolation* (1520). *PE* 1, 103-171.
[7] Cf. *WA* 6, 196.

toward Luther. Particularly, however, this was a matter of concern for the princes and ruling nobility.

Nor was this concern simply theoretical. The possibility of misunderstanding and distorting Luther's emphasis upon justification by faith alone was very real. When medieval man thought of faith he did so in terms of the concepts of *fides informis* (unfashioned, raw faith) and *fides formata* or *informata* (complete faith). The *fides informis* was held to be bare knowledge or assent which needed to be completed by the *fides formata,* faith adorned by good works by which men make themselves acceptable in the sight of God and win his favor. That many, both learned and unlearned, misunderstood Luther's teaching is forcefully illustrated in the personal tragedy of Karlstadt and the calamity of the libertine community in Münster.

Despite Spalatin's urgent prompting, Luther was not inclined to undertake the task. Only when he recalled that he had promised his congregation that he would do so did he set to work. Once the work got underway it grew far beyond the framework of a sermon. On March 25 he wrote to Spalatin saying that the work was likely to grow into a small book.[8] In subsequent letters he speaks of the growth of the material.[9] On June 8 a printed copy was in the hands of Melanchthon. Thus the work originally intended as a sermon for his congregation had grown into a substantial book for a much wider audience. Significantly, the book was dedicated to John, the brother of Elector Frederick, Luther's sovereign.[10]

At the very outset of the treatise Luther takes issue with the prevalent understanding of good works. This understanding regarded good works as those prescribed by the church and voluntarily assumed by the faithful: fasting, pilgrimages, fixed prayer

---

[8] *WA*, Br 2, 75.

[9] *WA*, Br 2, 101, 103.

[10] Probably as a result of Spalatin's urging. Luther had already dedicated his *Fourteen of Consolation* to Frederick. M. Reu suggests that the dedication to John, who succeeded to the electorate in 1525, was calculated to offset whatever unfavorable attitude toward Luther may have existed within the royal family. Duke George, another brother, is known to have formed an unfavorable impression of Luther from a sermon he had preached in Dresden. Cf. *PE* 1, 177-178. Luther commented on the duke's attitude in a letter to Spalatin, July 20, 1519. Cf. *WA*, Br 1, 423; *LW* 31, 324.

recitation, going to mass, etc. Such a concept established a false dichotomy of works. It led quite easily to the idea that there is a distinction in works in God's sight, by which certain works are superior or religious and therefore more acceptable to God, whereas others are inferior or secular and therefore less acceptable. To this Luther says unequivocally that there are no good works save those which God has commanded; that the first and most precious good work is faith in Christ; that in this faith one work is like another because there is no distinction between them; and that this faith is the source from which all truly good works issue. Thus the man who in faith stays at home to support his family and to care for his wife and children rather than make a pilgrimage does a truly good work, and one which is commanded by God. Prevalent teaching and popular piety, however, would have it the other way around. For Luther whatever is done in faith—even if it be to suffer and to endure the infirmities and loneliness of old age—is pleasing in God's sight, for faith "fulfils all commandments and makes all its works righteous. . . ."[11]

Firmly established on the foundation that faith is the source of all good works, Luther treats the works commanded by God in the two tables of the Decalogue with clarity and with a depth and breadth scarcely to be expected of a monk and professor. He goes to the very core of human life and the problems which beset it. He demonstrates not only the kinds of works commanded, but the abundant opportunities and occasions God gives for the exercise of faith in such works. Again and again Luther clearly points out that because of faith there is no distinction between "religious" and "secular" works. It is as much the work of the second commandment, for example, to speak up for the exploited and oppressed as it is to abstain from cursing. When Luther treats the fourth commandment he covers a wide area of social responsibility devolving upon the Christian in the station he occupies within his society. But with all of this Luther never fails to relate every good work to the source from whence it issues and whither it returns: faith in Christ alone. Without such faith good works not only avail

[11] See p. 31.

nothing, they are nothing. With this single treatise Luther obliterated the distinction between the "religious" and the "secular," and altered the whole system of Christian ethics.[12]

The present translation is a revision of that by W. A. Lambert in *PE* 1, 184-285. The German text, *Von den guten Werken,* is in *WA* 6, (196) 202-276. The revision is based on the *WA* text with comparison and reference to the text in *CL* 1, 227-298.

[12] Cf. Gustav Wingren, *Luther on Vocation* (Philadelphia: Muhlenberg Press, 1957), pp. 117-123.

TREATISE ON GOOD WORKS

Jesus

To the illustrious, highborn prince and lord, John, duke of Saxony, landgrave of Thuringia, margrave of Meissen, my gracious lord and patron.

Illustrious, highborn prince, gracious lord! To Your Princely Grace I offer my humble service, and my poor prayer is ever on your behalf.

Gracious prince and lord, for a long time I have earnestly desired to show my faithful loyalty and fulfil my duty toward Your Royal Highness by offering such spiritual wares as are at my disposal, but I have always considered my powers too feeble to undertake anything that was worth offering Your Royal Highness.

Since, however, my most gracious lord Frederick, duke of Saxony, grand marshal, elector, and vicar of the Holy Roman Empire, Your Grace's brother, has not despised but has graciously accepted my slight book[1] dedicated to His Royal Highness (a book now published though that was never my intention), I have gathered courage from his gracious example, and ventured to think that the princely spirit, like the princely blood, may be the same in both of you, especially with respect to gracious kindness and good will. I have hoped that Your Royal Highness likewise would not despise this my humble offering which I have felt needs publishing, perhaps more than any other of my sermons or books. For the greatest question has been raised, the question of good works, where immeasurably more trickery and deception is practiced than anywhere else, and where the simple-minded man is so easily misled that our Lord Christ has commanded us to watch carefully for the sheep's clothing under which the wolves hide themselves [Matt. 7:15]. There is no silver, gold, precious stone, or rare treasure that has as many substitutes and flaws as good works. Yet

[1] *The Fourteen of Consolation. PE* 1, 109-171.

of all things good works should have a single, simple goodness. Without that they are just color, glitter, and deceit.

And although I know full well and hear every day that many people think little of me and say that I only write little pamphlets and sermons in German for the uneducated laity, I do not let that stop me. Would to God that in my lifetime I had, to my fullest ability, helped one layman to be better! I would be quite satisfied, thank God, and quite willing then to let all my little books perish. Whether the making of many large books is an art and of benefit to Christendom, I leave for others to judge. But I believe that if I were of a mind to write big books of their kind, I could perhaps, with God's help, do it more readily than they could write my kind of little discourse. If following Christ had been as easy as persecuting him, Christ would long since have been cast down from heaven and the very throne of God overturned. If we cannot all be writers, then we all want to be critics! I will most gladly leave to anybody else the glory of greater things. I will not be ashamed in the slightest to preach to the uneducated layman and write for him in German. Although I may have little skill at it myself, it seems to me that if we had hitherto busied ourselves in this very task and were of a mind to do more of it in the future, Christendom would have reaped no small advantage and would have been more benefitted by this than by those heavy, weighty tomes and those *questiones*[2] which are only handled in the schools among learned schoolmen. Furthermore, I have never forced anyone or begged him to listen to me or read my sermons. I have served the church unstintingly with that which God gave me. This is my duty. If anybody so chooses, he is free to read others and listen to them. If people do not want to read my books or hear my sermons, that does not matter very much. As far as I am concerned it is quite enough, really more than enough, that some laymen—and those the most distinguished—are humble enough to read my sermons.

And if nothing else motivated me, this would be more than sufficient: that Your Grace, as I have heard, is pleased with such little books in German and is desirous of having them to get the instruction in good works and faith with which I am bound to

[2] Questions debated in the universities.

serve you diligently and humbly. Therefore in dutiful humility I pray Your Grace to accept this offering of mine with a gracious mind until, if God grant me the time, I prepare a complete exposition of the faith in German. In this present book I have wanted to show how we should practice and use faith in all good works, and how we should let faith be our chief work. If God permits I will on a later occasion handle the faith itself[3] and show how we are to use it as a prayer or recite it every day.

I am, Your Grace, your most obedient servant.

From Wittenberg, March 29, 1520

Your Princely Grace's humble chaplain
Dr. Martin Luther
Augustinian of Wittenberg

1. The first thing to know is that there are no good works except those works God has commanded, just as there is no sin except that which God has forbidden. Therefore, whoever wants to know what good works are as well as doing them needs to know nothing more than God's commandments. Thus in Matthew 19 [:17] Christ says, "If you would enter life, keep the commandments." And when the young man in Matthew 19 [:16-22] asks what he should do to inherit eternal life, Christ sets before him nothing else but the Ten Commandments. Accordingly, we have to learn to recognize good works from the commandments of God, and not from the appearance, size, or number of the works themselves, nor from the opinion of men or of human law or custom, as we see has happened and still happens because of our blindness and disregard of the divine commandments.

2. The first, highest, and most precious of all good works is faith in Christ, and as it says in John 6 [:28-29], when the Jews asked him, "What must we do, to be doing the good work of God?" Jesus answered, "This is the good work of God, that you believe in him whom he has sent." Now when we hear that or even preach it, we pass over it: we think nothing of it and think it easy to do, but actually we ought to pause a long time and think it over properly.

[3] Luther is referring to the Apostles' Creed. Cf. *PE* 1, 186.

For in this work all good works exist, and from faith these works receive a borrowed goodness. We must make this absolutely clear, so that men can understand it.

We find many who pray, fast, establish endowments, do this and that, lead a good life in the sight of their fellowmen, and yet, were you to ask them if they were quite certain that what they were doing was well pleasing to God, they would say no. They do not know, or at least are uncertain. And there are some very learned men who lead them astray and tell them it is not necessary to be certain of this, and yet these learned men do nothing else but teach good works. Now take careful note. All these works go on apart from faith; therefore they amount to nothing and are absolutely dead. For as their conscience stands in relation to God and as it believes, so also are their works which issue from it. Now that is not faith, nor is it a good conscience toward God; therefore, their works are pointless and their life and goodness all amount to nothing. This is the reason that when I exalt faith and reject such works done without faith they accuse me of forbidding good works. The fact of the matter is that I want very much to teach the real good works which spring from faith.

3. If you ask further whether they consider it a good work when a man works at his trade, walks, stands, eats, drinks, sleeps, and does all kinds of works for the nourishment of his body or for the common welfare, and whether they believe that God is well pleased with them, you will find that they say no, and that they define good works so narrowly that they are made to consist only of praying in church, fasting, and almsgiving. The other things they consider as worth nothing and think that God attaches no importance to them. And so, through their damnable unbelief, they deprive God of his due and despise faith, though God is served by all things that may be done, spoken, or thought in faith.

Ecclesiastes 9 [:7-9] teaches the same thing: "Go your way with joy, eat and drink, and know that your works are well-pleasing to God. Let your garments always be white, and let your head lack no ointment. Live joyfully with the wife you love all the days of this uncertain life that are given you." "Let your garments always be white," that is, let all our works be good whatever they may be, without any distinction. And they are white when I am certain and believe that they please God. Then shall the head of my soul never lack the ointment of a happy conscience.

So Christ says in John 8 [:29], "I always do the things that please him." How did he do that always, when he ate and drank and slept in turn? And St. John, I John 3 [:19-22], says, "By this we shall know we are of the truth when we can comfort our hearts before him and have a good confidence." And if our heart condemns or troubles us, God is greater than our heart, and we are confident that whatever we ask we shall receive, because we keep his commandments and do those things that are pleasing in his sight. Again, "Whosover is born of God (that means whosoever believes and puts his trust in God) does not commit sin and cannot commit sin" [I John 3:9]. Again, Psalm 34 [:22], "None of them that trust in him shall do sin." And in Psalm 2 [:12], "Blessed are all they that trust in him." If this be true, then all that they do must be good, or the evil that they do must be quickly forgiven. Now see why I exalt faith so much, include all works under it, and reject all works which do not flow from it!

4. Now everyone can notice and feel for himself when he does what is good and what is not good. If he finds his heart confident that it pleases God, then the work is good, even if it were so small a thing as picking up a straw. If the confidence is not there, or if he has any doubt about it, then the work is not good, even if the work were to raise all the dead and if the man were to give his body to be burned.[4] This is the teaching of St. Paul in Romans 14 [:23], "Whatsoever is not done of faith or in faith is sin." It is from faith as the chief work and from no other work that we are called believers in Christ. A heathen, a Jew, a Turk, a sinner may also do all other works; but to trust firmly that he pleases God is possible only for a Christian who is enlightened and strengthened by grace.

That these words seem strange, and that some people call me a heretic because of them, is due to the fact that they have followed blind reason and heathen ways of thinking. They have set faith not above but beside other virtues. They have made faith into a kind of work of its own, separated from all works of the other virtues, al-

[4] Cf. I Cor. 13:3.

though faith alone makes all other works good, acceptable, and worthy because it trusts God and never doubts that everything a man does in faith is well done in God's sight. In fact, they have not let faith remain a work but have made it a *habitus*,[5] as they call it, although the whole of Scripture gives the name good, divine work to no work except to faith alone. Therefore, it is no wonder that they have become blind and leaders of the blind.[6] And this faith soon brings along with it love, peace, joy, and hope. For God gives his spirit immediately to him who trusts him, as St. Paul says to the Galatians, "You have received the Spirit not from your good works but because you have believed the word of God" [Gal. 3:2].

5. In this faith all works become equal, and one work is like the other; all distinctions between works fall away, whether they be great, small, short, long, many, or few. For the works are acceptable not for their own sake but because of faith, which is always the same and lives and works in each and every work without distinction, however numerous and varied these works always are, just as all the members of the body live, work, and take their name from the head, and without the head no member can live, work, or have a name.

It further follows from this that a Christian man living in this faith has no need of a teacher of good works, but he does whatever the occasion calls for, and all is well done. As Samuel said to Saul, "You shall become another man when the spirit enters you; do whatever your hand finds to do, for God is with you" [I Sam. 10:6-7]. So also we read of St. Anna, Samuel's mother. When she believed the priest Eli, who promised her God's grace, she went home in joy and peace [I Sam. 1:17-18], and from that time paced the floor no longer: this means that whatever happened to her was all the same to her. St. Paul also says, "Where the Spirit of Christ is, there all is free" [Rom. 8:2]. For faith does not permit itself to be bound to any work or to refuse any work, but, as the first Psalm says, "it yields its fruit in its season" [Ps. 1:3], that is, in the normal course of events.

6. We may see this in an everyday example. When a husband

[5] An acquired perfect state or condition independent of works.
[6] Cf. Matt. 15:14.

and wife really love one another, have pleasure in each other, and thoroughly believe in their love, who teaches them how they are to behave one to another, what they are to do or not to do, say or not to say, what they are to think? Confidence alone teaches them all this, and even more than is necessary. For such a man there is no distinction in works. He does the great and the important as gladly as the small and the unimportant, and vice versa. Moreover, he does them all in a glad, peaceful, and confident heart, and is an absolutely willing companion to the woman. But where there is any doubt, he searches within himself for the best thing to do; then a distinction of works arises by which he imagines he may win favor. And yet he goes about it with a heavy heart and great disinclination. He is like a prisoner, more than half in despair, and often makes a fool of himself.

Thus a Christian man who lives in this confidence toward God knows all things, can do all things, ventures everything that needs to be done, and does everything gladly and willingly, not that he may gather merits and good works, but because it is a pleasure for him to please God in doing these things. He simply serves God with no thought of reward, content that his service pleases God. On the other hand, he who is not at one with God, or is in a state of doubt, worries and starts looking about for ways and means to do enough and to influence God with his many good works. He runs off to St. James,[7] to Rome, to Jerusalem, hither and thither; he prays St. Bridget's prayer,[8] this prayer and that prayer; he fasts on this day and that day; he makes confession here and makes confession there; he questions this man and that man, and yet finds no peace. He does all this with great effort and with a doubting and unwilling heart, so that the Scriptures rightly call such works in Hebrew *aven amal*, that is, labor and sorrow.[9] And even then they are not good works and are in vain. Many people have gone quite crazy with them and their anxiety has brought them into all kinds of

---

[7] Cf. p. 12, n. 9.

[8] St. Bridget of Ireland (d. 523), called "the Mary of the Irish," was second only to the Virgin Mary in popular esteem and devotion. Perhaps she is confused here with the Scottish Bridget (d. 1373), who wrote prayers which were circulated all over Europe.

[9] Cf. Ps. 90:10.

misery. Of these it is written in Wisdom [of Solomon] 5 [:6], "We have wearied ourselves in the wrong way and have followed a hard and bitter road; but God's way we have not acknowledged and the sun of righteousness has not risen upon us."

7. In these works faith is still slight and weak. Let us ask further whether, when everything goes wrong with their life, their goods, their honor, their friends, or whatever they have, they still believe that their works are well-pleasing to God, and that God in his mercy ordains their sufferings and difficulties for them, whether they be small or great. The great thing in life is to have a sure confidence in God when, at least as far as we can see or understand, he shows himself in wrath, and to expect better at his hands than we now know. Here God is hidden, as the bride says in the Song of Songs [2:9], "Behold there he stands behind our wall, gazing in through the windows." That means he stands hidden among the sufferings which would separate us from him like a wall, indeed, like a wall of a fortress. And yet he looks upon me and does not forsake me. He stands there and is ready to help in grace, and through the window of dim faith he permits himself to be seen. And Jeremiah says in Lamentations 3 [:32-33], "He casts men aside, but that is not the intention of his heart."

These people know nothing at all of this kind of a faith, and they give themselves over to thinking that God has forsaken them and is their enemy. They even lay the blame on other men or on the devil, and have simply no confidence at all in God. For this reason, too, their suffering is always an offense to them and harmful. And yet they go on doing their good works, as they think, quite unaware of their serious unbelief. But they who in such suffering trust God and hold on to a good, firm confidence in him, who believe that he is well-pleased with them, see in their sufferings and afflictions nothing but pure and precious merits, the costliest treasures which no man can assess. For faith and confidence make precious before God all that which others think most shameful, so that it is written even of death in Psalm 116 [:15], "Precious in the sight of the Lord is the death of his saints." And just as confidence and faith are better, higher, and stronger at this stage than in the first, so the sufferings which are borne in this kind of faith excel all works of faith. Therefore there is an immeasurable difference between such works and sufferings, and the sufferings are better.

8. Beyond all this is the highest stage of faith, when God punishes the conscience not only with temporal sufferings but with death, hell, and sin, and at the same time refuses grace and mercy, as though he wanted to condemn and show his anger eternally. Few men experience this as David did when he complained in Psalm 6 [:1], "O Lord, rebuke me not in thy anger." To believe at such times that God is gracious and well-disposed toward us is the greatest work that may ever happen to and in a man, but of this the work-righteous and the doers of good works know nothing at all. For how would they know to expect God's goodness and grace in these circumstances when they are not certain about the works they do and have doubts at the lowest stage of faith?

As I have already said, I have always praised faith and rejected all works which are done without such faith in this way in order to lead men from the false, pretentious, pharisaic good works done without faith, with which all monasteries, churches, homes, and the upper and lower classes are overfilled, and to lead them to the right, true, genuine, real works of faith. Nobody strives against me in this except the unclean beasts who do not part the hoof (as the law of Moses decrees)[10] and who will tolerate no distinction of any kind between good works, but go lumbering along. If only they pray, fast, establish endowments, go to confession, and do enough, everything is supposed to be all right, although in all this they have had no faith in the grace of God and no certainty of his approval. In fact, they regard these works most highly when they have done a great many major ones for a long time, without any such confidence, and they look for good only after the works have been performed. And so they build their confidence not on God's favor, but on the works they have done. That is building on sand and water, and in the end they must fall, as Christ said in Matthew 7 [:26-27]. This good will and favor, on which our confidence rests, was proclaimed by the angels from heaven when they sang on Christmas morn, "Glory be to God on high, peace on earth, good will to men" [Luke 2:14].

[10] Lev. 11:4.

9. Now this is the work of the first commandment, which enjoins, "Thou shalt have no other gods." This means, "Since I alone am God, thou shalt place all thy confidence, trust, and faith in me alone and in no one else." For you do not have a god if you [just] call him God outwardly with your lips, or worship him with the knees or bodily gestures; but [only] if you trust him with your heart and look to him for all good, grace, and favor, whether in works or suffering, in life or death, in joy or sorrow. As the Lord Jesus Christ said to the heathen woman in John 4 [:24], "I say to you, whoever wants to worship God must worship him in spirit and in truth." And this faith, this trust, this confidence from the heart's core is the true fulfilling of the first commandment. Without such faith no work at all can satisfy this command. And because this commandment is the very first of all commandments and the highest and the best, [the one] from which all others proceed, in which they exist and by which they are judged and assessed, so its work (that is, the faith or confidence that God is gracious at all times) is the very first, highest, and best from which all others must proceed, in which they must exist and abide, and by which they must be judged and assessed. Compared with this work the other good works are like the other commandments would be if they were without the first and as if there were no God. Therefore, St. Augustine speaks rightly when he says that the works of the first commandment are faith, hope, and love.[11] As I have said above, such faith and confidence brings along with it hope and love. In fact, when we see it properly, love comes first, or at any rate it comes at the same time as faith. For I could not have faith in God if I did not think he wanted to be favorable and kind to me. This in turn makes me feel kindly disposed toward him, and I am moved to trust him with all my heart and to look to him for all good things.

10. Now you see for yourself that all those who do not trust God at all times and do not see God's favor and grace and good will toward them in everything they do and everything they suffer, in their living or in their dying, but seek his favor in other things or even in themselves, do not keep this commandment. Rather, they practice idolatry, even if they were to do the works of all the rest

[11] *Enchiridion ad Laurentium. MPL* 40, 232.

of the commandments and had in addition all the prayers, fasting, obedience, patience, chastity, and innocence of all the saints combined. For the chief work is not there, the work without which all the others are nothing but mere sham, show, and pretense with nothing behind them. Christ warns us against these in Matthew 7 [:15], "Beware of false prophets who come to you in sheep's clothing." This is what they are who want to make God favorably disposed to them and want to buy God's grace directly from him with their many good works (as they call them), as if God were a huckster or a journeyman who did not want to grant his grace and favor for nothing. These are the most perverse people on earth; only with great difficulty will they be converted to the right way, or possibly never at all. The same is true of those who in adversity run hither and thither and seek counsel, help, and comfort everywhere, except from God, from whom they are most urgently commanded to seek it. The prophet Isaiah reproves such people: "The foolish people did not turn to him who smote them" [Isa. 9:13]. This means that God smote them and sent sufferings and all kinds of adversity upon them so that they should run and put their trust in him. But they run away from him and turn to men, now to Egypt, now to Assyria, perchance even to the devil. And much is written in the same prophet and in the books of the kings about this kind of idolatry. All the holy hypocrites do just the same when they come up against it. They do not run to God, but flee from him and away from him, and think only how they may get rid of their trouble through their own efforts or through the help of other men. Yet they consider themselves pious, and they let others regard them as such.

11. This is what St. Paul means in many places where he ascribes so much to faith. He says, "*Justus ex fide sua vivit,*" "The righteous man draws his life out of his faith, and faith is that whereby he is counted righteous before God" [Rom. 1:17]. If righteousness consists of faith, it is clear that faith fulfils all commandments and makes all its works righteous, since no one is justified unless he does all the commandments of God. Or again, works can justify no man before God without faith. So utterly and roundly does the holy Apostle reject works and praise faith that

some have taken offense at his words and said, "Well then, we shall do no more good works." He condemns such men as erring and foolish.[12]

And still it goes on. When we reject the great, pretentious works of our time, done without any faith at all, they then say that they should only believe and do nothing good. For nowadays they say that the works of the first commandment are singing, [devotional] reading, playing the organ, reading the mass, saying matins, vespers, and other [canonical] hours, founding and decorating churches, altars, and monasteries, collecting bells, jewels, garments, trinkets, and treasures, and running to Rome and the saints.[13] Further, we call it worshiping and praying to God when we are all dressed up and bow, kneel, pray the rosary and the Psalter, and do all this not before an idol, but before the holy cross of God or a picture of his saints. We think this is in accordance with the first commandment of having no other gods, although even usurers, adulterers, and all manner of sinners are able to do this and do it every day.

Now it may well be that if these things are done with such faith that we believe that they please God, then they are praiseworthy, not because of their virtue, but because of that very faith by which all works are of equal value, as has been said. But if we have any doubt about it, or do not believe that God is gracious to us and pleased with us, or if we presume to please him first and foremost by good works, then it is all pure deception. To all appearances God is honored, but in reality the self has been set up as an idol. That is the reason I have so often spoken against the display, magnificence, and multitude of such works and rejected them. It is as clear as day that these works are not only done in doubt or without the faith we are talking about, but that there is not one in a thousand who does not put his confidence in the works and presume that by having done them he wins God's favor and lays claim to his grace. They turn the whole thing into a fairground.[14] God can-

---

[12] Cf. Rom. 3:28; 6:15.

[13] In other words, making pilgrimages to shrines.

[14] Luther probably alludes to the bargaining and huckstering which takes place at a fair. *PE* 1, 197.

not tolerate this: God has promised his grace freely, and he wills that we start by trusting that grace and perform all works in that grace, whatever those works may be.

12. See for yourself what a difference there is between the fulfilment of the first commandment with outward works and fulfilment with inward trust. For it is the latter which makes true, living children of God; the former makes for a wretched idolatry and the most pernicious hypocrites on earth, who with their great show of righteousness lead countless folk into their way, yet they leave them without faith. So these folk are led astray pitiably and bogged down in external wailing and show. Christ speaks of their kind when he said in Matthew 24 [:23], "Beware then if any one says to you, 'Lo, here is the Christ!' or 'There he is!'" Or again, John 4 [:21-23], "I say to you, the time will come when you shall not worship God either on this mountain or in Jerusalem, for the Father seeks spiritual worshipers."

These and passages like them have moved me (and ought to move everybody else) to repudiate the ostentatious display of bulls, seals, flags, and indulgences, by which the poor people are led to build churches, to give, endow, and pray. Even then faith is not mentioned at all and is even suppressed, for since faith makes no distinction among works, then where faith is present such trumpeting and urging of one kind of work above another cannot exist. Faith desires to be the only way of serving God, and will allow this name and honor to no other work, except in so far as faith imparts it, as it does when the work is done in and by faith. This perversion is indicated in the Old Testament when the Jews left the Temple and sacrificed at other places, in gardens and on the mountains [Isa. 65:3, 66:17]. These men do exactly the same. They are zealous to do all works, but this chief work of faith they never have any regard for at all.

13. Now where are those who ask what works are good, what they shall do, how shall they be good? Yes, and where, too, are those who say that when we preach about faith we do not teach works or say they should be done? Does not this single first commandment give us more work to do than any one man can do? If a man were a thousand men, if he were all men in one, if he

comprised all creatures, there is still enough asked of him—and more than enough—since he is commanded to live and walk at all times in faith and trust toward God, to place such faith in no one else and in this way to have no other God, just the one and only true God.

Now since the being and nature of man cannot exist for an instant unless it is doing or not doing something, putting up with or running away from something (for as we know, life never stands still), well then, let him who wants to be holy and full of good works begin to exercise himself at all times in this faith in all his life and works. Let him learn to do and to leave undone all things in such continual faith. Then he will find how much work he has to do, and how completely all things are included in faith, and how he may never grow idle because his very idling must be the exercise and work of faith. In short, nothing can be in or about us and nothing can happen to us but what must be good and serviceable to us, as long as we believe (as we ought) that all things please God. So says St. Paul, "Dear brethren, all that you do, whether you eat or drink, do all in the name of Jesus Christ, our Lord" [I Cor. 10:31]. Now it cannot be done in this name except it be done in this faith. Likewise, Romans 8 [:28], "We know that all things work together for good to the saints of God."

Therefore, when some people say, as they do, that when we preach faith alone good works are forbidden, it is as if I were to say to a sick man, "If you had health you would have the full use of all your limbs, but without health the works of all your limbs are nothing," and from this he wanted to infer that I had forbidden the works of his limbs. Whereas on the contrary I meant that the health must first be there to work all the works of all his limbs. In the same way faith must be the master-workman and captain in all the works, or they are nothing at all.

14. You might ask, if faith does everything through the first commandment, why then do we have so many laws of the church and of the state, and so many ceremonies of churches, monasteries, and holy places, which urge and tempt men to do good works through them? The answer: Simply because we do not all have or heed faith. If every man had faith we would need no more laws.

Everyone would of himself do good works all the time, as his faith shows him.

Now there are four kinds of men. The first, just mentioned, who need no law, of whom St. Paul says in I Timothy 1 [:9], "For the righteous man (that is, the believing man) no law is laid down." Such men do willingly what they know and can, because they alone are distinguished for their firm confidence that God's favor and grace rests upon them in all things. The second class of men wants to abuse this freedom, put false confidence in it, and grow lazy. St. Peter says in I Peter 2 [:16] of these, "You should live as free men, but not use this freedom as a cover for sin." Or, in other words, the freedom of faith does not give license to sin, nor will it cover sin, but gives us the license to do all manner of work and to suffer everything just as it presents itself, so that no man is obliged to do one particular work or even many. St. Paul says the same thing in Galatians 5 [:13], "See to it that you let not this liberty be an occasion for the life of the flesh." Such men must be urged by laws and safeguarded by teaching and warning. The third class are wicked men, who are always ready to sin. They must be restrained like wild horses and dogs by spiritual and temporal laws, and where this does not help, they must be put to death by the temporal sword. As St. Paul says in Romans 13 [:3-4], the ruler bears the sword and serves God with it not as a terror to the good but to the evil. The fourth class are those who are still lusty and childish in their understanding of such faith and the spiritual life, and they must be coaxed like young children, enticed with external, definite concomitant adornment, with reading, praying, fasting, singing, churches, decorations, organs, and all those things commanded and observed in monasteries and churches, until such time as they too learn to know the teachings of faith. But still there is great danger here when the rulers (as is now unfortunately the case) busy themselves with these same ceremonies and external works, insist on them as if they were the true works, and neglect faith. They ought always to teach faith along with these works, just as a mother gives her child other food besides milk, until the child can eat solid food by itself.

15. Since we are not all alike, we must tolerate these people

and keep and bear [the same observances] they keep and bear, and not despise them, but instruct them in the right way of faith. So St. Paul teaches in Romans 14 [:1], "Welcome him who is weak in faith that you may teach him." He did so himself in I Corinthians 9 [:20], "Among those who were under the law I became as though I were under it too, although I was not." And Christ, in Matthew 7 [:24-27], when asked if he would pay the tax, which he was not obliged to pay, discusses with St. Peter whether the children of kings must give tribute or only other people. St. Peter answers, "Only other people." Christ said, "Then the sons are free. However, not to give offense to them, go to the sea and cast a hook, and take the first fish that comes up, and when you open its mouth you will find a shekel. Take that shekel and give it to them for me and for yourself."

Here we see that all works and all things are free to a Christian through his faith. And yet, because the others do not yet believe, the Christian bears and holds with them what he is not obliged to do. But this he does freely, for he is certain that this is pleasing to God also, and he does it gladly, accepts it as any other free work which presents itself without his selecting it, because he desires and seeks no more than to do in faith the works which are pleasing to God.

But since we have undertaken in this discourse to teach what good works rightly are, and are now speaking of the highest work, it is clear that we do not speak of the second, third, or fourth class of men but of the first, like whom all the others should become. Until the others become like them the first class must tolerate and instruct them. Therefore, we must not despise these men of little faith who cling to their ceremonies and perform them as though they were lost souls. These men would gladly do right and learn something better, but they are as yet unable to grasp it all. Rather we must blame their ignorant blind teachers who have never taught them what faith is, and have led them so deeply into a doctrine of works. They must be led back to faith again in a kindly manner and with gentle patience, just as a sick man is nursed. For the sake of their conscience they must be allowed for a while to go on clinging to some works and to perform them as necessary for salvation, as long as they grasp faith properly. Otherwise, if we try to tear them away too suddenly their weak consciences may be utterly shattered and confused, and consequently they end with neither faith nor works. But we shall have to let those hardheaded people who are set in their works and pay no regard to what is said about faith, and even fight against it, go their own way, as Christ did and taught, when he said the blind lead the blind [Matt. 15:14].

16. But you say, how can I be absolutely sure that all my works are pleasing to God, when at times I fall, talk, eat, drink, and sleep too much, or otherwise transgress in ways I cannot avoid? Answer: This question shows that you still regard faith as a work among other works and do not set it above all works. It is the highest work because it blots out these everyday sins and still stands fast by never doubting that God is so favorably disposed toward you that he overlooks such everyday failures and offenses. Yes, even if a deadly sin should arise (which, however, never or rarely happens to those who live in faith and trust in God), nonetheless faith always rises again and does not doubt that its sin is already gone. As it is written in I John 2 [:1-2], "My dear children, I am writing this to you so that you may not sin; but if any one does sin, we have an advocate before God, Jesus Christ, who is the forgiveness for our sins." And Wisdom [of Solomon] 15 [:2], "And though we have already sinned, we are still thine, and know that thou are great." And Proverbs 24 [:16], "A righteous man may fall seven times, but he always rises up as many times." Yes, this confidence and faith must be so high and strong that a man knows that all his life and works are nothing but damnable sins in the judgment of God, as it says in Psalm 143 [:2], "For no man living is found righteous before thee." He must despair entirely of his works, and believe that they cannot be good except through this faith which expects no judgment but only pure grace, favor, kindness, and mercy. As David said in Psalm 26 [:3], "Thy loving kindness is ever before my eyes, and I am cheered in thy truth." And in Psalm 4 [:6-7], "The light of thy countenance hovers over us (that is, the knowledge of thy grace through faith) and thereby thou hast made my heart glad." For as faith expects, so does it come to pass.

See, it is by the mercy and grace of God and not by their own nature that works are without guilt and are forgiven. They are good because of faith, which abandons itself to this same mercy. Therefore, we must fear because of the works, but take comfort because of the grace of God. As it is written in Psalm 147 [:11], "But the Lord takes pleasure in those who fear him, in those who hope in his steadfast love." So we pray with perfect confidence, "Our Father . . . ," and yet ask him to "forgive us our trespasses." We are [his] children, and yet sinners; we are acceptable, and yet do not do enough—all this is the work of faith firmly grounded in God's grace.

17. But if you ask where faith and confidence may be found or whence they come, it is certainly the most necessary thing to know. First, without any doubt it does not come from your works or from your merits, but only from Jesus Christ, freely promised and freely given. As St. Paul writes in Romans 5 [:8], "God shows his love toward us as exceedingly sweet and kind in that Christ died for us while we were yet sinners." This is as if Paul said, "Ought this not give us a strong, invincible confidence in that before we prayed about it or cared about it, yes, while we still continually walked in sin, Christ died for our sins?" [Paul] goes on, "If then Christ has died for us while we were yet sinners, how much more shall we be saved through him, being justified by his blood. And if, while we were still enemies, we were reconciled to God through the death of his Son, how much more, now that we are reconciled, shall we be preserved through his life" [Rom. 5:8-11].

Look here! This is how you must cultivate Christ in yourself, and see how in him God holds before you his mercy and offers it to you without any prior merits of your own. It is from such a view of his grace that you must draw faith and confidence in the forgiveness of all your sins. Faith, therefore, does not originate in works; neither do works create faith, but faith must spring up and flow from the blood and wounds and death of Christ. If you see in these that God is so kindly disposed toward you that he even gives his own Son for you, then your heart in turn must grow sweet and disposed toward God. And in this way your confidence must grow out of pure good will and love—God's toward you, and yours toward God. We never read that the Holy Spirit was given to anybody because he had performed some works, but always when men have heard the gospel of Christ and the mercy of God. Faith must arise at all times from this same word and from no other source—and in our own day, too. For Christ is the rock from which men suck oil and honey, as Moses says in Deuteronomy 32 [:13].

On the Second Good Work

18. So far we have treated the first work and the first commandment, but very briefly, simply, and hurriedly, for very much might be said of it. We will now trace the works further through the commandments that follow.

Next to faith the second work is the work of the second commandment, that we shall honor God's name and not take it in vain. This, like all the other works, cannot be done without faith. However, if it is done without faith, it is simply sham and show. After faith we can do no greater work than to praise, preach, sing, and in every way laud and magnify God's glory, honor, and name.

And though I have said above,[15] and it is true, that where faith is and does the work there is no difference between one work and another, it must be understood as true only in regard to works in contradistinction to faith and its works. There is a difference between works when they are compared with one another, and one work is greater than another. It is just as in the body one member needs to be healthy just as much as any other member, yet the works of the members are different, and one is higher, nobler, more useful than the other. So it is in this instance, too—to praise God's glory and name is better than the works of the other commandments which follow. And yet this work must be done in the same faith as inwardly motivates all the others.

But I know quite well that this work is lightly regarded, and what is more, has become almost unknown. Therefore, we must go further into it, and let suffice what has been said, that is, such work as is done in faith and confidence is well-pleasing to God. Indeed, there is no work in which faith and confidence are so much experienced and felt as in honoring God's name. Further, honor-

[15] See pp. 26-28.

ing God's name helps very much to strengthen and increase faith, although all works help to do this, as St. Peter says in II Peter 1 [:10], "Dear brethren, work hard so that you make your call and election certain through good works."

19. The first commandment forbids us to have any other gods. This means we are to believe in one God, the true God, with a firm faith, and with trust, confidence, hope, and love. These are the only works by which a man may have, honor, and hold the one God. A man can find God by no work other than faith and trust; a man can lose God by no work other than unbelief and doubt. No other work can bring a man to God. It is for this reason that the second commandment forbids us to use God's name in vain. But this will not be enough. We are also commanded to honor, call upon, praise, preach, and glorify his name. And indeed, it is impossible for God's name not to be dishonored where it is not rightly honored. For although it is already honored with the lips, bending of the knees, kissing, and other postures, if this is not done in the heart by faith, in confident trust in God's grace, then it is nothing more than a hypocritical semblance and pretense.

See now how many kinds of works a man can do under this commandment at all times! He need never be without the good works of this commandment if he so determines. There is no need at all to make a distant pilgrimage or to seek holy places. For, tell me, what moment can pass in which we do not unceasingly receive God's blessings, or, on the other hand, suffer adversity? But what else are God's blessings and adversities than a constant urging and stirring up to praise, honor, and bless God, and to call upon him and his name? Now if you had nothing else to do at all would you not have enough to do with this commandment alone, simply to bless, sing, praise, and honor God's name without ceasing? And for what other purpose have tongue, voice, language, and mouth been created? As Psalm 51 [:15] says, "Lord, open thou my lips, and my mouth shall show forth thy praise." Again, "And my tongue will sing aloud of thy deliverance" [vs. 14].

What work is there in heaven except that of this second commandment? As it is written in Psalm 84 [:4], "Blessed are those who dwell in thy house, they will praise thee forever." And David says in Psalm 34 [:1], "God's praise shall continually be in my mouth." And St. Paul in I Corinthians 10 [:31], "So whether you eat or drink, or whatever you do, do all to the glory of God." Also Colossians 3 [:17], "Everything you do, in word or deed, do in the name of our Lord Jesus Christ, giving thanks to God the Father." If we were to observe this work, we would have a heaven here on earth and always have enough to do, just as the saints in heaven.

20. The wonderful and righteous judgment of God is based on this, that at times in the privacy of his home a poor man, in whom nobody can see many great works, joyfully praises God when he fares well, or with entire confidence calls upon him when he is in adversity. He does a greater and more acceptable work by this than another who fasts and prays much, endows churches, makes pilgrimages, and burdens himself with great deeds in this place and that. Such a fool opens his mouth wide and looks for still bigger works to do. He is so blinded that he does not notice this greatest work at all, and for him praising God is a very small matter compared with the great picture he has of the works of his own devising, in which he perhaps praises himself more than God, or takes more pleasure in them than he does in God. Thus he storms against the second commandment and its works with his own good works. We have an exact picture of this in the gospel in the case of the Pharisee and the publican [Luke 18:10-14]. The publican calls upon God in his sins, praises him, and fulfils the two greatest commandments, faith and the honoring of God. The Pharisee misses the mark on both. He struts about with other good works by which he praises himself, not God, and puts his trust more in himself than in God. Therefore is he justly rejected and the other chosen.

It is always the case that the higher and better the works are, the less show they make. It is evident that everyone thinks that such works are easy to do because no one imagines he praises God's name and honor so much as the very men who never do it. These men make such a show of doing it, yet their heart is without faith and causes this precious work to be despised, so that the Apostle Paul dared say boldly in Romans 2 [:23] that those who make their boast in the law of God blaspheme his name the most. For it is an easy matter to name the name of God and to write his honor on paper or on a wall; but genuinely to praise and bless him in his good deeds and confidently to call upon him in all adversities is, next to faith, truly the rarest and highest of works, so that if we were to see how little of this there is in Christendom we might despair for the very sorrow of it. Yet in the meantime there is a constant increase of high, handsome, and glorious works which men have thought up, or of works which seem to look like those true works, but at bottom are all utterly without faith and trust, and, in short, have nothing good behind them. Thus Isaiah rebukes the people of Israel in Isaiah 48 [:1-2], "Hear this, you who bear the name Israel as if you were the people of Israel, you who swear by the name of God and think you still stand in truth and righteousness." That means that they did not act in true faith and confidence, which is real truth and righteousness, but trusted in themselves, their works, and in their own abilities, and yet called upon God's name and praised him. These two things do not go together.

21. So then the first work of this commandment is to praise God in all his benefits, which are so innumerable that such praise and thanksgiving ought rightly be unremitting and unending. For who can praise him perfectly for the gift of natural life, not to mention all other temporal and eternal blessings? And so, through this one part of the commandment, man is overwhelmed with good and precious works, and if a man does these works in true faith, his life on earth has certainly not been useless. And none sins in this matter nearly as much as the most ostentatious saints who are pleased with themselves and like to praise themselves or hear themselves praised, honored, and glorified before the world.

Therefore, the second work of this commandment is to be on one's guard, to flee from and to avoid all temporal honor and praise, and never to seek a name for oneself, or fame and a great reputation, so that everyone may sing your praises and talk about you. This is an exceedingly dangerous sin, yet the most common of all, and unfortunately too little attention is paid to it. So deeply is human nature sunk in the evil of its own conceit and self-confidence, contrary to these first two commandments, that everyone wants to be looked up to and not be the least no matter how insignificant he may be.

Now the world regards this terrible vice as the highest virtue, and this makes it extremely dangerous for those who have not fully understood the commandments of God and are not really knowledgeable in the histories of Holy Scripture to read heathen books and histories. For all heathen books are poisoned through and through with this seeking after praise and honor; in them men are taught by blind reason that they are not and could never be men of power and worth if they were not moved by praise and honor, and that those who disregard body and life, friend and goods, and everything else in an effort to win praise and honor are looked up to as the best people. All the holy fathers have complained of this vice and are united in the conclusion that it is the very last vice to be overcome. St. Augustine says all other vices are practiced in doing evil works: it is only honor and self-satisfaction that are practiced in good works and by means of them.[16]

Therefore if a man had nothing else to do except the second work of this commandment, he would still have to work his whole lifetime to fight this vice which is so common to us all, so deceiving, so slippery to grasp, and so insidious that it is difficult to drive it out. Now we all pass by this good work and practice many other lesser good works. Indeed, by doing other good works we even upset and forget this one. And so the holy name of God, which alone ought to be honored, is taken in vain and dishonored because of our own cursed name, our own self-approval and seeking of our own honor. This sin is more grievous in God's eyes than murder and adultery, but because of its subtlety we do not recognize this wickedness as readily as we do that of murder, for this wickedness is not accomplished in the raw flesh but in the spirit.

22. Some think it is a good thing for young people to be encouraged by reputation and honor and discouraged by shame and dishonor, and so be induced to do good. For there are many who do what is good and forswear what is evil for fear of shame or love of honor, and so they do what otherwise they would never do and avoid what they would never avoid. I leave these people to their own opinion. But at present we are seeking how true good works

[16] "All the vices abound in evil works, but only pride has to be avoided in good works." *Prosperi Aquitani sententia ex Augustino delibatae* 48. *MPL* 45, 1863.

are to be done, and those who are inclined to do them surely do not need to be driven by the fear of shame and the love of honor. They have, and ought to have, a far higher and nobler incentive, and that is God's commandment, God's fear, God's approval, and their faith and love toward God. Those who do not possess this motive, or who pay no regard to it and let shame or honor be the spur, have their reward, as the Lord says in Matthew 6 [:2]. And as is the motive, so is the reward: none of them is good, except in the eyes of the world.

Now I hold that a young man could be more easily trained and encouraged by the fear of God and by his commandments than by any other means. Yet where these do not help we just have to put up with their doing the good and leaving the evil for the sake of shame or of honor, just as we have to put up with wicked men too, or with the immature, whom we mentioned earlier.[17] In fact, we cannot do much more about it than tell them that what they are doing is not satisfactory and right in God's sight, and leave them alone until they, too, learn to do right for the sake of God's commandments. It is just as young children are encouraged to pray and fast and learn their lessons and so on by gifts and promises from their parents, yet it would not be right to motivate them all their lives by such methods lest they never learn to do good in the fear of God, or what is still worse, lest they become accustomed to doing good for the sake of praise and honor.

23. But it is true, nonetheless, that we must have a good name and reputation, and every man ought so to live that nobody can say anything evil of him, and that he gives offense to nobody, as St. Paul says in Romans 12 [:17], "We should be zealous to do good, not only before God but also before all men." And II Corinthians 4 [:2], "We walk so honestly that no man knows anything against us." But there must be great diligence and care lest such a reputation puff up the heart and make a man self-satisfied. Here the saying of Solomon holds, "As fire in the furnace proves gold, so man is proved by the mouth of him who praises him" [Prov. 27:21]. Those men must be few and very highly spiritual who through honor and praise alike remain indifferent and unchanged, so that

[17] Cf. p. 35.

they do not care for it or take pride and pleasure in it, but remain utterly free and unconcerned, ascribe all their honor and good name to God alone, offer it to him alone, and use it to no purpose other than the glory of God and the benefit of their neighbors and in no way to their own benefit or advantage. Men like this trust not in their own honor, nor exalt themselves above the most useless and despised man on earth, but acknowledge themselves as servants of God, who has given them the honor in order to serve God and neighbor, just as if he had commanded them to distribute gulden[18] to the poor for his sake. In Matthew 5 [:16] Christ says, "Your light should shine before men so that they may see your good works and glorify your Father who is in heaven." He does not say "that men may praise *you*," but "that your works shall serve only to help men, that through them they may praise God in you and in themselves." The correct use of honor and a good name is when God is praised through serving others. And if men want to praise us and not God working in us, we ought not to tolerate it, but do all we can to protect ourselves from their praise and avoid it as the very worst of sins and as the robbery of God's honor.

24. God frequently permits a man to fall into or remain in grievous sin so that he may be put to shame in his own eyes and in the eyes of all men. Otherwise he could not have kept himself free of this great vice of vain honor and a famous name if he had remained constant in his great gifts and virtues. Thus God must ward off this sin by means of other grievous sins that his holy name alone may be honored. And so one sin becomes a medicine for the other because of our perverse wickedness, which not only does that which is evil, but also misuses all that is good.

Now see how much a man has to do if he wants to do good works, for there are piles of them around, surrounding him on all sides, and, unfortunately, because of his blindness he leaves them lying there and seeks out and runs after others of his own high thinking and delight. No man can speak strongly enough against these and no man can adequately guard himself against them. The prophets had to contend with all this and were put to death because they rejected such self-devised works and preached only God's

[18] On the gulden, cf. E. G. Schwiebert, *Luther and His Times* (St. Louis: Concordia, 1950), p. 258.

commandments. As one of them, Jeremiah 7 [:21-23], says, "Thus does the God of Israel say to you, 'Take away your offerings and put them together with all your gifts, and eat your sacrifice and meat yourselves, for I have commanded you nothing concerning those things. But I have commanded you this: "You shall heed my voice (that is, not what seems right and good to you but what I bid you) and walk in the way which I have commanded you."'" And Deuteronomy 12 [:8, 32], "You shall not do what is right and good in your eyes, but what your God has commanded you."

These and countless similar passages of Scripture are spoken to tear men away not only from their sins but from the works which they think good and right, and to turn men to the plain meaning of God's commandment so that they shall diligently observe this only and always. As it is written in Exodus 13 [:9], "You shall let my commandments be to you as a sign in your hand and an example before your eyes"; and Psalm 1 [:2], "A godly man meditates upon God's law day and night." For we have more than enough to do, too much in fact, just to satisfy God's commandments. He has given us such commandments so that if we understand them aright, we dare not be idle for a moment. We could well forget all other works. But when the evil spirit, who never rests, cannot lead us into evil works on the left, he fights on our right through self-devised works which seem good. Deuteronomy 28 [:14] and Joshua 23 [:6], "You shall not stray from my commandments either to the right hand or to the left."

25. The third work of this commandment is to call upon God's name in every need. God considers his name hallowed and honored when we name it and call upon it in adversity and need. And in the final analysis this is why he sends us much trouble, suffering, adversity, and even death as well. He lets us live in many wicked, sinful affections so that he may thereby urge man and give him much reason to run to him, to cry aloud to him, to call upon his holy name, and so to fulfil this work of the second commandment, as he says in Psalm 50 [:15, 14], "Call upon me in your need, and I will help you; thus you shall honor me, for I desire a sacrifice of praise." And this is the way by which you can come to salvation, for through such works man perceives and learns what God's

name is, how powerful he is to help all those who call upon him, and how it is through this that confidence and faith increase mightily. The first and most important commandment is fulfilled by doing this. This is the experience of David in Psalm 54 [:7, 6], "You have delivered me out of all trouble, therefore will I praise thy name and confess that it is lovely and sweet." And in Psalm 91 [:14] God says, "I will deliver him because he sets his hope upon me: I will help him because he has acknowledged my name."

Now look, what man on earth would not have enough to do all his life in performing this work? For who lives an hour without trials? I will make no mention of the trials of adversity which are countless. The most dangerous trial of all is when there is no trial, when everything is all right and running smoothly. That is when a man tends to forget God, to become too independent and put his time of prosperity to a wrong use. In fact, at this time he has ten times more need to call upon God's name than in adversity. As it is written in Psalm 91 [:7], "A thousand fall at your side, ten thousand at your right side."

And so we see as clear as daylight that worse sin and vice occur in the everyday experience of all men when there is peace, when everything is going well and times are good, than when war, pestilence, illness, and all manner of misfortune burden us. Moses, too, is anxious about his people lest they forsake the slightest ground of God's commandment for no other reason than that they are too full, too well provided for, and had ease for too long, when he says in Deuteronomy 32 [:15], "My beloved people has become too rich, full, and fat: therefore have they resisted their God." As it is written in Judges 3 [:1-11], God allowed many of their enemies to remain and would not drive them out so that they should not have peace and would have to discipline themselves by keeping God's commandments. He deals with us in the same way when he brings all kinds of misfortune into our lives. Indeed, so mindful of us is he that he teaches and compels us to honor and call upon his name, to gain confidence and faith in him, and so fulfil the first two commandments.

26. In this respect foolish men run into danger, and especially the work-righteous saints and those who want to be somebody spe-

cial. They teach men to cross themselves. One arms himself with letters,[19] another runs to the fortune-tellers. One seeks this, another that, all in order to escape misfortune and be secure. It is beyond telling what devilish spirit is behind this, playing with sorcery, magic, and superstition. All of this happens only because it is God's name they do not heed and in which they put no trust. Here the name of God and the first two commandments are greatly dishonored, when men look to the devil, to man, or to creatures for that which should be sought and found in God alone through a pure faith and a simple confidence, in cheerful meditation and calling on his holy name.

Now take a close look at this and see whether it is not a gross, mad perversion. They have to believe the devil, man, or creatures and trust in them for all that is good. Without such faith or confidence nothing remains steady or helps them. How shall the good and faithful God reward us for not believing and trusting in him as much as or more than in man or the devil—and this in spite of the fact that he not only promises help and sure assistance but also commands us confidently to look for it and gives us every cause and reason to place such faith and confidence in him? Is it not lamentable and pitiable that the devil, or man, who commands nothing and compels nothing, but only bids fair and makes promises, is set over God, who gives the promises, constrains and commands us? And is it not lamentable that more is thought of them than of God himself? We ought to be thoroughly ashamed and learn from the example of those who trust the devil or man. For if the devil, who is a wicked lying spirit, holds faith with all those who ally themselves with him, how much more will God, who alone is the most gracious and most true of all, keep faith if a man trusts him! A rich man trusts and relies upon his money and possessions, and they help him; and are we not willing to trust and rely upon the living God in the faith that he would help us and wants to help us? They say that gold makes bold;[20] and it is true, as Baruch 3 [:17] says, "Gold is a thing in which men trust." But far greater

[19] I.e., indulgences and other dispensations. Cf. p. 155, n. 101.

[20] *Gut macht mut* (*WA* 6, 225, l. 6) is a clever play on the words *gut* and *mut*. It is *gut*, i.e., the world's goods, which gives a man *mut*, i.e., courage, but it is the divine *gut*, i.e., faith in God, which gives a man true courage.

is the courage which the highest eternal God gives, in whom not men, but only God's children trust.

27. Even if these adversities were to constrain none of us to call upon God's name and put our trust in him, yet sin alone is more than sufficient to give us practice in this work and spur us on. For sin has hemmed us in with three kinds of powerful and mighty armies. The first is our own flesh, the second the world, the third the wicked spirit. We are oppressed and attacked without respite by these three. In this God gives us unceasing occasion to do good works, that is, to fight these very enemies and sins. The flesh seeks pleasure and repose; the world seeks riches, favor, power, and honor; the wicked spirit seeks pride, glory, to think well of itself, and to despise other people.

And all the individual armies are so powerful in themselves that each one is sufficient in its own right to engage a man in warfare. Yet there is no way we can overcome them except by calling upon the name of the holy God in a firm faith. As Solomon says in Proverbs 18 [:10], "The name of the Lord is a strong tower; the righteous man flees to it and is set aloft over all." And David, in Psalm 116 [:13], "I will drink the cup of salvation and call upon God's name." Again, Psalm 18 [:3], "I will call upon God with praise: so shall I be saved from all my enemies." These works and the power of God's name have become unknown to us because we are not accustomed to it and have never seriously fought with sins and have not needed his name. That means we are practiced only in our self-devised works, which we were able to do by our own powers.

28. Further works of this commandment are that we should not swear, curse, lie, deceive, or conjure with God's holy name, or pursue other misuses. These are very simple matters and well known to everybody for they are the sins which have been almost exclusively preached and proclaimed in connection with this commandment. This also includes preventing others from making sinful use of God's name by lying, swearing, deceiving, cursing, conjuring, and the like. Here again much occasion is given for doing good and warding off evil.

But the greatest and most difficult work of this commandment is to protect the holy name of God against all who misuse it in a spiritual manner, as well as to proclaim it far and wide to all men. For it is not enough that I for myself and in myself praise God's name and call upon him in prosperity and in adversity. I must step forth and for the sake of God's honor and name bring upon myself the enmity of all men, as Christ said to his disciples, "You will be hated by all for my name's sake" [Matt. 10:22]. Here we must provoke father, mother, and the best of friends to anger. Here we must strive against spiritual and temporal authorities and be accused of disobedience. Here we must stir up against us the rich, the learned, the holy, and all that is of repute in the world. And although this is especially the duty of those who are commanded to preach God's word, yet every Christian is bound to do so too when time and place demand. For the holy name of God we must risk and give up all that we have and all that we can, and show by our deeds that we love God and his name, his honor and his praise, above all things, that we trust him above all else, and that we look to him for every good. By this we confess that we regard him as the highest good, for whose sake we renounce and give up all other possessions.

29. In this connection we must offer resistance to all wrong, wherever truth or righteousness are violated and abused. We dare make no distinction of persons, as do some who fight most actively and busily against the wrong which is done to the rich, the mighty, or their own friends, but who are quite quiet and patient when wrong is done to the poor, or to those of low estate, or to their own enemy. These people see the name and the honor of God not as it is but through a colored glass. They measure truth and righteousness according to the persons, and are not aware that their eye, which looks more on the person than on the truth of the matter, deceives them. They are hypocrites under the skin and only appear to be defending the truth. They know quite well that there is no danger in helping the rich, the mighty, the learned, and one's own friends. In turn, they can enjoy their help, and be protected and honored by them.

It is very easy to fight in this way against the wrong done to popes, kings, princes, bishops, and other big shots. Everybody wants to be the most pious in this, where the need is not so great. O how sly the deceitful Adam is with his importunity in such cases! How splendidly he cloaks his greed that he may profit by the name of truth and righteousness and the honor of God! But where anything goes against a poor, insignificant man, the deceitful eye finds little pleasure, though it sees the disfavor of the mighty well enough; therefore, he lets the poor man remain unhelped. And who could tell the extent of this vice in Christendom? In Psalm 82 [:2-4] God says, "How long will you judge unjustly and show partiality to the wicked? Judge the cause of the weak and fatherless; maintain the right of the afflicted and destitute. Rescue the weak and the forsaken from the power of the wicked." But nobody does it, and therefore the text continues, "They have neither knowledge nor understanding, they walk about in darkness" [vs. 5]. That is, they do not see the truth. Rather do they have regard for the great [of this world], however unrighteous they are; but they have no regard for the poor, no matter how righteous they are.

30. Look, there are plenty of good works to be done! Most of the mighty, most of the rich, and most of [their] friends are unjust and exercise their power over the poor, the lowly, and over their opponents. The more powerful they are, the worse their deeds. And where one cannot prevent this by force and help the truth, one can at least confess the truth and do something for it by our words, not the kind which please the unrighteous or agree with them, but those which speak the truth boldly.

What good would it be for a man to do all manner of good, make pilgrimages to Rome and to all the holy places, acquire all indulgences, build all churches and found all endowments,[21] if he were found guilty of sin against the name and honor of God by not speaking, by deserting the truth, and by regarding his possessions, honor, favor, and friends more highly than the truth, which is God's name and honor itself? Or who is he at whose door and into whose house such good works do not present themselves every day? There is no need for him to travel far or to inquire about good works. And if we consider the life of men, how very rashly and lightly men everywhere act in this respect, we are forced to cry

[21] *Stiffte,* that is, endowed institutions such as monasteries and convents.

out with the prophet, "*Omnis homo mendax,*" "All men are false: they lie and deceive" [Ps. 116:11]. They neglect the right and proper good works, yet they adorn and decorate themselves with the worst. They want to be pious and ascend to heaven in peaceful security.

But you might ask, "Why does God not do it all by himself, since he is able to help everyone and knows how to help everyone?" Yes, he can do it; but he does not want to do it alone. He wants us to work with him. He does us the honor of wanting to effect his work with us and through us. And if we are not willing to accept such honor, he will, after all, do the work alone, and help the poor. And those who were not willing to help him and who despised the great honor of doing his work he will condemn along with the unrighteous as those who made common cause with the unrighteous. Although he alone is blessed, he does us the honor of wanting to share his blessedness with us. And if he were to do it alone, his commandments would be given us in vain, because nobody would have occasion to exercise himself in the great works of these commandments, nor would anyone test whether he regards God and his name as the highest good and would sacrifice everything for his sake.

31. It is also the nature of this work to resist all false, seductive, erroneous, heretical doctrines and every misuse of spiritual power. Now this is much loftier, for these things use the holy name of God itself to fight against the name of God. For this reason it seems a serious and dangerous matter to resist them, for they assert that he who resists them resists God and all his saints, in whose place they sit and whose power they exercise. They say that Christ was speaking of them when he said, "He who hears you hears me, and he who rejects you rejects me" [Luke 10:16]. They lean heavily on these words and become insolent and bold to say, do, or leave undone whatever they like. They ban, curse, rob, kill, and practice all their wickedness without any hindrance in whatever way they like and can devise.

Now Christ did not mean that we should listen to them in all they say and do, but only at such a time when they present his word to us, the gospel, and not their own word, his work and not their own work. Otherwise how could we know whether their lies and sins were to be avoided? There must be some rule as to what extent we are to hear them and follow them. Such a rule cannot be established by them but must be imposed upon them by God, a rule by which we can direct ourselves, as we shall hear in the fourth commandment.

So it must be that the greater part of the clergy preach false doctrine and misuse their spiritual authority that we may have occasion to do the works of this commandment, and that we be tested to see what we are willing to do or not do against such blasphemers for the sake of God's honor.

O if only we were truly godly in this matter! How often would the official penances[22] have decreed their papal and episcopal excommunications in vain! How the Roman thunderbolts would have had their thunder stolen! How often must many have had to hold their tongue; now the world must lend its ears! How few preachers would be found in Christendom! But it[23] has got the upper hand. Whatever they assert (and in whatever way) must be absolutely right. There is no one who fights for God's name and honor on this issue, and I hold that no greater or more widespread sin exists in external works than in this. It is a matter so high that few understand it, and besides, adorned with God's name and power, it is dangerous to touch upon it. But the prophets of old were masters at this, and so were the apostles, especially St. Paul. It did not trouble them whether the highest or the lowest priest had said it or done it, in God's name or his own. They took the words and works at their face value and compared them with God's commandment, regardless of whether big Jack or little Nick had said it, or whether they had done it in God's name or in man's. And for this they, too, had to die. Much more ought to be said about this kind of dying these days, for things are much worse now. But Christ and St. Peter and St. Paul must cover all this with their holy names. No more shameful cover for infamy has been found on earth than the most holy and blessed name of Jesus Christ!

[22] *Die official bussen.* A variant reading noted by *WA* gives *official buben*, i.e., "official rascals [of Rome]." The meaning remains the same, although the variant text may well be closer to what Luther had in mind. Cf. *WA* 6, 228, note to l. 25.
[23] I.e., the assertion of preachers of false doctrine.

One shudders to be alive, if only because of the misuse and blasphemy of the holy name of God. If this misuse and blasphemy lasts much longer, I am afraid we shall be openly worshiping the devil as a god, so vilely beyond description do the spiritual authorities and the learned act in these matters. It is high time that we earnestly pray God that he hallow his name. But it will cost blood, and those who enjoy the inheritance of the holy martyrs, the inheritance which was won with the blood of the martyrs, must in their turn take on the role of martyr. More of this another time.[24]

On the Third Commandment

1. We have now seen how many good works there are in the second commandment, which, however, are not good in themselves, but must be done in faith and in the assurance of God's favor, and how much we have to do if we take heed of this commandment alone, and, unfortunately, how many people are busy with other works and have not the least understanding of what this commandment means. Now follows the third commandment: Thou shalt hallow the holy day.[25] The first commandment tells how our inmost heart should think about God; the second, how the words of our mouth should express this. The third tells us how we should relate ourselves to God in works. All this comprises the first and proper table of Moses on which these first three commandments are written, and directs man on the right path, namely, in the things which concern God. This means in those matters in which God has to do with man and man with God without the mediation of any other creature.

The first works of this commandment are plain and perceptible. We generally call them divine service, such as hearing mass, pray-

[24] Cf. especially *To the Christian Nobility of the German Nation,* in this volume, pp. 115-217, and the *Babylonian Captivity of the Church* in *LW* 36, 3-126.

[25] Luther uses the term *feyrtag* (in modern German *Feiertag*) here and in his catechisms. It means not only holy day, but also has connotations of a holiday, a day of rest, and festivity. By not using the word sabbath Luther shows that to a Christian the rather restrictive and legalistic sabbath has been superseded by the more joyous and festive Sunday.

ing, and hearing a sermon on holy days. Understood in this way there are very few works in this commandment; and these, if they are not done in the certainty and confidence of God's favor, are worth nothing, as was said before. It would be a good thing, therefore, if there were fewer saints' days, since in our times the works done on those days are for the greater part worse than those done on work days, what with idling about, gluttony, drunkenness, gambling, and other evil deeds. But worse than that, the mass and the sermon are heard without edification, and the prayer is said without faith. It has almost gotten to the point where we think it is enough to watch the mass with our eyes, hear the preaching with our ears, and say the prayers with our mouths. It has reached the stage that men try to gain heaven by outward acts! We do not think that we are to receive something out of the mass into our hearts, learn something from the sermon and appropriate it, or seek, desire, and expect something in prayer. Of course, the greatest blame in this matter attaches to the bishops and priests or those to whom the work of preaching is entrusted, because they do not preach the gospel and teach the people how they ought to watch the mass, listen to the sermon, and pray. Therefore, we shall briefly explain these three works.

2. In the mass it is necessary that we attend with our hearts also; and we do attend when we exercise faith in our hearts. Here we must listen to the words of Christ when he institutes the mass and says, "Take, eat; this is my body, which is given for you." In like manner he says over the cup, "Take it and all of you drink of it: this is a new everlasting testament in my blood, which is shed for you and for many for the remission of sins. Do this, as oft as you do it, in remembrance of me."[26] In these words Christ has made a memorial[27] or an anniversary[28] to be observed daily throughout Christendom. To it he has added a wonderful, rich, great testament in which are bequeathed and distributed not interest, money, or temporal possessions, but the forgiveness of all sins, grace and

[26] Cf. Matt. 26:26-28; Luke 22:17-19; I Cor. 11:23-24.

[27] Luther uses the term *Begencknisz*, that is, a requieum mass celebrated prior to interment or upon the anniversary of a death. The word is similar to the term *Begängnis* or *Gedächtnis* in modern German.

[28] I.e., an anniversary of his day of death, a celebration.

mercy unto eternal life, that all who come to this memorial shall have the same testament. He died with the intent that this testament become permanent and irrevocable. In proof and evidence of this he has left his own body and blood under bread and wine, instead of letter and seal.

A man must practice the first works of this commandment thoroughly. He not only must not doubt that it is true, but he must also consider the testament as sure, so that he does not make Christ a liar. For if you are present at mass and do not consider or believe that here Christ has bequeathed and given you forgiveness of all sins through his testament, then what else is it than as if you said, "I do not know or do not believe that it is true that forgiveness of my sins is here bequeathed and given me?" O how many masses there are in the world, but how few are they who hear them in such faith and with such profit! How grievously God is provoked to anger by such practices! It is for this reason that no one can benefit from attending mass unless his heart is deeply troubled and he longs for divine mercy and desires to be rid of his sins; or unless, if he has evil intentions, he is changed during the mass and comes to have a desire for this testament. This is the reason that in ancient times no open sinner was allowed to be present at mass.

When this faith is rightly present the heart must be made glad by the testament. The heart must grow warm and melt in the love of God. Then praise and thanksgiving will follow with a pure heart, from which the mass is called *eucharistia* in Greek, that is, thanksgiving. We praise God and give him thanks for this comforting, rich, blessed testament, just as a man is thankful and grateful and glad when a good friend has presented him with a thousand or more gulden. Christ more often fares like those who make several persons rich by their testament, and then these beneficiaries never think of them, or praise or thank them. And this is the case with our masses. They are merely celebrated. We do not know the why or wherefore of the service. Consequently, we neither give thanks, nor love or praise God, but remain arid and hard at the mass, contented with our own petty prayers. But more of this another time.

3. The sermon ought to be nothing else than the proclamation of this testament. But who can hear it if nobody preaches it? Those

who should be preaching it do not know it themselves. That is why sermons ramble off into good-for-nothing fables,[29] and thus Christ is forgotten. We are then in the position of the man in II Kings 7 [:19]: we see our riches but do not enjoy them. Ecclesiastes also speaks of this, "This is a great evil, when God gives a man riches, and does not let him enjoy them" [Eccles. 6:2]. And so we see countless numbers of masses, and yet we do not know whether the mass is a testament, or whether it is this thing or that thing, just as if it were any other ordinary good work in itself. O God, how utterly blind we are! But where this is rightly preached, it must be diligently heard, grasped, retained, pondered often, and faith must be strengthened against every temptation of sin, whether past or present or to come.

See here! This is the only ceremony or practice Christ has instituted for which his Christians are to assemble and the only ceremony they are to keep and observe with one accord. Further, he did not make this to be a mere work like other ceremonies but set within it a rich and exceedingly great treasure, which is to be offered and bestowed upon all who believe in it.

This preaching should induce sinners to grieve over their sins and should kindle within them a longing for the treasure. Therefore, it must be a grievous sin not to listen to the gospel, and to despise such a treasure and so rich a feast to which we are bidden. But it is a much greater sin not to preach the gospel, and to allow so many people who would gladly hear it to perish, for Christ has so strictly commanded that the gospel and this testament be preached that he does not even wish the mass to be celebrated unless the gospel be preached. As he says, "As often as you do this, remember me." And, as St. Paul says, "You shall preach his death" [I Cor. 11:26]. For this reason it is dreadful and horrible to be a bishop, pastor, and preacher in our times, for no one knows this testament any longer, not to mention that they ought to preach it, although this is their highest and only duty and obligation. They

[29] Luther makes frequent and adverse references to the popular preaching of his day. The sermons were often mere recitals of the legends of the saints and were often told in a ribald or comic way, seemingly to chastise the people gently as well as to amuse them. Luther never concealed his scorn of the popular preaching of his day. The emphasis on preaching the gospel developed into a characteristic of the entire Reformation movement as well as the authority of its existence.

will certainly have to account for the many souls who perish because of such feeble preaching!

4. We should pray not as we do now, by turning over many pages and counting many beads, but by fixing our mind on some pressing need, desiring it with all earnestness, and thereby exercising faith and confidence toward God and not doubting that we shall be heard. This is how St. Bernard[30] instructs his brethren and says: Dear brethren, you shall by no means despise your prayer as if it were in vain, for indeed I tell you that before you have uttered the words, the prayer is already written in heaven; and you shall confidently expect from God one of two things: either that your prayer will be granted, or that if it is not granted it is because to fulfil it would not have been a good and useful thing.

Prayer, therefore, is a special exercise of faith, and faith makes the prayer so acceptable that either it will surely be granted, or something better than what we ask will be given in its stead. St. James says, "He who asks of God should not waver in faith; for if he wavers, let not that man think that he shall receive anything from God" [Jas. 1:6-8]. This is a clear statement which straightforwardly says: he who does not trust receives nothing, neither that which he asks nor anything better.

And to call forth such faith Christ himself has said in Mark 11 [:24], "I say to you, whatever you ask in prayer, believe that you receive it, and you will." And Luke 11 [:9-13], "Ask, and it will be given you; seek, and you will find; knock, and it will be opened to you. For every one who asks, receives, and he who seeks finds, and to him who knocks it will be opened. What father among you, if his son asks for bread, will give him a stone? Or if he asks for a fish, will give him a serpent? Or if he asks for an egg, will give him a scorpion? Now if you know how to give good gifts to your children, and you yourselves are not naturally good, how much more shall your heavenly Father give a good spirit to all them that ask him!"

5. Who is so hard and stony that such mighty words shall not

[30] Bernard (1091-1153) was the founder of the Cistercian monastery at Clairvaux.

move him to pray joyfully, gladly, and with every confidence? But how many prayers must be reformed if we are to pray aright according to these words? Now indeed, all the churches and monasteries are full of praying and singing, but why is it that so little improvement and benefit result from it, and that things daily grow worse? The reason is none other than that which St. James indicates when he says, "You ask much and receive nothing, because you have not prayed aright" [Jas. 4:3]. For where this kind of faith and confidence is not in the prayer, the prayer is dead and is nothing more than a grievous labor and work. If anything is given as a result of this prayer, it is only temporal benefit and without any blessing and help for the soul. In fact, not only [is it] no blessing for the soul, but rather [is it] to the great damage and blinding of souls, so that they go on prattling away interminably with their lips regardless of whether they receive anything, or desire anything, or trust anybody. And they remain hardened in this state of unbelief, the frame of mind most opposed to the exercise of faith and the nature of prayer.

It follows from this that he who prays aright never doubts that his prayer is surely acceptable and is heard, although the very thing for which he prays may not be granted him. For we are to lay our need before God in prayer, but not prescribe to him the measure or the manner, the limits or the place. If he wills to give us something better or something other than we think, we are to leave it to him; for frequently we do not know what we pray, as St. Paul says in Romans 8 [:26]. "God works and gives above and beyond all that we understand," as he also says in Ephesians 3 [:20]. So there can be no doubt that the prayer is acceptable and heard, and yet we leave the time and place, the measure and the limit up to God: he will surely do it as it should be. "They are the true worshipers who worship him in spirit and in truth" [John 4:24]. For those who do not believe that they will be heard sin against this commandment on the left side, and go far astray with their unbelief. But those who prescribe a limit to him sin on the right side and come too close to tempting God. He has forbidden us to stray from his commandment either to the left or to the right, that is, neither with unbelief nor with tempting. He has commanded us to remain on the right path with simple faith, believing in him but at the same time setting him no limits.

6. Thus we see that this commandment, like the second, should be nothing other than a doing and a keeping of the first commandment, that is, of faith, trust, confidence, hope, and love toward God so that in all the commandments the first may be the captain, and faith the chief work and life of all other works, without which, as has been said, such works cannot be good.

But if you say, "What if I cannot believe that my prayer is heard and accepted?" I reply that faith, prayer, and all other good works are commanded so that you should know what you can do and what you cannot do. And when you find that you cannot believe [in this way] and do [what is commanded], humble yourself before God, deploring this fact, and in this way begin with a weak spark of faith and strengthen it more and more every day by exercising it in all your living and doing. For there is not a man living who does not have a full share in breaking the first and greatest commandment, i.e., the commandment to believe. Even the holy apostles in the gospel, and St. Peter in particular, were weak in faith, so that they also asked Christ and said, "Lord, increase our faith" [Luke 17:5]. And he very frequently rebukes them because they have so little faith.[31]

Therefore, you shall not despair or let up for a moment either in prayer or in other works if you find that you do not believe as firmly as you ought and want to. In fact, you should thank God with all your heart that he thus reveals to you your weakness, through which weakness he teaches and admonishes you what your real need is, that is, to exercise and strengthen yourself in faith every day. For how many do you see who go on praying, singing, reading, and working, and who have every appearance of being great saints, yet they never reach the point of knowing where they stand with respect to the chief work, faith. In this state they blind themselves and lead other people astray. They think that all is very well with them, and in their darkness they build without any faith

[31] Cf. Matt. 14:31; Mark 4:40.

at all on the sand of their own works and not on God's grace and promise through a firm, pure faith.

Therefore, however long we live, we shall always have our hands full if we remain pupils of the first commandment and of faith throughout all works and sufferings, and never cease to learn. Nobody knows what a great thing it is to trust God alone except him who begins to trust and tries to do faith's works.

7. Now just take a look! If no other work were commanded, would not prayer alone suffice to exercise a man's whole life in faith? The spiritual estate has been especially established for this work, as indeed in ancient times some fathers prayed day and night. In fact, there is no Christian man who does not have time to pray without ceasing. But I mean spiritual praying. That is, no man is so heavily burdened with his work that he cannot, if the will is there, speak with God in his heart while he is working, lay his need and that of other men before him, ask for help, make petition, and in all this exercise and strengthen his faith.

That is what the Lord means when he says in Luke 18 [:1] that we should pray without ceasing, although in Matthew 6 [:7] he forbids much speaking and long prayers and rebukes the hypocrites for so doing, not because long oral prayer is an evil thing, but because it is not the right prayer which must be made at all times, and which, without the inner prayer of faith, is nothing. For we must also practice outward prayer at its proper time, especially in the mass, as this commandment requires, and wherever it furthers the inner life of prayer and faith, whether in the house or in the field, in this task or in that. But we have no time to say more about that now, for this belongs to the Lord's Prayer, in which all requests and spoken prayer are summed up in few words.

8. Where now are those who desire to know and to do good works? Let them undertake just prayer alone and rightly exercise themselves in faith, and they will find that it is true, as the holy fathers have said, that there is no work like prayer. Mumbling with the mouth is easy, or at least considered easy. But to follow the words in deep devotion and sincerity of heart, that is, with desire and in faith, so that one earnestly desires what the words say and

does not doubt that they will be heard, that is a great deed in God's sight.

Here the evil spirit hinders men with all his powers. Oh, how often will he prevent here the desire to pray, not allow us to find time or place, and even raise doubts over whether a man is worthy to ask anything of such a majesty as God, so confusing us that a man does not know himself whether he is really praying or not, whether it is possible that his prayer is acceptable, and other similar strange thoughts. For the evil spirit knows well enough how powerful one man's truly believing prayer is, how it hurts him and benefits all men. Therefore, this evil spirit does not willingly let praying happen.

A man must indeed be wise when tempted in this way and not doubt whether he and his prayers are unworthy before such infinite majesty. In no wise dare he rely on his worthiness or relax because of his unworthiness. He must accept God's command and leave it to him. A man must resist the devil and say to him, "Because of my worthiness I undertake nothing, because of my unworthiness, I omit nothing. I pray and work only because God, of his pure mercy, has promised to hear and be gracious to all unworthy men. God has not only promised it, but most strongly commanded us to pray, trust, and receive on pain of his eternal displeasure and wrath. If it has not been too much for that High Majesty solemnly and seriously to make it incumbent on his unworthy worms to pray, to trust, and to receive from him, how shall it be too much for me to take such a command upon myself with all joy, however worthy or unworthy I may be?" Thus we must drive out the devil's suggestion with God's command. This is the only way the devil will ever relent—otherwise, never at all.

9. But what are the things and the necessities which a man must lay before Almighty God, cry to him over, and thereby exercise faith? Answer: First, every man's own besetting need and trouble, of which David says in Psalm 32 [:7], "Thou art my refuge in all trouble which compasses me; thou art my comfort to deliver me from all evil which surrounds me." Likewise in Psalm 142 [:1-2], "I cried to the Lord God with my voice; with my voice I make supplication to the Lord, I will spread out my prayer before his eyes

and will pour out before him all that gives me concern." At mass a Christian man should call to mind the failings or the excesses he feels. He should pour all these out freely before God with weeping and groaning as woefully as he can to his faithful Father, who is ready to help him. And if you do not know or recognize your need, or experience no spiritual attacks,[32] then you ought to know that you are in the very worst possible plight. For the greatest temptation is that you find yourself so hardened, hardhearted, and insensitive that no trouble moves you.

There is just no better mirror in which to see your need than the Ten Commandments, in which you will find what you lack and what you should seek. Therefore, where you find in yourself a weak faith, feeble hope, and little love toward God; where you find that you do not praise and honor God but love your own honor and fame, think much of the favor of men, do not gladly hear mass and sermon, are too lazy to pray (in which matters there is no one who has not sinned), then you must pay more heed to these infirmities than to all physical harm to goods, honor, and life, and believe that they are worse than death and all mortal sickness. You should earnestly lay these [infirmities] before God, lament and ask for help, and with all confidence expect help, believing that you are heard and that you will receive help and mercy.

Then proceed to the Second Table of the commandments. See how disobedient you have been and still are toward father and mother and all in authority; how you sin against your neighbor with anger, hatred, and evil words; how you are tempted to unchastity, covetousness, and injustice in word and deed against your neighbor. In this way you will without a doubt find that you are full of all need and misery, and that you have reason enough to weep even drops of blood, if you could.

10. But I know well that many are so foolish as not to want to ask for such things, unless they first know that they [themselves]

---

[32] *Anfechtung,* also translated in this paragraph as "temptation" and "trouble," means temptation in the sense of an attack, and not *Versuchung,* which means temptation in the sense of being led away. The attack may come from God as a testing of faith, or from the devil to destroy it. *Anfechtung* is a rich and complex idea to Luther, and the word is used to express the doubt, despair, and self-deception which assailed Luther. Cf. Ronald Bainton, *Here I Stand* (New York: Abingdon-Cokesbury Press, 1950), p. 42.

are pure, and believe therefore that God hears no one who is in sin. All this is the work of those false preachers who teach men to make a start not with faith and trust in God's favor, but with their own works.

Look here, wretched man that you are! If you have broken a leg, or if a deadly peril overtakes you, you call upon God then. You call on this saint and that one and you do not wait until your leg is healed or the danger is past. You are not so foolish as to think that God hears no one whose leg is broken or who is in bodily danger. On the contrary, you believe that God hears most of all when you are in the greatest need and fear. Why then are you so foolish in this instance, where there is immeasurably greater need and eternal hurt, that you do not ask for faith, hope, love, patience, obedience, chastity, gentleness, peace, and righteousness, unless you are already free from unbelief, doubt, pride, disobedience, unchastity, anger, covetousness, and unrighteousness? Well then, the more you find yourself lacking in these things, the more ought you diligently to pray and cry unto God.

How blind we are! We run to God with our body's sickness and need; with our soul's sickness we run from him, and will not come back to him before we are well again—just as if there were one god who could help the body and another who could help the soul, or as if we wanted to help ourselves in spiritual need, which is greater than bodily need. That is a devilish and expedient plan!

No indeed, my dear man. If you want to be cured of sin, you must not withdraw from God, but run to him and pray to him with much more confidence than if some physical distress had overtaken you. God is not hostile to sinners, only to unbelievers. That means to those who do not recognize and bewail their sin or seek help for it from God, but in their own presumption wish first to purify themselves, will not admit their need of his grace, and will not suffer him to be a God who gives to everyone and takes nothing for what he gives.

11. All this has been said of prayer for personal needs, and of prayer in general. But the prayer which really belongs to this commandment and is called a work of the holy day is far better and greater. This prayer is to be made for all Christendom, for all

the needs of all men, foe and friend alike, especially for those who live in the parish or the diocese.

St. Paul commanded his disciple Timothy: "I exhort you to see to it that prayers and intercessions be made for all men, for kings and all that are in authority, that we may lead a quiet, peaceable life in God's service and in purity. For this is good and acceptable in the sight of God our Savior" [I Tim. 2:1-3]. In the same manner Jeremiah 29 [:7] commanded the people of Israel to pray for the city and land of Babylon because the peace of the city was their peace also. And Baruch 1 [:11-12] says, "Pray for the life of the king of Babylon and for the life of his son that we may live in peace under their rule."

This common prayer is precious and the most effective, and it is for the sake of this that we assemble ourselves together. The church is called a house of prayer[33] because we are all there as a congregation and with one accord to bring our own needs as well as those of all men before God and to call upon him for mercy. But this must be done from the heart and with sincerity; we must take to heart the need of all men, and pray for them in real sympathy and in true faith and trust. Where such prayer does not take place in the mass, it would be better to omit the mass. By assembling together in a house of prayer we show that we ought to make common prayer and petition for the entire fellowship. What sense does it make for us to scatter those prayers and divide them up so that everyone prays only for himself, and nobody concerns himself with anybody else for another's need? Of what use can that prayer be, how can it be good, acceptable common prayer, or be called a work of the holy day and of the assembled congregation, the way they do it? They make their own petty prayers, one for this and one for that, and they have nothing but prayers for their own use and prayers to their own advantage. God is a foe of such prayers.

12. An indication of this common or collective prayer has been retained from ancient practice. [According to this ancient practice] the confession of sins is recited at the end of the sermon, and prayer is made from the pulpit for all Christendom. But this should not be the end of the matter, as is the custom and fashion nowadays. It

[33] Isa. 56:7; Matt. 21:13.

should be an exhortation to pray throughout the entire mass for such need as the preacher makes us feel. And in order that we may pray worthily, he first of all admonishes us because of our sins and thereby makes us humble. This should be done as briefly as possible; after that the entire congregation should commonly confess its own sin to God, and pray with earnestness and faith for all men.

O if any congregation, please God, were to hear mass in this way and pray in this way, so that a common, earnest, heartfelt cry of the whole people were to rise up to God, what immeasurable virtue and help would result from such a prayer! What more terrible thing could happen to all evil spirits? What greater work could be done on earth whereby so many pious souls would be preserved and so many sinners converted?

For indeed, the Christian church on earth has no greater power or work against everything that may oppose it than such common prayer. The evil spirit knows this well, and therefore he does all that he can to prevent such prayer. This is why he lets us build handsome churches, endow many colleges, make anthems, read and sing, celebrate many masses, and multiply ceremonies beyond all measure. This brings him no sorrow. On the contrary, he helps us to do it, so that we will regard such ways the best and think that in doing them we have done our whole duty. But when this common, effectual, and fruitful prayer suffers meanwhile, and remains unnoticed because of such hypocrisy, then he has gotten what he is after. For when prayer is subordinated, nobody takes anything from him and nobody resists him. But if he noticed that we wished to practice this prayer, even if it were under a straw roof or in a pigsty, he would not tolerate it for an instant. He would fear such a pigsty far more than all the high, great, and lovely churches, towers, and bells that ever were, if such prayer were not in them. What matters is not the places and buildings where we assemble, but this unconquerable prayer alone, and our really praying it together and offering it to God.

13. We see the power of this prayer in the fact that long ago Abraham prayed for the five cities, Sodom, Gomorrah, and the others, and thereby he accomplished so much, that if there had

been ten righteous people in them, two in each city, God would not have destroyed them [Gen. 18:32]. What then could many men do, if they united and called upon God earnestly and with sincere confidence?

St. James also says, "Dear brethren, pray for one another that you may be saved. For the prayer of a righteous man avails much, a prayer that perseveres and does not cease" [Jas. 5:16], that is, which does not cease asking ever more and more, as some faint-hearted men do, although what it asks does not immediately happen. And as an example in this matter he sets before us Elijah the prophet, who was a man, he says, as we are. Elijah prayed that it might not rain; and it did not rain for three years and six months. And he prayed again, and it rained, and everything became fruitful [Jas. 5:17-18]. There are many texts and examples in the Scriptures which urge us to pray with earnestness and faith. As David says, "The eyes of the Lord look upon the righteous, and his ears listen to their prayer" [Ps. 33:18]. Again, "God is near to all that call upon him, provided they call upon him in truth" [Ps. 145:18]. Why does he add "provided they call upon him in truth"? Because it is not prayer nor calling upon God when just the mouth is mumbling.

What can God do when you go at your prayer book[34] or Paternoster[35] with your mouth and think of nothing except finishing all the words and completing the number?[36] If someone were to ask you what it was all about, or what it was you prayed for, you yourself would not know; for you had not thought of laying this or that matter before God or desiring it. Your only reason for praying is that you are obliged to say so and so many prayers and this you intend to do in full. Little wonder, then, that thunder and lightning frequently set fire to churches when we make the house of prayer into a house of mockery by calling that prayer in which we bring nothing before God and desire nothing from him!

We should do as those do who wish to ask a favor of great princes. They do not plan merely to babble a certain number of

[34] The breviary used by the clergy.

[35] Luther probably means the bead of the rosary known as *paternoster*, the Lord's Prayer. Cf. *PE* 1, 236, n. 1.

[36] I.e., of prescribed prayers.

words, for the prince would reach a different decision: he would think that they were mocking him or that they were mad. On the contrary, they express themselves very plainly and present their need earnestly. They make direct appeal to his mercy in the certain confidence that he will grant what they ask. So we must deal with God about definite things. We must mention, for instance, some pressing need, commend it to his mercy and good will, and we must not doubt that our prayer is heard; for he has promised to hear such prayer. No earthly lord has done that.

14. We are masters of that form of prayer which springs from bodily need or illness. One man calls on St. Christopher, another on St. Barbara.[37] Another vows a pilgrimage to St. James[38] or to this or that shrine. When we go about like this we display earnest prayer and show good confidence and every good kind of prayer. But when we are at the mass in our churches we stand like blockheads.[39] We do not know what to say or what to bewail. The beads rattle, the pages rustle, and the mouth mumbles. And that is all there is to it.

But if you were to ask what you ought to bring up and bewail in your prayers, you could easily learn from the Ten Commandments and the Lord's Prayer. Open your eyes and look into your own life and into the life of all Christendom, particularly that of the spiritual estate. You will find how low faith, hope, love, obedience, chastity, and all virtue are, while all manner of heinous vice reigns supreme. You will find what a lack there is of good preachers and prelates; how only knaves, children, fools, and women rule. If you do this you will see that there is need every hour, everywhere, and without ceasing to pray with tears of blood to avert the terrible

---

[37] Two of the fourteen saints of medieval devotion who were supposed collectively to be the "defenders from all evils." Each of these saints was a defender against some particular disease or danger. Christopher, whose legend is well known, was invoked particularly by bookbinders, gardeners, and mariners against lightning, storms, epilepsy, and pestilence. Barbara was reputed to be an early Christian, beheaded by her pagan father. He was consumed by lightning in punishment. She came to be regarded as a protectress against thunderstorms and fire. Cf. *The Fourteen of Consolation*. *PE* 1, 103-171.

[38] The shrine of St. James at Compostella. Cf. p. 12, n. 9.

[39] *Olgotzen*, literally, the wooden images of saints which were painted with oil paints. The expression was transferred to any dull person and sometimes to priests, who were anointed with oil at their consecration.

wrath of God. In fact it is true that there has never been a greater need of praying than at present and increasingly so until the end of the world. If such terrible crimes do not move you to lament and complaint, do not let yourself be led astray by your rank, station, good works, or prayer: there is not a Christian streak in you however pious you may be. But it has all been foretold, that when God's anger is greatest and Christendom suffers her greatest need, then petitioners and supplicants to God shall not be found, as Isaiah says with tears, "Thou art angry with us, and unfortunately there is nobody who rises up and takes hold of thee" [Isa. 64:7]. Likewise Ezekiel 22 [:30-31] says, "I sought for a man among them, whether there be one who should make a hedge between us and stand against me and fend me off. But I have not found him. Therefore I have let my anger go against them, and have swallowed them up in the fire of my wrath." With these words God shows how he wants us to withstand him and turn away his anger from one another, as it is frequently written of the prophet Moses that he restrained God, lest his anger should overwhelm the people of Israel.[40]

15. Where then will they be who not only do not care about this misfortune in Christendom and do not pray to prevent it, but laugh at it, take pleasure in it, condemn, malign, sing, and talk of their neighbor's sins, and even then dare, unafraid and unashamed, to go to church, to hear mass, to say prayers, and to regard themselves as pious Christians and allow themselves to be so regarded? They really need us to pray twice as much for them where we only pray once for those whom they condemn, talk about, and laugh at. These people are foretold in the person of the thief on Christ's left hand. He blasphemed Christ in his suffering, weakness, and need. They are also foretold in all of those who reviled Christ on the cross when they more than all the others should have helped him.

O God, how blind, no, how insane we Christians have become! When will there be an end of wrath, O heavenly Father? Our folly makes us mock, blaspheme, and condemn the tragedy of

---

[40] Cf. Exod. 32:11-14; Num. 14:13-19, 21:7; Ps. 106:23.

Christendom, for which we are to pray when we are gathered together in church and at mass. If the Turk destroys cities, country, and people, and lays waste the churches, we think a great injury has been done Christendom. Then we start complaining, and urge kings and princes to wage war. But when faith collapses, love grows cold, God's word is neglected, and all manner of sin takes control, nobody thinks of fighting. In fact, pope, bishop, priests, and clergy, who ought to be the generals, captains, and standard-bearers in this spiritual warfare against Turks of a far deadlier spiritual kind, are themselves the very princes and leaders of such Turks, of a devilish army, just as Judas led the Jews when they took Christ prisoner. It had to be an apostle, a bishop, a priest, one of the best, who began the work of slaying Christ. And in the same way, too, Christendom is being destroyed not by the Turks, but by those who are supposed to defend it. And yet they go on being so senseless that they want to eat the Turk alive, and at the same time they set fire to their own house and sheep stall and let them burn away, sheep and all, and worry more about the wolf in the woods. That is how things are nowadays! This is the reward we have earned for our ingratitude for the unending grace Christ won for us freely with his precious blood, grievous labor, and bitter death.

16. Now then! Where are those idle fellows who do not know how to do good works? Where are those who run to Rome, to St. James, hither and thither? Take upon yourself this one single work of the mass, and look at your neighbor's sin and plight. Take pity on him, let it grieve you, plead to God for him, and pray for him. Do the same for every other need of Christendom, especially for the rulers, whom God, for the intolerable punishment and torment of us all, allows to fall and be misled so horribly. If you do this diligently, be assured that you are one of the best fighters and captains, not only against the Turks but also against the devils and powers of hell. But if you do not do it, what help would it be for you if you were to perform all the miracles of the saints and defeat all the Turks, and yet were found guilty of having disregarded your neighbor's need and of having thereby sinned

against love? For Christ at the last day will not ask how much you have prayed, fasted, pilgrimaged, done this or that for yourself, but how much good you have done to others, even to the very least [Matt. 25:40, 45].

Now without any doubt among these "least" are also those who are in sin and spiritual poverty, in captivity and in need, of whom there are now far more than those who suffer bodily need. Now see for yourself! Our own self-imposed good works lead us to and into ourselves, so that we just seek our own benefit and salvation. But God's commandments drive us to our neighbor's need, that by means of these commandments we may be of benefit only to others and to their salvation. Just as on the cross Christ prayed not for himself alone but rather for us when he said, "Father, forgive them, for they know not what they do" [Luke 23:34], so we must also pray for one another. From this discussion everybody can see how these slanderers, frivolous judges, and despisers of other people are a perverted, evil tribe who do nothing but heap abuse on those for whom they should pray. In this vice nobody is sunk as deeply as those very men who do many good works of their own devising, and who in men's eyes appear to be something rather special, and are held in high regard on account of their beautiful and splendid life full of good works.

17. This commandment, if understood in its spiritual intention, has a much deeper meaning which embraces the whole nature of man. Here it must be understood that in Hebrew "sabbath" means a festival or rest. Because God rested on the seventh day and ceased from all his works which he had created, Genesis 2 [:3], he commanded that man also should celebrate the seventh day, and that we should cease from our works which we do on the other six days. This same "sabbath" has been changed into Sunday for us, and the other days are called working days. Sunday means a day of rest, or a day of celebration, or a holy day. And would to God that in Christendom there were no holidays except Sundays, and that we made all the festivals of Our Lady and the saints fall on Sundays. The labor of the work days would prevent much vice. The land also would not be so poor and impoverished. But these

days we are plagued with many holy days, to the destruction of souls, bodies, and goods. A great deal more could be said of this matter.

This rest or pause from work is of two kinds, bodily and spiritual. For this reason this commandment is to be understood in two ways.

The bodily celebration or rest is what we have just discussed, that we put aside the work of our hands and rest from our labor so that we may gather in church, see mass, hear God's word, and offer common, single-minded prayer together. Neither is this festival, though intended for the benefit of the body, celebrated in Christendom by God's command. As the Apostle says in Colossians 2 [:16], "Let no man bind you by obligation to any kind of festival." For in ancient times these festivals were signs, but now the truth has been fulfilled, so that all days are holy days, as Isaiah 66 [:23] says, "One holy day shall follow another." Or put the other way around, all days are workdays. Yet it [Sunday] is a necessity and is ordained by the church for the sake of the imperfect laity and the working class so that they may also come [to hear] the word of God. For, as we see, the priests and clergy celebrate mass every day, pray at all hours, and train themselves in God's word by studying, reading, and listening. For this reason they are freed from the work which is done by others and are supported by tithes. They have a holy day every day, and they do the works of a holy day every day. For them there is no working day; every day is like the other. And if we were all perfect and knew the gospel, we might work every day if we wanted, or rest if we could. For a day of rest now is neither necessary nor is it commanded except for the teaching of God's word and prayer.

The spiritual rest which God especially intends in this commandment is that we not only cease from our labor and trade but much more—that we let God alone work in us and that in all our powers do we do nothing of our own. But how is this done? In this way: man, corrupted by sin, has much wicked love of and inclination to all sins. Man is as Scripture describes him in Genesis 8 [:21], "Man's heart and mind incline always to evil," that is, to pride, disobedience, anger, hatred, covetousness, etc. To sum up, in all that he does or leaves undone, he rather seeks his own advantage and his own way. He seeks his own honor, rather than God's and that of his neighbor. Therefore, all his works, all his words, all his thoughts, all his life are evil and not godly.

Now if God is to live and work in him, all this vice and wickedness must be choked and uprooted, so that in this event there is a rest from all our works, words, thoughts, and life, so that henceforth (as St. Paul says in Galatians 2 [:20]) it is no longer we who live, but Christ who lives, works, and speaks in us. This is not accomplished with comfortable, pleasant days. On the contrary, in these circumstances a man must hurt his own nature and let it be hurt. Here the strife between the spirit and the flesh begins, here the spirit resists anger, lust, and pride, while the flesh wants to enjoy pleasure, honor, and comfort. Of this St. Paul says in Galatians 5 [:24], "They that are our Lord Christ's have crucified the flesh with its affections and lusts." Only then do the good works ensue—fasting, watching, labor, about which some say and write so much, although they know neither the source nor the purpose of these good works. Therefore, we too will now discuss them.

18. The rest we are discussing, namely, that our works cease and that God alone works in us, is accomplished in two ways. In the first place through our own effort; in the second, through the effort or urging of others.

Our own effort is to be made and directed in such a way that in the first place we resist and do not heed our flesh, senses, will, and thoughts when we see that they are tempting us, as the wise man says, "Follow not your own desires" [Ecclus. 18:30]. And Deuteronomy 12 [:8], "You shall not do what is right in your own eyes."

Here a man must make daily use of those prayers David prayed, "Lord, lead me in thy path, and let me not walk in my own ways" [Ps. 119:35, 37], and many like prayers, which are all summed up in the prayer, "Thy kingdom come." For the desires are so many, so various, and besides, sometimes these desires appear in such an attractive, subtle, and desirable form through the suggestion of the evil one that it is not possible for a man to direct his own life. He must make a total commitment, commend himself to God's governance, and not trust his own reason at all, as Jeremiah says, "Lord, I know that the way of man is not in his own power" [Jer. 10:23]. That is demonstrated when the children of Israel went out of Egypt through the wilderness, where there was no road, no food, no drink, no help. Therefore, God went before them, by day in a bright cloud, by night in a fiery pillar, fed them from heaven with heavenly bread, and preserved their garments and shoes that they did not wear out, as we read in the books of Moses [Exod. 13:21; 16:4; Deut. 29:5]. For this reason we pray, Thy kingdom come; thou rule us and not we ourselves, for there is nothing more dangerous in us than our reason and will. The highest and first work of God in us and the best training is that we let our own works go and let our reason and will lie dormant, resting and commending ourselves to God in all things, especially when they appear spiritual and good.

19. After this comes the discipline of the flesh, the killing of its gross evil lust and giving it rest and relaxation. We must kill the flesh and subdue it with fastings, watchings, and labor. And it is from this that we learn how much and why we should fast, watch, and labor.

There are unfortunately many blind men who practice self-castigation, whether it be fasting, watching, or labor, and they do so only because they think that these are good works and that they earn much merit by doing them. This is why they travel about and at times do so much that they simply ruin their health and drive themselves mad. Far blinder still are those who measure their fasting not only by the quantity or duration as these do, but also by the nature of the food. They think that it is worth much more if they abstain from meat, eggs, or butter. In addition to these there are those who schedule their fasts by the saints and select special days: one fasts on Wednesdays, another on Saturdays, another on St. Barbara's day,[41] another on St. Sebastian's day,[42] and so on. All these people seek nothing beyond the work itself in their fasting. When they have performed that, they think they have done a good work. I will make no mention of those who fast, yet fill themselves

[41] December 4. Cf. p. 68, n. 37.

[42] January 20. St. Sebastian, a martyr of the third century, was supposed to ward off the plague.

with drink. Some fast so richly with fish and other foods that they would come much nearer to fasting if they ate meat, eggs, and butter. By doing this they would obtain far better results from their fasting. For such fasting is not fasting, but a mockery of fasting as well as of God.

Therefore, I am quite prepared to allow everybody to fast on any day he likes and choose which food and how much of it he likes, provided he does not stop there but pays attention to his own body. One must discipline the flesh with fastings, watchings, and labor only insofar as it is proud and self-willed, no more. Not even if the pope, the church, bishop, father confessor, or anybody else commands it. For nobody ought to measure and regulate fasts, vigils, and tasks, matters of amount or kinds of food, or special days. These matters should be regulated by the ebb and flow of the pride and lust of the flesh. For it was solely to kill and subdue the pride and lust of the flesh that fastings, vigils, and penances were instituted. If it were not for this lust, eating would be as meritorious as fasting; sleeping as watching; idleness as labor; and one would be as good as the other without any distinction.

20. Now if someone should find that more wantonness arose in his flesh from eating fish than from eating eggs and meat, let him eat meat and not fish. Or, on the other hand, if he found that he were going mad, or that his body and system were being ruined by fasting, or that it is no longer necessary to kill the wantonness of his flesh, then he must cease from fasting entirely and eat, sleep, and take it easy as far as it is essential to health, regardless of whether it is against the church's law or the rules of his order. For no commandment of the church, no rule of any order, can make fasting, vigils, and penances of more worth, or the pursuit of these activities, except inasmuch and insofar as they serve to subdue or destroy the flesh and its lusts. Where men go beyond this, and where fasting, eating, sleeping, and watching are imposed beyond the body's endurance or more than is necessary for the killing of lust, where the natural strength of the body is ruined and a man is driven out of his mind—then in these circumstances let no man imagine that he has done good works or excuse himself by referring to the church's command or the rule of his order. He will

be regarded as a man who takes no care of himself, and, as far as he is able, he has become his own murderer.

The body is not given to us to kill its natural life or work, but only its wantonness, unless its wantonness were so strong and powerful that we could not sufficiently resist it without ruin and harm to the natural life. For, as has been said, in the practice of fasting, vigils, and labors, we are not to look upon the works themselves, or the days, or the amount, or the [kind of] food, but only on the wanton and lustful Adam, that by these disciplines a man may be protected from the dominion of Adam.

21. In the light of this principle we can judge how wisely or foolishly certain women behave when they are pregnant, and also how one should deal with the sick. The foolish women cling so firmly to their fasting that they would rather run the risk of great danger to the child they carry, as well as to themselves, than not fast with the others. They make a matter of conscience where there is none, and when there is a matter of conscience they make none. This is all the fault of the preachers, for they are continually chattering about fasting, but they never indicate its right use, its limit, its fruit, its cause, and its purpose. By the same token, the sick ought to be allowed to eat and drink whatever they like every day. In brief, when the lust of the flesh ceases, every reason for fasting, watching, working, eating this or that has already ceased, and there is no longer any commandment whatever that is binding.

Yet on the other hand, a man has to watch himself lest a lazy indifference about killing the wantonness of the flesh grow out of this freedom, for Adam is crafty in his guile when he seeks freedom for himself or when pleading the ruination of the body or mind. This is what happens when men plunge in rashly and say that it is neither necessary nor commanded to fast or mortify the flesh, and are ready to eat this or that without reservation, just as if they had had much experience of fasting over a long period, though they have never even tried it.

We are to guard no less against offending those who do not have a proper grasp of the situation and think it is a great sin if we do not fast when they fast or eat when they eat. In cases like these we should teach them with kindness, and neither despise them with a superior mien, nor eat this and that despite them. But we must point out to them the reason it is right to do so, and lead them too into the same understanding as we have. If, however, they are stubborn and will not listen, we must let them go their own way and do what we know to be right.

22. The second form of discipline which we receive at the hands of others is when men or devils cause us suffering, as when our property is taken, our body is sick, and our honor is taken away; when everything moves us to anger, impatience, and unrest. For the work of God rules in us according to his wisdom and not according to our judgment; according to his purity and chastity, and not according to the will of our flesh. God's work is wisdom and purity, but our work is folly and impurity. It is these that we must cause to rest. So, then, we should be ruled by his peace and not by our anger, our impatience, or our unrest. For peace, too, is the work of God, but impatience is the work of our flesh. It is the works of the flesh that must rest and be made dead, so that we celebrate a spiritual holiday everywhere, let our own good works be idle, and let God work in us.

Therefore, to destroy such works of ours as well as the old Adam in us, God overwhelms us with those things which move us to anger, with many sufferings which rouse us to impatience, and last of all, even with death and the abuse of the world. By means of these he seeks nothing else but to drive out of us anger, impatience, and unrest, and to perfect his own work in us, that is, his peace. Thus Isaiah 28 [:21] says, "He takes upon himself an alien work, that he may do his own proper work." What does that mean? He sends us suffering and unrest to teach us to have patience and peace. He bids us die that he may make us live. He does this as long as and until a man, thoroughly trained, reaches such a pitch of peace and poise that he is no longer upset whether things go well or ill with him, whether he dies or lives, whether he is honored or dishonored. [In such a man] only God himself dwells; there there are no works of man. This is what it means to observe the day of rest and keep it holy. It is then that a man ceases to rule his own life, then that he desires nothing for himself, then that nothing disturbs him: God himself leads him. It is then that there is nothing but godly happiness, joy, and peace, and all other works and virtues as well.

23. God considers these works so great that he commands us not only to keep the day of rest, but also to hallow it or regard it as holy. In so doing he declares that there is nothing more precious than suffering, dying, and all manner of misfortune. They are something sacred, and set a man apart from his own works for the works of God, just as a church is set apart from natural works for the worship of God. Therefore, a man should recognize them as something holy too. When they fall to his lot, he should be glad and thank God. When they come they serve to make him holy, so that he [can] fulfil this commandment and become blessed, redeemed from his sinful works. Thus says David, "Precious in the sight of the Lord is the death of his saints" [Ps. 116:15].

To strengthen us for this discipline God has not only commanded us to keep such a rest (for nature is very unwilling to die and to suffer, and it is a bitter holy day for nature to cease from its own works and be dead), but he has also comforted us in the Scriptures with many words and told us in Psalm 91 [:15], "I am with him in all his suffering and will help him out of it." And again in Psalm 34 [:18], "The Lord is near to all who suffer and he will help them."

As if this were not enough, God has given us a powerful, strong example [in] his only dear Son Jesus Christ, our Lord. He lay [in the tomb] the entire day of rest free from all his works, and was the first to fulfil this commandment. He did not need to do this for himself, but solely to comfort us, that we, too, in all suffering and dying should be quiet and enjoy peace. Moreover, as Christ rose after his peace and rest, and now henceforth lives only in God and God in him, so we also shall be lifted up to God by the killing of our Adam, which is perfectly accomplished only through natural death and burial, that God may live and work in us forever. Look! these are the three parts of man: reason, desire, and dislike. All man's works are done under the impulse of these. These, therefore, must be slain by these three exercises: God's governance, our self-mortification, and the suffering inflicted on us by other people. This is how we must honor God and make way for his works.

24. But as has been said before,[48] such works are to be done and such suffering endured in faith and in the sure confidence of God's favor, so that all works remain within the sphere of the first commandment and of faith, which exercises itself in these sufferings and grows strong. It is for the sake of this faith that all other commandments and works have been instituted. See what a pretty golden ring these three commandments and their works make of themselves! See how the second commandment emerges from the first commandment and its subject, faith, and runs into the third, and the third in turn works back through the second into the first! The first work is to believe and to have a good heart and confidence in God. From this flows the second good work, to praise God's name, to confess his grace, to give all honor to him alone. Then follows the third, to worship God by praying, hearing the sermon, meditating upon and pondering God's benefits, and, in addition, chastising oneself and keeping the flesh subdued.

But when the evil spirit perceives such faith, such honor and worship of God, he rages and stirs up persecution, attacks body, goods, honor, and life. He brings upon us illness, poverty, shame, and death, which God allows and ordains to happen in this way. Now see, it is at this point that the second work or observance of the third commandment begins. By this observance faith is sorely tested, as is gold in the fire [Ecclus. 2:5]. It is a fine thing to hold on to a firm confidence in God, although he sends us death, shame, sickness, poverty. And while undergoing this horrible form of wrath it is a fine thing to regard him as our all-gracious Father, something which must be done in this work of the third commandment. In such circumstances suffering compels faith to call upon God's name and to praise him in such suffering. So faith comes right through the third commandment, and back into the second again. And through that very calling on the name of God and praising him, faith grows and comes into its own. In this way faith strengthens itself through the two works of the third and second commandment. Thus faith goes out into works and through works comes back to itself again, just as the sun goes forth to its setting and comes again at its rising. This is why the Scriptures associate the

[48] See pp. 40-41.

daytime with peaceful living in doing works, the night with a life of suffering and adversity. And so faith lives and works in both; it goes out and returns in both, as Christ says in John 9 [:4].

25. This is the order in which we pray for good works in the Lord's Prayer. The first is when we say, "Our Father, which art in heaven." These are the words of the first work of faith, which according to the first commandment does not doubt that it has a gracious Father in heaven. The second is "Hallowed be thy name," in which faith desires that God's name, praise, and honor be glorified, and that God's name be called upon in every need, as the second commandment says. The third is "Thy kingdom come," in which we pray for the proper sabbath and true, quiet rest from our own works, so that only God's work is done in us and that in this way God rules in us as in his own kingdom. As he says, "Behold, God's kingdom is nowhere else except in you yourselves" [Luke 17:21]. The fourth petition is "Thy will be done," in which we pray that we may keep and hold the seven commandments of the Second Table, in which faith is further exercised toward our neighbor, just as in the first three it is exercised in works toward God. Further, these are the petitions in which the little words "Thou," "Thy," and "Thine" stand, because these words seek only what belongs to God. All the others say "us," "our," "ours," etc., for in them we pray for our goods and blessedness.

Let this then suffice as a plain and simple explanation of the First Table of Moses to point out to ordinary people what are the highest of good works.

The Second Table follows

The First Commandment of the Second Table of Moses

Thou shalt honor thy father and mother

1. From this commandment we teach that after the excellent works of the first three commandments there are no better works than to obey and serve all those who are set in authority over us.

This is why disobedience is a sin worse than murder, unchastity, theft, dishonesty, and all that goes with them. There is no better way we can learn the difference between greater and lesser sins than from the order of God's commandments, although there are also distinctions within the works of each individual commandment. Who does not know that it is a greater sin to curse than to be angry, that to strike is worse than cursing, and that to strike father and mother is worse than striking anyone else? Thus these seven commandments teach us how we should exercise ourselves in good works toward men, above all, toward those set in authority over us.

The first work is that we should honor our own father and mother. This honoring does not consist in merely showing them all deference. It means that we obey them, have regard for what they do and what they say, esteem them highly, give way to them, and accept what they say. It means that we endure their treatment of us without complaint, so long as it is not contrary to the first three commandments, and, in addition, provide them with food, clothing, and shelter when they are in need. For it is not without purpose that he has said, "Thou shalt honor them." He does not say, "Thou shalt love them," although it means that as well. But honor is higher than mere love, and includes within it a kind of fear which unites with love and has such an effect upon a man that he fears offending them more than he fears the ensuing punishment. It is just as there is fear in the honor we pay a holy place, and yet we do not flee from it as from a punishment, but draw all the more near to it. True honor is such a fear mingled with love. The other kind of fear that is without love is the fear of those things which we despise or avoid, e.g., the fear of the hangman or of punishment. There is no honor in that, for it is fear without love: in fact, it is a fear mixed with hatred and hostility. We have a proverb of St. Jerome[44] about this: What we fear, we also hate.[45] God does not want to be feared or honored with that kind of fear, nor does he want our parents honored with this kind of fear, but rather with the first kind, the kind mingled with love and confidence.

[44] Jerome (*ca.* 340-420) was noted chiefly for his labors in revising and translating the Latin Bible. His translation, known as the Vulgate, was declared the official Bible of the Roman Catholic Church by the Council of Trent in 1546.

[45] *Epistola ad Theophilum. MPL* 22, 737.

2. This work appears easy, yet few see it rightly. For where the parents are truly godly and love their children not just in human fashion, but (as they ought) instruct and direct them by words and works to serve God in the first three commandments, then in these cases the child's own will is constantly broken. The child must do, not do, or put up with whatever his own nature would gladly have otherwise. Because of this he finds occasion to despise his parents, murmur against them, or worse. Love and fear depart when God's grace is not there. Likewise, when parents quite properly—though at times unjustly—punish and chastise, the soul's salvation is not imperiled; the evil nature is just unwilling to accept it. Besides all this, some are so wicked as to be ashamed of their parents because of their poverty, lowly birth, ugliness, or dishonor, and allow these things to influence them more than the high commandment of God, who is above all things and who has, with benevolent intent, given them such parents, to exercise and try them in his commandment. But the matter becomes still worse when the child in turn has children of his own. Then love for them increases, while the love and honor due to the parents declines.

But what is said and commanded of parents must also be understood of those who, when the parents are dead or not there, take their place, such as friends, relatives, godparents, temporal lords, and spiritual fathers. For everybody must be ruled and subject to other men. So we see here again how many good works are taught in this commandment, for in it all our life is made subject to other men. That is the reason obedience is so highly praised, and all virtue and good works are included in it.

3. There is still another kind of dishonoring of parents, much more dangerous and subtle than this first, [a dishonoring] which decks itself out and lets itself be regarded as a true honoring of parents. That is when a child has its own way and the parents allow it to do so out of natural love. In this case they honor one another and love one another. On all sides it is a precious thing; the mother and father are pleased and the child is pleased.

This plague is so common that instances of the first kind of dishonoring[46] are very rarely seen. This second kind of dishonoring

[46] See p. 81.

arises from the fact that the parents have been blinded and neither know nor honor God in the sense of the first three commandments. For this reason they cannot see what the children lack, or how they ought to teach them and bring them up. It is only to please men and to get ahead that they train their children for worldly honors, pleasure, and possessions. The children like this, and, of course, they obey very gladly without any back talk.

Thus God's commandment falls absolutely to the ground, unwittingly, and ostensibly for good reasons. Then is fulfilled that which is written in the prophets Isaiah and Jeremiah, that the children are destroyed by their own parents [Isa. 57:5; Jer. 7:31; 32:35]. They do what King Manasseh did. This king sacrificed his son to the idol Molech and burned him.[47] What else is it but to sacrifice one's own child to an idol and burn it when parents train their children more in the love of the world than in the love of God, and let their children go their own way and get burned up in worldly pleasure, love, enjoyment, lust, goods, and honor, but let God's love and honor and the love of eternal blessings be extinguished in them?

O how perilous it is to be a father or mother, where only flesh and blood are supreme! Indeed, it is because parents are commanded to teach their children that the knowledge and keeping of the first three and the last six commandments depend on this commandment. As Psalm 78 [:5-6] says, "How strictly has God commanded our fathers to make known his commandments to their children, that the generation to come might know them and declare them to their children's children." This is also the reason God bids us honor our parents, that is, to love them with fear; for that other love is without fear, therefore, it is more dishonor than honor.

Now see whether everyone does not have enough good works to do, whether he be father or child. But we, blind men that we are, neglect such works as these and seek elsewhere all sorts of other works which are not commanded.

4. Now children are not to obey parents who are so foolish that they bring up their children after the fashion of this world.

[47] II Kings 21:6. Although not mentioned by name in this passage, Molech was a god to whom children were sacrificed. Cf. Lev. 18:21, II Kings 23:10, and Jer. 32:35.

God is to be more highly regarded than parents according to the first three commandments. I call it being brought up after the fashion of the world when parents teach their children to seek nothing but the pleasure, honor, possessions, or power of this world.

To wear decent clothes and seek an honest living is a necessity, not a sin. Yet in his heart a child must be reconciled to the fact that it is an awful pity that this miserable earthly life cannot well be lived, or even begun, without the striving after more adornment and more possessions than are necessary to protect the body against cold and for nourishment. Thus the child must be taught to do against its own will what the world wants. The child must put up with fools and with that kind of evil for the sake of something better and to avoid something worse. Queen Esther wore her royal crown, but yet she said to God, "Thou knowest that the sign of my high estate which is upon my head has never at all delighted me, and that I abhor it as a filthy, menstruous rag. I never wear it when I am alone, but only when I have to and when I face the people."[48] The heart that is so minded wears adornment without peril, for it wears and yet does not wear, it dances yet does not dance, it lives well yet does not live well. And souls such as this are the secret hidden brides of Christ. But such souls are rare, for it is hard not to take delight in great adornment and display. Thus St. Cecilia[49] wore golden clothes at the command of her parents, but underneath she wore a hair shirt next to her skin.

Here some men say, "How then could I bring my children into society and make proper marriage settlements? I must make some show." Tell me, are not these the words of a heart which doubts God and trusts more in its own providing than in God's care? Yet St. Peter teaches and says, "Cast all your care on him and be certain he cares for you" [I Pet. 5:7]. It is a sign that they have never yet

---

[48] Esther 14:16. The canonical book of Esther concludes with 10:3. The Vulgate includes an additional six chapters. Jerome noted in the Vulgate that those chapters are not contained in the Hebrew text, but in the Septuagint.

[49] St. Cecilia, who lived during the second or third century, was the patron saint of music. What is known about her comes from fifth century legends. She is alleged to have converted her husband and her brother, both of whom were martyred. She too was a martyr, and it is said that her relics were moved from the catacombs in the ninth century to the church in Rome which bears her name. When this church was repaired in 1599 her body was said to have been found entire and uncorrupted.

thanked God for their children, have never yet rightly prayed for them, have never yet commended them to him. Had they done so, they would have known from their own experience that they should also ask God to settle the marriage of their children and wait upon his guidance. Because they do not do this, he just lets them go their own way, bringing cares and worries on themselves; and even then they do not order their lives well.

5. Thus it is true, as men say, that parents could attain salvation by training their own children, even if they were to do nothing else. If parents do this by rightly training them to God's service, they will indeed have their hands full of good works. For what are the hungry, the thirsty, the naked, the sick, the alien[50] if not the souls of your own children? With these God makes a hospital of your own house. He sets you over them as the hospital superintendent, to wait on them, to give them the food and drink of good words and works. [He sets you over them] that they may learn to trust God, to believe in him, to fear him, and to set their whole hope upon him; to honor his name and never curse or swear; to mortify themselves by praying, fasting, watching, working; to go to church, wait on the word of God, and observe the sabbath. [He sets you over them] that they may learn to despise temporal things, to bear misfortune without complaint, and neither fear death nor love this life.

Just think what a great lesson this is! How many good works you have at hand in your own home with your own child who needs all such things as these like a hungry, thirsty, naked, poor, imprisoned, sick soul! O what a blessed marriage and home that would be with such parents! That home would indeed be a true church, a chosen cloister, yes, a paradise! It was of such places that the psalmist sang in Psalm 128 [:1-4], "Blessed are they that fear God and walk in his commandments. You shall eat of the labor of your hands. On this account shall you be happy and all will go well with you. Your wife shall be like a fruitful vine in your house, and your children like the young shoots of laden olive trees around your table. Behold, thus shall the man be blessed who fears God." Where are such parents? Where are those who inquire after good works

[50] Matt. 25:35-36.

such as these? Nobody comes forward. Why? Because God has commanded these works! The flesh and the devil pull you away from these works. There is no pomp or show about them; therefore, we assume they are worth nothing. Husbands run to St. James, wives make vows to Our Lady. No one vows to train and teach himself and his child to honor God properly. Those whom God has commanded a man to keep in body and soul he leaves behind, and wants to serve God in some place or another, something that was never commanded. No bishop forbids and no preacher rebukes such a perverse practice. In fact, in the interests of their own covetousness the clergy endorse such practices. Every day they think up more and more pilgrimages, canonizations of saints, and indulgence fairs. May God have mercy on such blindness!

6. On the other hand, parents cannot earn hell more easily than by neglecting their own children in their own home and by not teaching them the things spoken of above. What use is it if they fast themselves to death, pray, go on pilgrimages, and do all manner of good works? After all, God will not ask them about these in the hours of death and on the day of judgment, but will require of them the children he entrusted to their care. This is shown by the word of Christ in Luke 23 [:28-29], "You daughters of Jerusalem, weep not for me but for yourselves and your children. The days will come when they will say, 'Blessed are the wombs that never bore, and the breasts which never gave suck!'" Why should they lament in this way if it does not mean that all their condemnation will come from their own children? If they had not had children, perhaps they might have been saved. These words certainly ought to open the eyes of parents and make them think about the souls of their children so that the poor children would not be deceived by the parents' human love and made to believe they had rightly honored their parents because they had not shown anger toward them or had been obedient to them in everyday affairs. This serves only to strengthen the children's self-will, although the commandment puts the parents in the place of honor so that the children's self-will is broken and they are made humble and meek.

It has been said in reference to the other commandments that they are to be fulfilled in relation to faith, the chief work. It is the same in this instance. Nobody must think that the training and teaching of his children is sufficient in itself. It must be done in confidence of God's favor. A man must have no doubt that he is well pleasing to God in what he is doing, and he should let work of this kind be nothing else but an expression and exercise of his faith. He should trust in God and look to him for blessings and a gracious will. Without faith of this kind no work is a genuine living work: it is neither good nor acceptable. Many heathen have brought their children up charmingly, but all that is lost because of their unbelief.

7. The second work of this commandment is to honor and obey our spiritual mother, the holy Christian church, and [its] spiritual authorities. We must conform to what they command, forbid, appoint, ordain, bind, and loose. We must honor, fear, and love the spiritual authorities as we do our natural parents, and yield to them in all things that are not contrary to the first three commandments.

Now things are almost worse with regard to this work than they are with regard to the first. The spiritual authorities should punish sin with the ban and with laws, and constrain their spiritual children to be pious, motivate them to do this work, to practice obedience, and to honor the authorities. You do not see this kind of zeal today. They [the spiritual authorities] behave toward their responsibilities like those mothers who forsake their children and run after their lovers, as Hosea 2 [:5] says. They do not preach, they do not teach, they do not restrain, they do not punish, and no spiritual government at all remains in Christendom.

What then can I say of this work? There are still a few fast days and feast days left which would be better abolished. But nobody pays any attention to this. Only the ban for debt is enforced here and there, although it should not be enforced. But spiritual authorities should see to it that adultery, unchastity, usury, gluttony, worldly show, excessive adornment, and other such blatant sin and shame are most severely punished and rectified. And further, the endowments, monastic houses, parishes, and schools should be properly managed and real worship maintained within them. The spiritual authorities should take care of the young people, both boys and girls, in schools and cloisters, and provide them with learned and pious men for teachers that they may all be well brought up. The older people should provide a good example, and Christendom would be filled and adorned with fine young people. St. Paul enjoins his disciple Titus that he should properly instruct and govern all classes, young and old, men and women [Titus 2:1-10]. But today everybody just does as he likes. The only one who has any education is the one who rules and teaches himself. Unfortunately it has come to such a sorry pass that those places where something good should be taught have become schools for scoundrels, and nobody takes any interest in the high-spirited youth at all.

8. If this state of affairs prevailed one could say how honor and obedience ought to be paid to the spiritual authorities. But now the situation is much the same as it is with those natural parents who let their children do as they like. Today the spiritual authorities issue decrees, make dispensations, and take money. They pardon beyond what they have power to pardon. I will say no more. We see more of it than is good. Greed sits in the saddle. What ought to be checked is actually taught. We see with our own eyes that the spiritual estate is more worldly in all points than the worldly estate itself. In the meantime, Christendom has to go to wrack and ruin, and this commandment has to go by the board.

If a bishop would devotedly take care of all these demands, see to them, make visitations, and fulfil all his responsibilities in the way that he should, then even one single city would be too much for him. For in the days of the apostles, when Christendom was at its best, each city had a bishop, even though Christians constituted the smallest part of the population. What will happen when one bishop wants this much and another that much, one wants the entire world and another half of it?

It is time we prayed to God for mercy. We have plenty of spiritual authorities, but little or no spiritual government. In the meantime, may he who is able give what help he can, so that institutions, monasteries, parishes, and schools may be well ordered and governed. It should also be one of the tasks of the spiritual authorities to reduce the [number of] institutions, monasteries, and schools where they cannot be properly cared for. It is much better to have no monastery or institution than one in which an evil system rules and provokes God to anger all the more.

9. Now since the spiritual authorities let their proper work go completely by the board and are so perverted, the inescapable consequence is that they misuse their power and take upon themselves alien and wicked works. They are just like parents who give a command which is contrary to God. In a state of affairs like this we have to be sensible. The Apostle has said that those times in which such authorities rule shall be perilous (I Tim. 4:1 ff., II Tim. 3:1 ff.). For if anybody does not do or leaves undone all that they prescribe, he gives the appearance of resisting their authority. Therefore, our first task is to take a firm hold of the first three commandments and the First Table, and be quite certain that no man, neither bishop, pope, nor even angel, may command or prescribe anything contrary to these three commandments and their works, whether it is contrary to them or does not further them. And if they attempt to impose such demands, we must consider their demands unauthorized and worthless. If we follow their demands and obey them, or even let such things go on, we are guilty of sin.

From this it is easy to understand that the commands on fasting do not apply to the sick, the pregnant, or those who for other reasons cannot fast without injury. And at a higher level, today nothing comes from Rome but a fair of spiritual wares which are bought and sold openly and shamelessly: indulgences, parishes, monasteries, bishoprics, deaneries, benefices, and everything else that was originally founded for the service of God throughout the world. As a result, not only is all the money and wealth of the world drawn and driven to Rome[51] (this is by no means the worst feature of the business), but the parishes, bishoprics, and prelacies are pulled to pieces and laid waste. Consequently, the people are neglected, and the word of God and God's name and honor perish and faith is destroyed. In the end such institutions and offices fall into the hands not only of unlearned and incompetent men, but the greater part are grabbed by Romans, the worst scoundrels in the world. Thus what was founded for God's service, for preaching

[51] Luther deals at length with this matter in *To the Christian Nobility of the German Nation*. Cf. pp. 141-157.

the gospel to the people and guiding and instructing them, is today put at the disposal of stableboys and mule skinners—in fact, because I dare not be more blunt, Roman whores and louts. Even then they thank us by mocking us as fools.

10. Now if such unbearable abuses are committed in the name of God and St. Peter, as if God's name and spiritual authorities were instituted to blaspheme God's honor and destroy the life and soul of Christendom, then we are certainly duty bound to offer appropriate resistance as far as we are able. We have to act as good children whose parents have lost their minds. In the first place, we must see by what right that which was founded for God's service in our own country or was provided for the welfare of our own children should be allowed to be spent in Rome rather than here, where it ought to be spent. How can we be so foolish?

Since bishops and spiritual prelates do nothing about this, and either offer no opposition or show fear, and thus allow Christendom to perish, it is our solemn duty in the first place humbly to call upon God to help to prevent this thing. In the second place it is our solemn duty to set our hand to the task and send those courtesans and those who held papal commissions on their way. [We must] inform them in a reasonable and gentle manner that if they want to look after their parishes honestly and sincerely, they shall have to live in them and help the people by preaching or by setting a good example for them. If they will not do this, but reside in Rome or anywhere else, plundering and wasting the churches, then let the pope feed them, for they are his servants. It simply is not right for us to support the pope's servants, his crew, indeed, his lackeys and whores, to the destruction and hurt of our souls.

Now these are the real Turks whom the kings, princes, and nobles ought to attack first, not in their own interest, but for the benefit of Christendom and to prevent blasphemy and the disgrace of the divine name. The nobility should deal with the spiritual estate as they would with a father who had lost his senses, who, if he were not restrained and resisted, might destroy child, heir, and everybody (yet with due respect and regard). Thus we are to honor Roman authority highly as our father superior. Yet at the same time, because the authorities at Rome had gone mad and lost their senses, we must not allow them to do what they want to do, lest Christendom be destroyed by their conduct.

11. Some think this should be referred to a general council. To this I say, No! We have had many councils in which this has been proposed, such as Constance, Basel, and the last Lateran council.[52] Nothing came of these councils and things are going from bad to worse. Moreover, such councils are of no use, for Roman cunning has contrived a device so that before a council starts, kings and princes must take an oath to let the Romans remain just as they are and keep what they have gotten. In this way they have set up a barrier to shield themselves from any reformation, as well as to provide them with protection and freedom for all their knavery. And yet, this very oath is demanded and imposed contrary to God and right. By this oath the doors are locked against the Holy Spirit who ought to rule the councils.

It would be best—in fact it is the only way—if kings, princes, nobles, cities, and communities made a start, so that bishops and clergy (who are now afraid) would have reason to follow. In this respect nothing else must be considered, or ought to be considered, except God's first three commandments, against which neither Rome, nor heaven, nor earth can either command or forbid anything. And all their bans and threats by which they think they can prevent this amount to nothing, just as it amounts to nothing if an insane father violently threatens his son when he restrains him or locks him up.

12. The third work of this commandment is to obey the temporal authority, as Paul teaches in Romans 13 [:1-7], and Titus 3 [:1], and St. Peter in I Peter 2 [:13–14], "Submit yourselves to the king as supreme and to the princes as his ambassadors, and to all

[52] Three "reform councils" had been convened during the fifteenth century. The Council of Pisa (1409) was convened by cardinals to resolve the schism caused by two rival popes. The result was the election of a third pontiff. The Council of Constance (1414-1418) successfully deposed the three rival popes and elected Martin V. It was at this council that John Huss was condemned and burned at the stake. The Council of Basel (1431-1439) was characterized by hostility between the council and Pope Eugene IV, who excommunicated its members and convened a countercouncil, attended by the emperor, at Ferrara (1438). The council which remained at Basel deposed Eugene and elected Felix V. Unable to find political support and recognition, Felix resigned within ten months of his election. The Fifth Lateran Council (1512-1517) is distinguished chiefly for its repeal of the Pragmatic Sanction (cf. p. 159, n. 112).

the ordinances of the worldly power." But the task of the temporal power is to protect its subjects and to punish theft, robbery, and adultery, as St. Paul says in Romans 13 [:4], "Authority does not bear the sword in vain; it serves God with it, [and is] a terror to evildoers, but the protector of the good."

Here men sin in two ways. First, if they lie to the government, betray it, or are disloyal to it, neither obeying it nor doing as it orders and commands, whether with their bodies or their possessions. For even when the government commits an injustice, as the King of Babylon did to the people of Israel,[53] God wants the government obeyed, without treachery or deception. Second, [we sin] when men speak evil of the government and curse it, and when a man cannot avenge himself and abuses the government with grumbling and evil words, in public or in private.

In all this we are to regard that which St. Peter bids us regard,[54] and that is that the power of the temporal authority, whether it does right or wrong, cannot harm the soul, but only our body and our property—unless, of course, it should try openly to compel us to do wrong against God or men, as it did in the early church when the rulers were not yet Christian, and as by all accounts the Turk still does. For to suffer wrong destroys no man's soul, in fact, it improves the soul, though it does inflict hurt to our body and our possessions. But to do wrong destroys the soul, even though all the world's wealth be gained.

13. This is the reason it is less disastrous when the temporal power goes wrong than when the spiritual power does. For the temporal power can do no real harm because it has nothing to do with the preaching of the gospel, or with faith, or with the first three commandments. But the spiritual power does harm not only when it does wrong, but when it neglects its duty and busies itself with something else altogether, even if these other works were better than the very best works of the temporal power. Therefore, we must resist the spiritual power when it does not do right, and not resist the temporal power even when it does wrong. For the poor people believe and behave just as they see their spiritual

[53] Jer. 27:6-7; Bar. 2:21-23.
[54] I Pet. 2:19-20.

overlords believing and behaving. If they see and hear nothing, then they believe nothing and do nothing, since this spiritual power is instituted for no other purpose than to lead the people in faith to God. This is not so with the temporal power. The temporal power may do or not do what it wants. My faith in God still pursues its own course and does its job, for I do not have to believe what the temporal power believes.

For this reason then the temporal power is but a very small matter in the sight of God, and too slightly regarded by him for us to resist, disobey, or become quarrelsome on its account, no matter whether the state does right or wrong. But on the other hand the spiritual power is an exceedingly great blessing and much too precious in his sight for the very least of Christian men to suffer silently when it deviates one hairsbreadth from its proper function. This is to say nothing of when it goes absolutely contrary to its real function, as we see for ourselves every day.

14. There are all kinds of abuse in this authority. In the first place, [it is subject to abuse] when it is influenced by flattery, a common and particularly harmful plague to which this power is subject and against which no one can adequately guard and protect himself. In these circumstances the government is led by the nose and rides roughshod over the common people. It turns into the kind of a government a heathen once described in the saying, "The spider webs catch the little flies all right, but the millstone rolls on through."[55] So the laws, ordinances, and government of one and the same authority keep a hold on the little men while the big fellows go scot-free. And in those cases where the prince is himself so wise that he needs no advice from his people, or so little regards advice that they are afraid of him, there will be, and of necessity must be, a childish government (unless God performs a special miracle).

For this reason God has considered evil, unfit rulers as the greatest of plagues, as he threatens in Isaiah 3 [:1-4], "I will take away from them every man of valor and will give children and childish lords [to rule over them]." God has named four plagues in

[55] *Die spynweb fahen wol die kleinen fliegen, aber die molstein fahren durch hin.* Cf. Karl F. W. Wander (ed.), *Deutsches Sprichwörter Lexicon* (5 vols.; Leipzig, 1867-1880), Nos. 1 ff.

Ezekiel 14 [:13-21]. The first and least, which David in fact chose,[56] is pestilence, the second is famine, the third is war, and the fourth is all manner of evil beasts, such as lions, wolves, serpents, dragons. These last mean wicked rulers. For where these things are, the land is destroyed, not only in respect to life and property, as in the case of the other plagues, but even in respect to honor, breeding,[57] virtue, and the soul's salvation. For pestilence and famine make people pious and rich, but war and bad government bring to naught everything that has anything to do with temporal or eternal blessings.

15. A prince must also be very wise and not always try to impose his own will, even if he has the right and the best of all reasons to do so. For it is a far nobler virtue to put up with a slight to one's own rights than [it is to risk damage] to life and property, where this is to the advantage of the subjects. As we know, worldly rights are valid only with respect to the things of this world.

Therefore, it is absolutely foolish to say, I have a right to it and will therefore take it by force and hold on to it, although all sorts of misfortune may come to others in doing so. In this connection we read of Caesar Augustus[58] that he did not want to wage war, however right he was, unless there were sure indications of greater benefit than harm, or at least of a bearable harm. He said that war can be likened to fishing with a golden net—you never catch as much as you risk losing.[59] He who drives a cart must act differently than if he were walking alone. When he is on his own he can walk, jump, and do what he likes, but when he is driving he must control and guide so that the horse and cart can follow. He has to pay greater regard to the horse and cart than to himself. A prince is in the same position. He stands at the head and leads the multitude, and must not go or do as he wants but as the multitude are able. He has to pay more regard to their needs and necessities than to his own will and pleasure. When a prince rules according to his own

---

[56] Cf. II Sam. 24:13-14.

[57] I.e., education.

[58] The Caesar Augustus of Luke 2:1 (63 B.C.-A.D. 14).

[59] J. C. Rolfe (trans.), Suetonius' *Lives of the Caesars,* Bk. II, XXV ("Loeb Classical Library," Vol. I [Cambridge: Harvard University Press, 1960]), p. 141.

mad will and follows his own opinion he is like a mad driver who rushes straight ahead with his horse and cart through bushes, hedges, ditches, streams, uphill and downdale, regardless of roads and bridges. He will not drive for very long. He is bound to smash up.

Therefore, it would be of the greatest value to the ruling class if from their youth up they were to read, or have read to them, history books, both sacred and secular. They would find in these books more by way of example about the art of ruling than in all the law books. We read in Esther 6 [:1] that the kings of Persia did this. Historical examples give and teach much more than laws and statutes. In the former a particular historical experience teaches, in the latter, untried and uncertain words.

16. There are three tasks particularly necessary for every government to do at the present time, especially in these lands.[60] First, put an end to the horrible gluttony and drunkenness, not only because of their excess, but because of their expense. For through seasonings and spices and the like, which we could well do without, no small loss of temporal wealth has come to our country, and [the loss] is increasing daily. To prevent two such great evils would truly give the worldly power enough to do, for these evils have made deep inroads into our country. How could those in power do God and themselves a better service and improve their country more?

Second, [the government should] combat the excessive cost of clothes on which so much wealth is wasted, and yet only the world and the flesh are served. It is a shocking thing to realize that such misuse of wealth is to be found among the people who have been pledged, baptized, and dedicated to Christ the Crucified, and who ought to bear the cross with him and prepare themselves for the life to come by daily dying to self. If some men erred through ignorance it would be more tolerable. But it is a most un-Christian state of affairs when this excess is practiced so freely, without punishment, without shame, without hindrance. In fact, praise and fame are sought in such finery.

Third, [the government should] drive out the usurious buying

[60] I.e., in the German territories.

of *tzingskauff*,[61] which brings ruin, trouble, and disaster to every country, every people, and every city by its crafty pretense that it is not usury. They pretend that it is not usury, while in actual fact it is a good deal worse than usury, for men are not on their guard against it as they are against open usury. See, these are the three Jews, as they call them, which suck the world dry. On these matters overlords ought not to sleep or be lazy, if they would give a good account of their office to God.

17. Here too ought to be mentioned the knavery which is practiced by officials and other episcopal and ecclesiastical officers, who, with a very heavy hand, put the ban on the poor laity, lay grievous burdens on them, hunt them down, and chase them around as long as they have a penny to their name. This sort of thing should be prevented by the temporal sword, since there is no other help or remedy.

O would to God in heaven that some government might be established that would only do away with brothels, as was done among the people of Israel![62] It is indeed an un-Christian sight, that public houses of sin are maintained among Christians, a thing unheard of in earlier times. It should be a rule that young people should be married in good time, and vice of this kind would be prevented. Both the spiritual and the temporal power ought to strive for such a rule and practice. If it was possible among the

[61] This technical term, which describes a practice no longer in existence, has no equivalent in modern English. The practice stems from the medieval transaction whereby a feudal landlord turned over a piece of land as a fief in perpetuity in return for a specified annual return in the form of livestock or produce called a *Rente*. From the landlord's standpoint this contractual arrangement was a *Rentenkauf* (the purchase of a rent). In the course of time, as properties other than acreage came to be the chief security in the transaction, and as money became the chief and ultimately the sole factor in the transaction, the terms *Zins* (literally, "interest") and *Zinskauf* (literally, "purchase of interest") were used interchangeably with *Rente* and *Rentenkauf*. Under these circumstances it became increasingly important to make a theological distinction between this type of contract and an interest-bearing loan, which was universally condemned as usury. According to this distinction the transaction came to be regarded as a sale (*Kauf*) rather than as a loan, and the *Zins* or *Rente* as a delayed cash payment rather than as interest on a loan. The creditor, then, was one who purchased a fixed and regular income or the right thereto, and the debtor was one who sold (for money or property) such income. This interpretation exempted the *Zinskauf* from the ban on usury. Cf. *LW* 45, 235-237.

[62] Luther probably had in mind such passages as Lev. 19:29 and Deut. 23:17, 18.

Jews, why should it not be possible also among Christians? In fact, if it is possible in villages, market towns, and some cities, as we can see for ourselves, why should it not be possible everywhere?

But there is no real government in the world. Nobody wants to work. Therefore, the employers have to lay off their workmen. Then they are free, and nobody can tame them. But if there were a rule that they had to do as they were told, and if no employer would take them on in other places, this evil would be corrected to a very large extent. May God help us! I am afraid the wish is stronger than the hope. But we are not thereby excused.

Now this only indicates a few tasks for the government. But there are so many additional good works that every moment of their lives they have an abundant number of tasks and opportunities to serve God. But these works, like the others, should also be done in faith, in fact, as an exercise of faith, so that nobody thinks he is pleasing to God on account of what he does, but rather by a confident trust in his favor he does such tasks for a gracious and loving God and to his honor and praise alone. And in so doing he serves and benefits his neighbor.

18. The fourth work of this commandment is the obedience of servants and workers to their lords and ladies, masters and mistresses. St. Paul referred to this in Titus 2 [:9-10], "You shall exhort slaves and servants to honor their masters highly, to be obedient, to do what pleases them, and not to cheat or strive against them." Another reason for showing obedience is that by so doing these workers give the teaching of Christ and our faith a good name, and as a consequence the heathen are not in a position to complain about us and be offended [I Tim. 6:1]. St. Peter also says, "You servants should be obedient to your masters for the fear of God, not only to the good and gentle, but also to the perverse and the harsh. For this is acceptable to God, if a man suffer grief though innocent" [I Pet. 2:18-19].

There is a very serious complaint in the world today against servants and the working class. The complaint is that they are disobedient, unfaithful, unmannerly, and interested only in themselves. This is a plague sent from God. And yet actually in the case of servants this is the one work by which they may be saved. They cannot make many pilgrimages, or do this and that. They have enough to do if their hearts are simply set on gladly doing or leaving undone what they know pleases their masters and mistresses, and to do all this in the simplest faith. Not that they want to earn great merit by their work, but they want to do it all in the confidence of divine favor (in which all merit exists), and to do it simply without any thought of reward, but out of love and good will toward God, which grow out of a faith of this kind. They should let all such works always be an exercise and encouragement to strengthen such faith and trust more and more. And, as has been said over and over again, faith of this kind makes all works good. Yes, faith must cause the works; faith is the man in charge.

19. On the other hand, masters and mistresses should not govern their servants, maids, and workers high-handedly. They should not scrutinize everything, but occasionally overlook some things and wink at their faults for the sake of peace. For as long as we live on earth in imperfection it is not possible for everything to go according to the rules in any class of men. St. Paul says of this in Colossians 3 [4:1], "You masters should deal equally and justly with your servants, remembering that you also have a Master in heaven." Therefore, as masters do not want God to deal most severely with them, but want many things overlooked through grace, they too should be all the more gentle toward their servants and overlook some things. But yet they should see to it that their servants do the right thing and learn to fear God.

Now see what kind of good works a householder and a mistress can do! How splendidly God shows us all good works so near at hand, in such a variety and so continuously that we need not ask for good works to do and could well forget all those works devised by men, the showy, far-flung works, such as making pilgrimages, building churches, seeking indulgences, and things like that.

Here I ought to say too that a wife ought to be obedient to her husband as her lord, be subject to him, yield to him, keep silent and agree with him as long as it is not contrary to God. On the other hand, the husband should love his wife, overlook some things, and not deal harshly with her. St. Peter and St. Paul have said much on this subject.[63] But this matter belongs to a further explanation of the Ten Commandments, and is easily inferred from these passages.

20. But all that has been said of these works is included in these two, obedience and considerateness. Obedience is the duty of subjects, considerateness, of masters, that they be diligent to rule their subjects well, deal kindly with them, and do everything to benefit and help them. That is their way to heaven, and these are the best works they can do on earth. In doing these works they are more acceptable to God than if they performed nothing but miracles instead. St. Paul says in Romans 12 [:6-8], "He who has the responsibility of ruling, let his work be considerateness." This is as if Paul were to say, "Let him not allow himself to be led astray by what other people or rulers do; let him not look to this work or that, be it splendid or obscure; but let him look to his own situation, and be alert only to how he may benefit those who are subject to him. Let him stick to this. Let no power tear him away from this, even if heaven were to stand open before him, nor let himself be driven from it, even if hell pursued him. This is the right road that leads him to heaven."

O if a man were so to regard himself and his office, and attend to its duties alone, how rich he would be in good works in a short time, so quietly and secretly that no one would notice it except God alone! But today we let all this go, and one runs off to be a Carthusian monk,[64] another runs to this place, and a third somewhere else, just as if good works and God's commandments had been thrown in a corner and concealed. It is written in Proverbs 1 [:20] that divine wisdom cries out her commandments publicly in the streets, in the midst of the people and at the gates of the cities. This signifies that they [i.e., good works and God's commandments] are abundantly present in all places, in all walks of life, and at all times. But we do not see them. In our blindness we seek them elsewhere. This Christ declared in Matthew 24 [:23, 26, 24], "If they say to you, 'Look, here is Christ,' or 'There,' you ought not

[63] Cf. I Pet. 3:1-7; Eph. 5:22-23; Col. 3:18.

[64] The Carthusian Order was founded by Bruno of Cologne in the latter part of the eleventh century. Its chief rule and aim is absolute detachment from the world.

believe them. If they shall say, 'Behold, he is in the wilderness,' do not go out there. [If they say] 'Look, he is in secret chambers,' just do not believe it. They are false prophets and false Christs."

21. On the other hand, it is the duty of subjects to obey. They must diligently and carefully do or leave undone what their superiors desire of them, and not allow themselves to be dragged or driven from this task, regardless of what others do. Let no man think that he is living properly or that he is doing good works, be it praying or fasting or whatever, if he does not earnestly and diligently discipline himself in this matter of obedience.

But if, as often happens, the temporal power and authorities, or whatever they call themselves, would compel a subject to do something contrary to the command of God, or hinder him from doing what God commands, obedience ends and the obligation ceases. In such a case a man has to say what St. Peter said to the rulers of the Jews, "We must obey God rather than men" [Acts 5:29]. He did not say, "We must not obey men," for that would be wrong. He said, "God rather than men." [It is] as if a prince desired to go to war, and his cause was clearly unrighteous; we should neither follow nor help such a prince, because God had commanded us not to kill our neighbor or do him a wrong. Likewise, if the prince were to order us to bear false witness, steal, lie or deceive, and the like, [we should refuse]. In such cases we should indeed give up our property and honor, our life and limb, so that God's commandments remain.

The Fifth Commandment

The four preceding commandments do their work in the mind. That is, they take a man captive, rule him, and bring him into subjection so that he does not rule himself, does not think himself good or hold himself in esteem, but rather he humbly recognizes himself for what he is and allows himself to be led so that he may resist pride. The commandments which follow deal with men's passions and lusts in order to kill them.

1. [There is] the angry and revenge-seeking passion of which

the fifth commandment says, "Thou shalt not kill." This commandment has one work which comprehends many others and excludes much wickedness. It is called meekness.

Now there are two kinds of meekness. The first kind looks pretty enough, but there is nothing behind it. This is the kind of meekness we practice toward our friends and those who are either useful to us and please us with goods, honor, and favor, or toward those who do us no harm in word or deed. Even irrational animals, lions and snakes, heathen, Jews, Turks, knaves, murderers, and bad women have this kind of meekness. All of these alike are quite content and quite gentle when we do what they want or let them alone. And there are even quite a few who are deceived by such meekness and cover up their anger and excuse themselves, saying, "I would not really be angry if only people would leave me alone." Of course, my dear fellow, the evil spirit himself would be meek if he had his own way. Discord and insult come your way to show you how much anger and wickedness are really in you and to warn you to strive for meekness and to drive out anger.

The second kind of meekness is good through and through. It is shown to opponents and enemies and does them no harm. It does not avenge itself, it does not curse or blaspheme, it speaks no evil of them and thinks no evil against them, even if they have taken away goods, honor, life, friends, and everything. In fact, where it can, this kind of meekness returns good for evil, speaks well, thinks the best of, and prays for those who do evil. Christ says in Matthew 5 [:44], "Do good to them that harm you. Pray for your persecutors and revilers." And Paul in Romans 12 [:14] says, "Bless those who curse you: never curse them back, but rather do good to them."

2. Now see how this precious and lofty work has been lost among Christians. Nothing but strife, war, quarreling, anger, hatred, envy, backbiting, cursing, slandering, injury, vengeance, and all manner of deeds and words of anger and violence prevail everywhere. And yet side by side with this we go on with our numerous holy days, hear masses, say our little prayers, found churches, and adorn them with churchly ornaments. God has commanded none of this. We shine so resplendently and magnificently as if we were

the holiest Christians who had ever lived. Through these mirrors and masks we let the commandment of God be trodden underfoot, so that no one considers or reflects upon how near or how far he is from meekness and the fulfilment of this commandment. Yet God has said that it is not he who does such works, but he who keeps his commandments who shall enter into eternal life [John 14:21; 15:10].

Since there is not a man living to whom God has not given some indicator of his own anger and wickedness, that is, an enemy or adversary who does harm to him in property, honor, life, or friend, and by so doing tests whether anger is still present, whether he can be well disposed toward his enemy, speak well of him, do good to him, and not intend any evil against him—let that man step forward who asks what he has to do to do good works, please God, and be saved! Let him set his enemy before him, keeping him constantly before the eyes of his heart as an exercise whereby he may curb his spirit and accustom his heart to think kindly of his enemy, wish him all the best, care for him, and pray for him; and later, when the opportunity occurs, speak well of him and do good to him. Let him who is willing try this, and if he does not find plenty to do as long as he lives, then let him make me a liar and say that what I said was wrong. But if this is what God wants, and if God will be paid in no other coin, of what use is it then for us to run around performing great works which are not commanded, and to neglect this? This is why God says in Matthew 5 [:22], "I say to you that he who is angry with his neighbor is subject to judgment. But whosoever says to his brother 'Raca!' (that is, to give a horrible exhibition of foul temper) is subject to the council. But he who says to his brother 'You fool!' (that is, all manner of invective, cursing, reviling, slandering) shall be subject to everlasting fire." If the thoughts and words of anger are so severely condemned, what is in store then for the actual deed such as striking, wounding, killing, injuring, etc.?

3. But where there is true meekness the heart feels compassion at every evil which befalls its enemy. And people who feel this are the true children and heirs of God and brethren of Christ, who felt compassion for us on the holy cross. We see that a godly judge

painfully passes sentence upon the criminal, and regrets the death penalty which the law imposes. In this case the act has every appearance of anger and disfavor. Meekness is so thoroughly good that it remains even in such wrathful works. In fact, the heart is most tormented when it has to be angry and severe.

But we have to be careful that we are not meek contrary to the honor and command of God. It is written of Moses that he was the meekest man on earth [Ecclus. 45:4], and yet, when the Jews had worshiped the golden calf and provoked God to anger, he put many of them to death, and thereby made atonement before God [Exod. 32:1-33]. Likewise, it is not right for the government to take a holiday and let sin rule and for us to say nothing about it. I must not regard my own possessions, my own honor, my own injury, nor get angry on their account; but we must defend God's honor and commandment, as well as prevent injury or injustice to our neighbor. The temporal authorities [have the responsibility of doing this] with the sword; the rest of us, by reproof and rebuke. But it is [to be done] with pity for those who have earned the punishment.

This lofty, noble, satisfying work may be learned very easily, if we do it in faith and bring faith to bear upon it. For if faith does not doubt the favor of God, and a man has no doubt that he has a gracious God, it will be quite easy for him to be gracious and favorable to his neighbor, however much the neighbor may have sinned against him. For we have sinned far more against God. See what a short commandment this is! Yet it is a long one, in which many possibilities to do good works and exercise faith are set forth.

On the Sixth Commandment

Thou shalt not commit adultery

1. In this commandment, too, a good work is commanded which embraces much virtue and drives out much vice. The work is called purity or chastity, of which much is written and preached. Chastity

is well known to everybody, but it is not as carefully observed and practiced as the other works which are not commanded. We are so ready to do what is not commanded and to leave undone what is commanded. We know that the world is full of shameful works of unchastity, indecent words, stories, and ditties, and that the temptation to unchastity is daily increased through gluttony and drunkenness, idleness, and excessive finery. Yet we still go about as if we were Christians. When we have been to church, said our little prayer, observed the fasts and feasts, we think that that is all we have to do.

Now if no other work but chastity were commanded we would have our hands full doing it, for unchastity is a serious and rabid vice. It rages in all our members: in the thoughts of our heart, in the seeing of our eyes, in the hearing of our ears, in the words of our mouth, in the works of our hands, our feet, and our whole body. To control all of these calls for labor and effort. And so the commandments of God teach us what a great thing it is to conceive true good works, or rather, that it is quite impossible for us to conceive a good work out of our own resources, to say nothing of attempting or fulfilling them. St. Augustine says that among all the conflicts of the Christian the conflict of chastity is the hardest, if only because unchastity continues daily without ceasing and is seldom far away.[65] All the saints have cried and complained about it, as St. Paul says in Romans 7 [:18], "I find in me, that is, in my flesh, no good thing."

2. If this work of chastity lasts, it will lead to many more good works: to fasting, temperance against gluttony and drunkenness, to watchfulness and early rising over against sloth and excessive sleep, and to work and labor over against idleness. Gluttony, drunkenness, lying in bed, loafing, and idling about are weapons of unchastity by which chastity is quickly overcome. On the other hand, the holy Apostle Paul calls fasting, watching, and working godly weapons by which unchastity is mastered [Rom. 13:12-14] But, as has been said above, these exercises must go no further than to overcome unchastity, and not be detrimental to the natural life.

Above all these aforementioned good works, the strongest de-

[65] Cf. *De vita eremitica. MPL* 32, 1460, cap. XXVI.

fense is prayer and the word of God. When evil lust begins to stir, a man must flee to prayer, call upon God's grace and help, read the gospel and meditate on it, and thereby behold the sufferings of Christ. Psalm 137 [:9] says, "Blessed is he who seizes the young of Babylon and dashes them on the rock." This means when the heart runs to the Lord Christ with its evil thoughts while they are still young and in their infancy. For Christ is a rock on which these thoughts are dashed to pieces and come to naught.

Every man will find for himself more than enough to do in this matter. He will discover plenty of good works which need doing in himself. But today it has come to such a state that nobody uses prayer, fasting, watching, labor for this purpose, but rather as ends in themselves. These works should be so ordered only to help to fulfil the works of this commandment and purify us more and more every day.

Some have indicated even more things to be avoided, e.g., soft beds and clothes, excessive adornment, the company of the opposite sex, speaking to them or even looking at them, and whatever else in the same vein that is conducive to chastity. In all these things no one can fix a definite rule or limit. Every man must find out what is conducive to chastity in his case. How much of what and for what length of time, he must decide for himself and observe. If he cannot do this, then let him submit himself for a time to the control of somebody else, who will hold him to such a rule until he is strong enough to govern himself. This was the purpose for which the monasteries were established in former times, to teach young people discipline and purity.

3. In the matter of chastity a good strong faith is a great help, and more noticeably so than in almost any other work. This is why Isaiah 11 [:5] says that faith is a girdle of the kidneys, that is, a guard of chastity. He who lives chastely and looks to God for all grace takes pleasure in spiritual purity. Therefore, he may much more easily resist the impurity of the flesh. When a man has faith like this the Spirit tells him in no uncertain way how to avoid evil thoughts and everything that opposes chastity. For just as the certainty of God's favor toward us never ceases to live and be active in us, so, too, that certainty never ceases to warn us in

those matters pleasing or displeasing to God. As St. John expresses it in his epistle, "You do not need anyone to teach you, for the divine anointing, that is, the Spirit of God, teaches you all things [I John 2:27].

Yet we must not despair if we are not quickly rid of the temptation. In fact, we must never assume that we shall have relief from temptation as long as we live. We must accept temptation as nothing else but an incentive and admonition to prayer, fasting, watching, laboring, and to the other disciplines to subdue the flesh, especially to the practice and exercise of faith in God. For that is no great chastity which enjoys peace and quiet. Real chastity is the kind which does battle with impurity, struggles against it, and unceasingly drives out all the poison injected by the flesh and the devil. St. Peter says, "I admonish you to abstain from fleshly desires and lusts, which continually war against the soul" [I Pet. 2:11]. And St. Paul says in Romans 6 [:12], "You should not obey the body according to its lusts," and so on. In these and like passages we are shown that nobody is without evil lust, but that everybody should and must fight against it daily. But although this brings restlessness and discomfort, chastity is nevertheless a work pleasing to God, and that should be our comfort and satisfaction. Those who think they can check temptation by yielding to it only arouse themselves all the more. And even if the temptation lets up for a time, it still comes back stronger at another time and finds their nature weaker than before.

The Seventh Commandment

Thou shalt not steal

1. This commandment also has a work which includes very many good works while opposing many vices. In German this work is called "selflessness,"[66] a willingness to help and serve all men with one's own means. Further, it fights not only against theft and robbery, but against every kind of sharp practice which men per-

[66] *Mildickeit.*

petrate against each other in matters of worldly goods. For instance, greed, usury, overcharging, counterfeit goods, short measure, short weight, and who could give an account of all the smart, novel, and sharp-witted tricks which daily increase in every trade! In these sharp practices everybody seeks his own advantage to the disadvantage of the other, and forgets the law which says, "What you want others to do to you, you do to them" [Matt. 7:12]. Everyone who keeps this rule before him, each man in his trade, in business, and in dealings with his neighbor, would soon find out how he ought to buy and sell, give and take, lend and give without return, promise and keep his promise, and the like. And when we look at the world as it really is and see how greed has the upper hand in all business, we would not only find enough to do to make a living with honor in the sight of God, but would also acquire a fear and dread of this dangerous and pitiable life which is so overburdened, entangled, and caught up with the cares of earning a living and the dishonest pursuit of gain.

2. It was not in vain that the wise man said, "Happy is the rich man who is found without blemish, who has not run after gold, and has not set his confidence in the treasures of money. Who is he? We will praise him because he has performed a miracle in his life" [Ecclus. 31:8-9]. This is as much as to say, "Nobody meets such a man, or at least very few indeed." There certainly are very few who notice and recognize such lust for gold in themselves. For in this case greed has a very pretty and attractive cover for its shame; it is called provision for the body and the needs of nature. Under this cover greed insatiably amasses unlimited wealth. As the wise man said, he who would keep himself pure in this respect must certainly do miracles or wondrous things in his life.

Look here! If a man wants to do not only good works but even miracles, which God may praise and be pleased with, what need is there to look further? Let him look to himself and see that he does not run after gold, or put his confidence in money. Rather, let the gold run after him and the money wait on his favor, and let him love none of these things or set his heart upon them. In this way he is the true, gentle, wonder-working, and blessed man; as Job 31 [:24] expresses it, "I have never yet relied on gold, and never yet made gold my comfort and confidence." And Psalm 62 [:10], "If your riches increase, you shall not set your heart upon them." Christ teaches the same thing in Matthew 6 [:31-32], that we should not be anxious as to what we eat, drink, and how we clothe ourselves, since God cares for all this and knows that we need these things.

But some people will say, "Well then, just rely on that, do not be concerned, and see whether a roasted chicken will fly into your mouth!" I do not say that a man need not work and seek his livelihood. But I do say that he is not to be anxious, not covetous; he is not to despair that he is not going to have enough. For in Adam we are all condemned to labor, as God says in Genesis 3 [:19], "In the sweat of your face you shall eat your bread," and Job 5 [:7], "As the bird is born to fly, so man is born to work." Now birds fly without anxiety and without covetousness, and so we should work without anxiety and without covetousness. But if you are anxious and greedy, and want the roast chicken to fly into your mouth, then go on worrying and coveting and see if you will fulfil God's commandment and find salvation.

3. Faith teaches this work of itself. If the heart expects and puts its trust in divine favor, how can a man be greedy and anxious? Such a man is absolutely certain that he is acceptable to God: therefore, he does not cling to money; he uses his money cheerfully and freely for the benefit of his neighbor. He knows full well that he will have enough no matter how much he gives away. His God, whom he trusts, will neither lie to him nor forsake him, as it is written in Psalm 37 [:25], "I have been young, and now I am old, yet have I never seen a man of faith who trusts God (that is, a righteous man) forsaken, or his child begging bread." The Apostle calls no other sin idolatry except covetousness [Col. 3:5], because this sin shows most starkly that a man does not trust God for anything, but expects more benefit from his money than from God. It is by confidence that God is truly honored or dishonored, as I have just said.

In fact, in this commandment it can clearly be seen that all good works must be done in faith and proceed from faith. In this instance everyone most certainly feels that the cause of covetousness is distrust, while on the other hand the cause of generosity is faith. A man is generous because he trusts God and never doubts but that he will always have enough. In contrast, a man is covetous and anxious because he does not trust God. Now faith is the master workman and the motivating force behind the good works of generosity, just as it is in all the other commandments. Without this faith, generosity is of no use at all; it is just a careless squandering of money.

4. We are also to know by this commandment that this kind of selflessness should extend even to enemies and opponents. What kind of good deed is it if we are kind only to our friends, as Christ teaches in Luke 6 [:32-36]? Even a wicked man is kind to one who is his friend. Besides, even the brute beasts are gentle and helpful to their own kind. Therefore, a Christian man must rise higher, letting his kindness serve even those who do not deserve it: evildoers, enemies, and the ungrateful, even as his heavenly Father makes his sun to rise on good and evil alike, and his rain to fall on the grateful and the ungrateful [Matt. 5:45].

But at this point you will discover how hard it is to do the good works God commands, how the natural man turns up his nose at them, wriggles out of them, and turns away from them, but yet does the good works of his own choosing easily and gladly. Therefore, take your enemies and the ungrateful and do good to them. Then you will find how near you are to keeping this commandment, or how far from it. You will find out that you will be occupied with the practice of this work for the rest of your life. If your enemy needs you and you do not help him when you can it is the same as if you had stolen what belonged to him, for you owe him your help. St. Ambrose says, "Feed the hungry: if you do not feed him, then as far as you are concerned, you have killed him."[67] And in this commandment are included the works of mercy which Christ will require at the last day [Matt. 25:35-46].

Nonetheless, the authorities and cities ought to see to it that vagabonds, Jacob's brethren,[68] and whatever strange beggars there

[67] *Expositio in psalmum CXVIII, sermo 12,* 44. *MPL* 15, 1449.

[68] A term referring to pilgrims to the tomb of St. James of Compostella. Cf. p. 12, n. 9.

may be should be barred, or permitted only to a limited extent and under certain conditions, so that scoundrels not be allowed to roam at large under the guise of mendicants,[69] and a stop be put to their knavery, of which there is far too much today. I have spoken at greater length about this commandment in my treatise on *Trade and Usury*.[70]

The Eighth Commandment

Thou shalt not bear false witness against thy neighbor

This commandment seems insignificant, and yet it is so great that he who would rightly keep it must risk life and limb, property and reputation, friends and all that he has. And yet it includes no more than the work of that tiny member, the tongue, and in German is called "telling the truth,"[71] which includes refuting lies when necessary, and thus many evil works of the tongue are forbidden by this commandment.

1. First of all [are those works] which are done by speaking, and those which are done by keeping silence. Take, for example, speaking: If a man has a poor case before the court and is determined to prove it and pursue it with false evidence, trap his neighbor with subtlety, produce everything that improves and furthers his own case, and withhold and discount everything that furthers the good cause of his neighbor, he does not do to his neighbor as he would have his neighbor do to him. Some men do this for pleasure, some to avoid loss or shame, and by so doing they seek their own advantage rather than [the keeping of] God's command, excusing themselves by saying, *"vigilanti jura subveniunt,"* "The law helps him who is vigilant." As if they were not just as much responsible for being as vigilant for their neighbor's interest as they are for

[69] Members of those monastic orders which renounced established sources of income and subsisted by soliciting alms.

[70] *LW* 45, 295-308.

[71] *Wahrheit sagen.*

their own! They deliberately allow their neighbor's cause to be lost, although they know his cause is right. This evil is so prevalent today that I am afraid that no court is held and no suit tried but that one party sins against this commandment. And even if they cannot bring it off, they still have the unrighteous spirit and determination to want the righteous cause of their neighbor to be lost and their own unrighteous cause to win. This sin happens particularly in those cases where the opponent is a prominent man, or an enemy. A man wants to avenge himself on his enemy, but no one wants to incur the ill will of a public figure. And then begins the flattering and fawning, or the suppression of the truth. No one is willing to run the risk of disfavor or displeasure, damage or danger, for the sake of truth. And so the commandment of God goes by the board. And this is the way of the world. He who would keep this commandment would have both hands full just keeping it in those matters concerning the tongue. And then, how many are there in addition who allow themselves to be silenced and led from the path of truth by presents and gifts! The result is that it is everywhere a noble, great, and rare work not to be a false witness against one's neighbor.

2. Over and above this there is another kind of bearing witness to the truth. This kind is greater, and through it we have to fight against evil spirits. It concerns not temporal matters but the gospel and the truth of faith which Satan has never been able to endure. He is always contriving to turn the leaders of the people against it, and compels them to persecute it. These [leaders] are the very hardest to resist. It is of them the psalmist writes in Psalm 82 [:3-4], "Release the poor from the power of the wicked, and help the forsaken to maintain his righteous cause."

Now if persecution of this kind has become a rarity, it is the fault of the spiritual prelates who do not awaken people with the gospel but just let it get buried. By doing this they have abandoned the very thing on account of which martyrdom and persecution should arise. In place of the gospel they teach us their own rules and whatever pleases them. Because of this the devil just sits still, for by vanquishing the gospel he has also vanquished faith in

Christ, and things go along just as he wants. But if the gospel should be revived and heard once again, no doubt the whole world would arise and bestir itself. The greater part of the kings, princes, bishops, doctors and clergy, and all the great ones would oppose it and grow furious, as has always happened when the word of God has come to light, for the world cannot tolerate what comes from God. This is proved in the case of Christ, who was and is the very greatest of all, the most loved and the very best of all that God has. Yet the world not only did not receive him, but persecuted him more cruelly than all the others who had ever come forth from God.

Therefore, as in his day, so at all times, there are few who stand by the divine truth and risk life and limb, goods and honor, and everything they have for it. As Christ has foretold, "You shall be hated by all men for my name's sake" [Matt. 24:9]. Or again, "Many of them shall take offense at me" [Matt. 24:10]. But if this truth were attacked by peasants, shepherds, stableboys, and people of no repute, who would not be willing and able to confess it and bear witness to it? But when the pope and the bishops, as well as princes and kings, attack the truth, then everybody runs away, keeps quiet, or pretends not to notice so as not to lose his possessions, his honor, his favor, and his life.

3. Why do they do this? For the simple reason that they have no faith in God and expect nothing good from him. For where there is such faith and confidence there is also a bold, defiant, fearless heart that risks all and stands by the truth, no matter what the cost, whether it is against pope or king, as we see that the dear martyrs did. For such a heart is satisfied and serenely sure that it has a gracious, kindly-disposed God. Therefore, he despises all the favors, grace, goods, and honor of men, and does not attach any value to these transitory things.[72] As it is written in Psalm 15 [:4], "He despises them who despise God, and honors those who fear him." That means he does not fear the tyrants, the mighty,

[72] *Lessit faren und kommen was nit bleyben will,* a figure of speech for which there is no terse English equivalent. The gist of the passage is that a God-fearing man is indifferent to the transitory glories of this life.

those who persecute the truth and despise God; he does not regard them, he despises them. On the other hand, he clings to those persecuted for the truth's sake, those who fear God more than men; he stands by them, protects and honors them, let it vex whom it may. It is written of Moses in Hebrews 11 [:24-27] that he stood by his brethren, regardless of the mighty king of Egypt.

Notice that in this commandment you see, though briefly, that faith must be the foreman behind this work. Without faith no one is able to do this work. In fact, all works are entirely comprised in faith, as I have often said. Therefore, apart from faith all works are dead, no matter how wonderful they look or what splendid names they have. For just as nobody does the work of this commandment unless he is firm and unshaken in the confidence of divine favor, so also he does no work of any of the other commandments without this same faith. Consequently, on the basis of this commandment, anyone may very easily try and find out whether he is a Christian and a true believer in Christ, and thus whether he is doing good works or not. We now see how Almighty God has not only set our Lord Jesus Christ before us that we should believe in him with such confidence, but we also see that in Christ God holds before us an example of the same confidence and of the same good works. God does this so that we believe in him, follow him, and abide in him forever, as he says in John 14 [:6], "I am the way, and the truth, and the life": the way, in which we follow him; the truth, that we believe in him; the life, that we live in him forever.

From all this it is now clear that all other works which are not commanded are dangerous and easily recognized. The works which are not commanded are the building of churches, beautifying them, making pilgrimages, and all those things of which so much is written in the ecclesiastical regulations. These things have misled and burdened the world, brought it to ruin, troubled consciences, silenced and weakened faith. It is also clear that a man has enough to engage all his strength to keep the commandments of God, and even if he neglects everything else, he can never do all the good works he is commanded to do. Why then does he seek other works which are neither necessary nor commanded, and yet neglect those that are necessary and commanded?

The Ninth and Tenth Commandments

The last two commandments are perfectly clear. They forbid the sinful lusts of the flesh and the coveting of temporal goods. These evil desires do no harm to our neighbor, and yet they persist to the grave. And the strife in us against these desires goes on until death. Therefore, these two commandments are drawn together by St. Paul into one in Romans 7 [:7]. These two commandments are set as a goal which we do not attain, and we reach out to them only in thought right up till death. For nobody has ever been so holy that he never felt some evil inclination within himself, especially when occasion and temptation were present together. For original sin is born in us by nature: it may be checked, but it cannot be entirely uprooted except through death. It is for this reason death is both profitable and desirable.

For this may God help us, Amen.

TO THE CHRISTIAN NOBILITY OF THE GERMAN NATION CONCERNING THE REFORM OF THE CHRISTIAN ESTATE

1520

Translated by Charles M. Jacobs

Revised by James Atkinson

INTRODUCTION

This treatise, one of the most significant documents produced by the Protestant Reformation, appeared at a critical point in Luther's career. The Leipzig Debate[1] with John Eck during the summer of 1519 had projected Luther into a position of prominence and attracted support from a wide variety of partisans and sympathizers in humanist circles, episcopal courts, universities, and among the imperial knights. After his return to Wittenberg, while awaiting the decision of the several universities appointed to referee the debate, Luther resumed the whole range of his pastoral and teaching activities. In the five and one-half months after the debate he also published sixteen treatises which, though not so intended, increased his reputation as a controversial figure.

One of these treatises, *The Blessed Sacrament of the Holy and True Body of Christ, and the Brotherhoods* (1519),[2] involved him in a quarrel with the bishop of Meissen and, indirectly, with Duke George of Saxony.[3] The settlement of this quarrel early in 1520, however, did not satisfy Elector Frederick, for he had known since the previous December that a new attack was being planned in Rome against himself and against Luther, and that this attack involved Eck, who had been summoned to Rome.[4] By the middle of March, 1520, the condemnation of Luther's position at Leipzig by the faculties of Louvain and Cologne reached Saxony. The elector urged Luther to address a proposal of peace to his opponents, but he refused on the ground that to withdraw from a controversy would be to deny God's Word.[5]

Early in May, 1520, the crude Latin polemic *On the Apostolic*

---

[1] Cf. *LW* 31, 307-325.

[2] *LW* 35, 47-73.

[3] The course and details of the quarrel are given in John W. Doberstein and Theodore G. Tappert (trans.), Heinrich Boehmer's *Road to Reformation* (Philadelphia: Muhlenberg Press, 1946), pp. 303-305.

[4] Eck was appointed to a commission to examine Luther's doctrine. This commission drafted the bull, *Exsurge, Domine,* which was published against Luther on June 15, 1520. Cf. *LW* 31, xix.

[5] Cf. Boehmer, *Road to Reformation,* p. 305.

See, written by Augustine von Alveld, a Franciscan friar, arrived in Wittenberg. Luther did not choose to issue a personal reply, and instead assigned the task to John Lonicer, his *famulus.* But when Alveld published a similar work in German, Luther replied himself, lest the German-speaking laity be misled. In the concluding section of his reply, *The Papacy at Rome, an Answer to the Celebrated Romanist at Leipzig,*[6] Luther wrote, "Moreover, I should be truly glad if kings, princes, and all the nobles would take hold, and turn the knaves from Rome out of the country, and keep the appointment to bishoprics and benefices out of their hands. How has Roman avarice come to usurp all the foundations, bishoprics, and benefices of our fathers? Who has ever read or heard of such monstrous robbery? Do we not also have the people who need them, while out of our poverty we must enrich the ass-drivers and stable boys, nay, the harlots and knaves at Rome, who look upon us as nothing else but arrant fools, and make us the objects of their vile mockery. . . . Oh, the pity that kings and princes have so little reverence for Christ, and his honor concerns them so little that they allow such heinous abominations to gain the upper hand, and look on, while at Rome they think of nothing but to continue in their madness and to increase the abounding misery, until no hope is left on earth except in the temporal authorities. About this, if this Romanist attacks me again, I will say more later. Let this suffice for a beginning."[7]

Although Alveld did not renew the attack himself, it did come. During the first week in June Luther received a copy of Prierias'[8] *Epitome of a Reply to Martin Luther,* which contained bold assertions of papal absolutism. Almost immediately Luther published an annotated reprint of this work.[9] In his preface to this reprint Luther wrote, "And now farewell, unhappy, hopeless, blasphemous Rome! The wrath of God has come upon you in the end, as you deserved,

[6] *PE* 1, 327-394. This reply was written during the last two weeks in May, 1520.

[7] *PE* 1, 392-393.

[8] Sylvester Prierias (1456-1523), a Dominican priest and professor, was the pope's counselor in matters of faith. He had been influential in securing the condemnation of Reuchlin and had been commissioned to examine Luther's writings.

[9] The text of Prierias' reply with Luther's notes is given in *Epitoma responsionis ad Martinum Luther* (1520). *WA* 6, 328-348.

and not for the many prayers which are made on your behalf, but because you have chosen to grow more evil from day to day! We have cared for Babylon and she is not healed. Let us then leave her that she may be the habitation of dragons, spectres, ghosts, and witches, and true to her name of Babel, an everlasting confusion, an idol of avarice, perfidy, apostasy, of cynics, lechers, robbers, sorcerers, and endless other impudent monsters, a new pantheon of wickedness."[10]

The tenor of these words gives significance to a letter written to Spalatin just before June 8, in which Luther states, "I have a mind to issue a broadside [*publicam schedam*] to [Emperor] Charles and the nobility of Germany against the tyranny and baseness of the Roman curia."[11] On June 23 Luther sent the manuscript of *To the Christian Nobility* to Nicholas von Amsdorf. By August 18 the first edition of four thousand copies had come from the press of Melchior Lotther in Wittenberg. Within a week a second, somewhat enlarged, edition was being prepared.

It would appear that *To the Christian Nobility* was occasioned by the attacks of Alveld and Prierias, and was the fulfilment of Luther's thinly veiled threat in the concluding section of *The Papacy at Rome* and of his intention expressed in the letter to Spalatin. Luther research over the last half century, however, has challenged this view.[12] Close scrutiny of the text of the treatise, of Luther's correspondence, and of other contemporary sources and documents has provided new insights into the general background and content of the treatise.

These insights indicate that the present treatise, originally intended as a small booklet,[13] actually came about as the result of urgent insistence from, and with the extensive co-operation of, un-

---

[10] *WA* 6, 329.

[11] *WA*, Br 2, 120.

[12] E. Kohlmeyer originally took the position that the attacks of Alveld and Prierias had motivated the intention expressed in the letter to Spalatin. He later modified this view and asserted that these attacks provided the psychological motivation for Luther to issue his broadside. Cf. Karl Bauer, "*Luthers Aufruf an den Adel, die Kirche zu reformieren,*" *Archiv für Reformationsgeschichte,* XXXII (1935), 172.

[13] Bauer goes to great lengths to demonstrate that the "broadside" (*publicam schedam*), of which Luther wrote to Spalatin, means a small booklet or brochure, longer than a tract, but by no means a major book. Cf. Bauer, *op. cit.*, p. 188.

identified members of the Saxon court, jurists, Wittenberg professors, and other widely respected men.[14] In Luther these men would have a spokesman who could give to the *Gravamina* of the German nation[15] the theological substance and expression which had been lacking previously.

Yet despite the urging and co-operation of others, *To the Christian Nobility* is the product of Luther's mind, heart, and soul. Firmly convinced of the priesthood of believers, and believing that the German nobility, as a whole, were of the same sincerity of spirit as those nobles he knew at the Saxon court, Luther, in the light of clear historical precedent, confidently conferred upon the crown and the nobility the responsibility and the right to intervene in ecclesiastical affairs to accomplish the reform of the church.

In the three sections of this treatise Luther laid the ax to the whole complex of ideas upon which the social, political, legal, and religious thought of the Western world had been developing for nearly a thousand years. The first section exposes and refutes theologically the three walls behind which the papacy was entrenched. By demolishing the first wall, the concept of spiritual and secular classes, Luther removed the medieval distinction between clergy and laity and conferred upon the state, the rulers of which (as Luther saw it) were Christians and therefore priests, the right and duty to curb evil no matter where it appeared. In rapid succession he demolishes the remaining two walls: the papal claim (most recently advanced by Alveld and Prierias) that only the pope can interpret Scripture, and that because only the pope could summon a council the decisions of a council were invalid without papal sanction. Luther declares that there is no biblical ground for the papal claim of the sole right to interpret Scripture, and he asserts the necessity for Rome to listen to those who can. The third wall collapses under the barrage of Luther's attacks drawn from Scripture, church history, and the assertion that "when necessity de-

---

[14] Bauer supports this view by citing a letter written to Johann Lang by Melanchthon at the time the second edition of *To the Christian Nobility* went to press. In this letter Melanchthon states that Luther had been motivated to write this treatise by many "whom we esteem." *Ibid.*, p. 173. The full text of the letter is in *CR* 1, 211.

[15] Cf. *LW* 48, 265, n. 5.

mands it, and the pope is an offense to Christendom, the first man who is able should, as a true member of the whole body, do what he can to bring about a truly free council."[16]

The second part of the work is a bill of particulars, a specific indictment of ecclesiastical abuses with which a general council should deal. These abuses range from the worldliness of the papacy and the curia to benefices and indulgences. For a long time it was assumed that Luther's portrayal of conditions in Rome derived from the recollection of his own stay there in 1510-1511. The evidence uncovered by modern research, however, suggests that he drew less upon his own memory than upon very recent information provided by Reuchlin's lawyer, Johann von der Wieck.[17]

Just as specific as the indictments are the proposals for reform which constitute the final section of the work. Here Luther's proposals range from the abolition of annates and the exclusion of the church from political power to popular piety, public provision for the poor, and the relationship between church and state. The latter part of this section deals with education and the economic and social ills afflicting the German nation.

The present translation is a revision of that by Charles M. Jacobs in *PE* 2, 61-164. The German text, *An den christlichen Adel deutscher Nation von des christlichen Standes Besserung,* is in *WA* 6, (381) 404-469.

---

[16] Cf. p. 137.
[17] Cf. Bauer, *op. cit.*, p. 196.

TO THE CHRISTIAN NOBILITY OF THE GERMAN NATION CONCERNING THE REFORM OF THE CHRISTIAN ESTATE

Jesus

To the Esteemed and Reverend Master, Nicholas von Amsdorf, Licentiate of Holy Scripture, and Canon of Wittenberg, my special and kind friend, from Doctor Martin Luther.

The grace and peace of God be with you, esteemed, reverend, and dear sir and friend.

The time for silence is past, and the time to speak has come, as Ecclesiastes says [3:7]. I am carrying out our intention to put together a few points on the matter of the reform of the Christian estate, to be laid before the Christian nobility of the German nation, in the hope that God may help his church through the laity, since the clergy, to whom this task more properly belongs, have grown quite indifferent. I am sending the whole thing to you, reverend sir, [that you may give] an opinion on it and, where necessary, improve it.

I know full well that I shall not escape the charge of presumption because I, a despised, inferior person, venture to address such high and great estates on such weighty matters, as if there were nobody else in the world except Doctor Luther to take up the cause of the Christian estate and give advice to such high-ranking people. I make no apologies no matter who demands them. Perhaps I owe my God and the world another work of folly. I intend to pay my debt honestly. And if I succeed, I shall for the time being become a court jester. And if I fail, I still have one advantage—no one need buy me a cap or put scissors to my head.[1]

[1] A jocular comparison of the monk's cowl and tonsure with the jester's cap and bells.

It is a question of who will put the bells on whom.[2] I must fulfil the proverb, "Whatever the world does, a monk must be in the picture, even if he has to be painted in."[3] More than once a fool has spoken wisely, and wise men have often been arrant fools. Paul says, "He who wishes to be wise must become a fool" [I Cor. 3:18]. Moreover, since I am not only a fool, but also a sworn doctor of Holy Scripture,[4] I am glad for the opportunity to fulfil my doctor's oath, even in the guise of a fool.

I beg you, give my apologies to those who are moderately intelligent, for I do not know how to earn the grace and favor of the superintelligent. I have often sought to do so with the greatest pains, but from now on I neither desire nor value their favor. God help us to seek not our own glory but his alone. Amen.

At Wittenberg, in the monastery of the Augustinians, on the eve of St. John Baptist [June 23] in the year fifteen hundred and twenty.

To His Most Illustrious, Most Mighty, and Imperial Majesty, and to the Christian Nobility of the German Nation, from Doctor Martin Luther.

Grace and power from God, Most Illustrious Majesty, and most gracious and dear lords.

It is not from sheer impertinence or rashness that I, one poor man, have taken it upon myself to address your worships. All the estates of Christendom, particularly in Germany, are now oppressed by distress and affliction, and this has stirred not only me but everybody else to cry out time and time again and to pray for help. It has even compelled me now at this time to cry aloud that God may inspire someone with his Spirit to lend a helping hand to this distressed and wretched nation. Often the councils have made some pretense at reformation,[5] but their attempts have been cleverly frustrated by the guile of certain men, and things have gone from

[2] I.e., who is the bigger fool.

[3] *Monachus semper praesens.*

[4] Luther often stressed that he had acquired his doctorate and its obligation to teach the gospel not out of his own desire but out of obedience to his superiors. Cf. *LW* 48, 6, n. 5.

[5] See p. 91, n. 52.

bad to worse. With God's help I intend to expose the wiles and wickedness of these men, so that they are shown up for what they are and may never again be so obstructive and destructive. God has given us a young man of noble birth as head of state,[6] and in him has awakened great hopes of good in many hearts. Presented with such an opportunity we ought to apply ourselves and use this time of grace profitably.

The first and most important thing to do in this matter is to prepare ourselves in all seriousness. We must not start something by trusting in great power or human reason, even if all the power in the world were ours. For God cannot and will not suffer that a good work begin by relying upon one's own power and reason. He dashes such works to the ground, they do no good at all. As it says in Psalm 33 [:16], "No king is saved by his great might and no lord is saved by the greatness of his strength." I fear that this is why the good emperors Frederick I[7] and Frederick II[8] and many other German emperors were in former times shamefully oppressed and trodden underfoot by the popes, although all the world feared the emperors. It may be that they relied on their own might more than on God, and therefore had to fall. What was it in our own times that raised the bloodthirsty Julius II[9] to such heights? Nothing else, I fear, except that France, the Germans, and Venice relied upon themselves. The children of Benjamin slew forty-two thousand Israelites[10] because the latter relied on their own strength, Judges 30 [:21].

That it may not so fare with us and our noble Charles, we must realize that in this matter we are not dealing with men, but with the princes of hell. These princes could fill the world with war and bloodshed, but war and bloodshed do not overcome them. We must tackle this job by renouncing trust in physical force and

[6] Charles V, who had been elected emperor in 1519 when only twenty years of age, and whom Luther appeared before at the Diet of Worms in 1521.

[7] Emperor Frederick Barbarossa (1152-1190).

[8] Frederick II (1212-1250), grandson of Barbarossa and last of the great Hohenstaufen emperors, died under excommunication.

[9] Pope Julius II (1503-1513) was notorious for his unscrupulous use of political power. Continually involved in war, he led his armies in person and was "the scourge of Italy."

[10] Luther's memory is not accurate here. The Book of Judges speaks of twenty-two thousand.

trusting humbly in God. We must seek God's help through earnest prayer and fix our minds on nothing else than the misery and distress of suffering Christendom without regard to what evil men deserve. Otherwise, we may start the game with great prospects of success, but when we get into it the evil spirits will stir up such confusion that the whole world will swim in blood, and then nothing will come of it all. Let us act wisely, therefore, and in the fear of God. The more force we use, the greater our disaster if we do not act humbly and in the fear of God. If the popes and Romanists[11] have hitherto been able to set kings against each other by the devil's help, they may well be able to do it again if we were to go ahead without the help of God on our own strength and by our own cunning.

The Romanists have very cleverly built three walls around themselves. Hitherto they have protected themselves by these walls in such a way that no one has been able to reform them. As a result, the whole of Christendom has fallen abominably.

In the first place, when pressed by the temporal power they have made decrees and declared that the temporal power had no jurisdiction over them, but that, on the contrary, the spiritual power is above the temporal. In the second place, when the attempt is made to reprove them with the Scriptures, they raise the objection that only the pope may interpret the Scriptures. In the third place, if threatened with a council, their story is that no one may summon a council but the pope.

In this way they have cunningly stolen our three rods from us, that they may go unpunished. They have ensconced themselves within the safe stronghold of these three walls so that they can practice all the knavery and wickedness which we see today. Even when they have been compelled to hold a council they have weakened its power in advance by putting the princes under oath to let them remain as they were.[12] In addition, they have given the

---

[11] Advocates of papal supremacy.

[12] Luther alludes here to the failure of the conciliar movement to reform the church. The movement failed chiefly because the papacy refused to submit to the authority of the council. Furthermore, the papacy refused to co-operate in the convening of councils unless the secular powers first swore not to deprive the pope of his authority. In brief, the papacy refused to submit to the authority of either church or empire. Luther felt that since the church had failed to take the initiative in the matter of reform, the emperor should do so.

pope full authority over all decisions of a council, so that it is all the same whether there are many councils or no councils. They only deceive us with puppet shows and sham fights. They fear terribly for their skin in a really free council! They have so intimidated kings and princes with this technique that they believe it would be an offense against God not to be obedient to the Romanists in all their knavish and ghoulish deceits.[13]

May God help us, and give us just one of those trumpets with which the walls of Jericho were overthrown[14] to blast down these walls of straw and paper in the same way and set free the Christian rods for the punishment of sin, [and] bring to light the craft and deceit of the devil, to the end that through punishment we may reform ourselves and once more attain God's favor.

Let us begin by attacking the first wall. It is pure invention that pope, bishop, priests, and monks are called the spiritual estate while princes, lords, artisans, and farmers are called the temporal estate. This is indeed a piece of deceit and hypocrisy. Yet no one need be intimidated by it, and for this reason: all Christians are truly of the spiritual estate, and there is no difference among them except that of office. Paul says in I Corinthians 12 [:12-13] that we are all one body, yet every member has its own work by which it serves the others. This is because we all have one baptism, one gospel, one faith, and are all Christians alike; for baptism, gospel, and faith alone make us spiritual and a Christian people.

The pope or bishop anoints, shaves heads,[15] ordains, consecrates, and prescribes garb different from that of the laity, but he can never make a man into a Christian or into a spiritual man by so doing. He might well make a man into a hypocrite or a humbug and blockhead,[16] but never a Christian or a spiritual man. As far as that goes, we are all consecrated priests through baptism, as St. Peter says in I Peter 2 [:9], "You are a royal priesthood and a priestly realm." The Apocalypse says, "Thou hast made us to be priests and kings by thy blood" [Rev. 5:9-10]. The consecration by pope or bishop would never make a priest, and if we had no

---

[13] *Spugnissen*, literally, "ghosts." The sense of the passage is that the Romanists have frightened the world with threats of purgatory and hell.

[14] Cf. Josh. 6:20.

[15] I.e., confers tonsure.

[16] *Olgotzen*. Cf. p. 68, n. 39.

higher consecration than that which pope or bishop gives, no one could say mass or preach a sermon or give absolution.

Therefore, when a bishop consecrates it is nothing else than that in the place and stead of the whole community, all of whom have like power, he takes a person and charges him to exercise this power on behalf of the others. It is like ten brothers, all king's sons and equal heirs, choosing one of themselves to rule the inheritance in the interests of all. In one sense they are all kings and of equal power, and yet one of them is charged with the responsibility of ruling. To put it still more clearly: suppose a group of earnest Christian laymen were taken prisoner and set down in a desert without an episcopally ordained priest among them. And suppose they were to come to a common mind there and then in the desert and elect one of their number, whether he were married[17] or not, and charge him to baptize, say mass, pronounce absolution, and preach the gospel. Such a man would be as truly a priest as though he had been ordained by all the bishops and popes in the world. That is why in cases of necessity anyone can baptize and give absolution. This would be impossible if we were not all priests. Through canon law[18] the Romanists have almost destroyed and made unknown the wondrous grace and authority of baptism and justification. In times gone by Christians used to choose their bishops and priests in this way from among their own number, and they were confirmed in their office by the other bishops without all the fuss that goes on nowadays. St. Augustine,[19] Ambrose,[20] and Cyprian[21] each became [a bishop in this way].

---

[17] *Ehelich. PE* and other English translations also render this word as "married." It can, however, also mean "legitimately born." Karl Benrath notes that according to canon law only one born in wedlock may receive ordination as a priest. Cf. *An den christlichen Adel deutscher Nation von des christlichen Standes Besserung. . . . Bearbeitet, sowie mit Einleitung und Erläuterungen versehen von Karl Benrath* (Halle: Verein für Reformationsgeschichte, 1884), p. 83, n. 7.

[18] Canon law, which Luther throughout this treatise and elsewhere calls the "spiritual law," is a general name for the decrees of councils and the decisions of the popes collected in the *Corpus Iuris Canonici.* It comprised the whole body of church law and embodied in legal forms the medieval theory of papal absolutism, which accounts for the bitterness with which Luther speaks of it, especially in this treatise. Cf. *PE* 2, 67, n. 2.

[19] Augustine, bishop of Hippo (395-430).

[20] Ambrose, bishop of Milan (374-397), was elected to the office by the people of Milan, even though he was not yet baptized.

[21] Cyprian, bishop of Carthage (247-258), was also elected to the episcopate by the laity.

Since those who exercise secular authority have been baptized with the same baptism, and have the same faith and the same gospel as the rest of us, we must admit that they are priests and bishops and we must regard their office as one which has a proper and useful place in the Christian community. For whoever comes out of the water of baptism can boast that he is already a consecrated priest, bishop, and pope, although of course it is not seemly that just anybody should exercise such office. Because we are all priests of equal standing, no one must push himself forward and take it upon himself, without our consent and election, to do that for which we all have equal authority. For no one dare take upon himself what is common to all without the authority and consent of the community. And should it happen that a person chosen for such office were deposed for abuse of trust, he would then be exactly what he was before. Therefore, a priest in Christendom is nothing else but an officeholder. As long as he holds office he takes precedence; where he is deposed, he is a peasant or a townsman like anybody else. Indeed, a priest is never a priest when he is deposed. But now the Romanists have invented *characteres indelebiles*[22] and say[23] that a deposed priest is nevertheless something different from a mere layman. They hold the illusion that a priest can never be anything other than a priest, or ever become a layman. All this is just contrived talk, and human regulation.

It follows from this argument that there is no true, basic difference between laymen and priests, princes and bishops, between religious and secular, except for the sake of office and work, but not for the sake of status. They are all of the spiritual estate, all are truly priests, bishops, and popes. But they do not all have the same work to do. Just as all priests and monks do not have the same

[22] The *character indelebilis* or "indelible mark," was given authoritative formulation in the bull *Exultate Deo* (1439). Eugene IV, summing up the decrees of the Council of Florence, wrote: "Among these sacraments there are three—baptism, confirmation, and orders—which indelibly impress upon the soul a character, i.e., a certain spiritual mark which distinguishes them from the rest" (Carl Mirbt, *Quellen zur Geschichte des Papstums* [2nd ed.], No. 150). The Council of Trent, in its twenty-third session, July 15, 1563 (Mirbt, *op. cit.*, No. 312), defined the correct Roman teaching as follows: "Since in the sacrament of orders, as in baptism and confirmation, a character is impressed which cannot be destroyed or taken away, the Holy Synod justly condemns the opinion of those who assert that the priests of the New Testament have only temporary power, and that those once rightly ordained can again be made laymen, if they do not exercise the ministry of the Word of God." Cf. *PE* 2, 68, n. 5.

[23] *Schwetzen*; literally, "to chatter nonsense."

work. This is the teaching of St. Paul in Romans 12 [:4-5] and I Corinthians 12 [:12] and in I Peter 2 [:9], as I have said above, namely, that we are all one body of Christ the Head, and all members one of another. Christ does not have two different bodies, one temporal, the other spiritual. There is but one Head and one body.

Therefore, just as those who are now called "spiritual," that is, priests, bishops, or popes, are neither different from other Christians nor superior to them, except that they are charged with the administration of the word of God and the sacraments, which is their work and office, so it is with the temporal authorities. They bear the sword and rod in their hand to punish the wicked and protect the good. A cobbler, a smith, a peasant—each has the work and office of his trade, and yet they are all alike consecrated priests and bishops. Further, everyone must benefit and serve every other by means of his own work or office so that in this way many kinds of work may be done for the bodily and spiritual welfare of the community, just as all the members of the body serve one another [I Cor. 12:14-26].

Consider for a moment how Christian is the decree which says that the temporal power is not above the "spiritual estate" and has no right to punish it.[24] That is as much as to say that the hand shall not help the eye when it suffers pain. Is it not unnatural, not to mention un-Christian, that one member does not help another and prevent its destruction? In fact, the more honorable the member, the more the others ought to help. I say therefore that since the temporal power is ordained of God to punish the wicked and protect the good, it should be left free to perform its office in the whole body of Christendom without restriction and without respect to persons, whether it affects pope, bishops, priests, monks, nuns, or anyone else. If it were right to say that the temporal power is inferior to all the spiritual estates (preacher, confessor, or any spiritual office), and so prevent the temporal power from doing its

[24] The sharp distinction drawn by the Roman church between clergy and laity made possible the contention that the clergy was exempt from the jurisdiction of the civil courts. This is known as *privilegium fori*, i.e., "benefit of clergy." It was further claimed that the governing of the clergy and the administration of church property were matters for church authorities, and that lay rulers could not make or enforce laws which affected the church in any way. Cf. *PE* 2, 70, n. 1.

proper work, then the tailors, cobblers, stonemasons, carpenters, cooks, innkeepers, farmers, and all the temporal craftsmen should be prevented from providing pope, bishops, priests, and monks with shoes, clothes, house, meat and drink, as well as from paying them any tribute. But if these laymen are allowed to do their proper work without restriction, what then are the Romanist scribes doing with their own laws, which exempt them from the jurisdiction of the temporal Christian authority? It is just so that they can be free to do evil and fulfil what St. Peter said, "False teachers will rise up among you who will deceive you, and with their false and fanciful talk, they will take advantage of you" [II Pet. 2:1–3].

For these reasons the temporal Christian authority ought to exercise its office without hindrance, regardless of whether it is pope, bishop, or priest whom it affects. Whoever is guilty, let him suffer. All that canon law has said to the contrary is the invention of Romanist presumption. For thus St. Paul says to all Christians, "Let every soul (I take that to mean the pope's soul also) be subject to the temporal authority; for it does not bear the sword in vain, but serves God by punishing the wicked and benefiting the good" [Rom. 13:1, 4]. St. Peter, too, says, "Be subject to all human ordinances for the sake of the Lord, who so wills it" [I Pet. 2:13, 15]. He has also prophesied in II Peter 2 [:1] that such men would arise and despise the temporal authority. This is exactly what has happened through the canon law.

So, then, I think this first paper wall is overthrown. Inasmuch as the temporal power has become a member of the Christian body it is a spiritual estate, even though its work is physical.[25] Therefore, its work should extend without hindrance to all the members of the whole body to punish and use force whenever guilt deserves or necessity demands, without regard to whether the culprit is pope, bishop, or priest. Let the Romanists hurl threats and bans about as they like. That is why guilty priests, when they are handed over to secular law, are first deprived of their priestly dignities.[26] This

---

[25] I.e., temporal.

[26] Church authorities insisted that clergy charged with infractions of the laws of the state first be tried in ecclesiastical courts. Priests found guilty by such courts were deprived of their priesthood and were surrendered to the temporal authorities. *PE* 2, 71, n. 1.

would not be right unless the secular sword previously had had authority over these priests by divine right. Moreover, it is intolerable that in canon law so much importance is attached to the freedom, life, and property of the clergy, as though the laity were not also as spiritual and as good Christians as they, or did not also belong to the church. Why are your life and limb, your property and honor, so cheap and mine not, inasmuch as we are all Christians and have the same baptism, the same faith, the same Spirit, and all the rest? If a priest is murdered, the whole country is placed under interdict.[27] Why not when a peasant is murdered? How does this great difference come about between two men who are both Christians? It comes from the laws and fabrications of men.

Moreover, it can be no good spirit which has invented such exceptions and granted sin such license and impunity. For if it is our duty to strive against the words and works of the devil and to drive him out in whatever way we can, as both Christ and his apostles command us, how have we gotten into such a state that we have to do nothing and say nothing when the pope or his cohorts undertake devilish words and works? Ought we merely out of regard for these people allow the suppression of divine commandments and truth, which we have sworn in baptism to support with life and limb? Then we should have to answer for all the souls that would thereby be abandoned and led astray!

It must, therefore, have been the chief devil himself who said what is written in the canon law, that if the pope were so scandalously bad as to lead crowds of souls to the devil, still he could not be deposed.[28] At Rome they build on this accursed and devilish

---

[27] The interdict prohibits the administration of the sacraments and the other rites of the church within a given territory. Its use was not uncommon in the Middle Ages, and at the height of papal power it proved an effective means of bringing rulers to terms. Innocent III imposed the interdict upon England in 1208, during the reign of King John. Interdicts of more limited local extent were quite frequent. The use of the interdict for trifling infractions of church law was a subject of complaint at the Diet of Worms in 1521 and of Nürnberg in 1524. Cf. *PE* 2, 72, n. 1.

[28] The statement about which Luther here complains is found in the *Decreti Prima Pars,* dist. XL, C. VI, *Si papa. CIC* 1, 146. In his *Epitome* Prierias had quoted this canon against Luther: "A *Pontifex indubitatus* [i.e., a pope not accused of heresy or schism] cannot lawfully be deposed or judged either by a council or by the whole world, even if he is so scandalous as to lead people with him by crowds into the possession of hell." Luther's comment is, "Be astonished, O heaven; shudder, O earth! Behold, O Christians, what Rome is!" *WA* 6, 336. Cf. *PE* 2, 72, n. 1.

foundation, and think that we should let all the world go to the devil rather than resist their knavery. If the fact that one man is set over others were sufficient reason why he should not be punished, then no Christian could punish another, since Christ commanded that every man should esteem himself as the lowliest and the least [Matt. 18:4].

Where sin is, there is no longer any shielding from punishment. St. Gregory writes that we are indeed all equal, but guilt makes a man inferior to others.[29] Now we see how the Romanists treat Christendom. They take away its freedom without any proof from Scripture, at their own whim. But God, as well as the apostles, made them subject to the temporal sword. It is to be feared that this is a game of the Antichrist,[30] or at any rate that his forerunner has appeared.

The second wall is still more loosely built and less substantial. The Romanists want to be the only masters of Holy Scripture, although they never learn a thing from the Bible all their life long. They assume the sole authority for themselves, and, quite unashamed, they play about with words before our very eyes, trying to persuade us that the pope cannot err in matters of faith,[31] regardless of whether he is righteous or wicked. Yet they cannot point to a single letter.[32] This is why so many heretical and un-Christian, even unnatural, ordinances stand in the canon law. But there is no need to talk about these ordinances at present. Since these Romanists think the Holy Spirit never leaves them, no matter how ignorant and wicked they are, they become bold and decree only

---

[29] Gregory the Great (590-604), in *Regula pastoralis,* II, 6. *MPL* 77, 34.

[30] Antichrist is the incarnation of all that is hostile to Christ and his kingdom and whose appearance is prophesied in II Thess. 2:3-10; I John 2:18, 22; 4:3; and Revelation 13.

[31] The doctrine of papal infallibility was never officially sanctioned in the Middle Ages, but the claim was repeatedly made by the champions of papal power, e.g., Augustinus Triumphus (d. 1328) in his *Summa de potestate Papae.* In his attack on the *Ninety-five Theses* (*Dialogus de potestate Papae,* December, 1517) Sylvester Prierias had asserted, "The supreme pontiff cannot err when giving a decision as pontiff, i.e., when speaking officially [*ex officio*]"; and also, "Whoever does not rest upon the teaching of the Roman church and the supreme pontiff as an infallible rule of faith, from which even Holy Scripture draws its vigor and authority, is a heretic" (*EA Var. arg.* 1, 348). In the *Epitome* Prierias had said, "Even though the pope as an individual [*singularis persona*] can do wrong and hold a wrong faith, nevertheless as pope he cannot give a wrong decision" (*WA* 6, 337). Cf. *PE* 2, 73, n. 5.

[32] I.e., a single letter of Scripture to support their claim.

what they want. And if what they claim were true, why have Holy Scripture at all? Of what use is Scripture? Let us burn the Scripture and be satisfied with the unlearned gentlemen at Rome who possess the Holy Spirit! And yet the Holy Spirit can be possessed only by pious hearts. If I had not read the words with my own eyes,[33] I would not have believed it possible for the devil to have made such stupid claims at Rome, and to have won supporters for them.

But so as not to fight them with mere words, we will quote the Scriptures. St. Paul says in I Corinthians 14 [:30], "If something better is revealed to anyone, though he is already sitting and listening to another in God's word, then the one who is speaking shall hold his peace and give place." What would be the point of this commandment if we were compelled to believe only the man who does the talking, or the man who is at the top? Even Christ said in John 6 [:45] that all Christians shall be taught by God. If it were to happen that the pope and his cohorts were wicked and not true Christians, were not taught by God and were without understanding, and at the same time some obscure person had a right understanding, why should the people not follow the obscure man? Has the pope not erred many times? Who would help Christendom when the pope erred if we did not have somebody we could trust more than him, somebody who had the Scriptures on his side?

Therefore, their claim that only the pope may interpret Scripture is an outrageous fancied fable. They cannot produce a single letter [of Scripture] to maintain that the interpretation of Scripture or the confirmation of its interpretation belongs to the pope alone. They themselves have usurped this power. And although they allege that this power was given to St. Peter when the keys were given him, it is clear enough that the keys were not given to Peter alone but to the whole community. Further, the keys were not ordained for doctrine or government, but only for the binding or loosing of sin.[34] Whatever else or whatever more they

---

[33] See the reference to the *Epitome* of Prierias on p. 132, n. 28.

[34] Matt. 16:19, 18:18, and John 20:23. Throughout his career Luther dealt with the office of the keys. He first mentioned it in 1517 in his *Ninety-five Theses* (*LW* 31, 27, 31) and devoted a substantial portion of his last treatise, *Against the Roman Papacy, An Institution of the Devil* (1545) to a discussion of the keys (*LW* 41, 315-320 *passim*). His clearest and most extensive treatment was set forth in his 1530 treatise *The Keys* (*LW* 40, 321-377).

arrogate to themselves on the basis of the keys is a mere fabrication. But Christ's words to Peter, "I have prayed for you that your faith fail not" [Luke 22:32], cannot be applied to the pope, since the majority of the popes have been without faith, as they must themselves confess. Besides, it is not only for Peter that Christ prayed, but also for all apostles and Christians, as he says in John 17 [:9, 20], "Father, I pray for those whom thou hast given me, and not for these only, but for all who believe on me through their word." Is that not clear enough?

Just think of it! The Romanists must admit that there are among us good Christians who have the true faith, spirit, understanding, word, and mind of Christ. Why, then, should we reject the word and understanding of good Christians and follow the pope, who has neither faith nor the Spirit? To follow the pope would be to deny the whole faith[35] as well as the Christian church. Again, if the article, "I believe in one holy Christian church," is correct, then the pope cannot be the only one who is right. Otherwise, we would have to confess,[36] "I believe in the pope at Rome." This would reduce the Christian church to one man, and be nothing else than a devilish and hellish error.

Besides, if we are all priests, as was said above, and all have one faith, one gospel, one sacrament,[37] why should we not also have the power to test and judge what is right or wrong in matters of faith? What becomes of Paul's words in I Corinthians 2 [:15], "A spiritual man judges all things, yet he is judged by no one"? And II Corinthians 4 [:13], "We all have one spirit of faith"? Why, then, should not we perceive what is consistent with faith and what is not, just as well as an unbelieving pope does?

We ought to become bold and free on the authority of all these texts, and many others. We ought not to allow the Spirit of freedom (as Paul calls him [II Cor. 3:17]) to be frightened off by the fabrications of the popes, but we ought to march boldly forward and test all that they do, or leave undone, by our believing understanding of the Scriptures. We must compel the Romanists to follow not their own interpretation but the better one. Long ago Abraham

[35] Literally, "the creed," referring to the Apostles' Creed.
[36] *Beten*; literally, "to pray."
[37] Luther means baptism. See p. 127.

had to listen to Sarah, although she was in more complete subjection to him than we are to anyone on earth [Gen. 21:12]. And Balaam's ass was wiser than the prophet himself [Num. 22:21-35]. If God spoke then through an ass against a prophet, why should he not be able even now to speak through a righteous man against the pope? Similarly, St. Paul rebukes St. Peter as a man in error in Galatians 2 [:11-12]. Therefore, it is the duty of every Christian to espouse the cause of the faith, to understand and defend it, and to denounce every error.

The third wall falls of itself when the first two are down. When the pope acts contrary to the Scriptures, it is our duty to stand by the Scriptures, to reprove him and to constrain him, according to the word of Christ, Matthew 18 [:15-17], "If your brother sins against you, go and tell it to him, between you and him alone; if he does not listen to you, then take one or two others with you; if he does not listen to them, tell it to the church; if he does not listen to the church, consider him a heathen." Here every member is commanded to care for every other. How much more should we do this when the member that does evil is responsible for the government of the church, and by his evil-doing is the cause of much harm and offense to the rest! But if I am to accuse him before the church, I must naturally call the church together.

The Romanists have no basis in Scripture for their claim that the pope alone has the right to call or confirm a council.[38] This is just their own ruling, and it is only valid as long as it is not harmful to Christendom or contrary to the laws of God. Now when the pope deserves punishment, this ruling no longer obtains, for not to punish him by authority of a council is harmful to Christendom.

Thus we read in Acts 15 that it was not St. Peter who called the Apostolic Council but the apostles and elders. If then that right had belonged to St. Peter alone, the council would not have been

---

[38] This is another contention of Prierias. On November 28, 1518, Luther appealed his cause from the decision of the pope, which he could foresee would be adverse, to the decision of a council to be held at some future time. In the *Epitome* Prierias discusses this appeal, asserting among other things that "when there is one undisputed pontiff, it belongs to him alone to call a council," and that "the decrees of councils neither bind nor hold [*nullum ligant vel astringunt*] unless they are confirmed by authority of the Roman pontiff." *WA* 6, 335; *PE* 2, 77, n. 1.

a Christian council, but a heretical *conciliabulum.*[39] Even the Council of Nicaea, the most famous of all councils, was neither called nor confirmed by the bishop of Rome, but by the emperor Constantine.[40] Many other emperors after him have done the same, and yet these councils were the most Christian of all.[41] But if the pope alone has the right to convene councils, then these councils would all have been heretical. Further, when I examine the councils the pope did summon, I find that they did nothing of special importance.

Therefore, when necessity demands it, and the pope is an offense to Christendom, the first man who is able should, as a true member of the whole body, do what he can to bring about a truly free council.[42] No one can do this so well as the temporal authorities, especially since they are also fellow-Christians, fellow-priests, fellow-members of the spiritual estate, fellow-lords over all things. Whenever it is necessary or profitable they ought to exercise the office and work which they have received from God over everyone. Would it not be unnatural if a fire broke out in a city and everybody were to stand by and let it burn on and on and consume everything that could burn because nobody had the authority of the mayor, or because, perhaps, the fire broke out in the mayor's house? In such a situation is it not the duty of every citizen to arouse and summon the rest? How much more should this be done in the spiritual city of Christ if a fire of offense breaks out, whether in the papal government, or anywhere else! The same argument holds if an enemy were to attack a city. The man who first roused the others deserves honor and gratitude. Why, then, should he not deserve honor who makes known the presence of the enemy from hell and rouses Christian people and calls them together?

But all their boasting about an authority which dare not be opposed amounts to nothing at all. Nobody in Christendom has

---

[39] A mere gathering of people as opposed to a *concilium,* i.e., a valid council.

[40] The Council of Nicaea (325), the first general council, was convened by Constantine to settle the Arian controversy on the relation of Christ to God. Luther's contention is historically correct.

[41] Luther is referring to the first four ecumenical councils: Nicaea, Constantinople (381), Ephesus (431), and Chalcedon (451).

[42] A council free of papal control. Cf. p. 126, n. 12.

authority to do injury or to forbid the resisting of injury. There is no authority in the church except to promote good. Therefore, if the pope were to use his authority to prevent the calling of a free council, thereby preventing the improvement of the church, we should have regard neither for him nor for his authority. And if he were to hurl his bans and thunderbolts, we should despise his conduct as that of a madman. On the contrary, we should excommunicate him and drive him out as best we could, relying completely upon God. This presumptuous authority of his is nothing. He does not even have such authority. He is quickly defeated by a single text of Scripture, where Paul says to the Corinthians, "God has given us authority not to ruin Christendom, but to build it up" [II Cor. 10:8]. Who wants to leap over the hurdle of this text? It is the power of the devil and of Antichrist which resists the things that serve to build up Christendom. Such power is not to be obeyed, but rather resisted with life, property, and with all our might and main.

Even though a miracle were to be done against the temporal authority on the pope's behalf, or if somebody were struck down by the plague—which they boast has sometimes happened—it should be considered as nothing but the work of the devil designed to destroy our faith in God. Christ foretold this in Matthew 24 [:24], "False Christs and false prophets shall come in my name, who shall perform signs and wonders in order to deceive even the elect." And Paul says in II Thessalonians 2 [:9] that Antichrist shall, through the power of Satan, be mighty in false wonders.

Let us, therefore, hold fast to this: no Christian authority can do anything against Christ. As St. Paul says, "We can do nothing against Christ, only for Christ" [II Cor. 13:8]. But if an authority does anything against Christ, then that authority is the power of Antichrist and of the devil, even if it were to deluge us with wonders and plagues. Wonders and plagues prove nothing, especially in these evil latter days. The whole of Scripture foretells such false wonders. This is why we must hold fast to the word of God with firm faith, and then the devil will soon drop his miracles!

With this I hope that all this wicked and lying terror with which the Romanists have long intimidated and dulled our conscience has been overcome, and that they, just like all of us, shall be made subject to the sword. They have no right to interpret Scripture merely by authority and without learning.[43] They have no authority to prevent a council, or even worse yet at their mere whim to pledge it, impose conditions on it, or deprive it of its freedom. When they do that they are truly in the fellowship of Antichrist and the devil. They have nothing at all of Christ except the name.

We shall now look at the matters which ought to be properly dealt with in councils, matters with which popes, cardinals, bishops, and all scholars ought properly to be occupied day and night if they loved Christ and his church. But if this is not the case, let ordinary people[44] and the temporal authorities do it without regard to papal bans and fulminations, for an unjust ban is better than ten just and proper absolutions, and one unjust, improper absolution is worse than ten just bans.[45] Therefore, let us awake, dear Germans, and fear God more than man [Acts 5:29], lest we suffer the same fate of all the poor souls who are so lamentably lost through the shameless, devilish rule of the Romanists. The devil grows stronger[46] every day, if such a thing were possible, if such a hellish regime could grow any worse—a thing I can neither conceive nor believe.

1. It is horrible and shocking to see the head of Christendom, who boasts that he is the vicar of Christ and successor of St. Peter, going about in such a worldly and ostentatious style that neither king nor emperor can equal or approach him. He claims the title of "most holy" and "most spiritual," and yet he is more worldly than the world itself. He wears a triple crown,[47] whereas the highest monarchs wear but one. If that is like the poverty of Christ and of

[43] *Kunst*; literally, "skill."

[44] *Der hauff*; literally, rank and file Christians without office or authority in the church.

[45] The sense of this passage is that if the ecclesiastical hierarchy will not do its duty and convene a council, then the secular authorities and the rank and file Christians must take the matter in hand regardless of ecclesiastical sanctions. Furthermore, to come under one such sanction for the sake of this good cause is better than to receive ten absolutions.

[46] *Zunympt*; literally, "grows larger" or "increases."

[47] The papal crown dates from the eleventh century; the triple crown or tiara, from the fourteenth. It was intended to signify the superiority of the pope over the rulers of this world, of which Luther complains. Cf. *PE* 2, 80, n. 2.

St. Peter, then it is a new and strange kind of likeness! When anybody says anything against it, the Romanists bleat, "Heresy!" They refuse to hear how un-Christian and ungodly all this is. In my opinion, if the pope were to pray to God with tears, he would have to lay aside his triple crown, for the God we worship cannot put up with pride. In fact, the pope's office should be nothing else but to weep and pray for Christendom and to set an example of utter humility.

Be that as it may, this kind of splendor is offensive, and the pope is bound for the sake of his own salvation to set it aside. It was because of this kind of thing that St. Paul said, "Abstain from all practices which give offense" [I Thess. 5:22], and in Romans 12 [:17], "We should do good, not only in the sight of God, but also in the sight of all men." An ordinary bishop's mitre ought to be good enough for the pope. It is in wisdom and holiness that he should be above his fellows. He ought to leave the crown of pride to Antichrist, as his predecessors did centuries ago. The Romanists say he is a lord of the earth. That is a lie! For Christ, whose vicar and vicegerent he claims to be, said to Pilate, "My kingdom is not of this world" [John 18:36]. No vicar's rule can go beyond that of his lord. Moreover, he is not the vicar of Christ glorified but of Christ crucified. As Paul says, "I was determined to know nothing among you save Christ, and him only as the crucified" [I Cor. 2:2], and in Philippians 2 [:5-7], "This is how you should regard yourselves, as you see in Christ, who emptied himself and took upon himself the form of a servant." Or again in I Corinthians 1 [:23], "We preach Christ, the crucified." Now the Romanists make the pope a vicar of the glorified Christ in heaven, and some of them have allowed the devil to rule them so completely that they have maintained that the pope is above the angels in heaven and has them at his command.[48] These are certainly the proper works of the real Antichrist.

---

[48] A statement made by Augustinus Triumphus in his *Summa de potestate Papae.* Cf. B. Ministeri, *"De Augustini de Ancona vita et operibus," Analecta Augustiniana,* Rome, XXII (1952-1953), 7-56, 148-262. In the year 1500 thousands of pilgrims died of plague on the way to Rome. A rumor began to circulate that Pope Clement VI had once given orders that the angels should immediately carry to heaven the souls of those who die on a pilgrimage. This rumor was based on a papal bull, most likely spurious. Luther referred to it in his *Defense and Explanation of All the Articles* (1521). *LW* 32, 74-75; *WA* 7, 421. Cf. *LW* 32, 75, n. 89.

Of what use to Christendom are those people called cardinals? I shall tell you. Italy and Germany have many rich monasteries, foundations,[49] benefices, and livings. No better way has been discovered of bringing all these to Rome than by creating cardinals and giving them bishoprics, monasteries, and prelacies for their own use[50] and so overthrowing the worship of God. You can see that Italy is now almost a wilderness: monasteries in ruins, bishoprics despoiled, the prelacies and the revenues of all the churches drawn to Rome, cities decayed, land and people ruined because services are no longer held and the word of God is not preached. And why? Because the cardinals must have the income! No Turk could have devastated Italy and suppressed the worship of God so effectively!

Now that Italy is sucked dry, the Romanists are coming into Germany.[51] They have made a gentle beginning. But let us keep our eyes open! Germany shall soon be like Italy. We have a few cardinals already. The "drunken Germans" are not supposed to understand what the Romanists are up to until there is not a bishopric, a monastery, a living, a benefice, not a red cent left. Antichrist must seize the treasures of the earth, as it is prophesied [Dan. 11:39, 43]. It works like this: they skim the cream off the bishoprics, monasteries, and benefices, and because they do not yet venture to put them all to shameful use, as they have done in Italy, they in the meantime practice their holy cunning and couple together ten or twenty prelacies. They then tear off a little piece each year so as to make quite a tidy sum after all. The priory of Würzburg yields a thousand gulden;[52] the priory of Bamberg also yields a sum; Mainz, Trier, and others. In this way one thousand or ten thousand gulden may be collected, so that a cardinal could live like a wealthy monarch at Rome.

When we have got that, we shall appoint thirty or forty cardi-

---

[49] *Stifft*; i.e., endowed institutions.

[50] For example, Pope Julius II, when a cardinal, held the revenues of the archbishopric of Avignon, the bishoprics of Bologna, Lausanne, Coutances, Viviers, Mende, Ostia, and Velletri, and the abbacies of Nonantola and Grottaferrata. Cf. *PE* 2, 82, n. 1.

[51] The complaint that the cardinals were provided with incomes by appointment to German benefices goes back to the Council of Constance (1414-1418). Cf. Luther's complaint in the *Treatise on Good Works*, p. 89.

[52] Cf. p. 144, n. 58.

nals in one day.[53] We shall give to one of them Mount St. Michael near Bamberg,[54] along with the bishopric of Würzburg, attach a few rich benefices to them until churches and cities are destitute, and then we will say, "We are Christ's vicars, and shepherds of Christ's sheep. The foolish, drunken Germans will just have to put up with it."

My advice is to make fewer cardinals, or to let the pope support them at his own expense. Twelve of them would be enough, and each of them might have an income of a thousand gulden.[55] How is it that we Germans must put up with such robbery and extortion of our goods at the hands of the pope? If the kingdom of France has prevented it,[56] why do we Germans let them make such fools and apes of us? We could put up with all this if they stole only our property, but they lay waste to the churches in so doing, rob Christ's sheep of their true shepherds, and debase the worship and word of God. If there were not a single cardinal, the church would not perish. The cardinals do nothing to serve Christendom. They are only interested in the money side of bishoprics and prelacies, and they wrangle about them just as any thief might do.

3. If ninety-nine per cent of the papal court[57] were abolished

---

[53] Luther puts these words into the mouths of the Romanists, hence the change from "they" to "we." The creation of cardinals was a lucrative matter for the popes. On July 31, 1517, Pope Leo X created thirty-one cardinals. He is reported to have received 300,000 ducats from the appointees. *WA* 6, 417, n. 1; *PE* 2, 82, n. 3.

[54] A famous Benedictine monastery located outside of Bamberg on Mount St. Michael (*Mönchberg*).

[55] The Council of Constance had suggested a yearly salary of three to four thousand gulden for cardinals.

[56] In the fourteenth century England and France enacted laws protecting themselves against these practices. There was a strong anti-clerical and anti-papal movement in England at that time, and much legislation was enacted under Edward I to prevent endowments going to Rome as well as to prevent the appointment of Roman puppets to English benefices. In France these laws were embodied in the *Pragmatic Sanction of Bourges*, issued by King Charles VII and a council of French clergy on July 7, 1438. This edict breathed the spirit of conciliarism, and was responsible for greatly reducing the receipts of nonresident benefice holders. See *The Cambridge Modern History* (14 vols.; New York: The Macmillan Company, 1903-1912), I, 385-386.

[57] The papal court (curia) consisted of all the officials engaged in the transaction of papal business and those who were in immediate attendance upon the person of the pope, the so-called "papal household." Karl Benrath states that according to a document printed in Rome in 1545 and found among the belong-

and only one per cent kept, it would still be large enough to give answers in matters of faith. Today, however, there is such a swarm of parasites in that place called Rome, all of them boasting that they belong to the pope, that not even Babylon saw the likes of it. There are more than three thousand papal secretaries alone. Who could count the other officials? There are so many offices that one could scarcely count them. These are all the people lying in wait for the endowments and benefices of Germany as wolves lie in wait for the sheep. I believe that Germany now gives much more to the pope at Rome than it used to give to the emperors in ancient times. In fact, some have estimated that more than three hundred thousand gulden a year find their way from Germany to Rome. This money serves no use or purpose. We get nothing for it except scorn and contempt. And we still go on wondering why princes and nobles, cities and endowments, land and people, grow poor. We ought to marvel that we have anything left to eat!

Since we have now come to the heart of the matter, we will pause a little and let it be seen that the Germans are not quite such crass fools that they do not see or understand the sharp practices of the Romanists. I do not at the moment complain that God's command and Christian law are despised at Rome, for the state of Christendom is such—Rome in particular—that we may not complain of such exalted matters now. Nor am I complaining that natural law, or secular law, or even reason count for nothing. My complaint goes deeper than that. I complain that the Romanists do not keep their own self-devised canon law, though it is in fact just tyranny, avarice, and temporal splendor rather than law. That I shall now show you.

In former times German emperors and princes permitted the pope to receive annates from all the benefices of the German nation. This sum amounts to one half of the revenue of the first year from

ings of John Eck, there were 949 curial positions obtained by the payment of a fee. This figure does not include those officials who had to do with the administration of the city of Rome and the papal states, or the members of the "papal household." Cf. Benrath, *op. cit.*, p. 88, n. 18. The *Gravamina* of the German nation presented by the Diet of Worms in 1521 complain that the increase of these offices had added greatly to the financial burdens of the German church. Cf. *WA* 6, 417, n. 4; and *PE* 2, 83, n. 3.

every single benefice.[58] This permission was given, however, so that by means of these large sums of money the pope might raise funds to fight against the Turks and infidels in defense of Christendom, and, so that the burden of war might not rest too heavily upon the nobility, the clergy too should contribute something toward it. The popes have so far used the splendid and simple devotion of the German people—they have received this money for more than a hundred years and have now made it an obligatory tax and tribute, but they have not only accumulated no money, they have used it to endow many posts and positions at Rome and to provide salaries for these posts, as though the annates were a fixed rent.

When they pretend that they are about to fight the Turks, they send out emissaries to raise money. They often issue an indulgence[59] on the same pretext of fighting the Turks. They think that those half-witted Germans will always be gullible, stupid fools, and will just keep handing over money to them to satisfy their unspeakable greed. And they think this in spite of the fact that everybody knows that not a cent of the annates, or of the indulgence money, or of all the rest, is spent to fight the Turk. It all goes into their bottomless bag. They lie and deceive. They make laws and they make agreements with us, but they do not intend to keep a single letter of them. Yet all this is done in the holy names of Christ and St. Peter.

Now in this matter the German nation, bishops and princes, should consider that they, too, are Christians. They should rule the

[58] The annates (*annatae, annalia*) were originally the various incomes a bishop received from the vacant benefices in his diocese. In 1317 Pope John XXII fixed the annates at one half of one year's income from the benefice, payable upon the incumbent's accession. Two years later the same pope claimed for himself the annates from all benefices falling vacant during the next two years. These annates were claimed regularly by his successors. After 1418 the term was extended to include the so-called *servitia,* payments which were made to the curia by bishops and abbots at the time of their accession. These charges soon became a fixed tax on all church offices which became vacant, and claims against overassessment and extortion were frequent. The Council of Constance (1415) restricted the obligation of annates to bishoprics, abbacies, and benefices with a yearly income of more than twenty-four gulden. The Council of Basel resolved to abolish them (1439), but could not enforce its decision because the supporters of the council ultimately yielded to Pope Eugene IV. Luther's complaint here is that the annates are not applied to their ostensible purpose, the Crusades. The complaint came up again at the Diet of Worms in 1521, as well as at other diets. Cf. *PE* 1, 383, n. 1; 2, 84, n. 1; cf. also Benrath, *op. cit.*, p. 88, n. 19.

[59] The Crusades indulgence was established by Urban II (1088-1099) and granted to those who personally went to Palestine. In 1198 Innocent III extended it to include those who supported the Crusades in other than military ways.

people entrusted to them in temporal and spiritual matters and protect them from these rapacious wolves in sheep's clothing who pretend to be their shepherds and rulers. And since the annates have been so shockingly abused, and not even kept for their original agreed purpose, [the bishops and princes] should not allow their land and people to be so pitilessly robbed and ruined contrary to all law. By decree either of the emperor or of the whole nation the annates should either be kept here at home or else abolished again.[60] Since the Romanists do not keep to their agreement, they have no right to the annates. Therefore, the bishops and princes are responsible for punishing such thievery and robbery, or even preventing it, as the law requires.

In such a matter they ought to help the pope and strengthen his hand. Perhaps he is too weak to prevent such abuse singlehandedly. Or, in those cases where he wants to defend and maintain this state of affairs, they ought to resist him and protect themselves from him as they would from a wolf or a tyrant, for he has no authority to do evil or fight on its behalf. Even if it were ever desirable to raise such funds for fighting the Turk, we ought to have enough sense at least to see that the German nation could be a better custodian of these funds than the pope. The German nation itself has enough people to wage the war if the money is available. It is the same with the annates as it has been with many other Romanist pretenses.

Then, too, the year has been so divided between the pope and the ruling bishops and chapters that the pope has six months in the year (every other month) in which to bestow the benefices which become vacant in his months.[61] In this way almost all the best benefices have fallen into the hands of Rome, especially the

[60] Cf. p. 144, n. 58.

[61] This whole section deals with the "right of reservation," i.e., the alleged right of the pope to fill vacant church positions by appointment. The papal theory held that the right of appointment belonged to the pope, who in some cases graciously yielded the right to others while reserving it to himself in other cases. The rule of the "papal months" provided that livings (except those of the cathedrals and the chief posts in the monasteries) which became vacant in the months of February, April, June, August, October, and December should be filled by the ordinary methods—election, presentation, and appointment by the bishop, etc. But vacancies occurring in the other months were to be filled by appointment of the pope. Cf. *PE* 2, 86, n. 3.

very best livings and dignities.[62] And when they once fall into the hands of Rome, they never come out of them again, though a vacancy may never occur again in the pope's month. In this way the chapters are cheated. This is plain robbery, and the intention is to let nothing escape. Therefore, it is high time to abolish the "papal months" altogether. Everything that has been taken to Rome in this way must be restored. The princes and nobles ought to take steps for the restitution of the stolen property, punish the thieves, and deprive of privilege those who have abused that privilege. If it is binding and valid for the pope, on the day after his election, to make regulations and laws in his chancery[63] by which our endowed chapters and livings are stolen from us—a thing he has absolutely no right to do—then it should be still more valid for Emperor Charles, on the day after his coronation,[64] to make rules and laws that not another benefice or living in all Germany should be allowed to pass into the hands of Rome by means of the "papal months." The livings which have already fallen into the hands of Rome should be restored and redeemed from these Romanist robbers. Charles V has the right to do this by virtue of his authority as ruler.

But now this Romanist See of avarice and robbery has not had the patience to wait for the time when all the benefices would fall to it one by one through this device of the "papal months." Rather, urged on by its insatiable appetite to get them all in its hands as speedily as possible, the Romanist See has devised a scheme whereby, in addition to the "annates" and "papal months," the benefices and livings should fall to Rome in three ways.

First, if anyone who holds a "free" living[65] should die in Rome or on a journey to Rome, his living becomes the property in per-

---

[62] A dignity or prelacy was originally an ecclesiastical office in which jurisdiction was exercised in the name of the incumbent. Cf. Albert Hauck (ed.), *Realencyklopädie für protestantische Theologie und Kirche* (3rd ed., 24 vols.; Leipzig: Hinrichs, 1896-1913), IV, 658.

[63] Luther refers to the "chancery regulations," which were the policies governing the conferring of reserved benefices, the permissibility of renouncing an office, etc. The pope established these policies, usually just after his ascension to the papal throne. The Germans had protested at the councils of Constance and Basel against the arbitrariness of these regulations, and insisted that such policies be fixed by legislation. Cf. Benrath, *op. cit.*, p. 96, n. 40.

[64] Charles V had not yet been crowned emperor when this treatise was written. Cf. *PE* 2, 87, n. 2.

[65] A living not hitherto filled by papal appointment. Cf. *PE* 2, 88, n. 1.

petuity of the Romanist—I ought to say roguish—See.[66] But the Romanists do not want to be called robbers on this account, though they are guilty of robbery of a kind never heard of or read about before.

Second, if anyone belonging to the household of the pope or cardinals holds or takes over a benefice, or if anyone who had previously held a benefice subsequently enters the household of the pope or cardinals, [his living becomes the property in perpetuity of the Romanist See].[67] But who can count the household of the pope and cardinals? If he only goes on a pleasure ride, the pope takes with him three or four thousand on mules, all emperors and kings notwithstanding! Christ and St. Peter went on foot so that their successors might have all the more pomp and splendor. Now Avarice has cleverly thought out another scheme, and arranges it so that many even outside Rome have the name "member of the papal household" just as if they were in Rome. This is done for the sole purpose that, by the simple use of that pernicious phrase "member of the pope's household," all benefices may be brought to Rome and tied there for all time. Are not these vexatious and devilish little inventions? Let us beware! Soon Mainz, Magdeburg, and Halberstadt will quietly slip into the hands of Rome, and then the cardinalate will cost a pretty penny![68] After that they will make all the German bishops cardinals, and then there will be nothing left.

Third, when a dispute has started at Rome over a benefice.[69] In my opinion this is the commonest and widest road to bring livings into the hands of Rome. Even when there is no dispute here, countless knaves will be found at Rome who will unearth a dispute and snatch the benefices at will. Thus many a good priest must lose his living or pay a sum of money to avoid having his benefice disputed. Such a living, rightly or wrongly contested, becomes the

[66] A rule found in the Concordat of Vienna. Cf. *WA* 6, 420, n. 3.

[67] The "household of the pope" included all who were in immediate attendance on the pope or the cardinals, and all to whom, by virtue of any special connection with the curia, the name "papal servant" could be made to apply. These are the "courtesans" to whom Luther later refers. Cf. *PE* 2, 88, n. 3.

[68] In 1513 Prince Albert of Brandenburg was made archbishop of Magdeburg. Later that same year he became administrator of Halberstadt. The following year he became archbishop of Mainz as well, and in 1518 was made a cardinal. The expenses attending this pluralism were defrayed by the sale of papal indulgences. Cf. *PE* 2, 88, n. 4.

[69] This rule is also mentioned in the Concordat of Vienna.

property of the Roman See forever. It would be no wonder if God would rain fire and brimstone from heaven and sink Rome in the abyss, as he did Sodom and Gomorrah of old [Gen. 19:24]. Why should there be a pope in Christendom if his power is used for nothing else than for such gross wickedness and to protect and practice it? O noble princes and lords, how long will you leave your lands and your people naked and exposed to such ravening wolves?

Since even these practices were not enough, and Avarice grew impatient at the long time it took to get hold of all the bishoprics, my Lord Avarice devised the fiction that the bishoprics should be nominally abroad but that their origin and foundation is at Rome.[70] Furthermore, no bishop can be confirmed unless he pays a huge sum for his pallium[71] and binds himself with solemn oaths to the personal service of the pope.[72] That explains why no bishop dares to act against the pope. That is what the Romanists were seeking when they imposed the oath. It also explains why all the richest bishoprics have fallen into debt and ruin. I am told that Mainz pays twenty thousand gulden.[73] That is the Romanists all over! To be sure, they decreed a long time ago in canon law that the pallium should be given without cost, that the number in the pope's household be reduced, disputes[74] lessened, and the chapters and bishops allowed their liberty. But this did not bring in money. So they turned over a new leaf and have taken all authority away from the bishops and chapters. These sit there like ciphers, and have neither office nor authority nor work. Everything is controlled by those arch-villains at Rome, almost right down to the office of sexton and

---

70 I.e., although the dioceses bear foreign names, they are constituted by and originate in Rome.

71 The pallium is a woolen shoulder cape. It is the emblem of the archbishop's office and must be secured from Rome. The bestowal of the pallium is a very ancient custom and was so referred to by Gregory I (590-604). Canon law prescribes that the archbishop-elect must secure the pallium from Rome within three months of his election; otherwise he is forbidden to discharge the duties of his office. Luther's contention that it was originally a free gift of good will is correct, as is his contention that the pallium (i.e., an archbishopric) was bought in his day at a fantastic price. Cf. *PE* 2, 89, n. 3; Benrath, *op. cit.*, p. 91, n. 22.

72 An oath of allegiance to the pope was required before the pallium was conferred.

73 Cf. p. 147, n. 68.

74 I.e., the contesting of benefices.

bell-ringer. Every dispute is called to Rome,[75] and everyone does just as he pleases, under cover of the pope's authority.

What has happened in this very year? The bishop of Strassburg[76] wanted to govern his chapter properly and reform it in matters of worship. With this end in view he established certain godly and Christian regulations. But our dear friend the pope and the Holy Roman See wrecked and damned this holy and spiritual ordinance, all at the instigation of the priests. This is called feeding the sheep of Christ![77] That is how priests are strengthened against their own bishop, and how their disobedience to divine law is protected! Antichrist himself, I hope, will not dare to shame God so openly. There is your pope for you! Just as you have always wanted! Why did the pope do this? Ah! If one church were reformed that would be a dangerous breakthrough. Rome might have to follow suit. Therefore, it is better that no priest be allowed to get along with another and, as we have grown accustomed to seeing right up to the present day, that kings and princes should be set at odds. It is better to flood the world with Christian blood, lest the unity of Christians compel the Holy Roman See to reform itself!

So far we have been getting an idea of how they deal with benefices which become vacant and free. But for tenderhearted Avarice the free vacancies are too few. Therefore, he has kept a very close watch even on those benefices still occupied by their incumbents, so that these too can be made free, even though they are not now free. He does this in several ways.

First, Avarice lies in wait where fat prebends or bishoprics are held by an old or sick man, or even by one with an alleged disability. The Holy See gives a coadjutor, that is, an assistant, to an incumbent of this kind. This is done without the holder's consent or gratitude, and for the benefit of the coadjutor, because he is a member of the pope's "household," or because he has paid for it or has otherwise earned it by some sort of service to Rome. In this case the free rights of the chapter or the rights of the incumbent are disregarded, and the whole thing falls into the hands of Rome.

[75] For adjudication.
[76] Wilhelm III, count of Honstein, was bishop from 1506 to 1541.
[77] Cf. John 21:15-17.

Second, there is the little word "commend." This means the pope puts a cardinal, or another of his underlings, in charge of a rich, prosperous monastery,[78] just as if I were to give you a hundred gulden to keep. This does not mean to give the monastery or bestow it. Nor does it mean abolishing it or the divine service. It means quite simply to give it into his keeping. Not that he to whom it is entrusted is to care for it or build it up, but he is to drive out the incumbent, receive the goods and revenues, and install some apostate, renegade monk[79] or another, who accepts five or six gulden a year and sits all day long in the church selling pictures and images to the pilgrims, so that neither prayers nor masses are said in that place any more. If this were to be called destroying monasteries and abolishing the worship of God, then the pope would have to be called a destroyer of Christendom and an abolisher of divine worship. He certainly does well at it! But this would be harsh language for Rome, so they have to call it a "commend," or a command to take over the charge of the monastery. The pope can make "commends" of four or more of these monasteries in one year, any single one of which may have an income of more than six thousand gulden.[80] This is how the Romanists increase the worship of God and maintain the monasteries! Even the Germans are beginning to find that out!

Third, there are some benefices they call *incompatabilia*,[81] which, according to the ordinances of canon law, cannot be held at the same time, such as two parishes, two bishoprics, and the like. In

[78] The commendation of these benefices did not obligate the recipient to exercise the duties attached to the benefice. The result was that these benefices suffered from the absenteeism of those into whose charge they were commended. Even Duke George of Saxony, an opponent of the Reformation, complained before the Diet of Worms in 1521 that such commendations greatly depleted the resources of the benefices. Cf. *PE* 2, 91, n. 2; Benrath, *op. cit.*, p. 92, n. 24.

[79] An apostate monk was one who left his monastery without permission and functioned as a secular priest (*MA*[3] 2, 395). There were quite a few such monks in Luther's day. They wandered about from place to place, often wearing garb and exercising the rights and privileges reserved to their order. They were a nuisance to the resident clergy because they often disrupted parish life. Carafa, who later became Pope Paul IV (1555-1559), regarded them as a great menace. Benrath, *op. cit.*, p. 92, n. 25.

[80] Cf. p. 45, n. 18.

[81] Offices which cannot be united in the hands of one man.

these cases the Holy Roman See of Avarice evades canon law by making glosses[82] to its own advantage, called *unio* and *incorporatio.* This means that the pope incorporates many *incompatabilia* into one single unity, so that each is a part of every other and all of them together are looked upon as one benefice. They are then no longer *incompatabilia,* and the holy canon law is satisfied because it is no longer binding, except upon those who do not buy these glosses from the pope or his *datarius.*[83] The *unio,* that is, the uniting, is very similar. The pope combines many such benefices like a bundle of sticks, and they are all regarded as one benefice. There is at present a certain court follower in Rome who alone holds twenty-two parishes, seven priories, as well as forty-four benefices.[84] All these are held by the help of that masterly gloss, which declares that this is not against canon law. What the cardinals and other prelates get out of it is anybody's guess. And this is the way the Germans are to have their purses emptied and their itch scratched.[85]

Another of these glosses is the *administratio.* This means a man may hold, in addition to his bishopric, some abbacy or dignity[86] and all its emoluments, without having the title attached to it. He is simply called the "administrator."[87] At Rome it is sufficient to change a word or two but leave the actuality what it was before. It is as if I were to teach that we were now to call the brothel-keeper the mayor's wife. She still remains what she was before. This kind of Romish regime Peter foretold in II Peter 2 [:1, 3],

[82] Glosses are more or less authoritative comments on canon law, which date from the time when the study of canon law became a part of the theological curriculum. Their chief aim is to show how the law applies to practical cases that may arise. The so-called *glossa ordinaria* in Luther's time had an authority almost equal to that of the *corpus iuris* itself. Cf. *PE* 2, 92, n. 3.

[83] The papal bureau that granted dispensations and was responsible for the issuing, registration, and dating (hence the name) of papal appointments. A fee had to be paid for the services of this bureau. Its headquarters were in a splendid building near St. Peter's.

[84] Jacobs cites the example of two such court followers, Johannes Zink and Johannes Ingenwinkel. Between 1513 and 1521 Zink received fifty-six appointments. Ingenwinkel received one hundred six appointments between 1496 and 1521. Cf. *PE* 2, 93, n. 3.

[85] I.e., have their pride deflated.

[86] Cf. p. 147, n. 68.

[87] Cardinal Albrecht of Mainz also had the title of "administrator" of Halberstadt. Cf. *PE* 2, 93, n. 5.

"False teachers will come who will deal with you in greed and lying words for their gain."

Our worthy Roman Avarice has devised another technique. He sells or disposes of livings on the condition that the vendor or disposer retains reversionary rights to them.[88] In that event, when the incumbent dies the benefices automatically revert to him who had sold, disposed, or surrendered them in the first instance. In this way they have made hereditary property out of the benefices. Nobody else can come into possession of them except the man to whom the seller is willing to dispose of them, or to whom he bequeaths his rights at death. Besides, there are many who transfer to another the mere title to a benefice, but from which the titleholder does not draw a cent. Today, too, it has become an established custom to confer a benefice on a man while reserving a portion of the annual income for oneself.[89] This used to be called simony.[90] There are many more things of this sort than can be counted. They treat benefices more shamefully than the heathen soldiers treated Christ's clothes at the foot of the cross.[91]

But all that has been said up till now has been going on for so long that it has become established custom. Yet Avarice has devised one more thing, which I hope may be his last and choke him. The pope has a noble little device called *pectoralis reservatio,* meaning mental reservation, and *proprius motus,* meaning the arbitrary will of his authority.[92] It goes like this. A certain man goes to Rome

[88] The name of the practice was "regression" (*regressus*). Cf. *PE* 2, 94, n. 1.

[89] The complaint was made at Worms in 1521 that it was impossible for a German to secure a clear title to a benefice from Rome unless he applied for it in the name of an Italian who demanded a lump sum, a yearly pension, or a percentage of the income in return for the use of his name.

[90] Simony (Acts 8:18-20) is the ecclesiastical name for the buying or procuring of an office in the church for money, favor, or any consideration or reward. In the primitive and earlier medieval church such activity invalidated the appointment and brought shame and punishment upon the perpetrator (*PE* 2, 94, n. 3). Aeneas Sylvius, who became Pope Pius II in 1458, complained that there was nothing which could not be had at Rome for money (Benrath, *op. cit.*, p. 94, n. 30).

[91] Cf. Matt. 27:35.

[92] The canonists taught that in theory the pope ultimately held all rights of appointment. This right could be exercised *per petitionem alterius,* i.e., by confirming the election or appointment by others, or by the pope's own right, *proprio motu.* Countless disputes arose and all sorts of agreements were arrived at, e.g., the "papal months," in which the pope invariably had the right of appointment (see p. 145, n. 61). Any given case could, of course, be made an exception, if the canonists' theory is supported, and in these cases the matter was "reserved in the heart of the pope," and the appointment then made "on his own motion." Cf. *PE* 2, 94, n. 4.

and succeeds in procuring a benefice. It is duly signed and sealed in the customary manner. Then another candidate comes along, who brings money or else has rendered services to the pope, which we shall not mention here, and desires the same benefice of the pope. The pope then gives it to him and takes it away from the other.[93] If anybody complains that this is not right, then the Most Holy Father has to find some excuse lest he be accused of a flagrant violation of the [canon] law. He then says that he had mentally reserved that particular benefice to himself and had retained full rights of disposal over it, although he had neither given it a thought in his life nor even heard of it. In this way he has now found his usual little gloss. As pope he can tell lies, deceive, and make everybody look like a fool. And all this he does openly and unashamedly. And yet he still wants to be the head of Christendom, but lets himself be ruled by the evil spirit in obvious lies.

The arbitrary and deceptive reservation of the pope only creates a state of affairs in Rome that defies description. There is buying, selling, bartering, changing, trading, drunkenness, lying, deceiving, robbing, stealing, luxury, harlotry, knavery, and every sort of contempt of God. Even the rule of the Antichrist could not be more scandalous. Venice, Antwerp, and Cairo have nothing on this fair at Rome and all that goes on there.[94] In these places there is still some regard for right and reason, but in Rome the devil himself is in charge. And out of this sea the same kind of morality flows into all the world. Is it any wonder that people like this are terrified of reformation and of a free council, and prefer rather to set all the kings and princes at enmity lest in their unity they should call a council? Who could bear to have such villainy brought to light?

Finally, the pope has built his own store for all this noble commerce, that is, the house of the *datarius* in Rome.[95] All who deal in benefices and livings must go there. Here they have to buy their glosses, and transact their business, and get authority to practice

[93] An instance of this giving and taking back was cited at Worms in 1521.

[94] These ports were the three great commercial centers of foreign trade in the fifteenth and sixteenth centuries. Their annual fairs brought the merchants together to transact their wholesale trade. The three cities were notorious. Cf. *PE* 2, 95, n. 2.

[95] See p. 151, n. 83.

such arch-knavery. There was a time when Rome was still gracious. In those days people had to buy justice or suppress it with money. But Rome has become so expensive today that it allows no one to practice knavery unless he has first bought the right to do so. If that is not a brothel above all imaginable brothels, then I do not know what brothels are.

If you have money in this establishment you can obtain all these things we have just discussed. Indeed, not just these! Here usury becomes honest money, the possession of property acquired by theft or robbery is legalized. Here vows are dissolved; monks are granted liberty to leave their orders. Here marriage is on sale to the clergy. Here bastards can be legitimized. Here all dishonor and shame can be made to look like honor and glory. Here every kind of iniquity and evil is knighted or raised to nobility. Here marriage is permitted which is within the prohibited relationships or otherwise forbidden. O what assessing and fleecing goes on there! It seems as though canon law were instituted solely for the purpose of making a great deal of money. Whoever would be a Christian has to buy his way out of its provisions.[96] In fact, here the devil becomes a saint, and a god as well. What cannot be done anywhere else in heaven or on earth, can be done in this place. They call these things *compositiones*! Compositions indeed! Better named confusions.[97] They put nothing together, but break everything all up! Compared with the exactions of this bureau, the Rhine toll[98] is but a drop in the bucket.

Let no one accuse me of exaggeration. It is all so open that even in Rome they have to admit that the state of affairs is more revolting and worse than anyone can say. I have not yet stirred the real hellish broth of their personal vices—nor do I want to. I speak only of general, current matters, and still words fail me. The bishops, priests, and above all the doctors in the universities ought

[96] I.e., has to buy exemptions from the provisions of canon law in the form of dispensations.

[97] The fees paid for the procurement of dispensations were called *compositiones*. Luther makes a play on the Latin words *compositiones* and *confusiones* (confusions). Cf. *WA* 6, 426, n. 1.

[98] The Rhine toll was a toll levied by the "robber barons" on the Rhine castles on all merchants who passed through their domains.

to have done their duty and with common accord written against such goings-on and cried out against them. This is what they are paid to do! Just turn the page over, and then you'll find out.[99]

One final word remains, and I am bound to say it. Since this boundless Avarice is not satisfied with all this wealth, wealth with which three great kings would be content, he now begins to transfer this trade and sell it to the Fuggers of Augsburg.[100] The lending, trading, and buying of bishoprics and benefices, and the commerce in ecclesiastical holdings, have now come to the right place. Now spiritual and secular goods have become one. I would now like to hear of somebody clever enough to imagine what Roman Avarice could do more than what it has already done, unless perhaps Fugger were to transfer or sell this present combination of two lines of business to somebody else. I really think it has just reached the limit.

As for what they have stolen in all lands, and still steal and extort, through indulgences, bulls, letters of confession,[101] butter letters,[102] and other *confessionalia*[103]—all this is just patchwork. It is like casting one devil into hell. Not that these bring in little money, for a powerful king could well support himself on such proceeds, but it is not to be compared with the streams of treasure referred to above. I shall say nothing at present about where this indulgence money has gone. I shall have more to say about that later. The

---

[99] *Ja, wend das blat umb, so findistu es.* Cf. *CL* 1, 383, which interprets this obscure expression to mean that the opposite is the case. Jacobs translates it, "but they have done the very opposite." *PE* 2, 97.

[100] The Fuggers were the greatest international bankers of the sixteenth century and bankers to the curia. They were zealous Romanists and supported Eck against Luther. Their control of large amounts of capital enabled them to advance large sums of money to the territorial rulers. In return they received monopolistic concessions. The spiritual lords as well as the secular lords availed themselves of the services of this accommodating firm. They were the pope's financial representative in Germany, and made the financial arrangements between the pope and Albrecht of Mainz which occasioned the indulgence controversy of 1517. Cf. *PE* 2, 97, n. 5.

[101] Certificates which entitled the holder to choose his own confessor and authorized the confessor to absolve him from certain classes of "reserved" sins.

[102] The *Butterbriefe* were dispensations alleviating the severity of fasts by permitting the eating of eggs and milk products. Such dispensations date back to 1338. Cf. Henry Charles Lea, *A History of Auricular Confession and Indulgences in the Latin Church* (Philadelphia, Lea Brothers & Co., 1896), III, 192 ff.

[103] *Confessionalia* is used here in the broad sense, and means dispensations of all sorts, including those relating to penance. Cf. *PE* 2, 98, n. 3.

Campoflore[104] and the Belvindere[105] and certain other places probably know something about that.

Since, then, such devilish rule is not only barefaced robbery, deceit, and the tyranny of hell's portals, but ruinous to the body and soul of Christendom, it is our duty to exercise all diligence to protect Christendom from such misery and destruction. If we want to fight against the Turks, let us begin here where they are worst of all. If we are right in hanging thieves and beheading robbers, why should we let Roman Avarice go free? He is the worst thief and robber that has ever been or could ever come into the world, and all in the holy name of Christ and St. Peter! Who can put up with it a moment longer and say nothing? Almost everything Avarice possesses has been gotten by theft and robbery. It has never been otherwise, as all the history books prove. The pope never purchased such extensive holdings that the income from his *officia*[106] should amount to one million ducats, over and above the gold mines we have just been discussing and the income from his lands. Nor did Christ and St. Peter bequeath it to him. Neither has anyone given or lent it to him. Neither is it his by virtue of ancient rights or usage. Tell me, then, from what source he could have got it? Learn a lesson from this, and watch carefully what they are after and what they say when they send out their legates to collect money to fight the Turks.

Now, although I am too insignificant a man to make propositions for the improvement of this dreadful state of affairs, nevertheless I shall sing my fool's song through to the end and say, so far as I am able, what could and should be done, either by the temporal authority or by a general council.

1. Every prince, every noble, every city should henceforth for-

---

[104] The Campo di Fiore, a Roman marketplace, was restored and adorned at great expense by Eugene IV (1431-1447) and his successors. It was here that Pope Alexander VI accidentally took the poisoned drink intended for a cardinal. See Benrath, *op. cit.*, p. 95, n. 35.

[105] A part of the Vatican palace notorious as the banquet hall of Alexander VI (1492-1503). Julius II (1503-1513) turned it into a museum to house his collection of ancient works of art. Luther is hinting that the indulgence money is spent on these and similar objects and not for the church. Cf. *PE* 2, 98, n. 6; cf. also *CL* 1, 384, n. 15.

[106] *Officia* were the host of positions which could be bought for fixed prices and which had substantial incomes. Cf. Benrath, *op. cit.*, p. 95, n. 36.

bid their subjects to pay annates to Rome and should abolish them entirely. The pope has broken the agreement and made the annates a robbery to the injury and shame of the whole German nation. He gives them to his friends, sells them for huge sums of money, and uses them to endow offices. In so doing he has lost his right to them and deserves punishment. Consequently the temporal authority is under obligation to protect the innocent and prevent injustice, as Paul teaches in Romans 13, and St. Peter in I Peter 2 [:14], and even the canon law in Case 16, Question 7, in the *de filiis* clause.[107] Thus it has come about that they say to the pope and his crowd, "*Tu ora,* thou shalt pray"; to the emperor and his servants, "*Tu protege,* thou shalt protect"; to the common man, "*Tu labora,* thou shalt work," not however as though everyone were not to pray, protect, and work. For the man who is diligent in his work prays, protects, and works in all that he does. But everyone should have his own special work assigned him.

2. Since the pope with his Romanist practices—his commends, coadjutors, reservations, *gratiae expectativae,*[108] papal months, incorporations, unions, pensions, pallia, chancery rules, and such knavery[109]—usurps for himself all the German foundations without authority and right, and gives and sells them to foreigners at Rome who do nothing for Germany in return, and since he robs the local bishops of their rights and makes mere ciphers and dummies of them, and thereby acts contrary to his own canon law, common sense, and reason, it has finally reached the point where the livings and benefices are sold to coarse, unlettered asses and ignorant knaves at Rome out of sheer greed. Pious and learned people do not benefit from the service or skill of these fellows. Consequently the poor German people must go without competent and learned prelates and go from bad to worse.

---

[107] Luther errs here. The clause is not *de filiis,* but *Filiis vel nepotibus.* The clause provides that in case the income from endowments bequeathed to the church is misused, and appeals to the bishop and archbishop fail to correct the misuse, the heirs of the testator may appeal to the royal courts. Luther wants to apply this same principle to the annates. Cf. *PE* 2, 99, n. 3.

[108] Promises to bestow livings not yet vacant. Complaints of the evils arising out of the practice were heard continually after 1416, and were made at Worms in 1521. Cf. *PE* 2, 100, n. 4.

[109] These items are discussed in the preceding paragraphs, beginning on p. 141.

For this reason the Christian nobility should set itself against the pope as against a common enemy and destroyer of Christendom for the salvation of the poor souls who perish because of this tyranny. The Christian nobility should ordain, order, and decree that henceforth no further benefice shall be drawn into the hands of Rome, and that hereafter no appointment shall be obtained there in any manner whatsoever, but that the benefices should be dragged from this tyrannical authority and kept out of his reach. The nobility should restore to the local bishops their right and responsibility to administer the benefices in the German nation to the best of their ability. And when a lackey comes along from Rome he should be given a strict order to keep out, to jump into the Rhine or the nearest river, and give the Romish ban with all its seals and letters a nice, cool dip. If this happened they would sit up and take notice in Rome. They would not think that the Germans are always dull and drunk, but have really become Christian again. They would realize that the Germans do not intend to permit the holy name of Christ, in whose name all this knavery and destruction of souls goes on, to be scoffed and scorned any longer, and that they have more regard for God's honor than for the authority of men.

3. An imperial law should be issued that no bishop's cloak[110] and no confirmation of any dignity whatsoever shall henceforth be secured from Rome, but that the ordinance of the most holy and famous Council of Nicaea[111] be restored. This ordinance decreed that a bishop shall be confirmed by the two nearest bishops or by the archbishop. If the pope breaks the statutes of this and of all other councils, what is the use of holding councils? Who has given him the authority to despise the decisions of councils and tear them to shreds like this?

This is all the more reason for us to depose all bishops, archbishops, and primates and make ordinary parsons of them, with only the pope as their superior, as he now is. The pope allows no proper authority or responsibility to the bishops, archbishops, and

110 The pallium.

111 Luther refers to canon 4 of this council. Cf. *PE* 2, 101, n. 3.

primates. He usurps everything for himself and lets them keep only the name and the empty title. It has even gone so far that by papal exemption[112] the monasteries, abbots, and prelates as well are excepted from the regular authority of the bishops. Consequently there is no longer any order in Christendom. The inevitable result of all this is what has happened already: relaxation of punishment, and license to do evil all over the world. I certainly fear that the pope may properly be called "the man of sin" [II Thess. 2:3]. Who but the pope can be blamed for there being no discipline, no punishment, no rule, no order in Christendom? By his usurpation of power he ties the prelates' hands and takes away their rod of discipline. He opens his hands to all those set under him, and gives away or sells their release.[113]

Lest the pope complain that he is being robbed of his authority, it should be decreed that in those cases where the primates or the archbishops are unable to settle a case, or when a dispute arises between them, then the matter should be laid before the pope, but not every little thing. It was done this way in former times, and this was the way the famous Council of Nicaea[114] decreed. Whatever can be settled without the pope, then, should be so settled so that his holiness is not burdened with such minor matters, but gives himself to prayer, study, and the care of all Christendom. This is what he claims to do. This is what the apostles did. They said in Acts 6 [:2-4], "It is not right that we should leave the Word of God and serve tables, but we will hold to preaching and prayer, and set others over that work." But now Rome stands for nothing else than the despising of the gospel and prayer, and for the serving of tables, that is, temporal things. The rule of the apostles and of

[112] "Exemption" was the practice by which monastic houses were withdrawn from the jurisdiction of the bishops and made directly subject to the pope. Apparently the practice originated in the tenth century with the famous monastery of Cluny, but it was almost universal in the case of the houses of the mendicant orders. It was a constant subject of complaint by the bishops, and the Fifth Lateran Council passed a decree (1516) abolishing all monastic exemptions. This decree seems not to have been effective. Cf. *PE* 2, 102, n. 1. Cf. also the fuller explanation in Benrath, *op. cit.*, p. 97, n. 42.

[113] I.e., release from their lawful superiors.

[114] A reference to canon 5 of the Council of Sardica (343), which was later incorporated in canon law as a canon of Nicaea. Cf. *PE* 2, 102, n. 4.

the pope have as much in common as Christ has with Lucifer, heaven with hell, night with day. Yet the pope is called "Vicar of Christ" and "Successor to the Apostles."

4. It should be decreed that no temporal matter is to be referred to Rome, but that all such cases shall be left to the temporal authority, as the Romanists themselves prescribe in that canon law of theirs, which they do not observe. It should be the pope's duty to be the most learned in the Scriptures and the holiest (not in the name only but in fact) and to regulate matters which concern the faith and holy life of Christians. He should hold the primates and archbishops to this task, and help them in dealing with these matters and taking care of these responsibilities. This is what St. Paul teaches in I Corinthians 6 [:7], and he takes the Corinthians severely to task for their concern with worldly things. That such matters are dealt with in Rome causes unbearable grief in every land. It increases the costs, and, moreover, these judges do not know the usage, laws, and customs of these lands, so that they often do violence to the facts and base their decisions on their own laws and precedents. As a result the contesting parties often suffer injustice.

In addition, the horrible extortion practiced by the judges in the bishops' courts[115] must be forbidden in every diocese so that they no longer judge anything except matters of faith and morals, and leave matters of money and property, life and honor, to the temporal judges. The temporal authorities, therefore, should not permit sentences of excommunication and exile to be passed where faith and morality are not involved. Spiritual authorities should rule over matters which are spiritual; this is just a matter of common sense. But spiritual matters are not money or material things; they are faith and good works.

Nevertheless, it might be granted that cases concerning benefices or livings be tried before bishops, archbishops, and primates. Therefore, to settle disputes and disagreements, it might be possible for the primate of Germany to hold a general consistory court with

---

[115] The complaint against these judges was that they assumed jurisdiction over cases which belonged in the secular courts and enforced their decision through ecclesiastical censure. The *Gravamina* of 1521 specify the charges against these episcopal courts. Cf. *PE* 2, 103, n. 2.

its auditors and chancellors.[116] This court should have control of the *signaturae gratiae* and *signaturae justitiae*,[117] which are now controlled at Rome, and to this court of appeal the cases in Germany would normally be brought and tried. These courts ought not to be paid for by chance presents and gifts, as is the practice at Rome, by which they have grown accustomed to selling justice and injustice. They are forced to do this at Rome because the pope does not pay them a salary, but lets them grow fat from gifts. The fact is that at Rome no one bothers now about what is right or wrong, only about what is money and what is not. This court, however, might be paid from the annates, or in some other way devised by those who are more clever and more experienced in these things than I. All I seek to do is to arouse and set to thinking those who have the ability and inclination to help the German nation to be free and Christian again after the wretched, heathenish, and un-Christian rule of the pope.

5. Reservations should no longer be valid, and no more benefices should be seized by Rome, even if the incumbent dies, or there is a dispute, or even if the incumbent is a member of the pope's household or on the staff of a cardinal. And it must be strictly forbidden and prevented for any member of the papal court to contest any benefice whatsoever, to summon pious priests to court, harass them, or force them into lawsuits. If, in consequence of this prohibition, any ban or ecclesiastical pressure should come from Rome, it should be disregarded, just as though a thief were to put a man under the ban because he would not let him steal. Indeed, they should be severely punished for blasphemous misuse of the ban and the divine name to strengthen their hand at robbery. They want to drive us with their threats, which are only lies and fabrications, to the point where we put up with, yes, even praise, such blasphemy of God's name and such abuse of spiritual authority. They want to force us to be partakers in their rascality in the sight of God. We

[116] This idea is not original with Luther. Jakob Wimpheling, the Alsatian-born humanist and German patriot, had made just such a suggestion to the emperor in 1510. Its effect would have been substantial independence of the German church from Roman control. Cf. Benrath, *op. cit.*, p. 98, n. 45.

[117] The *signaturae gratiae* and the *signaturae justitiae* were the bureaus through which the pope regulated those matters of administration which belonged to his own special prerogative. Cf. *PE* 2, 104, n. 1.

are responsible before God to oppose them, as St. Paul in Romans 1 [:32] reproves as worthy of death not only those who do such things, but also those who approve and permit them to be done. Most unbearable of all is the lying *reservatio pectoralis,*[118] whereby Christendom is so scandalously and openly put to shame and scorn because its head deals with open lies and for filthy lucre unashamedly deceives and fools everybody.

6. The *casus reservati,*[119] reserved cases, should also be abolished. They are not only the means of extorting much money from the people, but by means of them the ruthless tyrants ensnare and confuse many tender consciences, intolerably injuring their faith in God. This is especially true of the ridiculous, childish cases they make such a fuss about in the bull *Coena Domini,*[120] sins which should not even be called everyday sins, much less so great that the pope cannot remit them by indulgence. Examples of these sins are hindering a pilgrim on his way to Rome, supplying weapons to the Turk, or counterfeiting papal letters.[121] They make fools of us with such crude, silly, clumsy goings-on! Sodom and Gomorrah, and all those sins which are or may be committed against the commandments of God, are not reserved cases. But what God has never commanded, what they themselves have imagined—these must be reserved cases. The only reason for all this is to make sure that no one will be prevented from bringing money to Rome, so that the Romanists may live in the lap of luxury, safe from the Turks, and by their wanton, worthless bulls and letters keep the world subjected to their tyranny.

Every priest simply ought to know, and a decree publicly made, that no secret, undenounced sin constitutes a reserved case;

---

[118] Cf. p. 152, n. 92.

[119] Those cases in which a priest was forbidden to give absolution. Luther means specifically those cases in which only the pope could absolve.

[120] This papal bull was published annually on Maundy Thursday until the middle of the eighteenth century. It was directed against heretics, but to the condemnation of the heretics and their heresies was added a list of offenses for which absolution could be gotten only from the pope or by his authorization. Luther's name was added to the list of heretics after his excommunication. Cf. *PE* 2, 105, n. 4.

[121] The brief or letter is a papal decree of equal authority with the bull, but differing from it in form and usually dealing with matters of lesser importance. Cf. *PE* 2, 106, n. 1.

and that every priest has the power to remit every sin no matter what it is. Where sins are secret, neither abbot, bishop, nor pope has the power to reserve one to himself. If they did that, their action would be null and void. They ought even to be punished as men who without any right at all presume to make judgments in God's stead, and thereby ensnare and burden poor and ignorant consciences. In those cases, however, where open and notorious sins are committed, especially sins against God's commandment, then there are indeed grounds for reserved cases. But even then there should not be too many of them, and they should not be reserved arbitrarily and without cause. For Christ did not set tyrants in his church, but shepherds, as Peter said in the last chapter of his first epistle [I Pet. 5:2-3].

7. The Roman See should do away with the *officia*,[122] and cut down the creeping, crawling swarm of vermin at Rome, so that the pope's household can be supported out of the pope's own pocket. The pope should not allow his court to surpass the courts of all kings in pomp and extravagance, because this kind of thing not only has never been of any use to the cause of the Christian faith, but has kept the courtesans from study and prayer until they are hardly able to speak about the faith at all. This they proved quite flagrantly at this last Roman council,[123] in which, among many other childish and frivolous things, they decreed that the soul of man is immortal and that every priest must say his prayers once a month unless he wants to lose his benefice. How can the affairs of Christendom and matters of faith be settled by men who are hardened and blinded by gross avarice, wealth, and worldly splendor, and who now for the first time decree that the soul is immortal? It is no small shame to the whole of Christendom that they deal so disgracefully with the faith at Rome. If they had less wealth and pomp, they could pray and study more diligently to be worthy and diligent in dealing with matters of faith, as was the case in ancient times when bishops did not presume to be the kings of kings.

[122] See p. 156, n. 106.

[123] The Fifth Lateran Council (1512-1517). Convened by Pope Julius II, the main item on the agenda was the reformation of the church. Among the subjects under discussion were the authority of the council in relation to that of the pope; the reformation of religious orders; the decadence and reform of the church itself; reformation of the state; and heresy.

8. The harsh and terrible oaths which the bishops are wrongfully compelled to swear to the pope should be abolished. These oaths bind the bishops like servants, and are decreed in that arbitrary, stupid, worthless, and unlearned chapter, *Significasti.*[124] Is it not enough that they burden us in body, soul, and property with their countless foolish laws by which they weaken faith and waste Christendom, without also making a prisoner of the bishop both as a person as well as in his office and function? In addition, they have also assumed the investiture,[125] which in ancient times was the right of the German emperor, and in France and other countries investiture still belongs to the king. They had great wars and disputes with the emperors about this matter until finally they had the brazen effrontery to take it over, and have held it until now; just as though the Germans more than all other Christians on earth had to be the country bumpkins of the pope and the Romanist See and do and put up with what no one else will either put up with or do. Since this is sheer robbery and violence, hinders the regular authority of the bishop, and injures poor souls, the emperor and his nobles are duty-bound to prevent and punish such tyranny.

9. The pope should have no authority over the emperor, except the right to anoint and crown him at the altar just as a bishop crowns a king.[126] We should never again yield to that devilish pride which requires the emperor to kiss the pope's feet, or sit at his feet, or, as they say, hold his stirrup or the bridle of his mule when he mounts to go riding. Still less should he do homage and

---

[124] *Decretalium D. Gregorii Papae IX*, lib. i, tit. VI, C. IV (*CIC* 2, cols. 49-50). This chapter forbids the bestowing of the pallium on an archbishop-elect until he first shall have sworn allegiance to the Holy See.

[125] Investiture was the ceremony of inducting church officials into offices to which revenues and the exercise of certain temporal powers were attached. The right to appoint and invest these officials afforded frequent occasion for controversy between pope and emperor in the Middle Ages. The outstanding controversy was that between Pope Gregory VII and Emperor Henry IV in 1075. The Concordat of Worms (1122) ended the struggle by providing that the election of bishops and abbots be conducted according to the law of the church, but under imperial supervision; that the pope invest appointees with staff and ring; and that the emperor invest them with temporal authority by a touch of his scepter.

[126] Since the coronation of Charlemagne in 800 the German Empire had been regarded as the continuation of the Roman Empire, a fiction fostered by the popes. The right to crown an emperor was held to be the prerogative of the pope. Cf. *PE* 2, 108, n. 2.

swear faithful allegiance to the pope as the popes brazenly demand as though they had a right to it. The chapter *Solite*,[127] which sets papal authority above imperial authority, is not worth a cent,[128] and the same goes for all those who base their authority on it or pay any deference to it. For it does nothing else than force the holy words of God, and wrest them out of their true meaning to conform to their own fond imaginations, as I have shown in a Latin treatise.[129]

This most extreme, arrogant, and wanton presumption of the pope has been devised by the devil, who under cover of this intends to usher in the Antichrist and raise the pope above God, as many are now doing and even have already done. It is not proper for the pope to exalt himself above the temporal authorities, except in spiritual offices such as preaching and giving absolution. In other matters the pope is subject to the crown, as Paul and Peter teach in Romans 13 [:1-7] and I Peter 2 [:13], and as I have explained above.[130]

The pope is not a vicar of Christ in heaven, but only of Christ as he walked the earth. Christ in heaven, in the form of a ruler, needs no vicar, but sits on his throne and sees everything, does everything, knows everything, and has all power. But Christ needs a vicar in the form of a servant, the form in which he went about on earth, working, preaching, suffering, and dying. Now the Romanists turn all that upside down. They take the heavenly and kingly form from Christ and give it to the pope, and leave the form of a servant to perish completely. He might almost be the Counter-Christ, whom the Scriptures call Antichrist,[131] for all his nature, work, and pretensions run counter to Christ and only blot out Christ's nature and destroy his work.

It is also ridiculous and childish for the pope, on the basis of such perverted and deluded reasoning, to claim in his decretal *Pas-*

---

[127] *Decretalium D. Gregorii Papae IX*, lib. i, tit. XXXIII, C. VI. *CIC* 2, col. 196.

[128] *Heller*, a coin of little value.

[129] *On the Power of the Pope (de potestate papae)* (1520). *WA* 2, 217.

[130] Cf. pp. 129-130.

[131] Cf. p. 133, n. 30.

toralis[132] that he is rightful heir to the empire in the event of a vacancy. Who has given him this right? Was it Christ when he said, "The princes of the Gentiles are lords, but it shall not be so among you" [Luke 22:25-26]? Or did Peter bequeath it to him? It makes me angry that we have to read and learn such shameless, gross, and idiotic lies in the canon law, and must even hold them as Christian doctrine when they are devilish lies.

That impossible lie, the *Donation of Constantine*,[133] is the same sort of thing. It must have been some special plague from God that so many intelligent people have let themselves be talked into accepting such lies. They are so crude and clumsy that I should imagine any drunken peasant could lie more adroitly and skilfully. How can a man rule and at the same time preach, pray, study, and care for the poor? Yet these are the duties which most properly and peculiarly belong to the pope, and they were so earnestly imposed by Christ that he even forbade his disciples to take cloak or money with them [Matt. 10:9-10]. Christ commanded this because it is almost impossible for anybody to fulfil these duties if they have to look after one single household. Yet the pope would rule an empire and still remain pope. This is what those rogues have thought up who, under the cover of the pope's name, would like to be lords of the world and would gladly restore the Roman Empire to its former state through the pope and in the name of Christ.

10. The pope should restrain himself, take his fingers out of the pie, and claim no title to the kingdom of Naples and Sicily.[134]

[132] A decree of Pope Clement V issued in 1313 and subsequently incorporated into canon law in *Clementinarum,* lib. ii, tit. XI, C. II. *CIC* 2, cols. 1151-1153.

[133] This document purported to be the testament of Emperor Constantine (306-337). It conveyed to the pope title to the city of Rome, certain lands in Italy, and "the islands of the sea." Medieval pontiffs used the document to support their claims to temporal power. In 1440 Laurentius Valla, an Italian humanist, exposed the *Donation* as an eighth-century forgery. Ulrich von Hutten's 1517 republication of Valla's exposé came to Luther's attention just before he wrote the present treatise. Luther published an annotated translation of the *Donation* in 1537. *WA* 50, 60-89. Cf. *PE* 2, 109, n. 4.

[134] The papal claim to sovereignty over this little kingdom, which comprised the island of Sicily and certain territories in southern Italy, goes back to the eleventh century. This claim was steadily asserted during the later Middle Ages and was one of the issues in the conflict between Emperor Frederick II (1200-1260) and the popes. The popes claimed the right to award the kingdom to a ruler who would swear allegiance to the Holy See. At the time Luther wrote this treatise, sovereignty over this kingdom was contested by the royal houses of France and of Spain, of which latter house Charles V was head. Cf. *PE* 2, 110, n. 1.

He has exactly as much right to that kingdom as I have, and yet he wants to be its overlord. It is property gotten by robbery and violence, like almost all his other possessions. The emperor, therefore, should not grant him this realm, and where it has been granted, he should no longer give his consent. Instead, he should draw the pope's attention to the Bible and the prayer book, that he preach and pray and leave the government of lands and people—especially those that no one has given to him—to the temporal lords.

The same goes for Bologna, Imola, Vicenza, Ravenna, and all the territories in the March of Ancona, Romagna, and other lands which the pope has seized by force and possesses without right.[135] Moreover, the pope has meddled in these things against every express command of Christ and St. Paul. For as St. Paul says, "No one should be entangled in worldly affairs who should tend to being a soldier of God."[136] Now the pope should be the head and chief of these soldiers, and yet he meddles in worldly affairs more than any emperor or king. We have to pull him out of these affairs and let him tend to being a soldier. Even Christ, whose vicar the pope boasts he is, was never willing to have anything to do with tem-

[135] At the time Luther wrote the present work (1520), the pope claimed the right and authority to rule over large areas of land. Luther maintained that temporal government was solely the concern of temporal, not spiritual, leaders. Behind this papal claim lay a thousand years of history. When the administrative system of the western half of the Roman Empire collapsed in the fifth century, the sole surviving authority was the papacy. By the end of the sixth century the Roman See was in possession of large areas of Italy and Sicily. The responsibility for these territories involved not only administration but sometimes even war.

In 752 Pope Stephen II appealed to the Franks for military assistance against the Lombards. As a result of that engagement the exarchate of Ravenna was given to the papacy (754). It was this so-called donation of Pepin the Frank which was the origin of the Papal States. The fiction of the *Donation of Constantine* encouraged the growth of a mystique around Pepin's gift.

In 1115 Countess Matilda of Tuscany bestowed Southern Tuscany upon Pope Gregory VIII. There were other extensive donations of territory, and the papacy's sovereignty was upheld by the power of the Hapsburgs.

During the fourteenth century desperate confusion arose as the result of the "Babylonian Captivity" of the papacy and of the Great Schism. Popes Alexander VI (1492-1503) and Julius II (1503-1513) became involved in war and political alliances. In 1527 during the pontificate of Clement VII, Rome itself was sacked by the emperor's forces. By the nineteenth century the Papal States were reduced to the Patrimony of St. Peter, a tiny area in and around Rome. Under the terms of the Lateran Treaty of 1929 the papacy gave up claim to all sovereignty except in Vatican City. Cf. Benrath, *op. cit.*, p. 100, n. 57, and *The Catholic Encyclopedia* (New York, Robert Appleton Co.), XIV (1912), 257-268.

[136] The passage is a free rendering of the Vulgate version of II Tim. 2:4.

poral rule. In fact, when somebody sought a judgment from him in the matter of a brother's action, he said to that man, "Who made me a judge over you?" [Luke 12:14]. But the pope rushes in without invitation and boldly takes hold of everything as if he were a god, until he no longer knows who Christ is, whose vicar he pretends to be.

11. Further, the kissing of the pope's feet should cease.[137] It is an un-Christian, indeed, an anti-Christian thing for a poor sinful man to let his feet be kissed by one who is a hundred times better than himself. If it is done in honor of his authority, why does the pope not do the same to others in honor of their holiness? Compare them with each other—Christ and the pope. Christ washed his disciples' feet and dried them but the disciples never washed his feet [John 13:4-16]. The pope, as though he were higher than Christ, turns that about, and allows his feet to be kissed as a great favor. Though properly, if anyone wanted to do so, the pope ought to use all his power to prevent it, as did St. Paul and Barnabas, who would not let the people of Lystra pay them divine honor, but said, "We are men like you" [Acts 14:15]. But our flatterers have gone so far as to make an idol [of the pope] for us, so that no one fears or honors God as much as he fears and honors the pope. They will stand for that, but not for diminishing the pope's majesty by so much as a hairsbreadth. If they were only Christian and esteemed God's honor more than their own, the pope would never be happy to see God's honor despised and his own exalted. Nor would he let anyone honor him until he saw that God's honor was once more exalted and raised higher than his own.

Another example[138] of the same scandalous pride is that the pope is not satisfied to ride or be driven, but, although he is strong and in good health, he has himself borne by men like an idol and with unheard-of splendor. Dear readers, how does such

---

[137] Cf. p. 164, n. 125.

[138] The remainder of this eleventh section was not included in the first edition. Along with two other passages indicated in footnotes to the present edition, it was included in the second edition, published very soon after the first. Cf. *WA* 6, 397; 436, n. 10; *PE* 2, 59; and *CL* 1, 421-422.

satanic pride compare with Christ, who went on foot, as did all his disciples? Where has there ever been a worldly monarch who went about in such worldly pomp and glory as he who wants to be the head of all those who ought to despise and flee from the pomp and vanity of this world, that is, the Christians? Not that we should bother ourselves very much about him as a person, but we certainly ought to fear the wrath of God if we flatter this sort of pride and do not show our indignation. It is enough for the pope to rant and play the fool in this way. But it is more than enough for us to approve of it and let it go on.

What Christian heart can or ought to take pleasure in seeing that when the pope wishes to receive communion, he sits quietly like a gracious lord and has the sacrament brought to him on a golden rod by a bowing cardinal on bended knee? As though the holy sacrament were not worthy enough for the pope, a poor, stinking sinner, to rise and show respect to his God, when all other Christians, who are much holier than the Most Holy Father the pope, receive it with all due reverence! Would it be a wonder if God sent down a plague upon us all because we tolerate such dishonor of God by our prelates and praise them for doing it, and because we share in this damnable pride by our silence or by our flattery?

It is the same when the pope carries the sacrament in procession. He must be carried, but the sacrament is set before him like a flagon of wine on a table. At Rome Christ counts for nothing, but the pope counts for everything. And yet the Romanists want to compel us—and even use threats—to approve, praise, and honor these sins of the Antichrist, even though they are against God and all Christian doctrine. Help us, O God, to get a free, general council which will teach the pope that he, too, is a man, and not more than God, as he sets himself up to be!

12. Pilgrimages to Rome should either be abolished or else no one should be allowed to make such a pilgrimage for reasons of curiosity or his own pious devotion, unless it is first acknowledged by his parish priest, his town authorities, or his overlord that he has a good and sufficient reason for doing so. I say this not because

pilgrimages are bad, but because they are ill-advised at this time.[139] At Rome men do not find a good example, but, on the contrary, pure scandal. The Romanists themselves devised the saying, "The nearer Rome, the worse Christians." After a pilgrimage to Rome men bring back with them contempt for God and his commandments. They say the first time a man goes to Rome he seeks a rascal; the second time he finds one; the third time he brings him back home with him.[140] Now, however, the Romanists have grown so clever that they can make three pilgrimages in one! The pilgrims have brought back such a pretty mess of experiences from Rome that it would be better never to have seen Rome or known anything about it.

Even if this were not the case there is still another and a better reason: simple people[141] are led into error and misunderstanding of the divine command. Such people think that going on a pilgrimage is a precious good work. This is not true. It is a very small good work—frequently it is evil and misleading, for God has not commanded it. But God has commanded that a man should care for his wife and children, perform the duties of a husband, and serve and help his neighbor. Today a man makes a pilgrimage to Rome and spends fifty, maybe a hundred, gulden, something nobody commanded him to do. He permits his wife and child, or his neighbor at any rate, to suffer want back home. And yet the silly fellow thinks he can gloss over such disobedience and contempt of the divine commandment with his self-assigned pilgrimage, which is really nothing but impertinence or a delusion of the devil. The popes have encouraged this sort of thing with their false, feigned,

---

139 There were other famous shrines, but the holy places at Rome had long been favorite destinations of pilgrimages, and this practice had been zealously fostered by the popes through the institution of the "golden" or "jubilee" years. Cf. p. 171, n. 142.

140 Cf. Ulrich von Hutten's remark in *Vadiscus*, "Three things there are which those who go to Rome usually bring back with them: a bad conscience, a ruined stomach, and an empty purse." Eduard Böcking, *Ulrichs von Hutten Schriften* (Leipzig, 1860), IV, 169. Erasmus was another critic of pilgrimages. Cf. *PE* 2, 113, n. 3. Cf. also *Erasmi Colloquia*, Vol. II, *Encomium Moriae* (Leipzig, n.d.), pp. 341 ff.

141 *Die einfeltigen menschen*; literally, the simple, or those of untrained mind.

foolish "golden years,"[142] by which the people are excited, torn away from God's commandments, and enticed to follow the popes' own erroneous undertakings. The popes have done the very thing they ought to have prevented. But it has brought in money and fortified their illegitimate authority. That is why it has to go on, even if it is contrary to God and the salvation of souls.

To eradicate such false, seductive faith from the minds of simple Christian people and to restore a right understanding of good works, all pilgrimages should be dropped. There is no good in them: no commandment enjoins them, no obedience attaches to them. Rather do these pilgrimages give countless occasions to commit sin and to despise God's commandments. This is why there are so many beggars who commit all kinds of mischief by going on these pilgrimages. These people learn to beg when there is no need to beg, and they make a habit of begging. This accounts for vagabondage and many ills about which I shall not speak here.

If any man wants to go on a pilgrimage today or vow to make a pilgrimage, he should first show his reasons for doing so to his priest or his master. If it turns out that he wants to do it for the sake of a good work, then let the priest or master put his foot down firmly and put an end to the vow and the good work as a devilish delusion. Let priest and master show him how to use the money and effort for the pilgrimage for God's commandments and for works a thousand times better by spending it on his own family or on his poor neighbors. But if he wishes to make the pilgrimage out of curiosity, to see other lands and cities, he may be allowed to do

[142] The "golden" or "jubilee" years were inaugurated by Boniface VIII in 1300. Originally every hundredth year was to be a jubilee, but by 1473 this was reduced to every twenty-fifth year. During these jubilee years indulgences were granted to those who visited the churches of St. Peter and St. Paul in Rome. These indulgences were extended on a limited scale by Clement VI in 1350 to those who could not make the pilgrimage to Rome. Still later Boniface IX sent commissioners throughout Europe to dispense the indulgences for the cost of a journey to Rome and back. In a great many instances these indulgences were represented as offering pardon without penitential or sacramental formality. For this representation as well as for irregularity of their financial accounts a great many of these commissioners were punished by the pope. Cf. Lea, *A History of Auricular Confession and Indulgences in the Latin Church*, III, 63-66. Benrath notes that very large numbers of Germans participated in the pilgrimages of 1500. Cf. Benrath, *op. cit.*, p. 101, n. 59.

so. But if he made the vow during an illness, then that vow must be annulled and canceled. God's commandment should be emphasized so that henceforth he will be content to keep the vow made in baptism and the commandments of God. Nevertheless, he may be allowed to perform his foolish vow just once to quiet his conscience. Nobody wants to walk in the straight path of God's commandments common to all of us. Everybody invents new ways and vows for himself as if he had already fulfilled all of God's commandments.

13. Next we come to the masses who make many vows but keep few. Do not be angry, my noble lords! I really mean it for the best. It is the bittersweet truth that the further building of mendicant houses should not be permitted. God help us, there are already too many of them. Would to God they were all dissolved, or at least combined into two or three orders! Their running about the country has never done any good and never will do any good. My advice is to join together ten of these houses or as many as need be, and make them a single institution for which adequate provision is made so that begging will not be necessary. It is far more important to consider what the common people need for their salvation than what St. Francis, St. Dominic, and St. Augustine,[143] or anyone else has established as a rule, especially because things have not turned out as they planned.

The mendicants should also be relieved of preaching and hearing confession, unless they are called to do this by the bishops, parishes, congregations, or the civil authorities. Nothing but hatred and envy between priests and monks has come out of this kind of preaching and shriving, and this has become a source of great offense and hindrance to the common people. It ought to stop because it can well be dispensed with. It looks suspiciously as though the Holy Roman See has purposely increased this army lest the priests and bishops, unable to stand the pope's tyranny any

[143] Luther alludes here to the three leading mendicant orders: the Franciscan Minorites or "little brothers," founded by St. Francis of Assisi (d. 1226); the Dominican or "preaching brothers," founded by St. Dominic (d. 1221); and the Augustinian Hermits. This last named order originated during the thirteenth century when Innocent IV and Alexander IV united several small hermit societies under the so-called Augustinian *Rule*. Luther was himself an Augustinian.

longer, some day become too powerful for him and start a reformation. That would be unbearable to his holiness.

At the same time the manifold divisions and differences[144] within one and the same order should be abolished. These divisions have arisen from time to time for very trivial reasons; they have been maintained for even more trivial reasons, and they quarrel with each other with unspeakable hatred and envy. Nevertheless, the Christian faith, which can well exist without any of these distinctions, comes to grief because of both parties, and a good Christian life is valued and sought after only according to the standards of outward laws, works, and methods. Nothing comes of this but hypocrisy and the ruination of souls, as all can plainly see.

The pope must also be forbidden to found or endorse any more of these orders; in fact he must be ordered to abolish some and reduce the numbers of others. Inasmuch as faith in Christ,[145] which alone is the chief possession, exists without any kind of orders, there is no little danger that men will be easily led astray to live according to many and varied works and ways rather than to pay heed to faith. And unless there are wise superiors in the monasteries who preach and stress faith more than the rule of the order, it is impossible for that order not to harm and mislead the simple souls who have regard only for works.

But in our day the superiors who did have faith and who founded the orders have passed away almost everywhere. It is just as it was centuries ago among the children of Israel. When the fathers who had known the wonders and the works of God had passed on, their children, ignorant of God's works and of faith, immediately elevated idolatry and their own human works. In our day, unfortunately, these orders have no understanding of God's works or of faith, but make wretched martyrs of themselves by

[144] The sectarianism deplored here by Luther is illustrated in the case of the Franciscans. Within a few years after the founding of the order the movement divided into two groups: the Spirituals, who kept strictly to the rule of the order; and the Conventuals, who advocated relaxation of the rule as circumstances dictated. When Pope John XXII ordered the Spirituals to conform (1317-1318), this group splintered and the stricter party became schismatics known as *Fraticelli.* Following the papal exile at Avignon and the Great Schism the party of the Observants was recognized as the true order of St. Francis. At this time another reform led to the establishment of the Capuchins.

[145] *Der glaub Christi;* literally, "the faith of Christ."

striving and working to keep their own rules, laws, and ways of life. Yet they never come to a right understanding of a spiritually good life. It is just as II Timothy 3 [:5, 7] declares, "They have the appearance of a spiritual life, but there is nothing behind it: they are constantly learning, but they never come to a knowledge of what true spiritual life is." If the ruling superior has no understanding of Christian faith, it would be better to have no monastery at all; for such a superior cannot govern an order without doing hurt and harm, and the holier and better the superior appears to be in his external works, the more injury and ruin he causes.

To my way of thinking it would be a necessary measure, especially in our perilous times, to regulate convents and monasteries in the same way they were regulated in the beginning, in the days of the apostles, and for a long time afterward.[146] In those days convents and monasteries were all open to everyone to stay in them as long as he pleased. What else were the convents and monasteries but Christian schools where Scripture and the Christian life were taught, and where people were trained to rule and to preach? Thus we read that St. Agnes[147] went to school, and we still see the same practice in some of the convents, like that at Quedlinburg[148] and elsewhere. And in truth all monasteries and convents ought to be so free that God is served freely and not under compulsion. Later on, however, they became tied up with the vows and became an eternal prison. Consequently, these monastic vows are more highly regarded than the vows of baptism. We see, hear, read, and learn more and more about the fruit of all this every day.

I can well suppose that this advice of mine will be regarded as the height of foolishness, but I am not concerned about that at

---

[146] Luther knew perfectly well that convents and monasteries did not exist in apostolic times. He is arguing for a monastic system based on the apostolic teaching of the New Testament. See his treatment of this subject in *The Judgment of Martin Luther on Monastic Vows,* in this volume, p. 312.

[147] St. Agnes, a martyr of the early fourth century, was a popular medieval saint associated with youthful chastity and innocence. According to one legend she was placed in a brothel by a Roman official. Whenever men cast lascivious eyes upon her, they were immediately stricken. The story of St. Agnes which Luther mentions here is probably the highly legendary account of her martyrdom given in Ambrose's *Vita gloriosa Agnetis.* Cf. Alban Butler, *The Lives of the Fathers, Martyrs, and other Principal Saints,* Vol. I (Dublin, 1836), pp. 88-90.

[148] One of the most famous of the German convents, founded in 936.

the moment. I advise what seems good to me, let him reject it who will. I see for myself how the vows are kept, especially the vow of chastity. This vow has become universal in these monasteries, and yet it was never commanded by Christ. On the contrary, chastity is given to very few, as he himself says [Matt. 19:11-12], as well as St. Paul [I Cor. 7:7]. It is my heartfelt wish for everybody to be helped. I do not want to let Christian souls get entangled in the self-contrived traditions and laws of men.[149]

14. We also see how the priesthood has fallen, and how many a poor priest is overburdened with wife and child, his conscience troubled. Yet no one does anything to help him, though he could easily be helped. Though pope and bishops may let things go on as they are, and allow what is heading for ruin to go to ruin, yet I will redeem my conscience and open my mouth freely, whether it vexes pope, bishop, or anybody else. And this is what I say: according to the institution of Christ and the apostles, every city should have a priest or bishop, as St. Paul clearly says in Titus 1 [:5]. And this priest should not be compelled to live without a wedded wife, but should be permitted to have one, as St. Paul writes in I Timothy 3 [:2, 4] and Titus 1 [:6–7] saying, "A bishop shall be a man who is blameless, and the husband of but one wife, whose children are obedient and well behaved," etc. According to St. Paul, and also St. Jerome,[150] a bishop and a priest are one and the same thing. But of bishops as they now are the Scriptures know nothing. Bishops have been appointed by ordinance of the Christian church, so that one of them may have authority over several priests.

So then, we clearly learn from the Apostle that it should be the custom for every town to choose from among the congregation a learned and pious citizen, entrust to him the office of the ministry, and support him at the expense of the congregation. He should be free to marry or not. He should have several priests or deacons, also free to marry or not as they choose, to help him minister to the congregation and the community with word and sacrament, as is still the practice in the Greek church. Because there was sometimes

[149] Cf. Col. 2.20.

[150] Cf. Luther's understanding of I Cor. 4:1 expressed in *Concerning the Ministry* (*LW* 40, 35). The reference is to Jerome's *Commentary on Titus* [1:7]. *MPL* 26, 562; cf. also 22, 656.

so much persecution and controversy with heretics after the apostolic age, there were many holy fathers who voluntarily abstained from matrimony that they might better devote themselves to study and be prepared at any moment for death or battle.

But the Roman See has interfered and out of its own wanton wickedness made a universal commandment forbidding priests to marry.[151] This was done at the bidding of the devil, as St. Paul declares in I Timothy 4 [:1, 3], "There shall come teachers who bring the devil's teaching and forbid marriage." Unfortunately so much misery has arisen from this that tongue could never tell it. Moreover, this caused the Greek church to separate,[152] and discord, sin, shame, and scandal were increased no end. But this always happens when the devil starts and carries on. What, then, shall we do about it?

My advice is, restore freedom to everybody and leave every man free to marry or not to marry. But then there would have to be a very different kind of government and administration of church property; the whole canon law would have to be demolished; and few benefices would be allowed to get into Roman hands. I fear that greed is a cause of this wretched, unchaste celibacy. As a result, everyone has wanted to become a priest and everyone wants his son to study for the priesthood, not with the idea of living in chastity, for that could be done outside the priesthood. [Their idea is to] be supported in temporal things without work or worry, contrary to God's command in Genesis 3 [:19] that "in the sweat of your face you shall eat your bread." The Romanists have colored this to mean that their labor is to pray and say mass.

I am not referring here to popes, bishops, canons, and monks. God has not instituted these offices. They have taken these burdens upon themselves, so they will have to bear them themselves. I want to speak only of the ministry which God has instituted, the responsibility of which is to minister word and sacrament to a congregation, among whom they reside. Such ministers should be

[151] The first definitive and documented canon to prescribe and enforce clerical celibacy was that of Pope Siricius in 385. Cf. Henry Charles Lea, *History of Sacerdotal Celibacy in the Christian Church* (revised 3rd ed.; New York: The Macmillan Co., 1907), I, 64.

[152] The controversy over celibacy was involved in the schism between the Greek and Roman churches. Cf. *PE* 2, 120, n. 1.

given liberty by a Christian council to marry to avoid temptation and sin. For since God has not bound them, no one else ought to bind them or can bind them, even if he were an angel from heaven, let alone a pope. Everything that canon law decrees to the contrary is mere fable and idle talk.

Furthermore, I advise anyone henceforth being ordained a priest or anything else that he in no wise vow to the bishop that he will remain celibate. On the contrary, he should tell the bishop that he has no right whatsoever to require such a vow, and that it is a devilish tyranny to make such a demand. But if anyone is compelled to say, or even wants to say, "so far as human frailty permits," as indeed many do, let him frankly interpret these same words in a negative manner to mean "I do not promise chastity." For human frailty does not permit a man to live chastely, but only the strength of angels and the power of heaven. In this way he should keep his conscience free of all vows.

I will advise neither for nor against marrying or remaining single. I leave that to common Christian order and to everyone's better judgment. I will not conceal my real opinion or withhold comfort from that pitiful band who with wives and children have fallen into disgrace and whose consciences are burdened because people call them priests' whores and their children priests' children. As the court-jester[153] I say this openly.

You will find many a pious priest against whom nobody has anything to say except that he is weak and has come to shame with a woman. From the bottom of their hearts both are of a mind to live together in lawful wedded love, if only they could do it with a clear conscience. But even though they both have to bear public shame, the two are certainly married in the sight of God. And I say that where they are so minded and live together, they should appeal anew to their conscience. Let the priest take and keep her as his lawful wedded wife, and live honestly with her as her husband, whether the pope likes it or not, whether it be against canon or human law. The salvation of your soul is more important than the observance of tyrannical, arbitrary, and wanton laws which are not necessary to salvation or commanded by God. You should do

[153] Luther had cast himself in this role in the introduction. Cf. p. 123.

as the children of Israel did who stole from the Egyptians the wages they had earned;[154] or as a servant who steals from his wicked master the wages he has earned: steal from the pope your wedded wife and child! Let the man who has faith enough to venture this, boldly follow me. I shall not lead him astray. Though I do not have the authority of a pope, I do have the authority of a Christian to advise and help my neighbor against sins and temptations. And that not without cause or reason!

First, not every priest can do without a woman, not only on account of human frailty, but much more on account of keeping house. If he then may keep a woman, and the pope allows that, and yet may not have her in marriage, what is that but leaving a man and a woman alone together and yet forbidding them to fall? It is just like putting straw and fire together and forbidding them to smoke or burn!

Second, the pope has as little power to command this as he has to forbid eating, drinking, the natural movement of the bowels, or growing fat. Therefore, no one is bound to keep it, but the pope is responsible for all the sins which are committed against this ordinance, for all the souls which are lost, and for all the consciences which are confused and tortured because of this ordinance. He has strangled so many wretched souls with this devilish rope that he has long deserved to be driven out of this world. Yet it is my firm belief that God has been more gracious to many souls at their last hour than the pope was to them in their whole lifetime. No good has ever come nor will come out of the papacy and its laws.

Third, although the law of the pope is against it, nevertheless, when the estate of matrimony has been entered against the pope's law, then his law is already at an end and is no longer valid. For God's commandment, which enjoins that no man shall put husband and wife asunder [Matt. 19:6], is above the pope's law. And the commandments of God must not be broken or neglected because of the pope's commandment. Nevertheless, many foolish jurists, along with the pope, have devised impediments and thereby pre-

[154] Cf. Exod. 12:35-36.

vented, broken, and brought confusion to the estate of matrimony so that God's commandment concerning it has altogether disappeared.[155] Need I say more? In the entire canon law of the pope there are not even two lines which could instruct a devout Christian, and, unfortunately, there are so many mistaken and dangerous laws that nothing would be better than to make a bonfire of it.[156]

But if you say that marriage of the clergy would give offense, and that the pope must first grant dispensation, I reply that whatever offense there is in it is the fault of the Roman See which has established such laws with no right and against God. Before God and the Holy Scriptures marriage of the clergy is no offense. Moreover, if the pope can grant dispensations from his greedy and tyrannical laws for money, then every Christian can grant dispensations from these very same laws for God's sake and for the salvation of souls. For Christ has set us free from all man-made laws, especially when they are opposed to God and the salvation of souls, as St. Paul teaches in Galatians 5 [:1] and I Corinthians 10 [:23].

15. Nor must I forget the poor monasteries. The evil spirit, who has now confused all the estates of life and made them unbearable through man-made laws, has taken possession of some abbots, abbesses, and prelates. As a result they govern their brothers and sisters in such a way that they quickly go to hell and lead a wretched existence here and now, as do the devil's martyrs. That is to say, these superiors have reserved to themselves in confession, all, or at least some, of the mortal sins which are secret, so that no brother can absolve another on pain of excommunication and under the vow of obedience. Now nobody finds angels all the time in all places; but we do find flesh and blood which would rather undergo all excommunications and threats rather than confess secret sins to prelates and appointed confessors. Thus these people go to the

[155] The laws that governed marriage were entirely ecclesiastical and prohibited the marriage of blood relatives as far as the seventh degree of consanguinity. In 1204 the prohibition was restricted by the Fourth Lateran Council to the first four degrees; lawful marriage within these degrees was possible only by dispensation, which was not difficult to secure by those willing to pay for it. The relation of godparents to godchildren was looked upon as a "spiritual consanguinity" which might serve as a bar to lawful marriage. Cf. Benrath, *op. cit.*, p. 103, n. 74.

[156] This is exactly what Luther did. A copy of the canon law was burned with the papal bull of excommunication on December 10, 1520.

sacrament with such consciences that they become irregulars[157] and even worse. O blind shepherds! O mad prelates! O ravenous wolves!

To this I say: if a sin is public or notorious, then it is proper for the prelate alone to punish it, and it is only these sins and no others that he may reserve and select for himself. He has no authority over secret sins, even if they were the worst sins that ever are or can be found. If the prelate makes exceptions of these secret sins, then he is a tyrant. He has no such right and is trespassing upon the prerogative of God's judgment.

And so I advise these children, brothers and sisters: if your superiors are unwilling to permit you to confess your secret sins to whom you choose, then take them to your brother or sister, whomever you like, and be absolved and comforted. Then go and do what you want and ought to do. Only believe firmly that you are absolved, and nothing more is needed. And do not be distressed or driven mad by threats of excommunication, becoming irregulars, or whatever else they threaten. These disciplines are valid only in the case of public or notorious sins which none will confess. They do not apply to you. What are you trying to do, you blind prelates, prevent secret sins by threats? Relinquish what you obviously cannot hold on to so that God's judgment and grace may work in the people under your care! He has not given them so entirely into your hands as to let them go entirely out of his own! In fact, you have the smaller part under you. Let your statutes be merely statutes. Do not exalt them to heaven or give them the weight of divine judgments!

16. It is also necessary to abolish all endowed masses for the dead,[158] or at least to reduce their number, since we plainly see

[157] Irregulars are monks who have violated the rules of their order and in consequence have been deprived of the benefits enjoyed by those living within the *regula* or rule of the order; cf. Benrath, *op. cit.*, p. 102, n. 65. Among the violations is the concealing of sins in confession; cf. *MA*[3] 2, 398.

[158] *Jartag, begencknis, seelmessen,* translated here as "endowed masses for the dead," were masses endowed either by the descendants of the deceased or by testamentary bequest. The terms by which Luther referred to these masses indicate the occasion of their celebration: *jartag,* the annual anniversary of the beneficiary's death; *begencknis,* the appointed day of the year when all the benefactors of a religious order were commemorated; and *seelmessen,* the masses regularly offered in behalf of souls in purgatory. Cf. Adolph Franz, *Die Messe im Deutschen Mittelalter* (Freiburg im Breisgau: Herdersche Verlagshandlung, 1902), pp. 243–244; cf. also Benrath, *op. cit.*, p. 102, n. 67.

that they have become nothing but a mockery. God is deeply angered by these, and their only purpose is money-grubbing, gluttony, and drunkenness. What pleasure can God take in wretched vigils[159] and masses which are so miserably rattled off, not read or prayed. And if they were prayed, it would not be for God's sake and out of love, but for the sake of money and of getting a job finished. Now it is impossible for a work which is not done out of unconstrained love to please or suffice God. So it is altogether Christian to abolish, or at least diminish, everything we see which is growing into an abuse and which angers God rather than reconciles him. I would rather—in fact, it would be more pleasing to God and much better—that a chapter, church, or monastery combine all its anniversary masses and vigils and on one day, with sincerity of heart, reverence, and faith, hold one true vigil and mass on behalf of all its benefactors, than hold thousands every year for each individual benefactor without reverence and faith. O dear Christians, God does not care for much praying but for true praying. In fact, he condemns long and repetitious prayers, and says in Matthew 6 [:7; 23:14] "They will only earn the more punishment thereby." But greed, which cannot put its trust in God, brings such things to pass. Avarice is anxious lest it starve to death.

17. Certain penalties or punishments of canon law should be abolished, too, especially the interdict,[160] which without any doubt was invented by the evil spirit. Is it not a devilish work to correct one sin through many and great sins? It is actually a greater sin to silence or suppress the word and worship of God than if one had strangled twenty popes at one time, to say nothing of a priest, or had misused church holdings. This is another of the tender virtues taught in canon law. One of the reasons this law is called "spiritual"[161] is that it comes from spirit: not from the Holy Spirit but from the Evil Spirit.

---

[159] Originally the term "vigil" was applied to the night before a major festival. Gradually the term came to include the entire day, and finally was applied to the particular liturgical offices connected with the festivals. Luther probably was thinking of vigils in this liturgical sense. Cf. Benrath, *op. cit.*, p. 103, n. 68.

[160] Cf. p. 132, n. 27.

[161] The term Luther uses for canon law is *geystlich recht*, literally, "spiritual law."

Excommunication must never be used except where the Scriptures prescribe its use, that is, against those who do not hold the true faith or who live in open sin, not for material advantage. But today it is the other way around. Everybody believes and lives as he pleases, especially those who use excommunication to fleece and defame other people. All the excommunications are for material advantage, for which we have nobody to thank but the holy canon law of unrighteousness. I have said more about this in an earlier discourse.[162]

The other punishments and penalties—suspension, irregularity, aggravation, reaggravation, deposition, lightning, thundering, cursings, damnings, and the rest of these devices[163]—should be buried ten fathoms deep in the earth so that their name and memory not be left on earth. The evil spirit unleashed by canon law has brought such a terrible plague and misery into the heavenly kingdom of holy Christendom, having done nothing but destroy and hinder souls by canon law, that the words of Christ in Matthew 23 [:13] may well be understood as applying to them,[164] "Woe to you scribes! You have taken upon yourselves the authority to teach, and closed up the kingdom of heaven to men. You do not go in and you stand in the way of those who enter."

18. All festivals should be abolished, and Sunday alone retained.[165] If it were desired, however, to retain the festivals of Our Lady and of the major saints, they should be transferred to Sunday, or observed only by a morning mass, after which all the rest of the day should be a working day. Here is the reason: since the feast days are abused by drinking, gambling, loafing, and all manner of sin, we anger God more on holy days than we do on other days. Things are so topsy-turvy that holy days are not holy, but

---

162 *Sermon on Excommunication (Sermon von dem Bann)* (1520). *WA* 6, 61-75.

163 Luther cites a number of penalties imposed by the church upon priests. Aggravation is the threat of excommunication; reaggravation is excommunication itself. Deposition is a permanent expulsion from clerical office. Cf. *MA*³ 2, 399.

164 I.e., those who teach and enforce canon law.

165 Luther refers here to the numerous saints' days and minor religious holidays which fell on weekdays. These observances not only interfered with the working week but led to gambling, drinking, and vice. Cf. *Treatise on Good Works,* in this volume, p. 55.

working days are. Nor is any service rendered God and his saints by so many saints' days. On the contrary, they are dishonored; although some foolish prelates think that they have done a good work if each, following the promptings of his own blind devotion, celebrates a festival in honor of St. Otilie[166] or St. Barbara.[167] But they would be doing something far better if they honored the saint by turning the saint's day into a working day.

Over and above the spiritual injury, the average man incurs two material disadvantages from this practice. First, he neglects his work and spends more money that he would otherwise spend. Second, he weakens his body and makes it less fit. We see this every day, yet nobody thinks of correcting the situation. In such cases we ought not to consider whether or not the pope has instituted the feasts, or whether we must have a dispensation or permission [to omit them]. Every town, council, or governing authority not only has the right, without the knowledge and consent of the pope or bishop, to abolish what is opposed to God and injurious to men's bodies and souls, but indeed is bound at the risk of the salvation of its souls to fight it even though popes and bishop, who ought to be the first to do so, do not consent.

Above all, we ought to abolish church anniversary celebrations[168] outright, since they have become nothing but taverns, fairs, and gambling places, and only increase the dishonoring of God and foster the soul's damnation. It does not help matters to boast that these festivals had a good beginning and are a good work. Did not God set aside his own law, which he had given from heaven, when it was perverted and abused? And does he not daily overturn what he has set up and destroy what he has made because of the same perversion and abuse? As it is written of him in Psalm 18 [:26], "You show yourself perverse with the perverted."

19. The grades or degrees within which marriage is forbidden, such as those affecting godparents or the third and fourth degree

[166] The feast day of this obscure saint is observed in the territory of Strassburg on December 13. Cf. *The Roman Martyrology* (London: Burns Oates and Washbourne, Ltd., 1937), p. 342.
[167] Cf. p. 68, n. 37.
[168] *Kirchweye,* the anniversary celebration of the consecration of a church. These days had become feast days in the parish. Cf. *PE* 2, 128, n. 1.

of kinship,[169] should be changed. If the pope in Rome can grant dispensations and scandalously sell them for money,[170] then every priest may give the same dispensations without price and for the salvation of souls. Would to God that every priest were able to do and remit without payment all those things we have to pay for at Rome, such as indulgences, letters of indulgence, butter letters, mass letters, and all the rest of the *confessionalia* and skullduggery[171] at Rome and free us from that golden noose the canon law, by which the poor people are deceived and cheated of their money! If the pope has the right to sell his noose of gold and his spiritual snares (I ought to say "law")[172] for money, then a priest certainly has more right to tear these nooses and snares apart, and for God's sake tread them underfoot. But if the priest does not have this right, neither has the pope the right to sell them at his disgraceful fair.

Furthermore, fasts should be left to individuals and every kind of food left optional, as the gospel makes them.[173] Even those gentlemen at Rome scoff at the fasts, and leave us commoners to eat the fat they would not deign to use to grease their shoes, and then afterward they sell us the liberty to eat butter and all sorts of other things. The holy Apostle says that we already have freedom in all these things through the gospel.[174] But they have bound us with their canon law and robbed us of our rights so that we have to buy them back again with money. In so doing they have made our consciences so timid and fearful that it is no longer easy to preach about liberty of this kind because the common people take offense at it and think that eating butter is a greater sin than lying, swearing, or even living unchastely. It is still a human work decreed by men. You may do with it what you will, yet nothing good will ever come of it.

---

[169] Cf. p. 179, n. 155.

[170] Dispensations from the marriage laws were issued by the *Datarius*. Cf. p. 151, n. 83.

[171] On the *confessionalia*, see p. 155, n. 103; on butter letters, see p. 155, n. 102. Mass letters were certificates entitling the holder to the benefits of masses celebrated by sodalities (cf. p. 192, n. 94). Cf. Benrath, *op. cit.*, p. 103, n. 75.

[172] Here Luther makes a pun on *geistliche netz*, i.e., spiritual snares, and *geystlich gesetz*, i.e., spiritual or canon law.

[173] Cf. Matt. 15:11.

[174] I Cor. 10:23; Col. 2:16.

20. The chapels in forests and the churches in fields,[175] such as Wilsnack,[176] Sternberg,[177] Trier,[178] the Grimmenthal,[179] and now Regensburg[180] and a goodly number of others which recently have become the goal of pilgrimages, must be leveled. Oh, what a terrible and heavy reckoning those bishops will have to give who permit this devilish deceit and profit by it.[181] They should be the first to prevent it and yet they regard it all as a godly and holy thing. They do not see that the devil is behind it all, to strengthen greed, to create a false and fictitious faith, to weaken the parish churches, to multiply taverns and harlotry, to lose money and working time to no purpose, and to lead ordinary people by the nose. If they had read Scripture as well as the damnable canon law, they would know how to deal with this matter!

[175] Chapels built in the country not for congregations but only for pilgrimages.

[176] Wilsnack, a town sixty-seven miles northwest of Berlin, was a much frequented place of pilgrimage after 1383. There three hosts, singed only about the edges, survived a fire which destroyed the church. In the middle of each host was what appeared to be a drop of blood, taken to be the blood of Christ. When these hosts were taken to a neighboring church they were said to become fiery and luminous without burning. Soon large numbers of pilgrims were drawn to Wilsnack, where the bishop of Havelberg erected a new and impressive edifice. Opposition to the pilgrimages was soon voiced by many people, including John Huss, who wrote about it in his *De omni sanguine Christi glorificato*. Despite these and other protests from several universities, the shrine continued to have wide popular appeal for some years after 1548, when Joachim Ellefeld, a Protestant pastor, burned the hosts. Cf. *The New Schaff-Herzog Encyclopedia of Religious Knowledge*, ed. Samuel Macauley Jackson (New York: Funk and Wagnalls Company, 1912), XII, 375-376. Cf. also Benrath, *op. cit.* p. 104, n. 76.

[177] Sternberg, a monastery of the Augustinian Hermits, located in Mecklenburg, also displayed a bleeding host after 1491. Cf. Benrath, *op. cit.*, p. 104, n. 76.

[178] A garment alleged to be the seamless garment of Christ for which the executioners cast lots beneath the cross (John 19:23-24) was first exhibited in Trier in 1512. According to tradition the garment was presented to the cathedral church by the Empress Helena, mother of Constantine the Great. Cf. *PE* 2, 130, n. 1.

[179] Grimmenthal in Meiningen had attracted pilgrimages since 1499. An image of the Virgin, said to have been miraculously created, was displayed there and was alleged to work miraculous healings, especially of syphilis. Cf. *PE* 2, 130, n. 2.

[180] "The fair Virgin of Regensburg" was an image of the Virgin similar to that exhibited in Grimmenthal. The shrine was opened March 25, 1519, and within a month fifty thousand pilgrims are said to have worshiped there (*PE* 2, 130, n. 3). Regensburg had previously been the location of pilgrimages honoring SS. Erhard and Wolfgang, bishops of Ratisbon (*WA* 6, 447, n. 1).

[181] The pilgrimages provided a large revenue from the sale of medals which were worn as amulets, the fees for masses at the shrines, and the free-will offerings of the pilgrims. Most of this revenue accrued to the bishop of the diocese. The popes, however, did not overlook opportunities for the sale of indulgences at these shrines. The *Gravamina* of 1521 state that the bishops demanded at least 25 to 33 per cent of the offerings made at the shrines of pilgrimages. Cf. *PE* 2, 130, n. 4.

The miracles that happen in these places prove nothing, for the evil spirit can also work miracles, as Christ has told us in Matthew 24 [:24]. If they took the matter seriously and forbade this sort of thing, the miracles would quickly come to an end. But if the thing were of God their prohibition would not hinder it.[182] And if there were no other evidence that it is not of God, the fact that men come running to them like herds of cattle, as if they had lost all reason, would be proof enough. This could not be possible if it were of God. Further, God never gave any command about all this. There is neither obedience nor merit in doing it. The thing to do is to step in boldly and protect the people. For whatever has not been commanded and is done beyond what God commands is certainly the devil's doing. To their disadvantage the parish churches are held in less respect. In short, these things are signs of great unbelief among the people, for if they really had faith they would find all they need in their own parish churches to which they are commanded to go.

But what shall I say now? Every bishop thinks only of how he can set up and maintain such a place of pilgrimage in his diocese.[183] He is not at all concerned that the people believe and live aright. The rulers are just like the people. The blind lead the blind [Luke 6:39]. In fact, where pilgrimages do not catch on, they set to work to canonize saints,[184] not to honor the saints, who would be honored enough without being canonized, but to draw the crowds and bring in the money. At this point pope and bishops lend their aid. There is a deluge of indulgences. There is always money enough for these. But nobody worries about what God has commanded. Nobody runs after these things; nobody has money for them. How blind we are!

---

[182] Cf. Acts 5:39.

[183] Identification with a saint conferred distinction and status upon a church. Because of the income to be had from pilgrimages, church authorities were willing to pay handsome sums for the canonization of deceased clerical or other dignitaries Cf. *PE* 2, 131, n. 2.

[184] Canonization, the definitive sentence by which the pope declares a soul (previously beatified) to have entered into eternal glory, is said to confer a sevenfold honor: (1) enrolment among the saints; (2) invocation in public prayer; (3) dedication of churches in the saint's memory; (4) the mass and office publicly offered to God in the saint's honor; (5) festival days celebrated in the saint's memory; (6) pictorial representations of the saint in heavenly light; and (7) the honoring of the saint's relics. Cf. *The Catholic Encyclopedia,* II, 364-369.

We not only give the devil free rein for his mischief, but we even strengthen and multiply his mischief. I would rather the dear saints were left in peace and the simple people not led astray! What spirit gave the pope authority to canonize saints? Who tells him whether they are saints or not? Are there not enough sins on earth already without tempting God, without interfering in his judgment and setting up the dear saints as decoys to get money?

My advice is to let the saints canonize themselves. Indeed, it is God alone who should canonize them. And let every man stay in his own parish; there he will find more than in all the shrines even if they were all rolled into one. In your own parish you find baptism, the sacrament, preaching, and your neighbor, and these things are greater than all the saints in heaven, for all of them were made saints by God's word and sacrament. As long as we esteem such wonderful things so little, God is just in his wrathful condemnation in allowing the devil to lead us where he likes, to conduct pilgrimages, found churches and chapels, canonize saints, and do other such fool's works so that we depart from true faith into a novel and wrong kind of belief. This is what the devil did in ancient times to the people of Israel, when he led them away from the temple at Jerusalem to countless other places. Yet he did it all in the name of God and under the pretense of holiness. All the prophets preached against it, and they were martyred for doing so. But today nobody preaches against it. If somebody were to preach against it all, perhaps bishop, pope, priest, and monk would possibly martyr him, too. St. Antoninus of Florence[185] and certain others must now be made saints and canonized in this way, so that their holiness, which would otherwise have served only for the glory of God and set a good example, may be used to bring fame and money.

Although the canonization of saints may have been a good thing in former days, it is certainly never good practice now. Like many other things that were good in former times, feast days, church holdings, and ornaments now are scandalous and offensive. For it is evident that through the canonization of saints neither God's glory

[185] Antoninus (1389-1459) had been archbishop of his native city of Florence and won renown as reformer of the Dominican Order. At the time Luther wrote the present treatise the procedure for canonizing Antoninus was already underway. Cf. Benrath, *op. cit.*, p. 105, n. 77; cf. also *WA* 6, 449, n. 1.

nor the improvement of Christians is sought, but only money and reputation. One church wants to have the advantage over the other and would not like to see another church enjoy that advantage in common. Spiritual treasures have even been misused to gain temporal goods in these last evil days so that everything, even God himself, has been forced into the service of Avarice. Such advantage only promotes schisms, sects, and pride. A church that has advantages over others looks down on them and exalts itself. Yet all divine treasures are common to all and serve all and ought to further the cause of unity. But the pope likes things as they are. He would not like it if all Christians were equal and one with each other.

It is fitting to say here that all church licenses, bulls, and whatever else the pope sells in that skinning house[186] of his in Rome should be abolished, disregarded, or extended to all. But if he sells or gives special licenses,[187] privileges, indulgences, graces, advantages, and faculties[188] to Wittenberg, Halle, Venice, and above all to his own city of Rome, why does he not give these things to all churches in general? Is it not his duty to do everything in his power for all Christians, freely and for God's sake, even shed his blood for them? Tell me, then, why does he give or sell to one church and not to another? Or must the accursed money make so great a difference in the eyes of His Holiness among Christians, who all have the same baptism, word, faith, Christ, God, and all else? Do the Romanists want us to be so blind to all these things, though we have eyes to see, and be such fools, though we have a perfectly good faculty of reason, that we worship such greed, skullduggery, and pretense? The pope is a shepherd, but only so long as you have money, and no longer. And still the Romanists are not ashamed of this rascality of leading us hither and thither with their bulls. They are concerned only about the accursed money and nothing else!

[186] *Schindleich,* i.e., a place where the carrion of skinned animals is piled.

[187] *Indulta,* i.e., papal dispensations which conveyed advantages otherwise unobtainable through normal channels. Cf. Benrath, *op. cit.,* p. 105, n. 78.

[188] Faculties usually were extraordinary powers to grant indulgences and absolution in reserved cases. They were bestowed by the pope and could be revoked by him at any time. Sometimes they were given to local church officials, but were usually held by the legates or commissioners sent from Rome. Complaints were made at the diets of Worms (1521) and Nürnberg (1523) that the papal commissioners and legates interfered with the normal procedure of ecclesiastical jurisdiction and appointment. Cf. *PE* 2, 138, n. 2.

My advice is this: If such fool's work cannot be abolished, then every decent Christian should open his eyes and not permit himself to be led astray by the Romanist bulls and seals and all their glittering show. Let him stay at home in his own parish church and be content with the best; his baptism, the gospel, his faith, his Christ, and his God, who is the same God everywhere. Let the pope remain a blind leader of the blind. Neither an angel nor a pope can give you as much as God gives you in your parish church. The fact is, the pope leads you away from the gifts of God, which are yours without cost, to his gifts, for which you have to pay. He gives you lead for gold, hide for meat, the string for the purse, wax for honey, words for goods, the letter for the spirit.[189] You see all this before your very eyes, but you refuse to take notice. If you intend to ride to heaven on his wax and parchment, this chariot will soon break down and you will fall into hell, and not in God's name!

Let this be your one sure guide: Whatever you have to buy from the pope is neither good nor from God. For what God gives is not only given without charge, but the whole world is punished and damned for not being willing to receive it as a free gift. I mean the gospel and God's work. We have deserved God's letting us be so led astray because we have despised his holy word and the grace of baptism. It is as St. Paul says, "God shall send a strong delusion upon all those who have not received the truth to their salvation, so that they believe and follow lies and knavery" [II Thess. 2:11]. This serves them right.

21. One of the greatest necessities is the abolition of all begging throughout Christendom. Nobody ought to go begging among Christians. It would even be a very simple matter to make a law to the effect that every city should look after its own poor, if only we had the courage and the intention to do so. No beggar from outside should be allowed into the city whether he might call himself pilgrim or mendicant monk. Every city should support its own poor, and if it was too small, the people in the surrounding villages should also be urged to contribute, since in any case they have to feed so

---

[189] Luther alludes to the exchange of a papal bull for money. Lead was the leaden seal attached to the bull; hide, the parchment on which it was written; the string was the cord from which the seal hung; wax, the seal which held the cord to the parchment. Cf. *PE* 2, 134, n. 1.

many vagabonds and evil rogues who call themselves mendicants. In this way, too, it could be known who was really poor, and who was not.

There would have to be an overseer or warden who knows all the poor and informs the city council or the clergy what they needed. Or some other better arrangement might be made. As I see it, there is no other business in which so much skullduggery and deceit are practiced as in begging, and yet it could all be easily abolished. Moreover, this unrestricted universal begging is harmful to the common people. I have figured out that each of the five or six mendicant orders[190] visits the same place more than six or seven times every year. In addition to these there are the usual beggars, the "ambassador" beggars,[191] and the panhandlers.[192] This adds up to sixty times a year that a town is laid under tribute! This is over and above what the secular authorities demand in the way of taxes and assessments. All this the Romanist See steals in return for its wares and consumes for no purpose. To me it is one of God's greatest miracles that we can still go on existing and find the wherewithal to support ourselves!

To be sure, some think that if these proposals were adopted the poor would not be so well provided for, that fewer great stone houses and monasteries would be built, and fewer so well furnished. I can well believe all this. But none of it is necessary. He who has chosen poverty ought not to be rich. If he wants to be rich, let him put his hand to the plow and seek his fortune from the land. It is enough if the poor are decently cared for so that they do not die of hunger or cold. It is not fitting that one man should live in idleness on another's labor, or be rich and live comfortably at the cost of another's hardship, as it is according to the present perverted

---

[190] Franciscans, Dominicans, Augustinians, Carmelites, and Servites.

[191] I.e., wandering beggars who acted as ambassadors or messengers of a particular saint. Their practice was to enrol their benefactors on the list of beneficiaries of the saint they claimed to represent. This enrolment, they claimed, provided immunity from particular diseases, accidents, and other misfortunes. Protests were raised against this practice at the diets of Worms (1521) and Nürnberg (1523). Included in this protest were the *terminarii*, the collectors of alms sent out by these mendicants. Cf. the extensive note in Benrath, *op. cit.*, p. 105, n. 79; cf. also *WA* 6, 451, n. 1.

[192] I.e., men who spent their lives wandering from one place of pilgrimage to another subsisting on the alms of the faithful. Cf. *PE* 2, 135, n. 3.

custom. St. Paul says, "Whoever will not work shall not eat" [II Thess. 3:10]. God has not decreed that any man shall live off another man's property, save only the clergy who preach and have a parish to care for, and these should, as St. Paul says in I Corinthians 9 [:14], on account of their spiritual labor. And also as Christ says to the apostles, "Every laborer is worthy of his wage" [Luke 10:7].

22. It is also to be feared that the many masses which were endowed in ecclesiastical foundations and monasteries are not only of little use, but arouse the great wrath of God. It would therefore be profitable not to endow any more of these masses, but rather to abolish many that are already endowed. It is obvious that these masses are regarded only as sacrifices and good works, even though they are sacraments just like baptism and penance, which profit only those who receive them and no one else. But now the custom of saying masses for the living and the dead has crept in, and all hopes are built upon them. This is why so many masses are endowed, and why the state of affairs we see around us has developed out of it.

My proposal is perhaps too bold and an unheard-of thing, especially for those who are concerned that they would lose their job and means of livelihood if such masses were discontinued. I must refrain from saying more about it until we arrive again at a proper understanding of what the mass is and what it is for. Unfortunately, for many years now it has been a job, a way to earn a living. Therefore, from now on I will advise a man to become a shepherd or some sort of workman rather than a priest or a monk, unless he knows well in advance what this celebrating of masses is all about.

I am not speaking, however, of the old foundations and cathedrals, which were doubtless established for the sake of the children of the nobility. According to German custom not every one of a nobleman's children can become a landowner or a ruler. It was intended that these children should be looked after in such foundations, and there be free to serve God, to study, to become educated people, and to educate others.[193] I am speaking now of the new

---

[193] Bertram Lee Woolf notes that in this passage Luther touches upon a matter of much importance in the history of social structure, namely, the appointment of

foundations which have been established just for the saying of prayers and masses, and because of their example the older foundations are being burdened with the same sort of praying and mass celebrating so that even these old foundations serve little or no purpose. And it is by the grace of God that they finally hit the bottom, as they deserve. That is to say, they have been reduced to anthem singers, organ wheezers, and reciting decadent, indifferent masses to get and consume the income from the endowments. Pope, bishops, and university scholars ought to be looking into these things and writing about them, and yet it is precisely they who do the most to promote them. Whatever brings in money they let go on and on. The blind lead the blind [Luke 6:39]. This is what greed and canon law accomplish.

It should no longer be permissible for one person to hold more than one canonry or benefice. Each must be content with a modest position so that someone else may also have something. This would do away with the excuses of those who say that they must hold more than one such office to maintain their proper station. A proper station could be interpreted in such broad terms that an entire country would not be enough to maintain it. But greed and a secret lack of trust in God go hand in hand in this matter, so that what is alleged to be the needs of a proper station is nothing but greed and unbelief.

23. The brotherhoods,[194] and for that matter, indulgences, letters of indulgence, butter letters, mass letters, dispensations, and

---

the younger sons of the upper classes to ecclesiastical positions. These younger sons were embittered because appointments to the more substantial benefices were given to papal favorites. Luther's hope was that if these sons were given the opportunity to study the Bible and sound teaching they would infuse an evangelical spirit into priests and hierarchy. Cf. Woolf's *Reformation Writings of Martin Luther* (London: Lutterworth Press), I (1952), 175, n. 1.

[194] The brotherhoods flourished in the sixteenth century. Members of brotherhoods were obligated to recite certain prayers and to attend certain masses at appointed times. Membership in the association meant that each member participated in the benefits accruing from the good works of all the members. In the case of most of the brotherhoods, the membership enjoyed certain indulgences. In 1520 Wittenberg boasted of twenty such fraternities; Cologne, eighty; Hamburg, more than one hundred. In 1519 Degenhard Peffinger of Wittenberg was a member of eight such fraternities in his hometown and of twenty-seven in other places. Luther had expressed his views on these groups more fully in his *The Blessed Sacrament of the Holy and True Body of Christ, and the Brotherhoods* (1519). *LW* 35, 47-73 (*WA* 2, 742-758). Cf. the detailed footnote in Benrath, *op. cit.*, p. 106, n. 80.

everything of that kind, should be snuffed out and brought to an end. There is nothing good about them. If the pope has the authority to grant you a dispensation to eat butter, to absent yourself from mass, and the like, then he ought also to be able to delegate this authority to the priests, from whom he had no right to take it in the first place. I am speaking especially of those brotherhoods in which indulgences, masses, and good works are apportioned. My dear friend, in your baptism you have entered into a brotherhood with Christ, with all the angels, with the saints, and with all Christians on earth. Hold fast to this and live up to its demands, and you have all the brotherhoods you want. Let the others glitter as they will. Compared with the true brotherhood in Christ those brotherhoods are like a penny compared with a gulden. But if there were a brotherhood which raised money to feed the poor or to help the needy, that would be a good idea. It would find its indulgences and its merits in heaven. But today nothing comes of these groups except gluttony and drunkenness.

Above all, we should drive out of German territory the papal legates with their faculties,[195] which they sell to us for large sums of money. This traffic is nothing but skullduggery. For example, for payment of money they make unrighteousness into righteousness, and they dissolve oaths, vows, and agreements, thereby destroying and teaching us to destroy the faith and fealty which have been pledged. They assert that the pope has authority to do this. It is the devil who tells them to say these things. They sell us doctrine so satanic, and take money for it, that they are teaching us sin and leading us to hell.

If there were no other base trickery to prove that the pope is the true Antichrist, this one would be enough to prove it. Hear this, O pope, not of all men the holiest but of all men the most sinful! O that God from heaven would soon destroy your throne and sink it in the abyss of hell! Who has given you authority to exalt yourself above your God, to break and loose his commandments, and teach Christians, especially the German nation, praised throughout history for its nobility, its constancy and fidelity, to be inconstant,

[195] See p. 188, n. 188.

perjurers, traitors, profligates, and faithless? God has commanded us to keep word and faith even with an enemy, but you have taken it upon yourself to loose his commandment and have ordained in your heretical, anti-Christian decretals that you have his power. Thus through your voice and pen the wicked Satan lies as he has never lied before. You force and twist the Scriptures to suit your fancy. O Christ, my Lord, look down; let the day of your judgment break down and destroy this nest of devils at Rome. There sits the man of whom St. Paul said, "He shall exalt himself above you, sit in your church, and set himself up as God, that man of sin, the son of perdition" [II Thess. 2:3-5]. What else is papal power but simply the teaching and increasing of sin and wickedness? Papal power serves only to lead souls into damnation in your name and, to all outward appearances, with your approval!

In ancient times the children of Israel had to keep the oath which they had unwittingly been deceived into giving to their enemies, the Gibeonites [Josh. 9:3-21]. And King Zedekiah was miserably lost along with all his people because he broke his oath to the king of Babylon [II Kings 24:20—25:7]. In our own history, a hundred years ago, that fine king of Hungary and Poland, Ladislaus, was tragically slain by the Turk along with so many of his people because he allowed himself to be led astray by the papal legate and cardinal and broke the good and advantageous treaty and solemn agreement he had made with the Turk.[196] The pious Emperor Sigismund had no more success after the Council of Constance when he allowed those scoundrels to break the oath that had been given to John Huss and Jerome.[197] All the trouble between the Bohemians and ourselves stems from this. Even in our own times—God help us!

[196] Ladislaus III, king of Poland (1424-1444), and, as Uladislaus I, king of Hungary (1440-1444), forced the Sultan to sue for peace in 1443. The papal legate, Cardinal Caesarini, absolved the king from the fulfilment of the treaty's conditions. Ladislaus renewed the war and at the battle of Varna, 1444, the Hungarians were decisively defeated and Ladislaus and Caesarini both killed. Cf. *PE* 2, 139, n. 1.

[197] John Huss had come to Constance under the assurance of safe-conduct granted by Emperor Sigismund. Luther errs when he assumes that Jerome of Prague had a similar safe-conduct. In September, 1415, the council decreed that "neither by natural, divine, nor human law was any promise to be observed to the prejudice of the catholic faith." Both Huss and Jerome of Prague were subsequently executed. Cf. *PE* 2, 140, n. 1.

—how much Christian blood has been shed because of the oath and the alliance which Pope Julius made between Emperor Maximilian and King Louis of France, and afterward broke![198] How could I tell all the trouble the popes have stirred up by their devilish presumption with which they annul oaths and vows made between powerful princes, making a mockery of these things, and taking money for it? I hope that the day of judgment is at hand. Things could not possibly be worse than the state of affairs the Romanist See is promoting. The pope suppresses God's commandment and exalts his own. If he is not the Antichrist, then somebody tell me who is! But more of this another time.

24. It is high time we took up the Bohemian question[199] and dealt seriously and honestly with it. We should come to an understanding with them so that the terrible slander, hatred, and envy on both sides comes to an end. As befits my folly, I shall be the first to submit an opinion on this subject, with due deference to everyone who may understand the case better than I.

First, we must honestly confess the truth and stop justifying ourselves. We must admit to the Bohemians that John Huss and Jerome of Prague were burned at Constance[200] against the papal, Christian, imperial oath and promise of safe-conduct. This happened contrary to God's commandment and gave the Bohemians ample cause for bitterness. And although they should have acted as perfect Christians and suffered this grave injustice and disobedience to God by these people, nevertheless they were not obliged to condone such conduct and acknowledge it as just. To this day they would rather give up life and limb than admit that it is right to break and deal contrarily with an imperial, papal, and Christian oath. So then, although it is the impatience of the Bohemians that is at fault, yet the pope and his crowd are still more to blame for all the misery, error, and the loss of souls which have followed that council.

---

[198] In 1508 Pope Julius II, Louis XII of France, Emperor Maximilian I, and Ferdinand the Catholic of Spain entered into an alliance against Venice. When Venice capitulated to the pope in 1510, he broke the alliance and waged war on France. Cf. *The Cambridge Modern History*, I, 130-131.

[199] Luther refers to the Hussite movement in Bohemia; cf. p. 197, n. 201.

[200] Cf. p. 194, n. 197.

I will not pass judgment here on the articles of John Huss, or defend his errors, although I have not yet found any errors in his writings according to my way of thinking. I firmly believe that those who violated a Christian safe-conduct and a commandment of God with their faithless betrayal gave neither a fair judgment nor an honest condemnation. Without doubt they were possessed more by the evil spirit than by the Holy Spirit. Nobody will doubt that the Holy Spirit does not act contrary to the commandment of God, and nobody is so ignorant as not to know that the violation of good faith and of a promise of safe-conduct is contrary to the commandment of God, even though they had been promised to the devil himself, to say nothing of a mere heretic. It is also quite evident that such a promise was made to John Huss and the Bohemians and was not kept, and that he was burnt at the stake as a result. I do not wish, however, to make John Huss a saint or a martyr, as some of the Bohemians do. But at the same time I do acknowledge that an injustice was done to him, and that his books and doctrines were unjustly condemned. For the judgments of God are secret and terrible, and no one save God alone should undertake to reveal or utter them.

I only want to say this. John Huss may have been as bad a heretic as it is possible to be; nevertheless he was burned unjustly and in violation of the commandment of God. Further, the Bohemians should not be forced to approve of such conduct, or else we shall never achieve any unity. Not obstinacy, but the open admission of the truth must make us one. It is useless to pretend, as was done at the time, that the oath of safe-conduct given to a heretic need not be kept. That is as much as to say that God's commandments need not be kept so that God's commandments may be kept. The devil made the Romanists mad and foolish so that they did not know what they had said and done. God has commanded that a promise of safe-conduct shall be kept. We should keep such a commandment though the whole world collapses. How much more, then, when it is only a question of freeing a heretic! We should overcome heretics with books, not with fire, as the ancient fathers did. If it were wisdom to vanquish heretics with fire, then the public hangmen would be the most learned scholars on earth.

We would no longer need to study books, for he who overcomes another by force would have the right to burn him at the stake.

Second, the emperor and princes should send a few really godly and sensible bishops and scholars over to the Bohemians. On no account should they send a cardinal or a papal legate or an inquisitor, for officials like these are most unversed in Christian things. They do not seek to save souls, but, like all the pope's henchmen, only their own power, profit, and prestige. In fact, these very people were the chief actors in this miserable business at Constance. The men sent into Bohemia should find out from the Bohemians how things stand in regard to their faith, and whether it is possible to unite all their sects.[201] In this case the pope ought to use his authority awhile for the sake of saving souls and, in accordance with the decree of the truly Christian Council of Nicaea,[202] allow the Bohemians to choose an archbishop of Prague from among their number and let him be confirmed by the bishop of Olmütz in Moravia, or the bishop of Gran in Hungary, or the bishop of Gnesen in Poland, or the bishop of Magdeburg in Germany. It will be enough if he is confirmed by one or two of these, as was the custom in the time of St. Cyprian.[203] The pope has no right to oppose such an arrangement, and if he does oppose it, he will be acting like a wolf and a tyrant; no one ought to obey him and his ban should be met with a counterban.

If, however, in deference to the chair of Peter, it was desired to do this with the pope's consent, then let it be done that way, provided it does not cost the Bohemians anything and provided the pope does not put them under the slightest obligation or bind them with his tyrannical oaths and vows as he does all other bishops, contrary to God and right. If he is not satisfied with the honor of having his consent asked, then let them not bother any more about the pope or his vows and his rights, his laws and his tyrannies. Let

201 After the death of Huss a number of movements developed in Bohemia which held in varying degrees to the teachings of Huss. These movements caused considerable political and ecclesiastical turmoil in Bohemia for well over a century after Huss's death. A large number of Hussites looked favorably upon Luther. Cf. *The New Schaff-Herzog Encyclopedia of Religious Knowledge,* IV (1909), 419-420; cf. also II (1908), 213 ff.

202 Cf. p. 137, n. 40.

203 Bishop of Carthage (249-258).

the election suffice, and let the blood of all the souls endangered by this state of affairs cry out against him. No one ought to consent to what is wrong. It is enough to have shown courtesy to tyranny. If it cannot be otherwise, then an election and the approval of the common people can even now be quite as valid as confirmation by a tyrant, though I hope this will not be necessary. Someday some of the Romanists or some of the good bishops and scholars will take notice of the pope's tyranny and repudiate it.

I would also advise against compelling the Bohemians to abolish both kinds in the sacrament[204] since that practice is neither un-Christian nor heretical. If they want to, I would let them go on in the way they have been doing. Yet the new bishop should be careful that no discord arises because of such a practice. He should kindly instruct them that neither practice is wrong,[205] just as it ought not to cause dissension that the clergy differ from the laity in manner of life and dress. By the same token, if they were unwilling to receive Roman canon law, they should not be forced to so do, but rather the prime concern should be that they live sincerely in faith and in accordance with Holy Scripture. For Christian faith and life can well exist without the intolerable laws of the pope. In fact, faith cannot properly exist unless there are fewer of these Romanist laws or unless they are even abolished altogether. In baptism we have become free and have been made subject only to God's word. Why should we become bound by the word of any man? As St. Paul says, "You have become free; do not become a bondservant of men,"[206] that is, of those men who rule by man-made laws.

If I knew that the Pickards[207] held no other error regarding the sacrament of the altar except believing that the bread and wine are present in their true nature, but that the body and blood of Christ

---

[204] The administration of the sacrament in both kinds was one of the chief points of controversy between the Roman church and the Hussites.

[205] Luther had not yet reached the conviction that the administration of the cup to the laity was a necessity, but in 1521 he advocated that a general council should decree that the sacrament be administered in both kinds. Cf. *PE* 2, 144, n. 1, and *Defense and Explanation of All the Articles* in *LW* 32, 55-62.

[206] Cf. I Cor. 7:23; Gal. 5:1.

[207] The term Pickard, a corruption of Beghards, was a derisive name for the Bohemian Brethren, a Hussite sect.

are truly present under them, then I would not condemn them but would let them come under the bishop of Prague. For it is not an article of faith that bread and wine are not present in the sacrament in their own essence and nature, but this is an opinion of St. Thomas[208] and the pope. On the other hand, it is an article of faith that the true natural body and blood of Christ are present in the natural bread and wine. So then, we should tolerate the opinions of both sides until they come to an agreement because there is no danger in believing that the bread is there or that it is not. We have to endure all sorts of practices and ordinances which are not harmful to faith. On the other hand, if they believed otherwise, I would rather think of them as outside,[209] though I would teach them the truth.

Whatever other errors and schisms are discovered in Bohemia should be tolerated until the archbishop has been restored and has gradually brought all the people together again in one common doctrine. They will certainly never be united by force, defiance, or by haste. Patience and gentleness are needed here. Did not even Christ have to tarry with his disciples and bear with their unbelief for a long time until they believed his resurrection? If only the Bohemians had a regular bishop and church administration again, without Romanist tyranny, I am sure that things would soon be better.

The restoration of the temporal goods which formerly belonged to the church should not be too strictly demanded, but since we are Christians and each is bound to help the rest, we have full power to give them these things for the sake of unity and allow them to retain them in the sight of God and before the eyes of the world. For Christ says, "Where two are in agreement with one another on earth, there am I in the midst of them" [Matt. 18:19-20]. Would to God that on both sides we were working toward this unity, extending to each other the hand of brotherhood and humil-

[208] Thomas Aquinas (1225-1274) was then, as now, the foremost Roman Catholic theologian. It was the teaching of Thomas that the bread and wine were transubstantiated into the flesh and blood of Christ. The accidents of the elements, i.e., texture, color, taste, remained, but the substance was changed. Transubstantiation is still official Roman doctrine. Luther's views at this time were developed in *The Babylonian Captivity of the Church* (1520). *LW* 36, 28-35.
[209] I.e., outside of the church.

ity. Love is greater and is more needed than the papacy at Rome, which is without love. Love can exist apart from the papacy.

With this counsel I shall have done what I could. If the pope or his supporters hinder it, they shall have to render an account for having sought their own advantage rather than their neighbor's, contrary to the love of God. The pope ought to give up his papacy and all his possessions and honors, if thereby he could save one soul. But today he would rather let the whole world perish than yield one hairsbreadth of his presumptuous authority. And yet he wants to be the holiest! With that my responsibility comes to an end.

25. The universities, too, need a good, thorough reformation. I must say that, no matter whom it annoys. Everything the papacy has instituted and ordered serves only to increase sin and error. What else are the universities, unless they are utterly changed from what they have been hitherto, than what the book of Maccabees calls *gymnasia epheborum et graecae gloriae*?[210] What are they but places where loose living is practiced, where little is taught of the Holy Scriptures and Christian faith, and where only the blind, heathen teacher Aristotle rules[211] far more than Christ? In this regard my advice would be that Aristotle's *Physics, Metaphysics, Concerning the Soul,* and *Ethics,* which hitherto have been thought to be his best books, should be completely discarded along with all the rest of his books that boast about nature, although nothing can be learned from them either about nature or the Spirit. Moreover, nobody has yet understood him, and many souls have been burdened with fruitless labor and study, at the cost of much precious time. I dare say that any potter has more knowledge of nature

---

[210] I.e., places for the training of youth in the fashions of Greek culture. Cf. II Macc. 4:9.

[211] Scholars other than Luther were and had been against the Aristotelian domination in the medieval universities, e.g., Roger Bacon and Erasmus. In brief, Luther's animadversion sprang mainly from Aristotle's baleful effect on Christian soteriology. Aristotle taught that a man becomes good by doing good, and ultimately led theologians to a belief in man's power to save himself. Luther taught that it was only when a man lost all belief in himself that he ever knew what it was to have faith in Christ. Luther had no objection to heathen philosophy as such and saw its value in the discipline of logical reasoning, but his main objection to Aristotle was that he served to displace Christ who alone could save a man and give him true knowledge of natural and spiritual things.

than is written in these books. It grieves me to the quick that this damned, conceited, rascally heathen has deluded and made fools of so many of the best Christians with his misleading writings. God has sent him as a plague upon us on account of our sins.

Why this wretched fellow in his best book, *Concerning the Soul*, teaches that the soul dies with the body, although many have tried without success to save his reputation. As though we did not have the Holy Scriptures, in which we are fully instructed about all things, things about which Aristotle has not the faintest clue! And yet this dead heathen has conquered, obstructed, and almost succeeded in suppressing the books of the living God. When I think of this miserable business I can only believe that the devil has introduced this study.

For the same reasons his book on ethics is the worst of all books. It flatly opposes divine grace and all Christian virtues, and yet it is considered one of his best works. Away with such books! Keep them away from Christians. No one can accuse me of overstating the case, or of condemning what I do not understand. Dear friend, I know what I am talking about. I know my Aristotle as well as you or the likes of you. I have lectured on him and been lectured on him,[212] and I understand him better than St. Thomas or Duns Scotus[213] did. I can boast about this without pride and if necessary, I can prove it. It makes no difference to me that so many great minds have devoted their labor to him for so many centuries. Such objections do not disturb me as once they did, for it is plain as day that other errors have remained for even more centuries in the world and in the universities.

I would gladly agree to keeping Aristotle's books, *Logic*, *Rhetoric*, and *Poetics*, or at least keeping and using them in an abridged form, as useful in training young people to speak and to preach properly. But the commentaries and notes must be abolished, and as Cicero's *Rhetoric* is read without commentaries and notes, so Aristotle's *Logic* should be read as it is without all these commen-

---

[212] Luther lectured on Aristotle's *Nicomachean Ethics* four times a week during his first year in Wittenberg (1508-1509).

[213] Duns Scotus (d. 1308) was highly regarded in the fifteenth and sixteenth centuries as a rival to Thomas for first place among theologians.

taries. But today nobody learns how to speak or how to preach from it. The whole thing has become nothing but a matter for disputation and a weariness to the flesh.

In addition to all this there are, of course, the Latin, Greek, and Hebrew languages, as well as the mathematical disciplines and history. But all this I commend to the experts. In fact, reform would come of itself if only we gave ourselves seriously to it. Actually a great deal depends on it, for it is here in the universities that the Christian youth and our nobility, with whom the future of Christendom lies, will be educated and trained. Therefore, I believe that there is no work more worthy of pope or emperor than a thorough reform of the universities. And on the other hand, nothing could be more devilish or disastrous than unreformed universities.

I leave the medical men to reform their own faculties; I take the jurists and theologians as my own responsibility. The first thing I would say is that it would be a good thing if canon law were completely blotted out, from the first letter to the last, especially the decretals.[214] More than enough is written in the Bible about how we should behave in all circumstances. The study of canon law only hinders the study of the Holy Scriptures. Moreover, the greater part smacks of nothing but greed and pride. Even if there were much in it that was good, it should still be destroyed, for the pope has the whole canon law imprisoned in the "chamber of his heart,"[215] so that henceforth any study of it is just a waste of time and a farce. These days canon law is not what is written in the books of law, but whatever the pope and his flatterers want. Your cause may be thoroughly established in canon law, but the pope always has his chamber of the heart in the matter, and all law, and with it the whole world, has to be guided by that. Now it is

---

[214] Papal decrees.

[215] *Scrinium pectoris.* In the days of the Roman Empire official papers and documents were stored in a chest called the *scrinium.* This term was carried over into the Middle Ages and designated the chest in which the instruments of a monastery were stored. Boniface VIII (1294-1303), who added his own book to the five books of the decretals of Gregory IX, said with reference to his activity in canon law, "The Roman pontiff has all laws in the chamber [*scrinium*] of his heart." This statement was incorporated within canon law and meant that the pope claimed authority over canon law. Cf. *Decretalium D. Gregorii Papae IX*, lib. vi, tit. II, C. I. *CIC* 2, 937. Cf. *CIC* 2, 929. Cf. also Friedrich Maassen, *Geschichte der Quellen und der Literatur des Canonischen Rechts im Abendlande bis zum Ausgange des Mittelalters,* Vol. I (Leipzig, 1870).

often a villain, and even the devil himself, who rules the *scrinium*—and they proudly boast that it is the Holy Spirit who rules it! Thus they deal with Christ's poor people. They impose many laws upon them but obey none themselves. They compel others to obey these laws, or buy their way out with money.

Since then the pope and his followers have suspended the whole canon law as far as they themselves are concerned, and since they pay it no heed, but give thought only to their own wanton will, we should do as they do and discard these volumes. Why should we waste our time studying them? We could never fathom the arbitrary will of the pope, which is all that canon law has become. Let canon law perish in God's name for it arose in the devil's name. Let there be no more "doctors of decrees"[216] in the world, but only "doctors of the papal chamber of the heart,"[217] that is, popish hypocrites! It is said that there is no better temporal rule anywhere than among the Turks, who have neither spiritual nor temporal law, but only their Koran. But we must admit that there is no more shameful rule than ours with its spiritual[218] and temporal law, which has resulted in nobody living according to common sense, much less according to Holy Scripture any more.

The secular law[219]—God help us—has become a wilderness! Though it is much better, wiser, and more honest than the spiritual law, which has nothing good about it except its name, nevertheless, there is far too much of it. Surely, wise rulers, side by side with Holy Scripture, would be law enough. As St. Paul says in I Corinthians 6 [:5–6], "Is there no one among you who can judge his neighbor's cause, that you must go to law before heathen courts?" It seems just to me that territorial laws and customs should take

[216] *Doctores decretorum.*

[217] *Doctores scrinii papalis.*

[218] I.e., canon law; cf. p. 128, n. 18.

[219] Roman law had been introduced into Germany in the twelfth century and its application became more widespread as rulers sought to establish an effective legal system in the wake of feudal decay. By the end of the fifteenth century the application of Roman law was so widespread that it became the accepted legal system of the empire. But the conditions for which this system had been designed were vastly different than those to which it was applied in the Middle Ages. The result was a continual conflict between Roman law and the feudal customs and remnants of Germanic legal ideas, and a state of confusion which justified Luther's description of the law as "a wilderness." Cf. *PE* 2, 149. n. 2.

precedence over general imperial laws, and that the imperial laws be used only in case of necessity. Would to God that every land were ruled by its own brief laws suitable to its gifts and peculiar character. This is how these lands were ruled before these imperial laws were designed, and as many lands are still ruled without them! Rambling and farfetched laws are only a burden to the people, and they hinder cases more than they help them. But I hope that others have already given more thought and attention to this matter than I am able to do.

Our dear theologians have saved themselves worry and work. They just let the Bible alone and lecture on the sentences.[220] I should have thought that the sentences ought to be the first study for young students of theology, and the Bible left to the doctors. But today it is the other way round. The Bible comes first and is then put aside when the bachelor's degree is received. The sentences come last, and they occupy a doctor as long as he lives. There is such a solemn obligation attached to these sentences that a man who is not a priest may well lecture on the Bible, but the sentences must be lectured on by a man who is a priest. As I see it, a married man may well be a Doctor of the Bible, but under no circumstances could he be a Doctor of the Sentences. How can we prosper when we behave so wrongly and give the Bible, the holy word of God, a back seat? To make things worse, the pope commands in the strongest language that his words are to be studied in the schools and used in the courts, but very little is thought of the gospel. Consequently, the gospel lies neglected in the schools and in the courts. It is pushed aside under the bench and gathers dust so that the scandalous laws of the pope alone may have full sway.

If we bear the name and title of teachers of Holy Scripture, then by this criterion we ought to be compelled to teach the Holy Scripture and nothing else, although we all know that this high and mighty title is much too exalted for a man to take pride in it and let himself be designated a Doctor of Holy Scripture. Yet that title might be permitted if the work justified the name. But now-

---

[220] "Sentences" was the title given to the textbooks on theology. Theological instruction was largely a matter of commentary on the famous book of *Sentences* by Peter Lombard, (*ca.* 1100-1164), renowned medieval theologian and for a short time archbishop of Paris. Cf. *PE* 2, 150, n. 1.

adays, the sentences alone dominate the situation in such a way that we find among the theologians more heathenish and humanistic[221] darkness than we find the holy and certain doctrine of Scripture. What are we to do about it? I know of nothing else to do than to pray humbly to God to give us such real Doctors of Theology as we have in mind. Pope, emperor, and universities may make Doctors of Arts, of Medicine, of Laws, of the Sentences; but be assured that no man can make a Doctor of Holy Scripture except the Holy Spirit from heaven. As Christ says in John 6 [:45], "They must all be taught by God himself." Now the Holy Spirit does not ask for red or brown birettas[222] or other decorations. Nor does he ask whether a person is young or old, lay or cleric, monk or secular, unmarried or married. In fact, in ancient times he actually spoke through an ass against the prophet who was riding it [Num. 22:28]. Would to God that we were worthy to have such doctors given to us, regardless of whether they were lay or cleric, married or single! They now try to force the Holy Spirit into pope, bishops, and doctors, although there is not the slightest sign or indication whatever that he is in them.

The number of books on theology must be reduced and only the best ones published. It is not many books that make men learned, nor even reading. But it is a good book frequently read, no matter how small it is, that makes a man learned in the Scriptures and godly. Indeed, the writings of all the holy fathers should be read only for a time so that through them we may be led into the Scriptures. As it is, however, we only read them these days to avoid going any further and getting into the Bible. We are like men who read the sign posts and never travel the road they indicate. Our dear fathers wanted to lead us to the Scriptures by their writings, but we use their works to get away from the Scriptures. Nevertheless, the Scripture alone is our vineyard in which we must all labor and toil.

Above all, the foremost reading for everybody, both in the uni-

---

[221] The words "heathenish" and "humanistic" are not abusive epithets. The first refers to the dominance of the heathen Aristotle in schools; the second, to the dominance of canon law and other humanly devised doctrines over the gospel.

[222] The biretta is a square cap worn by a teacher. Red or scarlet is the academic color of theology; brown, of the liberal arts.

versities and in the schools, should be Holy Scripture—and for the younger boys, the Gospels. And would to God that every town had a girls' school as well, where the girls would be taught the gospel for an hour every day either in German or in Latin. Schools indeed! Monasteries and nunneries began long ago with that end in view, and it was a praiseworthy and Christian purpose, as we learn from the story of St. Agnes[223] and of other saints. Those were the days of holy virgins and martyrs when all was well with Christendom. But today these monasteries and nunneries have come to nothing but praying and singing. Is it not only right that every Christian man know the entire holy gospel by the age of nine or ten? Does he not derive his name and his life from the gospel? A spinner or a seamstress teaches her daughter her craft in her early years. But today even the great, learned prelates and the very bishops do not know the gospel.

Oh, we handle these poor young people who are committed to us for training and instruction in the wrong way! We shall have to render a solemn account of our neglect to set the word of God before them. Their lot is as described by Jeremiah in Lamentations 2 [:11-12], "My eyes are grown weary with weeping, my bowels are terrified, my heart is poured out upon the ground because of the destruction of the daughter of my people, for the youth and the children perish in all the streets of the entire city. They said to their mothers, 'Where is bread and wine?' as they fainted like wounded men in the streets of the city and gave up the ghost on their mothers' bosom." We do not see this pitiful evil, how today the young people of Christendom languish and perish miserably in our midst for want of the gospel, in which we ought to be giving them constant instruction and training.

Moreover, even if the universities were diligent in Holy Scripture, we need not send everybody there as we do now, where their only concern is numbers and where everybody wants a doctor's degree. We should send only the most highly qualified students who have been well trained in the lower schools. A prince or city council ought to see to this, and permit only the well qualified to be

---

[223] Cf. p. 174, n. 147.

sent. I would advise no one to send his child where the Holy Scriptures are not supreme. Every institution that does not unceasingly pursue the study of God's word becomes corrupt. Because of this we can see what kind of people they become in the universities and what they are like now. Nobody is to blame for this except the pope, the bishops, and the prelates, who are all charged with training young people. The universities only ought to turn out men who are experts in the Holy Scriptures, men who can become bishops and priests, and stand in the front line against heretics, the devil, and all the world. But where do you find that? I greatly fear that the universities, unless they teach the Holy Scriptures diligently and impress them on the young students, are wide gates to hell.

26.[224] I know full well that the pope and his gang will pretend and boast about how the pope took the Holy Roman Empire from the Greek emperor and bestowed it upon the Germans, for which honor and benevolence he is said to have justly deserved and obtained submission, thanks, and all good things from the Germans.[225] For this reason they will, perhaps, undertake to throw all attempts to reform themselves to the four winds, and will not allow us to think about anything but the bestowal of the Roman Empire. For this cause they have persecuted and oppressed many a worthy emperor so wilfully and arrogantly that it is a shame even to mention it. And with the same adroitness they have made themselves overlords of every secular power and authority, contrary to the holy gospel. I must therefore speak of this, too.

There is no doubt that the true Roman Empire, which the writings of the prophets foretold in Numbers 24 [:17-19] and Daniel 2 [:44], has long since been overthrown and come to an end, as Balaam clearly prophesied in Numbers 24 [:24] when he said, "The

[224] This section did not appear in the first edition of the treatise. Luther added it to the second edition. Cf. p. 168, n. 138. Cf. also *WA* 6, 397, and *PE* 2, 59.

[225] Charlemagne, king of the Franks, was crowned Roman emperor by Pope Leo III in the year 800. Although he was a German, he regarded himself as the successor of the emperors who had ruled at Rome, a fiction fostered by the popes. After this first papal coronation, the German kings were called Roman emperors. The popes of the later Middle Ages claimed the right to bestow the imperial dignity, and Pope Clement V (1313) even claimed that in the event of a vacancy upon the throne, the pope was the possessor of the imperial power. Cf. James Bryce, *The Holy Roman Empire* (2nd ed.; New York: Macmillan Co., 1904), pp. 89-131.

Romans shall come and overthrow the Jews, and afterward they also shall be destroyed." That happened under the Goths,[226] but more particularly when the Muslim empire arose almost a thousand years ago. Then eventually Asia and Africa fell away, and in time France and Spain. Finally Venice arose, and nothing was left to Rome of its former power.

Now when the pope could not subdue to his arrogant will the Greeks and the emperor at Constantinople, who was the hereditary Roman emperor, he invented a little device to rob this emperor of his empire and his title and to turn it over to the Germans, who at that time were warlike and of good repute. In so doing, the Romanists brought the power of the Roman Empire under their control so they could parcel it out themselves. And this is just what happened. The empire was taken away from the emperor at Constantinople, and its very name and title given to us Germans. Through this we became servants of the pope. There is now a second Roman Empire, built by the pope upon the Germans. The former Roman Empire, the first one, has long since fallen, as I said earlier.

So, then, the Roman See now gets its own way. It has taken possession of Rome, driven out the German emperor, and bound him by oaths not to dwell at Rome. He is supposed to be Roman emperor, and yet he is not to have possession of Rome; and besides, he is to be dependent on and move within the limits of the good pleasure of the pope and his supporters. We have the title, but they have the land and the city. They have always abused our simplicity to serve their own arrogant and tyrannical designs. They call us crazy Germans for letting them make fools and monkeys of us as they please.

All right! It is a small thing for God to throw empires and principalities about. He is so gentle with them that once in a while he gives a kingdom to a scoundrel and takes one from a good man, sometimes by the treachery of wicked, faithless men, and sometimes by inheritance. This is what we read about the kingdoms of Persia and Greece, and about almost all kingdoms. It says in Daniel 2 [:21] and 4 [:34-35], "He who rules over all things dwells in heaven,

[226] Rome was sacked by the Visigoths in A.D. 410.

and it is he alone who overthrows kingdoms, tosses them to and fro, and establishes them." Since no one, particularly a Christian, can think it a very great thing to have a kingdom given him, we Germans, too, need not lose our heads because a new Roman Empire is bestowed on us. For in God's eyes it is but a trifling gift, one which he often gives to the most unworthy, as it says in Daniel 4 [:35], "All who dwell on earth are as nothing in his eyes, and he has the power in all the kingdoms of men to give them to whom he will."

But although the pope used violence and unjust means to rob the true emperor of his Roman Empire, or of the title of his Roman Empire, and gave it to us Germans, yet it is nevertheless certain that God has used the pope's wickedness to give such an empire to the German nation, and after the fall of the first Roman Empire, to set up another, the one which now exists. And although we had nothing to do with this wickedness of the popes, and although we did not understand their false aims and purposes, nevertheless, we have paid tragically and far too dearly for such an empire with incalculable bloodshed, with the suppression of our liberty, the hazarding and theft of all our possessions, especially of our churches and benefices, and with the suffering of unspeakable deception and insult. We carry the title of empire, but it is the pope who has our wealth, honor, body, life, soul, and all that we possess. This is how they deceive the Germans and cheat us with tricks.[227] What the popes have gladly sought was to be emperors, and when they could not achieve this, they at least succeeded in setting themselves over the emperors.

Since the empire has been given us by the providence of God as well as by the plotting of evil men, without any guilt on our part, I would not advise that we give it up, but rather that we rule it wisely and in the fear of God, as long as it pleases him for us to rule it. For, as has been said already, it does not matter to him where an empire comes from; his will is that it be governed. Though the popes were wrong in taking it from others, we were not wrong in

[227] *Szo sol man die Deutschen teuschen und mit teuschen teuschenn,* an untranslatable pun on the words *Deutschen* ("German") and *teuschenn* ("to deceive").

receiving it. It has been given us through evil men by the will of God: it is the will of God we have regard for rather than the wicked intentions of the popes. Their intention when they gave it to us was to be emperors, indeed, more than emperors, and only to fool and mock us with the title. The king of Babylon also seized his kingdom by robbery and violence. Yet it was God's will that that kingdom be ruled by the holy princes Daniel, Hananiah, Azariah, and Michael.[228] Much more, then, is it God's will that this empire should be ruled by the Christian princes of Germany, no matter whether the pope stole it, got it by force, or established it fresh. It is all God's ordering, which came about before we knew about it.

Therefore, the pope and his followers have no right to boast that they have done the German nation a great favor by giving us the Roman Empire. In the first place, they did not mean it for our good. Rather, they took advantage of our simplicity when they did it in order to strengthen their proud designs against the real Roman emperor at Constantinople. The pope took this empire against God and right, which he had no right to do. In the second place, the pope's intention was not to give us the empire, but to get it for himself that he might bring all our power, our freedom, our wealth, our souls and bodies into subjection to himself, and through us (had God not prevented it) to subdue all the world. He clearly says so himself in his decretals, and has attempted to do so by means of many wicked wiles with a number of the German emperors. Thus have we Germans been taught our German.[229] While we supposed we were going to be masters, we became in fact slaves of the most deceitful tyrants of all time. We have the name, the title, and the insignia of empire, but the pope has its treasures, authority, rights, and liberties. The pope gobbles the kernel while we are left playing with the husk!

Now may God, who, as we have said, tossed this empire into our lap by the wiles of tyrants and has charged us with its rule, help us to live up to the name, title, and insignia, and to retrieve our liberty. Let the Romanists see once and for all what it is that we have received from God through them! If they boast that they have

[228] Dan. 1:6-7; 2:48; 5:29.

[229] I.e., "We Germans have been tricked."

bestowed an empire on us, let them! If that is true, then let the pope give us back Rome and all that he has gotten from the empire; let him free our land from his intolerable taxing and fleecing; let him give us back our liberty, our rights, our honor, our body and soul; and let the empire be what an empire should be, so that the pope's words and pretensions might be fulfilled.

If he will not do that, then what is he playing at with his false and lying words and his juggler's tricks? Has there not been enough of constantly and rudely leading this noble nation by the nose for these many centuries? It does not follow that the pope must be above the emperor because he crowns him or appoints him. The prophet St. Samuel anointed and crowned the kings Saul and David[230] at God's command, and yet he was their subject. The prophet Nathan anointed King Solomon,[231] but he was not set over the king on that account. Similarly, St. Elisha had one of his servants anoint Jehu[232] king of Israel, but they still remained obedient and subject to the king. It has never happened in all the history of the world that he who consecrated or crowned the king was over the king, except in this single instance of the pope.

If the pope lets himself be crowned by three cardinals who are beneath him, he is nonetheless their superior. Why should he then go against his own example, against universal practice, and against the teaching of Scripture by exalting himself above temporal authority or imperial majesty simply because he crowns or consecrates the emperor? It is quite enough that he is the emperor's superior in the things of God, that is, in preaching, teaching, and the administration of the sacraments. In these respects any bishop and any priest is over everybody else, just as St. Ambrose in his see was over the emperor Theodosius,[233] the prophet Nathan over David, and Samuel over Saul. Therefore, let the German emperor be really

[230] Cf. I Sam. 10:1; I Sam. 16:13.

[231] Cf. I Kings 1:39. Luther errs; Zadok the priest did the anointing.

[232] Cf. II Kings 9:6.

[233] The word translated here as "see" (*stuel*) could be taken to mean the confessional stool (*Beichtstuhl*), in which case the passage would mean that Ambrose was superior to Theodosius in the confessional. The general sense would be the same, but there might be a historical allusion to Theodosius' massacre of seven thousand men, for which he was compelled to do public penance. Cf. *WA* 6, 465, n. 1.

and truly emperor. Let neither his authority nor his power be suppressed by such sham pretensions of these papist deceivers as though they were to be excepted from his authority and were themselves to rule in all things.

27.[234] Enough has now been said about the failings of the clergy, though you may find more and will find more if you look in the right place. We shall now devote a section to the failings of the temporal estate.

In the first place, there is a great need for a general law and decree in the German nation against extravagant and costly dress, because of which so many nobles and rich men are impoverished.[235] God has certainly given us, as he has to other countries, enough wool, hair, flax, and everything else necessary for the seemly and honorable dress of every class. We do not need to waste fantastic sums for silk, velvet, golden ornaments, and foreign wares. I believe that even if the pope had not robbed us with his intolerable fleecing, we would still have more than enough of these domestic robbers, the silk and velvet merchants. We see that now everybody wants to be like everybody else, and pride and envy are thereby aroused and increased among us, as we deserve. All this misery and much more besides would be happily left behind if only our desire to be noticed would let us be thankful and satisfied with the good things God has already given us.

It is also necessary to restrict the spice traffic,[236] which is another of the great ships in which money is carried out of German lands. By the grace of God more things to eat and drink grow in our own land than in any other, and they are just as nourishing and good. Perhaps my proposals seem foolish, impractical, and give the impression that I want to ruin the greatest of all trades, that of commerce. But I am doing my best, and if there is no improvement

[234] This section followed immediately after section 25 in the first edition and was numbered 26. Cf. *WA* 6, 465, n. 2.

[235] Such a law was proposed to the Diet of Worms in 1521. Cf. *PE* 2, 158, n. 2.

[236] Spices were one of the chief articles of foreign commerce in the sixteenth century. The discovery of the Cape route to India had given the Portuguese a practical monopoly of this trade. A comparative statement of the cost of spices over a period of years was reported to the Diet of Nürnberg (1523). Cf. *PE* 2, 159, n. 1.

in these matters, then let him who will try his hand at improving them. I do not see that many good customs have ever come to a land through commerce, and in ancient times God made his people Israel dwell away from the sea on this account, and did not let them engage in much commerce.

But the greatest misfortune of the German nation is certainly the *zynskauf*.[237] If that did not exist many a man would have to leave his silks, velvets, golden ornaments, spices, and display of every kind unbought. This traffic has not existed much longer than a hundred years, and it has already brought almost all princes, endowed institutions, cities, nobles, and their heirs to poverty, misery, and ruin. If it goes on for another hundred years, Germany will not have a penny left, and the chances are we shall have to eat one another. The devil invented the practice, and by confirming it[238] the pope has brought woe upon the whole world.

Therefore, I beg and pray at this point that everyone open his eyes and see the ruin of his children and heirs. Ruin is not just at the door, it is already in the house. I pray and beseech emperor, princes, lords, and city councilors to condemn this trade as speedily as possible and prevent it from now on, regardless of whether the pope with all his law—"unlaw" rather—objects or whether benefices or monasteries are based upon it. It is better for a city to have one benefice supported by honest legacies or revenue than to have a hundred benefices supported by *zynskauf*. Indeed, a benefice supported by a *zynskauf* is more grievous and oppressive than twenty supported by legacies. In fact, the *zynskauf* must be a sign and proof that the world has been sold to the devil because of its grievous sins and that at the same time we are losing both temporal and spiritual possessions. And yet we do not even notice it.

In this connection, we must put a bit in the mouth of the Fuggers[239] and similar companies. How is it possible in the lifetime of one man to accumulate such great possessions, worthy of a king,

---

[237] Cf. p. 96, n. 61. Cf. also Benrath's extensive discussion of the significance of this passage in *op. cit.*, p. 109, n. 99.

[238] The *zynskauf* was legalized by the Fifth Lateran Council in 1512. Cf. Benrath, *op. cit.*, 109, n. 99, and *MA*[3] 2, 401.

[239] See p. 155, n. 100.

legally and according to God's will? I don't know. But what I really cannot understand is how a man with one hundred gulden can make a profit of twenty in one year. Nor, for that matter, can I understand how a man with one gulden can make another—and all this not from tilling the soil or raising cattle, where the increase of wealth depends not on human wit but on God's blessing. I leave this to men who understand the ways of the world. As a theologian I have no further reproof to make on this subject except that it has an evil and offending appearance, about which St. Paul says, "Avoid every appearance or show of evil" [I Thess. 5:22]. I know full well that it would be a far more godly thing to increase agriculture and decrease commerce. I also know that those who work on the land and seek their livelihood from it according to the Scriptures do far better. All this was said to us and to everybody else in the story of Adam, "Cursed be the ground when you work it; it shall bear you thistles and thorns, and in the sweat of your face you shall eat your bread" [Gen. 3:17-19]. There is still a lot of land lying unworked and neglected.

Next comes the abuse of eating and drinking,[240] which gives us Germans a bad reputation in foreign lands, as though it were a special vice of ours. Preaching cannot stop it, so deeply is it rooted and so firmly has it got the upper hand. The waste of money would be its least evil, were it not followed by all the vices that accompany it—murder, adultery, stealing, blasphemy, and every other form of immorality. Government can do something to prevent it; otherwise, what Christ says will come to pass, that the last day shall come like a secret snare, when they shall be eating and drinking, marrying and wooing, building and planting, buying and selling.[241] It is so much like what is now going on that I sincerely hope the day of judgment is at hand, although very few people give it any thought.

Finally, is it not lamentable that we Christians tolerate open and common brothels in our midst, when all of us are baptized unto

---

[240] The diets of Augsburg (1500) and Cologne (1512) had passed edicts against drunkenness. The Diet of Worms (1521) adjourned before a recommendation that these earlier edicts be reaffirmed could be acted upon. Cf. *PE* 2, 161, n. 1.

[241] Luther may have had in mind such passages as Luke 21:34, 12:45, and Matt. 24:36-44.

chastity? I know perfectly well what some say to this, that is, that it is not a custom peculiar to one nation, that it would be difficult to put a stop to it, and, moreover, that it is better to keep such a house than that married women, or girls, or others of still more honorable estate should be outraged. Nevertheless, should not the government, which is temporal and also Christian, realize that such evil cannot be prevented by that kind of heathenish practice? If the children of Israel could exist without such an abomination, why cannot Christians do as much? In fact, how do so many cities, country towns, market towns, and villages do without such houses? Why can't large cities do without them as well?

In this matter of brothels, and in other matters previously mentioned, I have tried to point out how many good works the temporal government could do, and what the duty of every government should be, so that everyone may learn what an awful responsibility it is to rule and sit in high places. What use would it be if an overlord were as holy in his own life as St. Peter, if he did not diligently try to help his subjects in these matters? His very authority will condemn him. It is the duty of authorities to seek the best for those they govern. But if the authorities were to give some thought to how young people might be brought together in marriage, the hope of marriage would greatly help every one of them to endure and resist temptation.

But today everybody is attracted to the priesthood or the monastic life, and among them, I am sorry to say, there is not one in a hundred who has any other reason than that he seeks a living and doubts that he will ever be able to support himself and a family. Therefore, they live wildly enough beforehand, and wish, as they say, to get it out of their system, but experience shows that it is only more deeply embedded in them. I find the proverb true, "Despair makes most monks and priests."[242] That is what happens and that is how it is, as we see.

I will, however, sincerely advise that to avoid the many sins which entice so shamelessly, neither youth nor maid should be

---

[242] *Desperatio facit monachum.* Cf. Burton Stevenson (ed.), *The Home Book of Proverbs, Maxims, and Familiar Phrases* (New York: The Macmillan Company, 1948), p. 1619.

bound by the vow of chastity or a vow to adopt the religious life before the age of thirty.[243] Chastity, as St. Paul says, is a special gift [I Cor. 7:7]. Therefore, I would advise those upon whom God has not conferred his special gift not to enter religious orders or take the vows. Furthermore, I say that if you trust God so little that you cannot support yourself as a married man and wish to become a religious only because of this distrust, then I beg you for your own soul's sake not to become a religious at all, but rather a farmer or anything you like. For where a single measure of faith in God is needed to earn your daily bread, there must be ten times that amount of faith to remain a religious. If you do not trust God to support you in temporal things, how will you trust him to support you in spiritual things? Alas, unbelief and distrust spoil everything and lead us into all kinds of misery, as we see in all walks of life.

Much more could be said of this pitiable state of affairs. The young people have nobody to look after them. They all do as they please, and the government is as much use to them as if it never existed. And yet the care of young people ought to be the chief concern of the pope, bishops, the ruling classes, and of the councils. They want to exercise authority far and wide, and yet they help nobody. For just this reason a lord and ruler will be a rare sight in heaven, even though he build a hundred churches for God and raise up all the dead!

That is enough for the moment. [I think I have said enough in my little book *Treatise on Good Works*[244] about what the secular authorities and the nobility ought to do. There is certainly room for improvement in their lives and in their rule, yet the abuses of the temporal power are not to be compared with those of the spiritual power, as I have shown in that book.][245]

I know full well that I have been very outspoken. I have made many suggestions that will be considered impractical. I have at-

---

[243] In the *Discussion of Confession (Confitendi Ratio)* (1520) Luther sets the minimum age for men at eighteen or twenty, and for women at fifteen or sixteen (*WA* 6, 159-169). Cf. *PE* 1, 100. In *The Judgment of Martin Luther on Monastic Vows* (1521) Luther sets the minimum age at sixty. Cf. in this volume, pp. 387-388.

[244] Cf. in this volume, pp. 15-114.

[245] The bracketed sentences did not appear in the first edition.

tacked many things too severely. But how else ought I to do it? I am duty-bound to speak. If I had the power, these are the things I would do. I would rather have the wrath of the world upon me than the wrath of God. The world can do no more to me than take my life. In the past I have made frequent overtures of peace to my enemies, but as I see it, God has compelled me through them to keep on opening my mouth wider and wider and to give them enough to say, bark, shout, and write because they have nothing else to do. Well, I know another little song about Rome and the Romanists.[246] If their ears are itching to hear it, I will sing that one to them, too—and pitch it in the highest key! You understand what I mean, dear Rome.

Moreover, many times have I offered my writings for investigation and hearing, but to no avail. Nevertheless, I know full well that if my cause is just, it must be condemned on earth and be justified only by Christ in heaven, for all the Scriptures show that the cause of Christians and of Christendom must be judged by God alone. Moreover, no cause has ever yet been justified on earth by men because the opposition has always been too great and too strong. It is still my greatest concern and anxiety that my cause may not be condemned, by which I would know for certain that it is not yet pleasing to God.

Therefore, just let them go hard at it, pope, bishop, priest, monk, or scholar. They are just the ones to persecute the truth, as they have always done.

God give us all a Christian mind, and grant to the Christian nobility of the German nation in particular true spiritual courage to do the best they can for the poor church. Amen.

Wittenberg, in the year 1520.

---

[246] This little song is *The Babylonian Captivity of the Church* (1520), written shortly after the present treatise was published. *LW* 36, 3-126.

AN INSTRUCTION TO PENITENTS CONCERNING THE FORBIDDEN BOOKS OF DR. M. LUTHER

1521

Translated by James Atkinson

INTRODUCTION

On June 15, 1520, the papal bull *Exsurge, Domine* was published in Rome against Luther and his books were burned in a public Roman square. This bull gave Luther sixty days to recant or be condemned. It also required all bishops and prelates to seek out and to burn publicly all of his writings. Eck was charged with publishing the bull in Germany, and that it was not well received there was demonstrated by the antagonism exhibited toward Eck and other papal minions by Germans of all classes. When Albert, the archbishop of Mainz, announced that he would condemn Luther's books, such a crowd gathered outside his residence that the prelate fled for his life. In Leipzig Eck was insulted in verse. The Leipzig faculty published the bull only on the orders of Duke George of Saxony, and when it was posted, it was smeared with mud and otherwise defaced.[1] Despite this unwelcome reception and defiance of its publication, the bull was enforced where the hold of the church was strongest: in the privacy of the confessional. Here, acting upon the orders of their superiors, confessors sought to establish whether penitents possessed or had read Luther's writings. If they did possess them, absolution was withheld until the offending books were surrendered.[2]

Many felt that they could not in good conscience disown Luther. At the same time, however, they regarded absolution highly,[3] and were reluctant to be subjected to the spiritual and temporal discipline of the canon law.[4]

---

[1] Cf. Schweibert, *Luther and His Times*, pp. 484 ff.

[2] Cf. *WA* 7, 284, and Woolf, *Reformation Writings of Martin Luther*, II (1956), 91.

[3] Luther himself still regarded it as a sacrament (*WA* 7, 284). Nonetheless, he was not unaware of the shaky ground on which absolution was founded. Cf. in this volume, pp. 134-135.

[4] To be disciplined by the church was a very serious matter. Should the penitent prove recalcitrant, certain bans could be imposed upon him and extended to his family and even to his village, which could mean that no sacraments would be administered and no burial offices conducted. From an economic standpoint it could mean that no one would be allowed to buy from or sell to the offender, and he would be reduced to begging.

After the Leipzig Debate and the papal bull of excommunication Luther was under increasing pressure from his work. He is reported to have kept three printing presses busy.[5] Despite this pressure, and at Spalatin's urging, Luther decided early in February to give what counsel he could to the many who looked to him for guidance. On February 17, 1521, the writing was completed, and ten days later the printer was bringing copies to Worms.

In this book Luther addresses three groups of people. First there are those whose consciences are terrified. For them he writes what almost amounts to a script. He advises them to remind an inquiring priest that the matter of Luther perplexes many great minds, and that it is unlikely that priest and penitent will resolve the issue; therefore, why discuss it? After all, one need only confess what conscience demands, and inquiry of this sort has no place in the confessional. Should the priest threaten with the bull, the penitent should remind the confessor that no one is obliged to follow a vacillating papacy which decrees one thing today and another tomorrow. Finally, if the priest still will not grant absolution, let him keep it; the penitent should regard the priest as a thief who has robbed him of what is rightfully his.

The second group of people whom Luther addresses are those who are firmly convinced of the correctness of his teaching. They have no need of advice, Luther says, yet he ventures to give them some anyway. They are to demand absolution at their own risk and are to obey God rather than man. If the priest will not administer communion to them because they are not absolved, they should demand it with dignity, but be assured that though they be deprived of the sacrament, they cannot be deprived of its grace.

Finally, Luther addresses himself to the clergy. It is God's prerogative, he says, not theirs, to search and inquire into the hearts of men. Therefore it is not right for them to burden the consciences of their people. The priest's duty is to absolve and to minister God's pardon, not to impose conditions and restrictions upon God's grace. The Christian's duty is to obey God rather than man.

The present translation is based on the German text, *Ein Unterricht der Beichtkinder über die verbotenen Bücher*, in WA 7, (284) 290-297.

---

[5] WA 7, 284.

AN INSTRUCTION TO PENITENTS CONCERNING THE FORBIDDEN BOOKS OF DR. M. LUTHER

Jesus

To all Christian men into whose hands this little book comes, I, Martin Luther, wish grace and peace in Jesus Christ our Lord.

It has been brought to my attention that certain father-confessors are not satisfied with having bewildered their poor people by publicly putting them under the ban on account of my books, but even go on to say that these poor people are under the condemnation of God. What is more, these same father-confessors take it upon themselves to pry into the consciences of their penitents, a thing they have no right to do. Actually their proper duty is to pronounce the absolution desired of them. Consequently Christian faithfulness and concern compel me to give counsel and instruction, that in so doing I may discharge my responsibility and leave nothing undone to help another's soul. Should anyone disregard this advice and instruction, let him know that I shall not be responsible for him before God. And with this, I commend you to God. Amen.

1. Since my teaching is from God, and I have never thought it otherwise, one must really consider why it is condemned by the majority, particularly by the prelates and those we call learned. What is happening now is exactly what happened to all the prophets, the apostles, and to Christ himself. As it is written in Daniel 13, "Wickedness comes from the rulers."[1] These men were esteemed as rulers of the people. Therefore I do not give this warning to everyone, for I have no intention of making everyone read my books or of burdening people with their contents. I speak only to those whose consciences tell them my teaching is true, but who are nonetheless disturbed by my many and mighty opponents and are influenced to act against their good though weak consciences.

2. Now if the father-confessor should inquire whether a person

[1] The free quotation is from the apocryphal story of Susanna, verse 5.

has my little books in his possession, or whether he is reading them, thereby offending him in his simpleness, the penitent must answer him quite humbly and say, "My dear sir, I beg you, cease from hounding me into dangerous snares. I have come to confession not to be trapped but to be absolved. Inasmuch as a great many learned and important men are still struggling with this matter and up till now nothing has been finally settled, I and you are much too insignificant to settle the issue here."

3. You can add this, if it proves necessary, "My dear sir, you are a father-confessor, not an officer.[2] I am obliged to confess what my conscience prompts me to confess. It is not your duty to force me to confess; neither is it your duty to probe the secrets of my heart. You might just as well inquire how many pennies I have in my pocket. If I do not tell something I know, then the risk is mine—what business is it of yours? Absolve me as is your duty, and after that argue with Luther, the pope, or whomever you like. Do not make the holy sacrament of confession the occasion for a quarrel, or a disputation, or a source of danger for me. This kind of matter does not belong to the confessional. I will answer these charges at the proper place and time."

4. I also make the same request of the father-confessors and ask them to restrain themselves and not snatch at God's jurisdiction. The secrets of the heart are reserved for him alone, as Psalm 7 [:9] says, "He searches the reins and the heart." They should thank God that they are through with a line of inquiry so fraught with danger and are obliged to do nothing more than to hear confession and pronounce absolution. There is no need to force anyone to disclose the secrets of his heart. As the saying goes, no one shall be compelled to faith; he is only called to it. If anyone does come to faith, it is really because God is moving him through your calling. If God is not moving him, what can you do by forcing him? St. Paul taught this too. He said that for the sake of those with weak consciences we should not pursue our inquiries lest we confuse such people or cause them anxiety.[3]

---

[2] *Stockmeister*; literally, a jailer or police officer. Cf. Luther's German Bible, Luke 12:58.

[3] Cf. I Cor. 8:9-13; Rom. 14:1-4.

5. Where the father-confessor will not grant remission and threatens the penitent with the bull, the penitent shall say this to him, "My dear father, the bull is not esteemed by many pious people, as you know, for the pope's opinion is wont to vacillate. He institutes something or other one day and rescinds it the next. Therefore, I will not be driven by you onto such sandy ground or into such vacillation that today I confess something and tomorrow deny it. I will not let myself be tossed to and fro by every change of wind. I am not obliged to follow you in such vacillation and uncertainty of action. Give me absolution. For me that is something that is certain. Let the other matter first be as certain as that, and then compel me to obey."

6. In those cases where he still will not grant remission I would just let him keep his absolution. I would go away from him as from one who, together with Lucifer, goes beyond his duty and authority and usurps the jurisdiction of God by probing into the secrets of the heart, a thing he has no right to do and something with which he should not concern himself. Where man does not absolve, there God absolves. It is as though somebody asked the priest for baptism and the sacrament of the altar and he did not want to give them. In that case the suppliant's faith and desire are sufficient cause for assurance that he has fully partaken [of the sacraments]. So, although the father-confessor is not willing to grant absolution, absolution is still fortunately quite certainly experienced because the penitent has made his confession and both desires absolution and has sought it. In such a case you must regard the father-confessor as a robber and a thief, who by this action is taking and withholding from us what is ours. We may greatly rejoice that we are absolved in the sight of God and not doubt that we have received the sacrament.

7. Where consciences are brave and strong, however, and understand the truth and dare to confess it, there is no need of my advice. Such people will know how to conduct themselves. Yet, in an excess of zeal, I will still offer my opinion. When this slave driver of the confessional knows for certain that they possess the forbidden books or do not possess them, and will not grant absolution unless they promise never to possess or read such books, the penitent

should say, "Give me absolution at my own risk. I will not leave the books alone, for if I were to do so, I would sin against my conscience. Now you ought not to force me to act against my conscience, as you know yourself, or ought to know, Romans 14 [:1-4]."

8. If he refuses and harps about the bull, then you will have to draw his attention to the words of St. Peter in Acts 5 [:29], "We must obey God rather than men." Even if all the world were to side with the pope and his bull, we still ought not to obey them because they so palpably condemn the gospel and faith. Yes, even if they consign us to the flames and blot us out! Look at the example of Christ. All the world persecuted him, but he was not wrong on that account. In the same way Luther's teaching has not been defeated yet and proved wrong. Up to the present it has only been attacked with violence.

9. If he will not give absolution, let him keep it. Let him give a solemn reckoning on the Day of Judgment for the ministry he neglected and the sacrament of which he deprived men and which was his responsibility to give. Such a penitent must bother himself no further about absolution. On the strength of the confession he has made and the absolution he has sought, the penitent may feel quite free to go to the sacrament. He is most certainly absolved in the sight of God and will have to endure the theft of his absolution with cheerful patience, just as he would have to endure the theft of any of his worldly possessions. They can take the sacrament from us by denying it to us or forbidding us to receive it, but they must leave the unrestricted and undiminished power and grace of the sacrament to us. God did not deliver our salvation and his grace into their arbitrary power, but to our faith. As Christ says, "Only believe that you have received what you ask for, and you have most certainly received it," Mark 11 [:24].

10. If, however, the priest denies you communion on the alleged grounds that you have not received absolution, you shall still quite humbly ask him to give it to you. You must always fight against the devil and all his works with humility, and yet at the same time maintain a bold faith. And if that is no help, then do without the sacrament, the altar, the priest, and the church, because the word

of God, condemned in the bull, is far more than all the rest put together. The soul cannot do without the word of God, but it can do quite well without the sacraments. In this way your true bishop, Christ himself, will feed you spiritually with this very sacrament. Let that not seem strange to you, although you may not go to the sacrament that year. It is not your fault. You want it very much but are prevented from going and are deprived of your rights. The commandment of the church[4] should not trouble you, because they are driving you against the word of God and the dictates of your conscience by this course of action. Nothing may be commanded that is contrary to the word of God and one's conscience. Nor is any such commandment valid. They teach this themselves.

11. Therefore, take care. Let nothing on earth, even if it were an angel from heaven, be so great as to drive you against your conscience and away from the teaching you recognize and regard as God's. St. Paul says in Galatians 1 [:8], "Even if an angel from heaven were to preach any other gospel than we preached, let him be accursed." You are not the first, you are not even the only one, nor will you be the last to be persecuted for the sake of the word of God. Christ says, "Blessed are you when you are persecuted for righteousness' sake" [Matt. 5:10]. Again, "You will be hated by all nations for my sake" [Matt. 24:9]. Again, "The time will come that whosoever persecutes you will think that by this act he is doing God a service." [John 16:2]. We have to take a firm hold of such texts and strengthen ourselves by them. In fact, we ought to praise and thank God for persecution, and pray to prove worthy of suffering for the sake of his word. Remember, it is foretold that in the day of the Antichrist no one will be permitted to preach, and that all who speak and listen to God's word shall be regarded as outcasts. That is what is happening now, and it has been going on for more than a hundred years.[5]

12. However, when they insist that you obey the decrees issued by some of the prelates which prohibit the reading of all kinds of

[4] Canon 21 of the Fourth Lateran Council makes yearly confession mandatory for everyone over the age of "discretion."

[5] No doubt Luther is alluding to John Huss, who was burned at the stake in 1415.

blasphemous books and libelous writings, you should most humbly obey.[6] For he who recognizes the word of God and is a believer will never have any interest in blasphemous books or malicious writings. The emperor's law prescribes that such wicked authors shall lose their heads along with all those who read their works, listen to them, or possess them. Therefore, since no one can read such things in good conscience, I, too, urge everyone to keep away from such books and to avoid them as you would a deadly poison. But no one could accuse my books of that, nor will he be allowed to; and no one can class them with that kind of book either and get away with it. Now this is the definition of a blasphemous book and a malicious libel, as it is clearly defined by imperial law: where any man, mentioned by name, has his reputation stained by evil, and where the writer does not disclose his name because he does not want to conduct himself decently and, fearing the light, prefers to work his wickedness in secret by biting surreptitiously like a poisonous snake, as Solomon says.[7]

Now in my case I have openly subscribed my name to all my books and have freely gone about my work in broad daylight. I have conducted myself as a law-abiding citizen and still do so. And although I have impugned the pope's regime, I have never insulted his person, nor that of any of his prelates or those of lower rank. I have never secretly slandered any person in particular, but have decried open shortcomings, as befits a preacher and as all the prophets have done. If that is what they mean by harmful books, then we shall never again be able to punish anyone for wickedness; and even the gospel and the whole Bible, in which so many and such severe penalties are prescribed for wickedness, would be called wicked. Unfortunately it is true that today there are many blasphemous books going the rounds, without the author's name and title, which are rightly banned and ought to be banned, for they are not only contrary to Christian love, but even contrary to natural law.

13. Finally, I beseech all prelates and father-confessors, as I

[6] Luther probably has in mind the defamatory writings and pamphlets which originated in the sixteenth century. Such a publication was known as a *libellus famosus*. Cf. *The Catholic Encyclopedia,* IX, 210.
[7] In Prov. 23:32.

have said, to refrain from ferreting people's consciences, and in the spirit of the holy gospel not to fall on the people with violence, but to rule them with kindness and gentleness and instruct them. They are not to violate the consciences of their penitents or torture them, for that is the work of the devil. They ought to do this lest the people raise questions and stir up an inquiry as to where their power in this matter comes from and from whence private confession arose. A tumult could arise out of this kind of questioning which would be too grievous for them to bear. For although private confession is one of the most salutary of practices, we know perfectly well[8] that the authority on which it is based is quite shaky. It is therefore essential that such a salutary and holy institution not be undermined by the fury and violence of wicked rulers. Just remember how many things would have remained as they were if the pope had not dealt so wickedly and violently with me, and that they can never regain what they have lost. And with that I shall have admonished everyone, and urged against violence and force. Coercion has its limits. Be careful and act wisely. God give us all his grace. Amen.

[8] Luther uses a colorful figure of speech: *Weisz man doch wol, wye der peltz auff den ermelen stat;* literally, "one knows how the fur lies on the ermine." Cf. Ernst Thiele, *Luthers Sprichwörtersammlung* (Weimar, 1900), No. 301.

A SERMON ON THE THREE KINDS OF GOOD LIFE FOR THE INSTRUCTION OF CONSCIENCES

1521

Translated by James Atkinson

INTRODUCTION

It is not possible to state the exact date or occasion when this discourse was delivered. Scholars are generally agreed, however, that it was preached in the year 1521, in all probability shortly before Luther's appearance at Worms on April 17. The sermon was published in that same year.

The sermon speaks in simple, graphic terms to men and women who were confused by the steady proclamation of justification by faith alone, which was at the heart of Luther's theology. They found it extremely difficult, if not impossible, to disengage themselves from old ideas and ways. They were accustomed to ceremonies, fast days, holy days, and to the kind of good works taught by the church. The people leaned heavily upon these external observances. To cast them off would work havoc, confusion, and even despair. Luther was aware of these people's feelings and it was to them that he addressed himself.

Luther begins with a brief description of the three main parts of the Hebrew tabernacle: the court, the holy place, and the holy of holies. This scheme of construction, he says, corresponds to that of Christian churches, which have a churchyard, a nave, and the sanctuary. In a manner of exposition to which the people were accustomed[1] Luther states that through this scheme of construction the Holy Spirit teaches us that there are three kinds of doctrine, which in turn teach that there are three kinds of conscience and sin as well as three kinds of good life or works. A Christian must not confuse these with each other, but must know how to distinguish among them.

First there is the doctrine of the churchyard. This doctrine is concerned with external things: ceremonies, fastings, the wearing of special garb, and the performance of specifically "religious" works. To dwell upon these matters is to be a "churchyard saint" and subject to constant uncertainty of conscience about whether

[1] Cf. John W. Doberstein's introduction in *LW* 51, xi-xxi, particularly the discussion of Luther's sermon structure, pp. xvi-xviii.

there have been enough observances and whether they have been properly and correctly kept. A churchyard saint, Luther says, is blind to sound doctrine, and his soul is tied to empty externals.

It is necessary to graduate from the churchyard and its religion of works and externals to the nave, and thereby learn of better and sounder doctrine. Here men learn what truly good works, virtue, and conscience are and to distinguish between the grain and the chaff and to put behind them the works and the superficialities of the courtyard. Here men learn that the joyful, willing performance of the really good works, the works God commands, is found in no man's heart; men need God to put them there.

Finally there is the sanctuary, which represents the final stage of evangelical doctrine and Christian life. Here Christ and his promises are held before us. Here we learn to deny ourselves and to call upon Christ in true faith. Here the Holy Spirit comes to the believer, creating and giving the "pure, free, cheerful, glad, and loving heart, a heart which is simply gratuitously righteous, seeking no reward, fearing no punishment."[2]

The present translation is based on the German text, *Sermon von dreierlei gutem Leben, das Gewissen zu unterrichten,* in WA 7, (792) 795-802.

---

[2] Cf. p. 241.

A SERMON ON THE THREE KINDS OF GOOD LIFE FOR THE INSTRUCTION OF CONSCIENCES[1]

1. It should be noted first of all how God Almighty commanded through Moses in the Old Testament that a tabernacle be built and divided into three parts. The first part was the holiest part of all and was called the holy of holies. It was ten cubits in length, breadth, and height and cubical in shape. The next was called the holy place, and that was the same height and width and twenty cubits long. These two parts were joined together in one building made of wooden boards so one could go into one from the other as easily as going from one room into another. The third part was called the atrium, the courtyard, which was one hundred cubits long, fifty wide, and five high, and there was a white curtain, transparent like a net, hanging around the tabernacle. No doubt our churches have developed from this pattern. We divide them into three parts, too: the churchyard, the nave, and the sanctuary. The sanctuary is the holiest, then the nave, and after that the churchyard. The same three parts are to be found in a house. First there is the yard, second the house, and third the study or bedchamber.

2. In this way the Holy Spirit shows that there are three kinds of preaching or teaching which make for three kinds of conscience and three kinds of sin, as well as three kinds of the good life with three kinds of good works. All these differences are helpful, and a Christian needs to know them lest he confuse one with the other and do nothing properly. He must not mistake the sanctuary for the churchyard, nor the churchyard for the nave. To understand these things better we propose to call the holy of holies the sanctuary, the holy place the nave, and the court the churchyard.

3. We start with the churchyard. It is preaching or teaching which is concerned only with outward works which are bound up with time and place. These matters are the ceremonies, the outward performances and techniques in matters of dress or food which

[1] This sermon is based on Exod. 25:9–27:18.

cause severe damage to the conscience if a preacher does not alert his people about them. As a result of this kind of teaching, people become hardened and blind, and in this state you can tell them nothing. Let us give a few examples. Priests, monks, nuns, bishops, and all the clergy[2] wear clothes different from the general run of people. They also do other kinds of jobs, wear sacred vestments in church, pray, sing, and so on. These are all outward works linked to dress and occasion. Now he who does these things holds that such teaching has been established by law and that they are called good works, the good life, the spiritual office. When he has done them he believes that he has most certainly earned a good conscience (for what it is worth) and that he has done the right thing. The opposite is true, too—if he overlooks one of them or neglects to do it, for example, if he does not wear his garb properly or does not observe the hours,[3] he gets a bad conscience, like a man who has not kept the commandments.

4. We act the same way when we observe or break the prescribed commandments, fasts, and feasts, until, through the neglect of the clergy, who are asleep on the job, we reach the point where we make it a more serious matter of conscience for someone to eat a morsel of bread on the eve of a fast than to soak himself in drink, or curse and swear, lie, deceive, or commit adultery or some other serious sin, so inseparably does this kind of teaching bind life and conscience to food and external things. In fact today there are many clergy who would have pangs of conscience ten times worse if they were to celebrate the mass without a maniple or a chasuble or an altar stone[4] or a silver chalice and things like that, than if they had spoken five times in a scurrilous and scandalous fashion or told lies or spoken behind somebody's back, or otherwise injured their neighbor, so inseparably bound up with these external things is their conscience and so far removed from the things that matter. And what layman or man in the street does not endure worse pangs of conscience if he eats eggs or butter or meat on the eve of a saint's

[2] *"Gantz geystlicher stand,"* i.e., "spiritual estate."

[3] The canonical hours.

[4] Luther is referring to the marble tablets carried about by clergy, on which mass was celebrated when no episcopally consecrated altar was available, e.g., on military expeditions. Cf. *WA* 7, 796, n. 1.

day or other fast day than if he had killed or been unchaste by word or deed? Yes, things are in such a state, owing to certain blind teachers, that no layman dare touch the chalice or corporal. A great fuss and matter of conscience is made of it if anybody unwittingly does touch it. It is worse than that! If an ordinary man were incautiously to touch the holy sacrament with his finger, they skin that finger for him. They make such a matter of conscience out of this affair that there is not a command or prohibition that I regard, they have become so ridiculous.

5. Just think it over. Such a view of conscience and such error arise from the fact that people have got everything confused and do not differentiate one thing from another in the right way. Then sound instruction and the capacity to differentiate are gone, and before we know where we are, we have reached the stage where the worst is upheld as the best, and the best as the worst. Then the fear of God goes out, human presumption takes over, and the hardening and blinding of men to their sins goes on apace. This is easy to see everywhere in the world. Is it not true that everybody, spiritual and secular estate alike, is unfaithful, prideful, avaricious, hateful, unchaste, and commits all the sins there are, and that nobody takes the slightest notice of them? They have the audacity to think that they live in the fear of the Lord and do his works, although they do not seek to improve themselves in these particular items. They think that they are in a right relationship with God, and that they are doing quite well so long as they exercise their office, pray the canonical hours, wear their clerical garb, and do the right thing in church.

The laity think the same, that all they have to do is to keep their fasts and feasts. As if our God were bothered in the slightest whether you drink beer or water, whether you eat fish or meat, whether you keep the feasts or fasts! It was of people like this that Christ spoke in Matthew 23 [:23-24], "Woe to you, scribes and Pharisees, hypocrites! for you tithe mint and dill and cummin, and have neglected the weightier matters of the law, justice and mercy and faith; these you ought to have done, without neglecting the others. You blind guides, straining out a gnat and swallowing a camel!"

6. Has our Lord himself not depicted here the foolish, perverted conscience which offends God by making important matters trifles and trifles important? How is it that a man can take such a careful sip of outward works that he even strains out a gnat, and can take such a gulp of the right works that he even swallows a camel? It is because he makes things which matter little if at all into strict matters of conscience, but has a very free and easy conscience in things of great importance on which everything depends. People who do this are all *Atrienses Sancti,* churchyard saints. They are only five cubits high. This means that their holiness is circumscribed by their five senses and their bodily existence. And yet, this very holiness shines brighter in the eyes of the world than does real holiness. That is why many stand in this court, for the churchyard is more than three times the length of the nave and ten times as long as the sanctuary. Further, the fact that there are such vast numbers in the courtyard constitutes a great inducement to follow such erroneous, perverted ideas of conscience, works, and life. Indeed, the office of the preacher and pastor is a very serious matter, for the clergy will have to render a solemn account of their failure here if they are not vigilant and active now, and are not striving against such a state of affairs and giving their people true instruction in these matters. But there is another side to it. If they resolve to do this, they will have to suffer persecution from the pope, the bishops, and the prelates. For that gang is itself in such a "churchyardish" state of spiritual life, utterly drowned in grave sin, that they will not let anyone teach anything different. They want to strain gnats and swallow camels.

7. Anybody can see for himself that such a "churchyardish" external system betters nobody, and that all the performances bound up with food and clothes, occasion and place, make nobody righteous. For everybody can see that such people continue to be unfaithful, avaricious, impatient, proud, unchaste, angry, and envious. In fact, nobody is more deeply involved in those sins than these very people who have equated righteousness with matters of food, clothing, and observances of time and place. We can see this all around us. Is it not time we called a halt and thought things over? This cannot be the right road to becoming righteous. There

must be another way somewhere. And because these people take such a light view of transgressing in very serious matters, we ought to be wise enough to despise the transgressions of their external pomposities in which we see so much that is corrupt. We must get into the habit of looking in the right direction.

Imagine you were to meet a slanderer or a vulgar gossip, and then you were to meet another man who happened not to have kept the fast or feast or who had eaten nonprescribed foods. Would you not be ten times more shocked by the first man than by the second? Would you not regard the second man as one who had swallowed a gnat, and the first a camel? It is grievous and aggravating that the pope is so concerned about eating butter and eggs that people have to buy letters[5] from him, and yet at the same time he is not bothered about whether a man sins against God. The bishops and the prelates follow suit in this, and aid and abet him. If they themselves confuse these matters and get them upside-down, strain gnats and swallow camels, how shall the poor people extricate themselves? How indeed, when their rulers and teachers fight against them in this by their doctrine, example, and authority?

8. Let us now leave the atrium or churchyard and proceed into the holy place, the nave. This means teaching, works, and concepts of conscience which are really good. These are humility, meekness, gentleness, peace, fidelity, love, propriety, purity, and the like. These are not bound up with food and clothing, or with place, time, or person. For in these matters a layman may do more of value than a priest, a priest more than a pope, a woman more than a man, a boy more than an adult, a poor man more than a rich man, a naked man more than a man richly clad; more of value may be done in the field than in the home, more in the secret chamber than in the church. This is what God looks for. He who takes this course is traveling on the right road to heaven, apart from what he does or leaves undone in the atrium, for God does not ask him about what happened there, so long as he journeys rightly in this holy place. On the other hand, it is in the nave that we ought to make it a matter of conscience if anybody blasphemes, swears, or speaks uncleanly, or if anybody hears, sees, does, or thinks anything improper.

[5] Cf. p. 155, n. 102.

That constitutes the true conscience. It is here that a man strains camels and swallows gnats. It is here that a man gathers up the corn and casts away the chaff. It is here that Abel sacrifices a lamb and lets Cain sacrifice his straw. It is here that a man must fight against pride, avarice, immodesty, anger, hatred, and the like. Here must we keep ourselves fully occupied as long as we live, so as to forget the churchyard altogether and not want it. Here we see what is the proper road to piety and holiness, for we see for ourselves that those who practice this become truly righteous, but those who practice "churchyard" piety do not. That proves that this way and not the other must be the right way.

9. Some do these works in a living and selfless way. Others, however, set about them in the wrong way. They drag their dead works in with them on their backs and bury them. These are the ones who maintain a pious posture not of their own desire, but because they fear disgrace, punishment, or hell. For many a man is chaste. But if there were no shame or punishment attached to unchastity, then they would go in for it just like those who pay no regard to shame or punishment. In a similar way, many a man controls his anger or temper not gladly or because he loves gentleness, but because he could not very well vent his anger and does not like to confess it. Many a man even gives to the church and endows services, not from generosity but for the sake of glory or to satisfy his vanity. And this false ground is so deep that no saint has ever fathomed its bottom, but shows uncertainty about it and says, "Lord God, create in me a clean heart, and renew a right spirit or will in my inmost being" [Ps. 51:10]. Or again in Psalm 19 [:12], "Lord, who can know all his faults? Cleanse me from secret sins." God does not just want such works by themselves. He wants them to be performed gladly and willingly. And when there is no joy in doing them and the right will and motive are absent, then they are dead in God's eyes. Such work is riddled with errors; it is service under compulsion, necessity, and duress and is not pleasing to God. As St. Paul says, "God loves a cheerful giver" [II Cor. 9:7].

10. Such gladness, love, joy, and willingness are not found in the heart of any man on earth. As far as our nature goes, we are

all sinners. We do not really want to be righteous; we only pretend because we are afraid of being punished or disgraced, or because we seek our own ends and pleasure in these works. And no one is righteous solely and alone for God's sake, the way it ought to be. The natural man wants to and has to seek something whereby he may be righteous: he is not able and has no desire to be righteous for righteousness' sake. He does not allow himself to be content with righteousness, as he ought to do, but is determined by means of it either to earn something or escape something. But that is wrong in God's sight. As St. Paul concludes in Romans 3 [:10], quoting Psalm 14 [:1], "Therefore no man is righteous in God's sight." We ought not be good to earn something or avoid something, for that is to behave no better than a hireling, a bondsman, a journeyman, and not as willing children and heirs who are righteous for the sake of righteousness itself. Children and heirs are righteous only for righteousness' sake, that is, for God's own sake alone, for God himself is righteousness, truth, goodness, wisdom, holiness. He who seeks nothing other than holiness is the one who seeks God himself, and he will find him. He who seeks reward, however, and avoids pain, never finds him at all and makes reward his God. Whatever it is that makes a man do something, that motive is his god.

11. For these reasons a man has to go down on his knees for grace and deny himself. To this end, then, God has built the sanctuary and *Sanctum sanctorum*[6] for us. Here he has set Christ before us and promised that he who believes in him and calls on his name shall at once receive the Holy Spirit. As he says in John 16, "The Father will send the Holy Spirit in my name."[7] A man who denies himself and calls upon Christ in genuine trust is certain to receive the Holy Spirit. Where Christ's name is, there the Holy Spirit follows. He who calls on Christ in faith, however, possesses his name, and the Holy Spirit most certainly comes to him. When the Spirit comes, however, look, he makes a pure, free, cheerful, glad, and loving heart, a heart which is simply gratuitously righteous, seeking no reward, fearing no punishment. Such a heart is holy for

[6] Holy of holies.

[7] A conflation of John 16:7 and 26.

the sake of holiness and righteousness alone and does everything with joy. Look! Here is really sound doctrine! This shows what a conscience is and what good works are! It is to go into the *Sanctum sanctorum,* to pass into the sanctuary. That is the last thing on earth that any man can do. This is the road to heaven. No man remains wicked; on the contrary, all become righteous. This road is quite the opposite of the atrium, for it has no regard for the external things of the churchyard. Indeed, one sees only what enemies of this road they are and how dangerous they are.

12. Christ referred to this when he said in Mark [16:16], "He that believes shall be saved." Faith alone saves. Why? Faith brings with it the Spirit, and he performs every good work with joy and love. In this way the Spirit fulfils God's commandments, and brings a man his salvation, all of which is signified by the sanctuary and the nave (the *Sanctum* and the *Sanctum sanctorum*) being built in one and the same structure. But the atrium, the churchyard that lies apart, is to show that good works without faith cannot happen, and that faith without works cannot endure. A preacher should not try to separate the two, although he should push faith to the fore. Further, faith and good works may well exist without the continuance of those external things, such as sacred foods, sacred garments, sacred times, sacred places. It is for this reason that it is written in the Apocalypse that in the new dispensation the court would be handed over to the heathen [Rev. 11:2], because in the new covenant external matters of this kind should rest with the free and unfettered choice of each individual. Consequently, only the nave and the sanctuary would really be used.

Tragically has it come to pass that there has never been a people on the face of the earth that has had a bigger atrium, more holy foods, more holy garments, more holy days, more holy places, than Christians now have! It is the fault of the pope and of his canon law, in which so many worthless, dangerous, and aggravating regulations are laid down to the unspeakable detriment and obscuring of faith and good works. May God redeem us from them and protect us with his grace. Amen.

THE JUDGMENT OF MARTIN LUTHER ON MONASTIC VOWS

1521

Translated by James Atkinson

INTRODUCTION

Although Luther had touched upon monastic life and clerical celibacy in *To the Christian Nobility,*[1] he did not pursue the theme to any extent, probably because a compelling occasion for dealing with these matters simply had not presented itself. During his stay at the Wartburg, however, a situation developed in Wittenberg which forced Luther to think through the whole problem of vows and monasticism. The marriage of three priests in the dioceses of Magdeburg and Meissen touched off a lively debate on the subject of clerical celibacy. Karlstadt quickly published a number of theses and a book[2] in which he proposed that all priests should be married. As he interpreted I Tim. 5:9, no one under the age of sixty should be permitted to enter the monastic life, and those monks and nuns under the age of sixty should be permitted to marry. In these works Karlstadt admitted that it was a sin to revoke one's vows, but at the same time he held that to do so was less sinful than to engage in secret impurity.[3] He called for an academic discussion of the subject.

In the meantime Wittenberg became directly involved in the case of the married priests, one of whom was Bartholomew Bernhardi, a priest at a village not far from Wittenberg, who had been a student of Luther.[4] Bernhardi's ecclesiastical superior[5] demanded that Elector Frederick surrender the offending priest. The elector refused to surrender the priest and instead referred the case to a commission of jurists for study. To this commission Melanchthon

---

[1] Cf. in this volume, pp. 177-179.

[2] *On Celibacy (Super Coeliba).*

[3] Cf. *WA* 6, 315; cf. also Hermann Barge, *Andreas Bodenstein von Karlstadt* (Leipzig, 1905), I, 264 ff.

[4] The other two priests were Jacob Seidler of Glasshütte in Meissen, and an unidentified priest from Mansfeld. Seidler, a subject of Duke George of Saxony, a bitter foe of the Reformation, was imprisoned and later executed. The fate of the Mansfeld priest is unknown. Cf. Lea, *History of Sacerdotal Celibacy in the Christian Church,* p. 42; cf. also Clyde Leonard Manschreck, *Melanchthon: The Quiet Reformer* (New York, Abingdon Press, 1958), p. 72.

[5] Albert, archbishop of Mainz, was also archbishop of Magdeburg, Cf. p. 147, n. 68.

submitted a defense brief[6] which argued the propriety of Bernhardi's action on the ground that both Scripture and the tradition of the early church warranted clerical marriage. Melanchthon argued further that because of the frailty of the flesh, Bernhardi could not keep the vow of celibacy, and that even canon law made exceptions in such cases.

Although Luther was removed from the immediate scene, he was kept informed of what was going on. In letters to Melanchthon he expressed the opinion that priestly celibacy was of human, not divine, institution, and was not binding upon Christians. On the basis of I Tim. 4:3 Luther said that he would allow priests to exercise their freedom.[7] Although Luther professed substantial agreement with Karlstadt's views, he was uneasy over the scriptural evidence mustered by Karlstadt and over his exegesis.[8] At the same time Luther was skeptical about Melanchthon's argument based on the frailty of the flesh. As Luther saw it, such a position could lead to the nullification of God's law.[9]

Luther soon abandoned the stance of an observer and entered the discussion with his *Theses on Vows,* addressed to "the bishops and deacons of the church at Wittenberg."[10] Arguing from the basic premise of justification by faith, he held that vows which contradict this Christian fundamental are impious and not binding. Although he did not condemn the monastic life as such, he did state that it could lead to a perversion of the gospel, and that as monasticism was then practiced it was almost universally pernicious. These theses, together with a second set which soon followed,[11] were published early in October, 1521, and are the foundation of the treatise presented here.

In a letter to Spalatin dated November 11, 1521, Luther gave notice of a forthcoming work on monastic vows. In another letter to

---

[6] This defense was published in German under the title, *Das die Preester Eeweyber nemen mögen und sollen.* The Latin text of the documents and letters connected with this case is given in *C. R.* 1, 421-440. Melanchthon's defense, along with a letter signed by him, Agricola, and Karlstadt, probably saved Bernhardi's life. Cf. Manschreck, *op. cit.,* p. 72.

[7] Cf. *LW* 48, 277-279.

[8] Cf. *LW* 48, 293.

[9] Cf. *LW* 48, 297-304.

[10] *Themata de Votis* (1521). *WA* 8, 323-329.

[11] *WA* 8, 330-335.

Spalatin, which accompanied the manuscript of the preface, Luther explained the more immediate circumstances which motivated him to write the book. He explained that word had come to him that a number of monks had already laid aside the cowl and were leaving their monasteries.[12] Luther did not object to their action, but he was concerned that those who left should act with the certainty of a good conscience, which he greatly feared was not the case. Because of his concern for such monks he decided to deal with the problem in a book. Thus *The Judgment of Martin Luther on Monastic Vows* was intended not as a polemical work, but as a guide to those who had already left or were thinking of leaving their monasteries and convents.[13]

On a secret visit to Wittenberg early in December, 1521, Luther was disturbed to learn that Spalatin (presumably at the command of the elector) had withheld several manuscripts, including this one,[14] from the press. He made it very clear to Spalatin that if these manuscripts were not published in Wittenberg, they would be published elsewhere and in even stronger language. Spalatin yielded, and the book came off the press in February, 1522. By the following month it had reached Basel, where Pellican[15] commented favorably upon it and where Leo Jud[16] translated it from Latin into German. Shortly after June 13, 1522, Luther revised the work and a second edition went to press in Wittenberg. From this second edition Justus Jonas[17] prepared a German translation, which was published in the same year.

Luther's preface to the work is a letter to his father,[18] who had

---

[12] *LW* 48, 337-338. Luther's own monastery in Wittenberg was among those affected. When he returned there in the spring of 1522, Prior Helt was the only monk who had remained.

[13] *LW* 48, 328.

[14] *LW* 48, 350-352.

[15] Konrad Pellican (1478-1556), priest, monk, and Hebrew scholar, was a close associate of Zwingli. He was well known as an exegete and translator.

[16] Leo Jud (1482-1542) was to Zwingli what Melanchthon was to Luther. He is renowned chiefly for his part in producing the Zurich translation of the Bible into German and for his translation of the Old Testament into Latin.

[17] Justus Jonas (1493-1555) was a devoted admirer of Erasmus. He accompanied Luther to Worms and the following year he was appointed to the Wittenberg faculty. In that capacity he became actively involved in the Reformation. His chief literary activity was translating the writings of Luther and Melanchthon into Latin and German.

[18] The text of the letter is given in *LW* 48, 330-336.

been unhappy about Martin's entering monastic life. In this preface Luther confesses that by taking vows he had sinned against God's commandment to honor his parents, but that now, sixteen years later, he realizes that his monastic vows were "not worth a fig."[19] The Lord himself has delivered him from the bondage of those vows. Now he is a monk, but not a monk; the cowl belongs to him, not he to the cowl.[20] And now it is Luther's hope that through him God will free the many sons torn from their fathers by false faith.

In a very brief introduction, which followed this letter, Luther invokes divine blessing and states his position. He does not deny that there is scriptural warrant for the making and keeping of vows. Indeed, making and keeping vows is not the issue at stake. The issue is what vows are truly vows, and how may we distinguish between true and false vows?

Luther treats the problem under five major headings. First, monastic vows are not commanded by God's word, but are contrary to it. To go beyond what Christ commands and enjoins is not faith, but sin. Those things a monk vows are not peculiar to the monastic life, but are required of all Christians. True Christian obedience is that which makes a man humble and unites him to his neighbor. True poverty is to seek not one's own, but to employ what one has for the welfare of one's neighbor. Monasticism's understanding of these vows is superficial and external, and does not proceed from faith.

In the second section Luther develops the thesis that monastic vows conflict with faith. The very taking of perpetual vows as a necessity of salvation is a denial of Christ and is the embracing of work-righteousness. On this basis Luther does not hesitate to declare that monastic vows are null and void.

The third section stresses that the compulsory and perpetual nature of monastic vows is a violation of Christian freedom. He does not advocate the abolition of the monastic life, but says it must be a life led voluntarily and with a conscience freed from reliance upon and trust in works. The cloistered life and all that belongs to

[19] *LW* 48, 332.
[20] *LW* 48, 335.

it must be chosen just as freely as other men choose to be farmers or mechanics, and it must be clearly recognized that the monastic life is in no way superior to a non-monastic way of life. Above all, the monastic life should be like other ways of life in that it is devoted to the welfare of neighbor and contemplation of the word of God. The only difference between the "religious" life and the "secular" life is the form, not the content.

In section four Luther argues that monastic vows violate the first commandment in a number of ways. They displace faith with works; they elevate the founders of religious orders above Christ himself; and they not only deny the Christian's responsibility and obligation to his neighbor, they actually impede it. They prevent the son from caring for his parents and exonerate those who have taken vows from all those works of mercy and love which Christ has enjoined upon all.

Finally, Luther holds that monastic vows are contrary to common sense and reason. He demonstrates clearly and at length that where for some reason it is impossible to keep a vow (e.g., because of sickness, imprisonment, the lack of financial means), dispensations can be granted. But there is no dispensation in the matter of celibacy. This one monastic vow does more than anything else to torture body and soul.

In the final passages Luther expounds the nature of poverty, chastity, and obedience as faith understands them. The Appendix is an exposition of I Timothy 5, which Luther says is the last weapon his opponents might use against him on the matter of monastic vows. Here he advocates that no one should be permitted to enter the monastic life before the age of sixty.

The present translation is based on the Latin text, *De votis monasticis Martini Lutheri iudicium,* in *WA* 8, (564) 573-669, with comparison to the text of *CL* 2, 188-298.

THE JUDGMENT OF MARTIN LUTHER ON MONASTIC VOWS

Jesus

At the very outset I want to declare that those who have an inveterate hatred of my name and condemn even truth itself if it is associated with me, will find nothing for themselves in this book. I do not wish to charm with my incantation those deaf adders that have stopped up their ears [Ps. 58:4], and waste my breath against them, or, like Solomon, to pour forth words which no one hears [Ecclus. 32:4]. I neither want to give that which is holy to the dogs, nor to cast pearls before swine [Matt. 7:6]. Let such people read the decretals of him[1] who created them and the books of their own wisdom any time they want. I serve only those who burn in the iron furnace of Egypt and the fierce fires of Babylon.[2] This means people tortured under the tyranny of conscience and sin. We shall deal with the subject of monastic vows because we see them multiplied and spread abroad to the utter ruination of Christendom and the wholesale destruction of souls.

God be merciful unto us and bless us and cause his countenance to shine upon us, that we may know his way on earth, his saving health among all nations, that the people may confess him, and the heathen rejoice and be glad, for he has righteously freed them from the traditions of men, and judges them in equity and governs the nations on earth. Amen [Ps. 67:1-4].

The Question Is Not Whether a Vow Ought to Be Kept, But What Vows Are True Vows

[1] The pope.

[2] Cf. Deut. 4:20 and Dan. 3:6.

No one can deny that the command to offer vows was instituted by divine authority. Scripture says, "Make your vows and keep them" [Ps. 76:11], so there is no point is disputing whether a vow may be offered. Nor do we dispute whether a vow ought to be offered. What we are trying to show is how to distinguish one vow from another and recognize which vows are godly, good, and pleasing to God. Only these must be considered as vows. They are named and demanded in Scripture. Further, we are trying to show how we may distinguish which vows are ungodly, evil, and displeasing to God, vows which would not otherwise be regarded as vows; for example, if a man were to vow to kill his neighbor or commit adultery and call that godliness. In such a case there is no need to discuss whether vows of this kind are to be kept or broken. Nothing has ever been instituted—no matter how godly and holy it was—that has not been perverted by distorted zeal and godless hypocrisy. In fact, the holier a thing is the more it is assailed by the perverted copying of blasphemous hypocrites. What is more holy than the worship of God, the highest and the first commandment? And yet, what is more widespread than superstition, that is, false, feigned worship? It must be feared that by this very perversity even the godliness of vows may degenerate into godless hypocrisy and superstition. True godliness and a sincere vow is no everyday occurrence, especially these days, these dangerous, godless, and desperate times, when it was foretold faith and love shall perish.[8]

I

Vows Do Not Rest on the Word of God: They Run Counter to the Word of God

There is no doubt that the monastic vow is in itself a most dangerous thing because it is without the authority and example of Scripture. Neither the early church nor the New Testament knows anything at all of the taking of this kind of vow, much less do they approve of a lifelong vow of very rare and remarkable chastity. It is purely a most pernicious invention of men no different

[8] Cf. Matt. 24:12 and Luke 18:8.

from all the other inventions of men. St. Paul, having made a vow, purified himself along with four other men [Acts 21:23-26]. Who cannot see that it was a vow left over from the old law? For the moment I shall pass over the fact that it was only a temporal vow, for this very apostle was in the habit of observing all the other parts of the old law along with his fellow Jews, but he had no intention of setting a pattern for the New Testament. As we all know, he did not observe the law in the company of Gentiles.

St. Anthony,[4] the very father of monks and the founder of the monastic life, most wisely and in a Christian manner believed and taught that absolutely nothing should be observed which did not have the authority of Scripture.[5] He knew absolutely nothing about monastic vows and ceremonial of this kind, but willingly chose to live as a hermit, and of his own will chose to live unmarried, after the pattern of the gospel. Pursuing human wisdom, his successors have made this way of life into a vow, into a matter of obligation and compulsion. This way of life is but a specious copy and a mistaken observance of the rule of Anthony, which is the rule of Christ.

The same may be said of St. Paul, too. When he speaks, as he so often does, of the form and tradition given to the churches through his ministry, and demands that they follow him, he does not want them to follow him, but Christ in him. As he says, "Be imitators of me, as I am of Christ" [I Cor. 11:1]. Certainly no other master has been given us than he in whom the wondrous glory of the father was testified to with these words, "Hear him" [Matt. 17:5]. By these words Christ was made the master of us all, and all are subject to him and set beneath him, just as Micah 5 [:2] had prophesied earlier when he said that the prince who was to rule the people of God would come out of Bethlehem. Therefore, he bears witness himself with his father and says, "He who follows me does not walk in darkness," and again, "I am the light of the world" [John 8:12]. And it is he who stands as an ensign of the people which God set up to gather together the scattered outcasts of Israel [Isa. 11:12]. Again in John 6 [14:6; 10:7], "No one comes

[4] Anthony was born around the middle of the third century. He is said to have renounced his inheritance and taken up the ascetic life out of a desire to imitate the apostles.

[5] *Vita Antonii. MPL* 73, 135.

to the Father except through me. I am the door. I am the way, the truth, and the life."

These and similar pronouncements of Scripture are clearer than the light of day and utterly reliable. The Scriptures clearly compel us to condemn whatever is only a matter of rules, statutes, orders, schools of thought, and, in addition, whatever falls short of, is contrary to, or goes beyond Christ, even if these things had been handed over by angels from heaven or confirmed by mighty miracles. He who said, "I am the way," will not allow another way to be chosen. By these words he has rescinded all other ways, past, present, and future. He has made them null and void. He who said, "Hear him," does not permit another leader or master to arise, whether he tries to offer anything better or even worse. Any law or tradition apart from Christ is condemned by these words. Christ says the same thing in John 10 [:8], "All who ever came before me were thieves and robbers."

These examples clearly show that one is not at liberty to take monastic vows. All vows of this sort have their very basis knocked from under them by this thunderbolt from heaven; they are both prohibited and condemned. No one can deny that in monasticism many things, indeed, all things and only those things are vowed which are far removed from Christ and have nothing to do with Christ (that is, they are without the Way, without the Light, without the Truth, without Life, without God). Proudly, without shame, they confess that they are people who go further than Christ and live a loftier and more perfect life! What inconceivable blindness!

Therefore, to begin with, let this principle be laid down: Whatever is commanded which is contrary to or beyond Christ[6] is condemned, whether a man takes it upon himself or whether he is following the example and teaching of the saints. This is but a human course, long forbidden by divine authority. Moreover, a man is not at liberty to take vows or set himself under oath or a compulsory rule of life. And, if a man has taken the vows already, he must neither fulfil them nor keep them, but must be released and set free. For this rock stands unassailed: "I am the way," and there is none other. Any other way is wrong, slippery, and dark.

[6] *Ultra et praeter Christum.*

But even St. Francis, a most admirable man of fervent spirit, wisely said that his rule was the gospel of Jesus Christ.[7] But the gospel holds chastity to be a matter of free choice, not one of the things these little brothers now observe, unbelievable hypocrites that they are. When Francis wanted his brethren to live according to the gospel he clearly wanted them to be as free from vows as from all human traditions. He wanted those little brothers to have the choice of living as celibates or as noncelibates on the strength of their vow and rule, and of remaining in monasteries and under their own regulations as long as they wanted. Those who vowed the gospel vowed nothing other than this and could vow nothing else. But now there is no one more superstitious and overscrupulous than this class of men, who ought to be freest of all men; they are held captive by countless statutes, regulations of one kind or another, and by childish, ridiculous customs.

For all that, this saintly man was deceived either by the great number of those in the world who despise the gospel, or by the misguided effort of procuring the support and approval of the pope. Consequently, he made the universal gospel intended for all the faithful into a special rule for the few. What Christ wanted to be universal and catholic, Francis made schismatic. When a Franciscan takes his vow he vows nothing more than that which he already vowed at the start in his baptism, and that is the gospel. It could be that the error of Francis was rather that he believed there were many counsels in the gospel, as the ungodly papist schools profess, and that he translated these counsels into commands through his rule. I will say later on why I do not entrust myself to such a man.

If, therefore, you were to ask a Franciscan why he lives as a celibate and why he will not handle money, although he professes the gospel, although Christ commanded that celibacy be a matter of free choice, and although Christ handled money (at any rate as far as to discuss Caesar's coinage), he will only reply that he discerns human wisdom. In the rule of Francis, this regulation was vitiated by papal tyranny. Yet why does he not keep what he knows

[7] The rule of St. Francis begins with the sentence, "The rule and life of the little brothers is this: to keep the holy gospel of our Lord Jesus Christ, by living in obedience, without property, and in chastity." Heinrich Böhmer, *Analekten zur Geschichte des Franziskus von Assisi* (Tübingen and Leipzig, 1904), p. 29.

to be of divine authority, namely, the gospel, which is his rule? So you see, it has been proved that Francis erred as a man when he established his rule. If you say, "The rule of the little brothers is the gospel," what else is it but to establish the principle that only the little brothers are Christians? If the gospel belongs only to them, there are no Christians except Franciscans. And yet without a doubt the gospel belongs only and wholly to Christian people. Francis must have been under an illusion when he taught his followers (if ever he did) to vow a second time that which both they and everybody else had vowed already in baptism, namely, that which we hold most in common, the gospel.

The Basic Ideas of Those who Take Vows

In this connection there are two articles of their belief, or rather unbelief, to be treated. The first is that the gospel is not common to all, but is divided into counsels and precepts. Their monasticism follows the counsels rather than the precepts. The precepts are meant for ordinary men. In holding this view they labor under no small error. I shall not mention that in making this distinction they show that they do not know what the gospel really is (because they make precepts and counsels of it). The gospel is simply the promises of God declaring the benefits offered to man. Among these benefits are those declarations of God's commandments and the exhortations to keep them, which Christ made in Matthew 5, 6, and 7. What would they say to those words of Christ in the last chapter of Mark, "Go into all the world and preach the gospel to every creature" [Mark 16:15]? Will they make anything else of this except a command to preach, anything else than a command to obey? Why does Christ command them to preach to every creature in the whole world what [St. Francis] demands be observed only by a few? Time and again Paul boasts that he has been set apart for the gospel [Rom. 1:1], that the gospel had been promised [Rom. 1:2], that the gospel is the power of God for salvation to every believer [Rom. 1:16], and that clearly all will perish from whom the gospel of Christ is hidden [II Cor. 4:3]. He teaches in nearly all his writings that there is nothing more universal, nothing more essential, than the gospel.

But just as they do not know what the gospel is, inasmuch as they make a law of it, so they do not at all grasp these words of Paul. Let us then descend to their level, to their horrible place of darkness. Let us prattle with these babes in the gospel, and what are exhortations in the gospel let us call counsels and precepts. It is Moses who has the precepts. As John 1 [:17] says, "The law was given through Moses." But it is the gospel that possesses grace. As John says in the same text, "Grace and truth came through Jesus Christ." Let us then see what happens to those who presume to fly higher than Christ, and let us see where the error of their impious presumption brings them. For if we could prove that what they assert and take vows to observe are not counsels, would we not detect them in damnable error and prove that their vows are based on impious lies? What is it to assert as counsels things that are not counsels and to abolish divine commands, but to deny the truth of God and turn it into a lie, in fact, even to blaspheme God? Is it not blasphemy when God says, "This is my commandment," and they say, against the Lord but in his name, "This is not a command but a counsel?" They go beyond this blasphemy and take the vows of monastic life. They color their eyes with powder and paint their lips with scarlet [Jer. 4:30], and say, "I have done nothing wrong, only good" [Prov. 30:20]. For who does not know that those who think the commandments of God are counsels make their vows with a sacrilegious and blasphemous conscience? Certainly the vows of all monks are of such a kind, for the monks are persuaded that this sacrilegious and blasphemous distinction between counsels and precepts is true.

Now let us proceed to uncover this godlessness. Counsels, as they imagine, are for the most part those things which Christ teaches in Matthew 6 [5:25, 39-44], that is, not to take revenge, not to return evil for evil, not to go to litigation in court, to give one's cloak as well as coat, to turn the other cheek, to go two miles with him who compels you to go one, in all matters not to resist evil, and to agree with an adversary while on the way with him. Also, to love one's enemies, do good to those who hate you, and pray for those who persecute and abuse you. Also, to give to everybody who asks of you, as well as to him who borrows. To sell everything, to leave everything, and follow Christ; to submit oneself to all men, even the most unworthy. To these add virginity and continence. There are some who include the eight beatitudes of Matthew 5 among these so that they do not break or deny all commandments of God. More about chastity and their contention that it is a counsel later. For the moment let us take a look at the rest.

That all these sayings are not counsels but necessary commandments is immediately shown by Matthew when he wrote that Christ went up into a mountain, sat down, opened his mouth, and taught [Matt. 5:1-2]. Now to teach is not to prescribe counsels. It is to state what a man must do. And further on Christ himself said, "I came not to destroy the law but to fulfil it" [Matt. 5:17]. Thus, whatever else he teaches in that text, in this text he teaches that the law must be fulfilled, not that counsels are to be enumerated. He says here, putting his finger on what he was then teaching for emphasis, "Whoever therefore shall break one of the least of these commandments and teaches men to do the same will be called least in the kingdom of heaven. But whoever shall do them and teach them shall be called great in the kingdom of heaven" [Matt. 5:19]. Here you see that he distinctly calls the things he is teaching commandments. Moreover, he explains that his teaching is the delivering of commandments.

Then, when he turned to those things they call "counsels," Christ says, "Unless your righteousness exceeds that of the scribes and Pharisees you will not enter the kingdom of heaven" [Matt. 5:20]. Is not the kingdom of heaven denied only to those who do not keep the commandments? And this he asserts is true of what he himself taught, beyond what the scribes and Pharisees had taught. I ask you, who could be so presumptuous as to regard what is written there as counsels when Christ, by teaching, commanding, and earnest warnings, concludes that everything written there must be kept? By what authority do they assert that these are "counsels"? Where is it stated? Let them offer one iota of proof in support of their testimony! And these godless people are so brazen as to make up counsels out of their own heads without any support of Scripture and contrary to all the fulminations of Christ's teaching, commanding, warning, and promising. Or perhaps we should follow the insanity of Paris,[8] that Gomorrah, where they have reached the lovely conclusion that the Christian law is too great a burden. O Sodom, O Gomorrah, where they assess the commandments of God in relation to the strength of their free will rather than in relation to the grace of God and the commandments themselves!

But further, he destroys their presumptuousness by the very nature of the counsels themselves when he says, "Be obliging to your adversary lest he deliver you to the judge, and the judge deliver you to the officer and you be cast into prison. Truly, I tell you, you will not leave there till you have paid the last penny" [Matt. 5:25-26]. To this the moles and bats of Paris would be likely to raise the question whether any punishment is imposed when a counsel has been neglected. What about punishment so terrible and eternal that he who has not agreed with his adversary will be handed over to the Judge, then to the officer, then to prison, from whence he will never come out? Or again when he says, "If you love only those who love you, what reward will you have? Do not even the publicans and sinners do the same?" [Matt. 5:46]. Does this not mean that not to have obeyed counsels and not to have a reward is to be the same as publicans and sinners? Our Lord has affirmed this at some length in Luke 6 [:20-38].

It is clear, therefore, that all their counsels we have just been discussing are, truly and without a shadow of doubt, obligatory precepts taught by Christ in Matthew 6 [5]. Peter says the same thing, too, in I Peter 5 [:5], "Be humble toward each other." Also in Romans 12, "Let everyone assume others better than himself."[9] That this statement, we ought to humble ourselves to people humbler than ourselves, is no counsel is proved by the way Peter introduces it and then adduces the reason. He says, "Because God

[8] Luther's uncomplimentary references to the theological faculty of the Sorbonne in Paris stem from that faculty's decision against his arguments in the Leipzig Debate with John Eck in 1519. The Parisians did not arrive at or announce their decision until April 14, 1521. Luther wrote the present treatise in November of the same year.

[9] Phil. 2:3; cf. Rom. 12:3.

opposes the proud, but gives grace to the humble." Do you still think it is a counsel when Peter calls it pride, saying that God opposes you if you do not submit yourself to those who are lowlier? To sell all and give to the poor is not the poverty these fellows call monastic poverty, which is proved by Peter's starting to fish again after the resurrection, just as he used to do, although he had forsaken everything. Not only do monks not sell all they have and give to the poor, these monks are the very people who accumulate everything belonging to everybody else, and have more than everyone else.

Not only should the godlessness and blasphemy of the schools and monasteries be condemned for daring to teach such sacrilegious ideas, but still more should their snoring, yawning, and shameful laziness, their arrogant certainty of salvation, be detested because these belly-centered creatures have not had enough concern for the gospel to open the books [gospels] at any time, to turn the pages, or even to look up a single word. If they had looked up the words of the gospels just once they could have avoided the monstrous sacrilege of their blasphemies because the words are so clear and straightforward. What are these schools and monasteries but playgrounds and places of loneliness? They are playgrounds because these people play with and are led astray by lies. They are places of loneliness because their occupants are men who are alone, without Christ, and set far apart from the universal way of Christian truth.[10]

You understand now with what faith and with what piety these brothels of Satan take their vows and live their life. Paul says, "Even if you speak with the tongues of men and of angels, give all your goods to feed the poor, give your body to be burned, you are nothing and effect nothing, unless you have love" [I Cor. 13:1-3]. You are less than nothing and do less than nothing if you become a monk and vow these counsels, if by so doing you deny God's truth with a blasphemous and godless conscience, as you see them doing!

[10] *Scholae, quia ludentes et illusi mendaciis, monasteria, qui solitaria sine Christo, extra communem viam Christianae veritatis longissima posita.* Luther makes a pun on the original meanings of the words for "school" and "monastery." The word for school is *ludus*, which comes from *ludare*, "to play." This play on *ludare* carries over to *illusi*, "illuded" or "led astray by lies." The root of monastery is *monos*, "alone," which Luther interprets as bereft of Christ.

We read that Pelagius[11] was a man of praiseworthy life, but because he denied the grace of God, this single impiety, he lived to no purpose. If anyone denies that Mary was a virgin, or any other single article of faith you will name, he is condemned, even if he has the virginity and sanctity of Mary herself. How much more will the monks, this mob of perdition, be damned for denying and altering the divine commandments, for making them null and void.

Just look! The very foundation of the monastic vows is godlessness, blasphemy, sacrilege, which has befallen them because they spurn Christ, their leader and light, and presume to follow other things they think better. What else can he who deserts truth as his guide pursue but untruth? He who does not pursue the glory of God deserves to pursue blasphemies. This then is the second reason monastic vows are to be avoided and banished from under heaven, and why all who have vowed them should return to the road all other Christians take and follow Christ in a confident and good conscience. It is God himself who calls them to return, God who forbids their vows, God who condemns them, God who convicts them of the worst godlessness.

On Virginity

"But virginity and celibacy is a counsel," [they say]. Clearly Christ did not counsel it, but rather discouraged it. It was only when eunuchs had been mentioned that he referred to it and praised it by saying, "He who is able to receive this precept, let him receive it" [Matt. 19:12]. And again, "Not all can receive this precept" [Matt. 19:11]. Are these not the words of someone who prefers to advise against virginity and celibacy and discourage their application? He neither invites anyone to take up celibacy, nor calls men to it. He simply refers to it. Paul, however, says, "I give this counsel . . . " [I Cor. 7:25], but he does not invite anyone to take up celibacy either; rather, he discourages them and deters them when he says, "But each has his own special gift from God"

[11] Pelagius was a fifth-century British monk who taught that man's initial steps toward salvation are without divine assistance.

[I Cor. 7:7]. Paul neither persuades nor dissuades; he leaves the matter open. But our unchaste celibates will not interpret the word "counsel" as having any other meaning than to invite, exhort, call, or persuade to celibacy, and at the same time to dissuade, discourage, renounce, and refrain from marriage. This they also do in all their sermons and writings. But now let us come to the heart of the matter. If celibacy is an evangelical counsel, what is the sense of your making a vow that goes beyond the gospel and makes a rigid commandment out of a counsel? For now you live not according to the gospel but beyond it. In holding this you even live contrary to the gospel and no longer have a counsel. If you obey the gospel, you ought to regard celibacy as a matter of free choice: if you do not hold it as a matter of free choice, you are not obeying the gospel. It is quite impossible to make an evangelical counsel into a precept, and it is equally impossible for your vow to be a counsel. A vow of chastity, therefore, is diametrically opposed to the gospel.

Thus since God, who is the Author of the evangel, accepts only what is evangelical, it is impossible for him to approve the vow of continence: he can only detest it. Have you got an answer for that, you monks? Either deny that the counsel of the evangel is a counsel, or else admit that your vow is not evangelical. You will not dare assert that God would let anybody make a precept of his counsel, or approve of and demand anything but the gospel. This is why we have to declare that your vow is not approved by God. And this is the third firm and powerful buttress that stands in support of our position against monastic vows. In addition, we see that monastic vows are found to be nothing but a terrible mistake. They only deceive a man and lead him astray. This mistake must be avoided or abandoned by the Christian. The monastic vow is only without harm to those who are spiritually minded, who practice it to good purpose. But this is possible only for the elect, whom neither errors nor sins can harm in the long run.

There is another article of their unbelief: they divide the Christian life into a state of perfection and a state of imperfection. To the common people, they ascribe a life of imperfection; to themselves, a life of perfection. And they measure this difference not by Spirit, faith, and love, which are certainly markedly predominant among ordinary people. They measure it by the show and appearance of outward works and by their vows, in which there is nothing at all, neither Spirit, faith, nor love. In fact, they destroy the spirit of faith and love. With a living faith the state of perfection despises death, life, glory, and all the world, and serves all men in fervent love. And yet you could not find anyone more covetous of life and glory —and consequently more devoid of faith and more horrified of death —than the dyed-in-the-wool monk. It could not be otherwise (as we shall argue later) than that those who trust in works and vows destroy their own faith in the process. They put their trust in the things they consider essential; they are afraid when they have not done these things, and they are hopeful when they have done them. Fear and hope depend on the same thing. But more about that another time. It is pure fabrication to talk about the states of perfection and imperfection. It is a mockery. It comes from knowing nothing about faith and only leads the simple people astray. Therefore, when we see monkery crammed to overflowing with godlessness, errors, and ignorance, so that wherever you see it, you see ignorance, godlessness, and error, can you any longer doubt that it is displeasing to God, and that vows made within it are null and void and should be completely cancelled? These are the false Christs who say, "Here is Christ," and "There is Christ." They lead many people astray, even the elect, by their false signs and wonders [Matt. 24:23-24].

It is a mistake and colossal ignorance to measure the state of perfection by counsels and not by precepts. For the situation is not as they make it out to be, that counsels are superior to precepts. It is quite the opposite. The counsel of chastity (no other counsel exists) takes second place to his precept. For instance, it is commanded not to lust. Yet there has never been a virgin or an unmarried person in the world who has been utterly free from lust. But this ignorant, wretched crowd does not even know why this counsel was given. They keep that particular counsel because [they believe] that chastity is in itself the most praiseworthy of works in which is salvation and glory. This is why they hold themselves in a class apart from all other Christians.

But Christ and Paul teach otherwise. They glory in faith alone.

They praise celibacy not because the chaste are more perfect than others because they are chaste, and not because they do not lust contrary to the command, but because they are free from the cares and tribulation of the flesh which Paul attributes to marriage [I Cor. 7:32], and may freely and without hindrance dedicate themselves day and night to the word and faith. The married man, in his concern for his wife, his children, his family, and the material affairs of this world, is torn between them and is drawn into matters which detract him from the word. Thus Christ praises eunuchs not because they castrate themselves, but because they castrate themselves for the sake of the kingdom of heaven [Matt. 19:12]—but not for the sake of the kingdom of heaven in the sense that they are saved by their chastity, otherwise everybody would have to be castrated before they could enter the kingdom. Faith alone saves. It is for the sake of the gospel, which Christ calls here "the kingdom of heaven," that celibacy is praised. The man who most effectively serves the kingdom by preaching the gospel and propagating the faith among the people is one who is unmarried,[12] who is free of family responsibilities and who lives a celibate life.

It is therefore Christ's intent that chastity should be a servant of the kingdom of heaven, and a willing servant, not something which earns the kingdom, for it already possesses the kingdom. Such chastity labors in joyful service to bring the kingdom to others, or in any case to increase the kingdom for the kingdom's own sake. Such chastity is always ready to die and depart from this world for the sake of the kingdom. And Paul [says that the unmarried state is a good thing because of the impending distress [I Cor. 7:26], not on account of a halo in heaven. The demands of this life, the Christian life particularly, are more easily borne by those who are unmarried and free than by those who are married and bound. And again Paul][13] says the same thing, "The virgin and the unmarried woman is concerned for the things of the Lord, how she may please God, that she may be holy in body and soul" [I Cor. 7:32, 34]. What does it mean "to be concerned for the things of the

[12] Luther uses the Greek word *agamos*.

[13] The section in brackets is an insertion from the revised 1522 Wittenberg edition. *WA* 8, 585.

Lord"? Certainly not to live alone in profitless chastity! It means to meditate, to serve the word of God, to preach, bear witness, to be ready to risk one's life for the word. What is more alien and further removed from this purpose of chastity than these monks? Of all men they are the most ignorant of this use of chastity, for they are chaste for nobody but themselves. They serve in the temples with noise and murmuring, promising themselves halos in heaven for a faith that is dead.

Quite clearly, once you think the matter over, you can see that by this kind of talk Satan has thought up this figment about counsels and the state of perfection so as to adorn this perverted monkery. When he saw that nothing is vowed or ever could be vowed in monkery which Christians had not already vowed in their baptism (with the exception of continence), he began to think up the idea of perfection and counsels to make the ordinary way despised and by a lot of make-believe make this extraordinary way very glamorous. He did this so that men would not see that the vows concerned trivialities. And he succeeded in fostering this error.

And what is even more scandalous, they have selected only three out of all those many things just referred to which they call counsels: obedience, poverty, and chastity. The rest of the counsels they neither vow nor keep. They undertake ligitation as they will; they avenge themselves; they hate their enemy; they demand their rights, never give and never lend. And yet, on the strength of further lies and still worse deceit, they go on boasting of their state of perfection and of their counsels. Certainly since they hold that obedience, poverty, and chastity are counsels and matters of perfection, then it is proper and right to vow the rest of these things if the institution of vows is the state of perfection and counsels.

Now surely, if you look very carefully at those three counsels they have chosen for themselves, you will see that their obedience and poverty bear no resemblance to what their counsels say. For the counsels teach that each is to be subject to all and is to think of everyone else as superior to himself. But their vow of obedience releases them absolutely from the universal humility taught by the gospel and subjects them only to their own superiors, and not even to them unless it is in accordance with the rule of their order. Even

St. Bernard asserts that a monk is not obliged to obey even his abbot if he commands him other than his rule allows.[14] I ask you, what sort of obedience is that which excuses from obedience to all and requires obedience only to one, and then only in some things? Is not this kind of a vow of obedience just a magnificent illusion? The gospel commands all men, always and in all situations, to yield, submit, and obey. Those who have vowed to keep these counsels submit themselves neither to their equals nor to their inferiors, but to one superior only, and this not in everything, only some things. There again you see what happens to those who devise for themselves better things than Christ taught, who despise Christ and run their own lives their own way.

Peter is referring to these things when he says in II Peter 3 [:3] that deceitful scoffers shall come who walk according to their own desires. Beguiling in their deception, they boast of their obedience, but they teach and practice disobedience. They make sport of everybody's common sense, and deceive the souls of the simple with their pomp. Thus you see that the monastic life, with all its confusion of errors, lies, ignorance, laziness, deception, and illusion, represents the true Babylon, in which the elect are miraculously saved, like the three youths in the furnace [Dan. 3:20-26].

What then does a monk vow? His words (if you take the sense) will be something like this: "O God, I vow to thee, not that I shall be subject to everyone in accordance with thy gospel, but only to someone greater, and even then only so far as the rule prescribes. In this way I vow to thee to keep thy gospel." What else is this but rejecting the gospel by one's vows and establishing a gospel of one's own? Here you could say with Isaiah that their vow is like a man who slays the son before the father's eyes [Isa. 66:3]. Do they not in fact sacrifice the Son of God when they deny his gospel so blasphemously, and yet presume to offer him to God in the sacrifice?[15] They profess obedience and yet at the same time they refuse to obey. Do you think these blasphemous vows are worth anything in the sight of God? Do you really think God wants such vows?

---

[14] Cf. *MPL* 182, 866; on Bernard, see in this volume, p. 58, n. 30.

[15] Luther alludes to the sacrifice of the mass.

The same can be said of the vow of poverty. Evangelical poverty means to desire nothing in spirit and to serve freely for the good of others. How can they vow anything more than this unless they vow an outward use of things? For the inner lust has been renounced in baptism; the outward ordering of things has been committed to the gospel, and not even they can dispense with that usage. But it is just at this point that they deceive themselves and everybody else as well. For just as nobody administers more things than they, nobody uses more things than they, not in the interests of others, but of themselves. Under this holy vow of poverty they have become the most greedy of men and are rolling in wealth. Yet they boast that they have vowed these counsels, though no layman is more removed from poverty than they.

The fact that they get other people to look after their affairs does not alter the situation one bit. Their agent looks after their affairs under their instructions. While they, having forsaken Christ, fly higher than the gospel and rush headlong in the opposite direction into an abyss of the most perverse false doctrine, claiming that they live in obedience and poverty when they are really the most disobedient and wealthy of all people. Nobody can grope his way through this maze. And yet, these deceivers enthral our minds with their fictitious "obedience," "poverty," "counsels," "perfection," "religious obligations," and the like.

And so it is shown that there is nothing of the nature of counsels among those who have vowed them. All of them, with the single exception of chastity, are the exact opposite of precepts, and even chastity has no function or purpose in the gospel. Because Satan could in no way turn a thing like chastity into its opposite, as he did in the case of obedience and poverty, he left it untouched, though he turned it into the greatest danger. Satan abolished its natural use, extolled it far above ordinary faith, and then he spread the error far and wide so that through the weakness of human nature he has entangled countless souls in his net and brought them to perdition. And so, only chastity is left to those who profess counsels; but it is a perverted and godless chastity, almost totally corrupted by lust. Woe to that accursed vowing of counsels and to the state of perfection! What do all its claims amount to except error, deception, and blasphemy? But "righteous art thou O Lord, and thy judgment is right" [Ps. 119:137]. All those who not only want to be like, but even want to be superior to the highest, and who forget the covenant of their God, ought to fall under the judgment of God like the woman in Proverbs 7 [2:17] who forsook the guide of her youth.

Even though, as I have just said, I blame St. Francis[16] and the other fathers for claiming the gospel for themselves as a class apart because of their spiritual fervor, yet I acquit them of further error. I do not believe that they would approve of lies and fictions about counsels, perfection, feigned obedience, poverty, and perverted chastity. For while St. Francis and the other fathers were being driven under the power of the Holy Spirit and in complete faith and consuming love to only that point where they could respond most fully and worthily to the gospel, they did not consider whose gospel it was and to whom it pertained. They considered only how it could be fulfilled. They believed that they possessed the kingdom of God not in word but in power [I Cor. 4:20]. Yet their successors have rushed in and taken over their outward practices, but have abandoned the spirit and faith of the early founders. The same thing has happened to them as happened to the Chaldeans who lit the furnace in Babylon [Dan. 3:22]. It is they themselves who perish and the saints who are saved, for the simple reason that, as Psalm 28 [:5] puts it, "They did not understand the acts of God or the works of his hands, and therefore he destroyed them and did not build them up." For it says in Psalm 77 [:19], "Thy paths are in many waters, and thy footsteps are not known." And in Psalm 4 [:3], "Be it known that the Lord has done wondrously with his saints." And in Psalm 68 [:35], "The Lord is wonderful in his saints." And in Psalm 16 [:3], "As for the saints on earth, they are the excellent, all my delight is in them."

We learn from these testimonies that in the lives of God's saints it is not the outward appearance of the works, but faith that has to be heeded. God rules them by faith and wonderfully redeems them, allowing them to sin quite often and make mistakes in matters of external behavior. Yet these modern successors of the saints regard these external things as the works of God, believe that

---

[16] Francis of Assisi (1182-1226) was the founder of the Franciscan Order. Cf. p. 255, n. 7.

these things are the proper course to take, and go down into an abyss of errors. And the Apostle in Hebrews 13 [:7], when he commanded them to consider the end of those set over them, added his reason—"that we may imitate their faith." In God's sight this principle stands firm and unshakable: all saints live by the same Spirit and by the same faith, and are guided and governed by the same Spirit and the same faith, but they all do different external works. For God does not work through them at the same time, in the same place, in the same work, or in the sight of the same people. He moves at different times, in different places, in different works, and in different people, but he always rules them by the same Spirit and in the same faith. So that his ways may be hidden and his footsteps unrecognizable [Ps. 77:19], he provides each one with other works in other times and places, just as he did with other saints. And each one is compelled by the work, place, time, persons, and circumstances, previously unknown to him, to follow God as he rules and guides him.

This is the true knowledge of faith in which all saints are instructed, each one in his own vocation. It is impossible, therefore, for these outdated imitators of the saints not to go disastrously wrong when they copy even the best works of the fathers rather than the faith and Spirit of the fathers, not to mention when they pick up the errors and sins of the fathers. For they are all like men who stand in the entrance of their tent and see the back of Moses as he goes into the tabernacle of the covenant [Exod. 33:8]. They think they will find God in these works which belong to the forecourt, so to speak.[17] As it is written, "The Lord is in his holy place" [Ps. 68:5]. Also, "The Lord has declared that he would dwell in thick darkness" [I Kings 8:12]. Read the Bible from cover to cover, and see whether the works of the saints have been the same.

It seems to me that Psalm 62 has been revealed particularly for this matter, and it would not be unprofitable to review it.

1. For God alone my soul waits in silence,
   my salvation comes from him.

[17] For an explanation of this allusion, see *A Sermon on the Three Kinds of Good Life,* in this volume, pp. 235-239.

2. He alone is my rock and my salvation,
    my fortress, I shall not be greatly moved.
3. How long will all of you rush upon a man to destroy him,
    as if you were pushing over a leaning wall
        or a tottering fence?
4. They think only on how they may thrust him out of
        his exalted position,
    they will delight in lying,
    they will bless with their mouth,
    but they will curse with their heart. Selah.
5. Keep silent, O my soul, before God,
    For from him alone comes my hope.
6. He alone is my rock and my salvation,
    my fortress, I shall not be moved.
7. In God is my salvation and my glory,
    he is the rock of my strength; my hope is in God.
8. All of you, hope in him always,
    pour out your heart before him.
    God is our refuge.
9. But the sons of men are vanity,
    the sons of men are liars,
    they are found wanting in the balances,
    they are altogether lighter than vanity.
10. Put not your trust in deceit and pillage,
    and seek not to become vain.
    If riches increase, do not set your heart upon them.
11. Once has God spoken, and twice have I heard it,
    That power belongs to God.
12. And to thee, O Lord, belongs mercy.
    Thou rewardest a man according to his works.[18]

There is no other psalm in which hope, trust, and waiting upon God are so often repeated and so much inculcated. A full twenty times the psalmist repeats it. The whole psalm rings with faith in God, which of all things most powerfully opposes the example of

[18] The psalm has been translated just as Luther gives it, but his text corresponds neither to the Vulgate nor to the Hebrew, nor even to his own later translation of the Bible.

works in the saints. The true way of salvation is to be subject to God, to yield to him in faith, to stand silent before him, to set aside the offensive presumption of good works whereby the ungodly seek to find him, and to yield ourselves to God's guidance so that he can work in us and not we ourselves. For we see in those followers of the saints nothing but a tumultuous confusion of works which they have seen in the saints. Day and night they wear themselves out with these works. But they are never still in the presence of God or subject to him in faith. For that reason they are troubled and their hearts are unsteady, for the heart cannot find peace by doing good works. Their confidence is in the works they strive to do following the example of the saints. They believe that by doing these works they can attain what the saints attained by faith alone.

The psalmist, however, cries out against their headlong blindness. They rush in to imitate the work of some great man or other. They rather ought to learn to keep silence before God and to have faith in God. Why, God asks, do you fall over yourselves to do what is merely a semblance of good works? Why do you all kill yourselves doing these works? You are all rushing around and plunging to your death. God is a high wall and sure defense. As Solomon says, "The name of the Lord is a high tower (that is, high and opposing); the righteous man runs to it and he will be saved" [Prov. 18:10]. But the name of the Lord is set over against you, and whatever you undertake will be like a tottering wall and a creaking fence. Whoever leans on his own undertaking will collapse with it: he will be ruined and utterly shattered. They want the words "rush in" to mean the same as "to congregate," in other words, "to go wrong." Either meaning supports the sense just discussed.

What follows is both obscure and ambiguous: "They think only how they may thrust him out of his exalted position." Our text[19] has, "But they have thought to cast away my dignity"; the Roman Psalter has "my honor"; Jerome, "my part," that is, my oblation. Offerings and certain holy things get the name "oblations" from the word *elevando*, to raise up. I think this means that the godless not only do not follow what alone is precious, honorable, and the best in the examples of the saints, or, for that matter faith,

[19] The Vulgate.

which is the essence of holiness, but by common consent—or rather common madness—they do their best to cast out and destroy faith and, at the same time, boast and preach the outward show of works. Nobody follows the example of the saints less, and nobody does more to obliterate it than those who follow only the works and not the faith of the saints. And so these days no one is less Franciscan than those Franciscans who are called the Observants.[20] In fact, these are Francis' bitterest enemies and are consumed with throwing out his idea of faith.

Then come the words, "They will delight in lying," that is, they preserve the outward appearance but blot out faith. They are proud of this. They are full of complacency and think themselves holier than all other men. They bless with their lips, but curse with their hearts. They praise God, Christ, St. Francis, Dominic,[21] and others, whose followers they boast they are. But this praise is blasphemy of the highest order, for they cast out faith and cherish the outward appearance instead of truth. From all of this the whole psalm becomes transparently clear. It teaches us to have faith in God, and tells us that without faith all else is a lie.

Isaiah 30 [:9-13] repeats this psalm, or at least interprets it, saying, "For it is a people who provoke to wrath, children who lie, children who do not want to hear the law of God. They tell the seers not to see, and the prophets not to prophesy the truth to us, but to tell us pleasant things and to prophesy falsehood! Take me from the way, lead me away from the path! Take from before us the Holy One of Israel. Therefore, the Holy One of Israel says, 'Because you have rejected this word and trusted in oppression and confusion, and relied on them, this iniquity shall be to you as a crack breaking out in a high wall and calling out for repair, and, suddenly, when least expected, the crash comes.'" And further on he says, "If you return and be quiet, you will be saved. In quietness and confidence shall be your strength" [vs. 15], etc.

---

20 Cf. p. 173, n. 144.

21 Dominic (1170-1211) founded the Dominican Order.

II
Vows Are Against Faith

Enough has been said about monastic vows being contrary to the word of God. We shall now try to show that they also contradict Christian faith. When this is proved we shall recognize more fully that this is the chief function of the abomination which stands in the holy place [Matt. 24:15]. Here let us lay our rock and foundation, our first principle of faith, namely, the words of Paul in Romans 14 [:23], "Everything that is not of faith is sin." From this we infer that monastic vows, if not of faith, are sins. Moreover, if these vows are lifelong, compulsory, and not optional, they are not of faith. One ought to be in a position to keep them at one time or to renounce them at another.

But because these pages will fall into the hands of adversaries or those who are weak [in the faith], their way of escape must be stopped and the waters of this Jordan taken before they do, lest these princes of the Midianites escape from our hands [Judg. 7:24]. In the first place they will deny that faith in this context[22] is Christian faith. They have their little human gloss, sometimes more obscure than the text itself, sometimes never understood even by themselves, and because of this practice the real force of Scripture eludes them with comments of this kind. They believe these glosses more than they do the pure, clear word of God for no other reason than to uphold the basic principle of their unbelief. By their unbelief they have decided that not everything which is not of faith is sin. Since Paul opposes this lie they had set up against God, they had to mask Paul's meaning with a gloss, and Paul's words had to give way to their interpretation. Now the gloss runs something like this: "faith" must be taken here for "conscience."[23] Therefore, not to be of faith means to act against one's conscience.

[22] I.e., in the context of Rom. 14:23.

[23] Cf. Thomas Aquinas, *Summa Theologica*, II, 2, ques. 10, art. 4, where Thomas discusses whether every act done without faith is sin. His conclusion is that all works done without faith are sin. Luther's complaint is that Aquinas glosses the text of Rom. 14:23 in such a way as to equate conscience with faith, thus losing the real meaning of Scripture.

Acting against one's conscience paves the road to hell. I only mention this so that they will not think we have not read and are unacquainted with their magnificent wisdom.

Furthermore, they will also vigorously deny that obligatory vows are without faith. These people hold to every conceivable kind of faith; general faith, special faith, acquired faith, infused faith, unformed faith, formed faith, universal faith, particular faith, implicit and explicit faith. This is the most utterly confused Babel of errors and opinions that ever was! Therefore, lest these Amorites and frogs[24] think I know nothing about their [teachings], I am forced to dispute against these things. I do this not to strengthen the rock[25] on which I stand, but to show them how unshakable this rock is when the smoke, clouds, and fog stirred up by men have been dispersed.

In the last chapter of Mark [16:16] Christ says, "He that believes not shall be condemned." And in John 8 [:24], "If you do not believe that I am he, you shall die in your sin." And in John 16 [:8], "He will convict the world of sin because they do not believe on me." Take then any monk. Though he be chaste, obedient, poor, and full of all virtues, and doing all the works you like to name, yet without faith, will he not be condemned in spite of the works? Does not the judgment "He that believes not shall be condemned" still hold good? Is a man not in sin if the Spirit convicts him? Shall he not die in his sin? Death, damnation, and censure are not imputed to the man who has no sin.

They cannot get around this by saying that the sin of unbelief would indeed be condemned, but not everything that happens in the state of unbelief would be condemned. Does a corrupt tree bear good fruit?[26] Are not those things sin which are done in sin? To give bread

---

[24] The expression "Amorite" is parallel to our description of a man as a Philistine. It refers to the inhabitants of Palestine who were doomed because of their idolatries and iniquities and who were supplanted by the Israelites. Luther, in applying the term to his opponents, means that they are idolatrous and immoral and will lose their place to true Christians. By bracketing the Amorites with frogs Luther alludes to the inane loquacity of frogs, implying that the Amorites want to hear only their own voices, instead of God's voice. Cf. *Praelectio in librum Judicum* (1516) (*WA* 4, 536, ll. 23 ff.) and *Dictata super Psalterium* (1513-1516), Ps. 77:3 (*WA* 3, 587, ll. 9 ff.).

[25] The rock is Rom. 14.23. Cf. 273.

[26] Cf. Matt. 7:17.

to the needy with the intention of committing adultery is sin, yet is it not sin to take vows with no intention of believing? But John 3 [:18] puts a stop to this blasphemous talk when it says, "He who believes not is judged already, because he does not believe in the name of the only begotten Son of God." I ask you, now, what kind of faith is he talking about here? Infused faith? Acquired faith? General faith? Any of their other kinds of faith?[27] Is he not speaking of the faith which gives life? He who is without this kind of faith is already judged. And again, "He who does not believe in the Son shall not see life, but the wrath of God rests on him" [John 3:36]. But the wrath of God does not rest on those who do no sin. Therefore if the works done apart from faith are not sins, the wrath ceases to work upon him who does them, and by his works he averts the wrath of God from himself so that faith is not necessary! What can be more blasphemous?

Our rock therefore is found to be solid, and when the clouds are dispelled, the ground of their unbelief is laid bare, and Paul stands immovable: "Everything that is not of faith is sin." Nor does Paul care if his statement might seem hard to them. The death of Christ, undertaken on our behalf, was hard, too! It was a wonderful thing for the Son of God to take on flesh and to be offered for us! Nevertheless, we believe it actually happened. It is not proper for us to follow our judgment in the things of God, nor may we define something as difficult or easy, serious or unimportant, good or bad, righteous or unrighteous because it seems so to us. It says in Deuteronomy 12 [:8], "You shall not do what seems right to you." Yet this is exactly what these utterly godless university faculties do. They assess all the things of God by the limitations of their own human judgment, and found their faith not on the rock of faith but on the sands and swamps of their own unbelief. But what we

[27] These terms were used by Gabriel Biel (1420-1495), one of the last great scholastics and a professor at Erfurt. "Acquired faith" is that which natural man acquires for himself without the operation of divine grace. "Infused faith" means the inpouring of divine grace into this natural or general faith, as milk is poured into a jug. This divine action was necessary to transform "unformed faith" into "formed faith," i.e., a faith acceptable to God. For Luther "acquired faith" was trust in man and his works. Cf. *Disputation Concerning Infused and Acquired Faith* (1520) *(Disputatio de fide infusa et acquisita)* (WA 6, 85-86), and *Explanation of the Disputation Concerning Infused and Acquired Faith* (1520) *(Resolutio disputationis de fide infusa et acquisita)* (WA 6, 88-98).

think must be in accordance with the words of faith, and our understanding must be brought into captivity to the obedience of Christ [II Cor. 10:5].

This is exactly what our Parisian street whore,[28] with her brazen effrontery and her virtue, long since prostituted, has not done. She has recently been bold enough to open her legs and uncover her nakedness before the whole world,[29] and say that the law about not returning evil for evil ought now to be regarded as a counsel, not because Holy Scripture so teaches, but because human opinion states that this makes the Christian law too difficult.[30] Just as piously they assert that there is no hell, that the Scriptures only threaten as much on the ground that human reason recoils at the idea of a man tormented throughout eternity. They say Origen made the same mistake.[31] What schools! What faculties! What theologians! What bilge! What newfangled rubbish! So much for your understanding of the words of God, namely, captivity to the obedience of Christ. (It is captivity to the obedience of your own understanding.) By divine authority we confidently conclude and boldly declare: Thus says the Lord of Hosts, monastic vows made and kept apart from faith are sins, and therefore such vows are pointless and blameworthy. They should be revoked and abolished, or, as an alternative, professed anew and observed in some different way.

When they make faith mean conscience in this context they act out of pure human temerity. They do not draw one iota of proof from the Scriptures that faith is sometimes understood in this way. I have never found a place where faith is understood other than as Christian faith. It is understood in this sense at all times and in all places. But to prove this would take us further than the present argument permits. Let us then put up with this obscure gloss of theirs, and by the spirit God has given us put this man-made evil to a good use. If they had properly understood con-

---

[28] Cf. p. 259, n. 8.

[29] Cf. Ezek. 16:25; 23:18.

[30] Cf. pp. 265-267.

[31] Origen (*ca.* 182-251) believed that everybody would be saved eventually, even the devil.

science when they glossed the text, they would not have made such a mistake. For it is most certainly true that if you have done something and believe you have done wrong in so doing, then you have sinned, and, as the saying goes, you pave the way to hell. But they make this mistake. They do not make this matter of conscience apply to all works done apart from faith in Christ. They restrict it to only those instances in which they declare a person has a guilty conscience.

They are wrong in this because they have eyes only for those coarser sins such as lust, anger, covetousness. But they never apply this conscience to those great and deep sins of the heart. Let us see whether we can do any better. If you do something you are not absolutely convinced is pleasing to God, or if you doubt that it is pleasing to God, are you not acting against conscience? You are doing a work, and you do not believe that that work is pleasing to God. If you do not believe you are pleasing God, then you have a conscience which tells you the work is not pleasing to God. And so, by your own admission, you are doing against your conscience a work which is not pleasing to God.

But are not all such vows, and works performed in fulfilment of vows, works done apart from faith? Show me one single person who would presume to assert that his vow was pleasing and acceptable to God. Indeed, they teach that it is presumption to claim this, for they want us to be fearful and uncertain. But God has commanded us to put our whole trust in his mercy, and with utter certainty and without any doubt to have faith that both we ourselves and all our works are pleasing to him, not because of our worthiness or merit but because of his goodness. This is the conscience of a sound faith which holds firmly and unshakably to the promise and command of God. On the other hand, the kind of faith that does not believe—or, what is the same thing, doubts—that both it and its works are pleasing to God, devastates the conscience and sins against it. For that matter, in doing what it does not believe is pleasing to God, such a faith sins both against itself and the conscience.

Who frees us then from this ungodly conscience which sins against itself? The natural man cannot do it. No matter what good works you do, even if you shed your blood, there is always the trembling conscience which says, "Who knows whether this is pleasing to God?" How true is that text from the book of Wisdom [9:14], "The thoughts of mortal man are fearful, and our counsels are uncertain." Therefore, the natural man is not in command of the situation, and works do not secure a good and certain conscience. The truth is that in the hearing of his word Christ himself has been manifested to the inner man; that it is he who was made a priest on our behalf, he who was given for us, who poured out his blood, who bore our sins and accepted us as his own. It is he and none other, I say, who, when his word has been heard within, rejoices the human heart and stirs the conscience so that it is emboldened to glory in him and cry out, "If Christ is for me and is mine, who is against me?"[32] How shall I, and all the works I do, not please God if Christ is mine and I am Christ's? Can Christ ever be displeasing to God?

Look! This is the faith Scripture teaches. If a man has this faith, he cannot act against his conscience because he can no longer have any doubt that he is pleasing to God because of Christ who was given for him. If a man does not have this faith, he cannot but act against his conscience all the time because he doubts that he is pleasing God. For what he lacks is both the promise of God and Christ, who is the pledge of God's promise. All he has left to him is his own nature, which is uncertain what God thinks of it. But when a man has both the promise and Christ himself, he is absolutely certain of what God thinks about him: thoughts of peace and reconciliation because the blood of Christ declares the remission of sins and says, "Abba, Father"[33] in our hearts.

So, then, the thoughts of mortal men are fearful. But God does not want us to base our life on these thoughts. This is why he gave us a promise of mercy and commanded us to have faith. He added as an inestimable pledge his only begotten Son, so that we should put our trust in his thoughts which are made known in the promise and sealed by Christ, and stand undoubting and unflinching even

[32] Cf. Rom. 8:31.

[33] A reference to Rom. 8:15.

against the gates of hell. What is more, if ever we lapse and sink in sin, we shall soon rise again, always knowing that because of Christ we cannot be but pleasing to God, though on our own account we could never be pleasing at all.

Interpreted in this sense that gloss of theirs is godly and will be of good use, and, moreover, is in full agreement with Paul and the whole of Scripture. For truly, he who does not believe in Christ, or who does not possess him, is doing works contrary to his conscience and is in sin. The opposite is true also. He who acts contrary to conscience is truly an unbelieving man. Consequently, the text still holds good, "He who does not believe will be condemned," because he does not believe unreservedly that his sins have been forgiven. This conscience plunges him into damnation and remains burdened with its sins.

Now it must be seen more generally that monastic vows are without faith. It has been proved, and established by irrefutable testimonies, that everything which is not of faith is sin, and that it is faith alone which effects the remission of sins and restores certainty, serenity, and freedom from sins to the conscience. Good works, however, or, to give them their proper name, the fruits of faith, do not really pertain to the remission of sins and a serene conscience, but are the fruits of a forgiveness already granted and still present, as well as of a good conscience. I beg you, dear reader, to remember most carefully that works done before faith are sins, and that only faith apart from works effects the remission of sins, justification, and a good conscience. But the works done after faith are the fruits of a man who is already justified, and these works come out of the remission of sins and a good conscience, that is, from faith and love.

Remember these things, I say, for this is the wind which blows on the grass and flower of vows, the grass which will wither and the flower which will fade [Isa. 40:7]. We depend upon divine, not human, things. For it is unchallengeable that prior to faith and without that living and glorious Christian faith, you not only cannot have remission of sins or a good conscience by means of works or vows, but that of necessity everything you do is sin. Now you will see with what godliness these men make their vows, and with what faith—general, acquired, infused[34]—they make their vows. You will begin to wonder whether you ought to consider them Jews or Christians. Paul says to the Galatians in the third chapter [:12], "The law is not of faith." And again, "By the works of the law shall no flesh be justified in his sight" [Rom. 3:20]. And again, "Those who follow after the righteousness of the law do not attain the righteousness of the law" [Rom. 9:31].

All this, together with what has gone before, makes this certain: he who attributes forgiveness, satisfaction for sins, and justification to anything but faith alone, and who seeks a way other than through faith—this man denies Christ and, like an apostate, throws away grace and abandons the gospel. Thus Paul cries out to the Galatians, "You who are justified by the law are fallen from grace" [Gal. 5:4]. Vows and the works of vows are but law and works. They are not faith, nor do they issue from faith, for what else is a vow but some kind of law? In their own words they say, "What was a matter of choice before the vow, is a matter of obligation after the vow: it is no longer a counsel but a precept."

Is it not clear that those who take their vows in the belief that they will live good lives and earn their salvation by this way of life, and that they will wipe away their sins and become rich in good works, are blasphemous Jews and apostates from the faith, indeed, who rather blaspheme and deny the faith? They attribute to their laws and good works what properly belongs to faith alone. Paul prophesied wonderfully about these people: "In the latter days some shall depart from the faith, giving heed to seducing spirits and to doctrines of devils who tell them lies in hypocrisy" [I Tim. 4:1, 2]. He also recalls that departure and apostasy from true faith in the Epistle to the Thessalonians [II Thess. 2:3]. Where, then, is that departure if it is not when a man runs after works and attributes to works what belongs to faith?

If we were to ask all those who have taken their vows what they believed when they took them, we would find them all holding this ungodly belief, namely, that they think the grace of baptism has become worthless, and that now the shipwreck must be avoided

[34] Cf. p. 275, n. 27.

by the "second plank of penance."[35] For that reason they seek not only to become good and to abolish their sins, but even to confess more and become better than other Christians through a way of life under vows. It is absolutely certain that they seek to find all these things in works and vows, not in faith. Their own words bear this out when they say, "If I did not seek these things and find them, what would I seek in a monastery? What should I strive for?"

If they had known that these things could be both performed and acquired by faith alone, then they would have inferred, "What is the necessity of taking vows and becoming a monk?" They would have understood immediately that this kind of life was superfluous and unnecessary not only for the attainment of justification but also of salvation. When once the truth about faith is made known, everything else is found unnecessary for righteousness. And if they had known this, they would never have taken their vows. After all, nobody wants to work for no purpose, particularly when it involves the work of one's entire life. So they are convinced by this testimony that they took their vows because they believed that this kind of life under vows was useful and essential for achieving righteousness or living the good life. In fact, they held that nothing was better or more useful. But this opinion is blasphemous, sacrilegious, and contrary to faith. Faith alone is necessary and of any avail. Nothing is more useful and more necessary for righteousness than faith.

But what convinces them much more effectively and completely is this: they take their vows and live their lives under nothing but the faithless and blasphemous idea that man is able to obtain grace and remission of sins by his natural works. They teach and declare this principle of their unbelief quite openly. They are all convinced of this and even take their vows to obtain the grace of God by this kind of life in accordance with the principle of [their] unbelief.

[35] In the belief that subsequent sin nullified the forgiveness conveyed by baptism, early Christians laid hold of the idea of penance as a vehicle of forgiveness for postbaptismal sins. This idea gradually developed into the Roman doctrine of penance and was regarded as the "second plank"—baptism was considered the "first plank"—by which a man might be saved when he was shipwrecked by his sin. Cf. Jerome's use of this term in his *Commentary on Isaiah* (*MPL* 24, 65, and 22, 1115); cf. also Peter Lombard, *Sententiarum Libri Quatuor,* dist. XIV*a* (*MPL* 192, 868-872).

Now what else are they doing but denying Christ and departing from faith? [Why, with my own ears I have actually heard some of the most renowned of them teach that a religious is so very rich in this grace that as often as he renews the vow of his order in his heart through some petty act of contrition or another, he enters into his order anew. But the person who said this equated entering [an order] with baptism, as they all do.[36] These poor lost souls, believing in justification by works, have a flood of baptisms! Faith, however, has but one baptism, and this they hold is lost by but one single sin!][37]

If there are any among them who do not know these things, because they neither hear nor see anything else, they will have to be saved miraculously in the midst of their blasphemous doctrine and life of unbelief, as were the youths in the fiery furnace of Babylon [Dan. 3:23-27]. They can be saved only by the power of God, who teaches truth in the inward parts and is mighty to save. Therefore, if there were no other reason for revoking and abandoning the monastic vow, this blasphemy which denies Christ and repudiates faith would be sufficiently urgent and compelling. No one can overestimate the urgency and importance of those words of Paul which we quoted, "In the last days some shall depart from the faith, giving heed to seducing spirits and doctrines of devils, who speak lies in hypocrisy, having their conscience burned, forbidding people to marry, making them abstain from meats which God created to be received with thanksgiving by the faithful and those who have known truth" [I Tim. 4:1-3].

On the authority of this text alone (since it is a word of the Holy Spirit, who is our God blessed forever, Amen), I am bold enough to declare that all monks be absolved from their vows, and I pronounce with confidence that their vows are unacceptable and worthless in the sight of God. Before this I used to absolve only priests from celibacy on the strength of this text, but as I looked at the matter more closely and considered the words of Paul more

[36] Both Jerome and Bernard taught that the taking of monk's orders was a second baptism. *WA* 8, 596, n. 1. Cf. *MPL* 182, 620, col. 889; 183, 570, col. 640.

[37] This bracketed passage is found only in the revised Wittenberg edition. *WA* 8, 596, n. to l. 18.

carefully, it occurred to me that his teaching is quite general and applies to all celibates, monks as well as priests. Therefore, it was advantageous to look at these words of Paul a little more closely.[38]

But first, let us thoroughly refute those who, to honor the pope, priests, and monks, distort this passage to make it refer to the Tatians,[39] and will not permit it to be understood as referring to the celibacy we are discussing. These words cannot be interpreted as applying to the Tatians at all, for the Tatians did not just prohibit marriage, but condemned marriage outright, maintaining that it is evil and a sin. In a like fashion the Manicheans[40] not only prohibited certain foods but condemned them on the grounds that these foods had been concocted in part by the powers of darkness. But the pope and the papists do not condemn food or even marriage; they just prohibit marriage and teach abstention from certain foods which are good in themselves and which they confess were created by God. And they do this under the pretext of a greater godliness. This is what Paul clearly referred to when he said, "telling lies in hypocrisy" [I Tim. 4:2].

Now the papists do not teach that it is necessary or a divine precept to abstain from certain foods and from marriage. Knowingly and intentionally they prohibit these on their own authority to establish hypocrisy. The Tatians and Manicheans wanted to make their fiction appear as necessary and as a demand of God. They did not realize that what they taught was their own invention. They

---

[38] Luther makes a pun on *paulo* ("a little") and the name of the Apostle, *Paulum.*

[39] Luther refers to Tatian and his followers. Tatian was a Christian apologist and Gnostic of the second century (*ca.* A.D. 160), remembered mainly for his *Diatessaron,* a history of the life of Christ taken from the four gospels but based on St. John's Gospel. Tatian is also remembered for his attack on the Hellenization of the Christianity of his day, which he refuted with his apology *Oratio ad Graecos.* He carried his doctrines and his asceticism to an extent that was deemed heretical by his contemporaries. He is believed to have founded the Encratites, a group of ascetics who refused to partake of wine or meat, and generally opposed marriage. To Luther, Tatian's views on marriage, fasting, and the like seemed to be a prototype of the practices he was attacking.

[40] Manicheans were followers of the Persian Manicheus (*ca.* 215-275). His teaching was a type of Gnosticism similar to the ancient Persian dualism of Light and Darkness, combined with stringent ascetic practices, including vegetarianism. This system posited a hierarchy of grades of spiritual achievement, and its adherents were noted for their austerity. As a young man and before his conversion, Augustine had been under the influence of Manicheism.

believed that they were motivated not by the semblance of a greater godliness, but by truth and the need for a universal godliness. We are left, therefore, with this passage of Paul which clearly refers to the celibates among us—our pope, priests, monks, and nuns.

Finally, to say that Paul is speaking of the Tatians and Manicheans in this passage makes it impossible to deny that he is also referring to the papists insofar as the papists are in agreement with the Tatians and Manicheans. For the same reason can it be denied that John the Evangelist is not arguing against Sabellius[41] on the subject of Christ's divinity because he is arguing against the Arians?[42] Or that John is not arguing against Cerinthus[43] because his words refute the Jews? Or, are his arguments any the less valid against the Turks because they are valid against the Gentiles? In short, to a greater or a lesser extent they are valid against and combat all—whatever their name, whatever their sect—insofar as they deny Christ as God. So then, this passage of Paul condemns all who prohibit marriage and teach abstinence from foods, whether they are Tatians, Manicheans, Turks, papists, or something else. Even the Turk abstains from wine under the pretext of piety!

Since then it cannot be denied that the pope has prohibited marriage and even certain foods, it is clear from this text of Paul that the pope is resisting the Holy Spirit and that his teaching is devilish, erroneous, and pure hypocrisy. Has anyone anything to say against these words? Are they not perfectly clear and unchallengeable? It goes without saying that the papists are not Turks, nor are they Manicheans or Tatians. Nor do we accuse them of being such. But we do accuse them of thinking like Turks, Mani-

[41] Cf. John 1:1-18. Sabellius, a theologian of the early third century, taught a modalistic monarchianism which sought to safeguard the "monarchy" or monotheism of the Godhead. This teaching portrayed the Godhead as a succession of modes or operations and thus failed to do full justice to the independent existence of the Son. The logic of this doctrine made the Father suffer as the Son, an error which earned modalists the epithet of Patripassionists.

[42] Arius (*ca.* 250-*ca.* 336) taught that the Son of God was not eternal, but a creation of God, and therefore not God by nature, but a creature. This denial of the divinity of Christ spread widely. It was refuted at Nicaea in 325 by the use of the famous term "of one substance [*homoousios*] with the Father."

[43] Cerinthus (*ca.* 100) was a Gnostic heretic who taught that the world as it is could not have been created by God. He postulated the Demiurge, a much less exalted being, or even the angels, as responsible for creation. Jesus, he taught, was a man upon whom the Christ descended in baptism and from whom Christ departed at the crucifixion.

cheans, and Tatians. They are not Turks, yet they do and teach what the Turks teach.

Since monastic vows are declared illusory, satanic, and hypocritical teaching by the divine judgment of the Spirit, why do you hesitate any longer to revoke and abandon them? Are you afraid to hear the Spirit, your creator, and to follow him? Are you afraid that the Spirit of Truth [John 14:16-17] will lie to you, or be angry with you if you obey his voice? If you knew that you had taken a vow to commit sacrilege, would you not annul it and change it? Why then do you not change and annul this one, too? Perhaps what holds you back is what has held me back until now: the monks do not teach this doctrine but give themselves up to this kind of teaching and hypocrisy of their own free will, while priests do not take the vows of their own free will but are compelled to do so by decree of the pope. This idea of a voluntary vow not imposed upon them by someone else has strongly influenced me until now. But it influences me no longer, first, because Paul affirms so freely that these are doctrines of erring spirits and the lies of demons, and because the whole business confirms the words of Paul and proves his point. For they teach justification and salvation by works, and depart from faith. They not only think that their obedience, poverty, and chastity are certain roads to salvation, but that their ways are more perfect and better than those of the rest of the faithful. This is an open, obvious lie, and an error and sin against faith. All they have is hypocrisy and a branded conscience.[44]

And then, so as not to allow anyone to doubt that Paul is actually speaking of them, they rave even more madly and brazenly proclaim their lies. They sell and exchange their good works, their merits, and their brotherhoods[45] to others, as if they were men who not only were advancing by a better way, but who could, out of their abundance, even save others along with themselves. Can anyone deny that they do these things openly and everywhere? Could anything more blasphemous and more insane be thought up against Christ and against faith in him than to attribute so much to works—not only that these works wipe out their own sins, but also

[44] Cf. I Tim. 4:2.

[45] Cf. p. 192, n. 194.

the sins of others, and are profitable not only to their own salvation, but to that of others? What Jews, what heathen, what Turks, are as mad? Does this not mean that they lure and entice not only their own consciences but those of others to put their trust in their own works and merits? And what else is this but to believe the most damnable lie? And yet, in return for this lie, they devour the wealth of the world in luxury and idleness.

Lately they have reached the peak of their insanity by promising entry to heaven to men about to die if they don the monk's cowl.[46] If this is not an abomination, then what is? Look, it is as clear as daylight! Not only have they departed from faith, they have seduced the whole world with their abominable lies. A man's own faith is essential and all that is required for the remission of sins and for salvation. Faith brings Christ to us, makes us one flesh with him, bone of his bones. Faith causes us to have all things in common with him so that our conscience glories in him and on account of him. We live as justified men solely because of his blood and merits, and we shall live redeemed in eternity, without any works of our own or the works of others.

Faith in Christ cannot tolerate grace and justification coming from our own works or the works of others, for faith knows and confesses continually that grace and justification come from Christ alone. If they taught as much they would not be able to sell their works to others, and they would jolt themselves and everyone else from trust in works into faith in Christ alone. At the same time they would show that nothing in their life of vows is necessary for righteousness, salvation, and the remission of sins. Faith alone is necessary.

Christ truly prophesied in Matthew 24 [:5], "Many shall come in my name, saying, I am the Christ." Note very carefully, I beg you, Christ's actual words, "In my name they shall come and say, I am the Christ." These papist monks never actually call themselves by that word "Christ." None of them says, "I am called or wish to be called 'Christ.'" Nevertheless, they all say, "I am Christ"; they abstain from using the name, but arrogate to themselves the office,

[46] Cf. Erasmus' comment on this practice in *The Seraphic Funeral* (*Exequiae Seraphicae*). Craig R. Thompson (trans.), *The Colloquies of Erasmus* (Chicago: The University of Chicago Press, 1965), pp. 503-516.

the work, and the person.[47] You may ask, "But how do they do this?" Well, just listen! It is Christ's work alone to help and save others by his merits and works. The works of others help no one, not even those who do them, for the text still stands, "The just shall live by his faith" [Rom. 1:17].

Now faith establishes us on the foundation of the works of Christ without our own works, and transfers us from the exile of our own sins into the kingdom of his righteousness. This is faith, this is the gospel, this is Christ. But what do the papists, in contrast, make of this kind of faith? Do they not make it into faith in themselves? They teach us to trust in their merits, and they portion out their own works and brotherhoods to other sinners that they might bear and remit the sins of others and make them righteous and redeemed.[48] Is this not the same as saying, "I am the Christ?" Is this not doing what Christ does? These people are no longer just Christians, they are Christ himself! This is the definition of being a Christian: simply believing you are justified by the works of Christ alone without any works of our own, believing you have been freed from your sins and saved. Similarly, by definition this is what Christ is: "He who saves his people from their sins" [Matt. 1:21], he who gives them his own merits and complete justification. But this is exactly what our monks do! "In my name they shall come," said Jesus. That is, they do these things not as heathen, but as Christians, indeed, as Christians of the highest order, for they do not allow anyone else to boast more proudly of the name of Christian than they boast themselves.

At this point I recall how often I have heard that some of these people have given all their own good works to dying sinners with the words, "Look, I give you whatever good I have done in my life." They want to do a great work of charity by this madness, but what they have done is to pull the poor wretch away from Christ, and made him put his trust in the works of man. O what horrible darkness! What pitiable blindness! What revolting delusions! Is this the way you play with lost and perishing souls, Satan?

I believe these rapacious wolves will be recognized by their

[47] Luther makes the same point in his *Theses on Vows* (1521) (*Themata de Votis*), Thesis 137. *WA* 8, 329.
[48] Cf. p. 192, n. 194.

fruits [Matt. 7:20]. It will be seen in what frame of mind they make their vows and live their lives, so that no one could deny that to become a monk (unless one is saved by a miracle) is to become an apostate from faith, to deny Christ, and to become a Jew,[49] and as Peter prophesied, to return to one's heathen vomit [II Pet. 2:22]. So you see, these lost souls seek after nothing except works, the kind they equate with the works of Christ. They do so because under the pretext of the name "Christian" they think that what they have done are Christian works by Christian men, done in that blasphemous and abominable faith they call general faith and unformed faith.

Therefore, as I have said, the voluntary nature of the monk's vow no longer prevents me from believing that it should and ought to be abolished. After all, what is that vow except a pact made with devils? The Holy Spirit your God says that you have vowed teachings of devils, delusions, and lies, and do you still doubt whether you ought to rescind and relinquish your vows? Look at Paul, who has in mind not only those who teach the doctrine or compel others to do so, but even those giving heed to such a doctrine. In fact, he speaks in the most emphatic terms of those who give heed. He says, "They shall depart from the faith, giving heed to erring spirits and doctrines of devils" [I Tim. 4:1]. You see here that it is the hearers and the ready followers who are mentioned first of all. But monks certainly, because they take their vows voluntarily, do not teach these lies; they are followers who have been indoctrinated and misled. Thus, Paul addresses all these celibates without exception, and he exempts none.

Shall we say any more? What will suffice that man for whom it is not enough that the Holy Spirit defines the things which are vowed as the doctrines of devils, lies, delusion, and hypocrisy? Who would keep a pact with the devil, and not abrogate it and renounce it at the earliest possible moment for his salvation? I quite agree that a man is wonderfully saved by a pure faith when he makes his vows and lives under them, just as Bernard[50] and many others have

[49] By "to become a Jew," Luther means to forsake the gospel and revert to a religion of law.
[50] Cf. p. 325.

been saved. But in these cases the poison did them no harm because of the faith in Christ with which they were filled. Nevertheless, when it is established by divine authority that these are doctrines of devils which by their very nature deceive and lead astray since they cannot teach anything else but works, you can and you ought to break off the vow you made to keep these things. You cannot make doctrines of God from the doctrines of men through the example of a holy man. The doctrine of God teaches faith; these men under vows boast that they teach something more than faith. And that something more is nothing but a work, and can be nothing else but a work. But you cannot teach works unless you hurt faith, since faith and works stand at opposite extremes in the matter of justification.

And so it comes about that the teaching of works is necessarily a doctrine of devils and a departure from faith. No one teaches works because he thinks they are unnecessary for righteousness and salvation, for unless he thought them necessary, he would be teaching for no purpose. To what end would he teach works? And who would follow them and do them if he knew of another way of righteousness and salvation? Paul rightly said, "The law is not of faith" [Gal. 3:12], and, "By the works of the law shall no man be justified" [Rom. 3:20]. By the same reasoning a vow is not faith, nor is any man justified by a vow. Everything which Paul in his Epistle to the Galatians argues against—the law and the works of the law—pertains exactly to the vow and its works. Whether vows were taken with godly or ungodly intent, they must be broken off, for they have been rejected by God and were undertaken with respect to things rejected by God.

And so Bernard and others who took their vows and lived under them in a godly frame of mind are like those two hundred men who went out from Jerusalem to Hebron with Absalom, who had planned a rebellion against the kingdom of his father David. They knew nothing of Absalom's plans and went out in simple trust [II Sam. 15:1-11]. It is quite certain, though, that if they had known they would have had second thoughts. Had they been intercepted in the affair they could have been accused of treason. But if you considered their work and their way of life and what was in their mind, they would have to be absolved. This story is a beautiful allegory for us in this matter, but this is neither the time nor the place to dwell on it. Plainly, Absalom is the papist kingdom incited against the kingdom of Christ. The pope has expelled this kingdom and sits ensconced in the heart of Jerusalem. It goes without saying, the godly men who consent to him do not give their consent to this insanity.

I am certain in the case of Bernard, not to mention others, that he was like those two hundred men, as he himself clearly showed once when he was at the point of death. He uttered no other confession than this, "I have lost my time because I have wasted my life. But one thing gives me solace. A broken and a contrite heart thou dost not despise."[51] And elsewhere, "Christ possesses the kingdom by a double right: in the first place, because he is the Son; and in the second place, because he has suffered. But there was no need of this second right in his case. He gave it to me and all who believe in him."[52] You see, these are the words of a great Christian soul, because he put all his faith in Christ and despaired absolutely of his own works. He takes no pride in his vow of poverty, obedience, and chastity; in fact, he calls his life wasted. Moreover, it is by this faith that Bernard is both saved and justified along with all the rest of the saints. Do you think he lied or spoke lightly when he said his life had been wasted? He is aware of the judgment of God before whom no one stands save Christ alone and his righteousness. It was for that reason he abandoned his own righteousness and betook himself to Christ, declaring that his own righteousness was wasted.

If you were to hear it preached that the vows and lives of the monks were wasted and of no use to anybody in attaining righteousness and salvation, who would take vows? Who would continue under vows? Yet unless you admit your righteousness is wasted and lost, you will be lost indeed. You will not be keeping any part of the vows of the holy fathers in the spirit in which they kept them. All the holy and pious monks must have been like Bernard, so you

[51] *MPL* 183, 867; Ps. 51:17.

[52] *MPL* 185, 491. Luther often quoted this saying of Bernard.

can see clearly that all were wonderfully saved and in the last resort had to say that their vows were nothing and were subject to damnation, for it is by faith alone that they were justified and redeemed. Yet the godless regard this faith of the fathers with contempt. They establish and make a great show of works which the fathers condemned, and under the pretext of the example of the saints the godless teach a departure from faith. Contrary to the examples of the fathers they dupe the whole world with their lies. That is what the text, "God is wonderful in his saints" [Ps. 68:35], means.

In as much as they want monasticism to appear to have God's approval because the saints lived a moral and happy life under monastic discipline, why do they not teach that fire, sword, cold, wild beasts, the cross, and death are approved of by God and should be the subject of vows? Did not the holy martyrs live well under those conditions? St. Agnes[53] remained a virgin in a brothel. Further, how many souls does God allow to fall into sin so that they can learn humility and recognize their true nature? Paul confesses in Romans 7 [:18] that sin dwells in his flesh, and yet in the midst of sin he leads a good life and uses the sin to advantage. And which of the saints did not lead a good life when they lived in the flesh, in the world, and in the midst of demons? But is that any reason to make the works of the world, the flesh, and the devil a subject of vows?

But these godless people not only want the monastic life to be regarded as a way of life in which a man may lead the good life, but rather as the way of life through which a man leads the good life—or, still better, the way of life which is good in itself. They teach that this kind of life, and all that goes to make it up, is the good life, and that by practicing it men become good and are saved. This is sacrilege, godlessness, and blasphemy. It is lies they have trumped up. It is delusion, hypocrisy, and satanic invention. They lead the hearts of the simple astray by this teaching, and by the vanity and conceit of their speech, as Peter says [II Pet. 2:18]. Not a single saint has been made good by this teaching, and they

[53] See p. 174, n. 147.

cannot give one example of this. All were made good and all were saved in Christ alone through faith, as we have shown in the case of Bernard.

But St. Augustine, too, says, "Woe to the life of men, be it ever so praiseworthy, if it be judged without the mercy of God."[54] And again, "I am disturbed though not perturbed when I think of the wounds of the Lord."[55] You see, even this man condemns his own life and everybody else's as well, but yet he flees to the wounds of Christ. And Paul says in Galatians 1 [2:20], "I live, yet not I, but truly Christ lives in me." It is in Christ alone that all men live, in him all take their vows, in him they all believe and glory and think nothing of their own works. And on the same grounds we too say, Let him be anathema who teaches anything else but that justification and salvation are in faith alone. Is this not clear enough?

It is now quite clear, therefore, that monastic vows, when they cannot be taught as being not more than and not other than faith, are ungodly, heathen, Jewish,[56] sacrilegious, lying, erroneous, satanic, hypocritical, apostate, and even contrary to the examples of the saints. On these grounds they ought to be revoked and given up in complete confidence, even if they were taken with godly and serious intent. For if the Apostle forbids the teaching of the works of the divine law, and with burning zeal constrains the Galatians and Romans to abandon it, how much more then ought these self-chosen works and vows of men to be forbidden and abandoned!

To sum the whole matter up: works and vows can be taught and recommended only if you can say they are wholesome and useful to salvation and justification. For what are you teaching when you say that works and vows are not useful to salvation and not necessary? Who would listen? Who would embrace them? Yet to have taught that they are useful to salvation is devilish and apostasy, since only faith is necessary and only faith saves. Monastic vows and works, then, cannot be seriously taught and learned without those who teach them and those who learn them becoming

[54] Augustine, *Confessions*, IX, chap. 13, 34. Cf. *LCC* 7, 199.
[55] The quotation is from Bernard. *MPL* 40, 960.
[56] Cf. p. 288, n. 49.

apostates from Christ and falling from faith. And then Paul firmly maintains that they are teachings of devils, lies and delusions, and that if you do not turn from them in the end as St. Bernard did, you will perish eternally.

All these arguments, since they are true and weighty and based on godly foundations, prove irrefutably that in the sight of God the mental attitude of the person making vows, if he does so without faith, is as follows, "Look, O God, I vow to thee that I no longer want to be a Christian. I revoke the vow made in my baptism, and will no longer depend on Christ or live in him. All these things are useless and outdated. I vow to thee, however, a new and much better vow, better than Christ and other than Christ, that is, to live by my own works of chastity, obedience, poverty, and by this entire rule. For by these works I shall be justified and saved, and will help myself and others toward righteousness and salvation." Are you horrified, and do you deny that a person who makes vows thinks like this? But if you deny this you will at the same time deny the truth of what has been said earlier. For the heart which is not grounded in a pure faith in Christ and presumes to take vows is not able to do anything other than what has just been said. Necessity has an eye on works and esteems them, otherwise it would not take vows. But to esteem works is to deny faith, revoke baptism, and repudiate Christ, and enough has been said about that already. And you believe that this most godless of vows can please God and is demanded by him, rather than held in utter odium by him and condemned by him? So it goes for those who strut about without faith and run after works.

But consider something much more grievous and wretched in their method. Those who come closest to this ungodliness are considered the very best among them: those who live in chastity, poverty, and obedience and keep all the rules are few and far between. How many penances are there, how many chainings of the body, how many punishments, how many sorrows, for those who do not attain this ungodliness? What a burdened conscience they have when they have not observed their rule! Just think for how much sweat Satan sells his perdition. The very thing that ought to be avoided with the maximum of effort and in all conscience is actually sought after with the maximum of effort and in all conscience. Truly did Moses say, "There you will serve foreign gods who will give you no peace, day or night" [Deut. 28:64-66]. Christ, too, seems to have preached about this, "Strive to enter by the narrow gate, for many will seek to enter but will be unable to do so" [Luke 13:24].

It appears, however, that God in his mercy works against them to keep them from attaining their goal of perfection, that is, the peak of godlessness. He allows them to fall by the wayside and hedges their way with thorns (as he says in Hosea), so that in the midst of their troubles they may realize they are but sinners and come to their senses and go back to their former husband where it was better for them than it now is [Hos. 2:6-7]. Is this not then an unbelievable reversal? The first are last and the last first [Matt. 20:16]. The apostates are the devout religious and the devout are apostate. Those who keep the vows least actually keep them more, and those who keep them more actually keep them least. This is how it is when the Lord casts down the haughty [Ps. 18:27]. Thus is Psalm 14 [:3] fulfilled, "Sorrow and unhappiness lie across their paths, and the way of happiness have they not known."

Further, a man taking his vows in a Christian and godly way would of necessity think thus in the presence of God, "Look, O God, I vow to thee this kind of life, not because I think this is a way to attain righteousness and salvation or to make satisfaction for my sins. Such an attitude might turn away thy mercy from me. This would cause harm to my Lord Christ, since it would be to deny his merits and profane his blood, and to hold thy Son as a reproach.[57] To him alone belongs the glory of being the Lamb of God who takes away the sin of the world. He washes and justifies all with his blood. I will not so blasphemously reject thy grace. My expectations and hopes I shall set in him alone, never at all trusting in myself or in any other creature, to say nothing of trusting in my vows and good works. I do this because I must live in the flesh and cannot be idle. I take this way of life upon myself for the sake of disciplining my body to the service of my neighbor and meditating upon thy word. I do this just as another man may take up farming

[57] Cf. Heb. 6:6; 10:29.

or a trade—every man a job—without any thought of merits or justification. Justification exists first and foremost in faith. It will always be the most important and will always reign supreme, etc."

You understand from what just has been said that if such is not the mind of him who takes vows, his vow cannot be holy, and it is not really a vow at all. The reason is that if faith is present, it demands this attitude of mind. Otherwise, the vow is without faith. The text stands unchallengeable, "The just shall live by faith" [Rom. 1:17]. No man shall live by his works, and, by the same token, no man shall live by his vows. Just think how many there are who take their vows in this way: to be sure, no one, or only those who have been miraculously led into it.

Such an attitude holds vows in contempt and regards them as no better than working on a farm or any other kind of manual work—and what monk ever takes a vow without regarding the work of the vow as a work of supererogation and perfection which has no like or equal? This is the doctrine these people brazenly teach.

Furthermore, he who has such an attitude lives this kind of life for its usefulness and discipline, not for the substance of the thing itself. He holds that faith is the thing and substance. Just as a man is the substance, his natural work is the use of his substance. And so faith uses the activity and work of all. But these other people take an opposite view. They live for the thing itself, not to put it to use.[58] To be a religious, they argue, means to stand absolutely right with God, a status which must never be put to any use, but which uses everybody else! This is the top and bottom of the whole matter. It sums up the whole business from A to Z![59]

III
Vows Are Against Evangelical Freedom

So far we have seen that our monasticism is as much against the word of God as it is against the Christian faith. And although

[58] I.e., the man who makes his vows in what Luther calls a "Christian and godly way" makes vows a means to an end. He who makes his vows in a contrary way pursues them as ends in themselves.

[59] This passage may also be rendered, "He [Christ] himself is the head, the first and the last, the beginning and the end, the Alpha and Omega." Cf. Rev. 22:13.

by reason of these two charges it has been rightly condemned, rejected, and detested by everybody everywhere, nevertheless we shall prove this very fact at greater length to those who cannot find it out for themselves. (If an idea is found to be contrary to God and his word it may readily be assumed that there is nothing it will not contradict; it will even be self-contradictory.) And now for this third point we shall seek to prove that monastic vows resist the fruit of the word and of faith, namely, Christian, evangelical freedom. To have violated this and not preserved it intact is no less ungodly than to have denied the faith and to have apostacized, as we learn from Paul's letter to the Galatians.

We repeat therefore what we have said earlier, and submit it as a matter of sound principle that a vow cannot be pleasing to God, nor can it be regarded as a vow by him unless it is intrinsically Christian and godly. God can no more easily acknowledge what runs counter to Christian godliness than he can deny himself, for he enjoined Christian godliness as the first and greatest commandment. A vow is Christian and godly only when it is not destructive of faith. Faith remains unhurt only when a vow is regarded as a matter of free choice and not as necessary to attain righteousness and salvation. Most certainly righteousness and salvation are not achieved by any laws or works, but only by faith in Christ. We have already proved convincingly enough and clearly demonstrated all these things.

Righteousness and salvation have to exist before any works can exist. But not the righteousness and salvation you offer, but what God offers, that is, eternal righteousness and salvation, which abide throughout eternity. Only God can give and effect that in us. Moreover, because it is a work of God alone in us, it can only be hindered by any works we do; it cannot be acquired by our works. John 6 [:29] says, "This is the work of God, that you believe in him whom God has sent." And farther on, "No one comes to me unless the Father who sent me draws him" [John 6:44]. And again, "It is written in the prophets: And they will all be taught of God. Every one who has heard from my Father and has learned from him comes to me" [John 6:45]. And again, "For this reason I said to you: No one can come to me unless it has been granted him by my

Father" [John 6:65]. He also said this to Peter in Matthew 16 [:17], "You are blessed, Simon bar Jonah, for flesh and blood has not revealed it to you, but my Father who is in heaven." And Paul calls faith a gift of God because it does not come of ourselves [Eph. 2:8].

Therefore, this kind of righteousness and salvation is far too great to be acquired by us mortal men. It is the work of the divine majesty alone. What we mortal men achieve is closer to iniquity than righteousness, to perdition than salvation. As Hosea 13 [:9] says, "Your perdition is your own, O Israel. Your salvation comes from me." So, then, all those vows taken on to acquire righteousness and salvation are nothing but iniquity and perdition. They work contrary to the righteousness and salvation of God, whose function and office they arrogate to themselves.

What Christian Liberty Is

Since therefore it is absolutely certain from these arguments that no vow is acceptable to God unless it is a kind not deemed necessary for righteousness and salvation, and since God has not commanded the taking of any vow, it clearly follows that this kind of vow is a matter of free choice and can be laid aside. For the two statements—that a vow is not necessary for righteousness and salvation, and that a vow cannot be set aside without endangering righteousness and salvation—are clearly at odds with each other. If a vow cannot be set aside, it is necessary; if it is not a matter of necessity, it can be set aside. So then, as God sees the matter, the form of a vow that is godly and Christian would appear to be this: "I vow to thee this kind of life, which by its very nature is not necessary to attain righteousness, neither can it ever become a matter of necessity." Unless the vow were something like this, it could not be a godly vow, as is sufficiently clear from what has been said. What then will God say to this? Will he not say, "Why make such foolish vows then? Have you not plenty of vows already which you owe me?"

But here it will be strongly objected that the works of the divine law commanded in the decalogue, such as chastity, gentleness, generosity, and obedience to parents, do not justify, nor are they necessary for righteousness and salvation, since Paul says, "No flesh is justified by the works of the law" [Rom. 3:20]. Yet they are necessary, as Christ says in Matthew 16 [19:17], "If you wish to enter life, keep the commandments." Nor can these works be set aside even where faith, which alone justifies, is present, since they are the fruits of a justifying faith. For faith without works is dead and worth nothing.[60] And Peter requires virtue in the man of faith [II Pet. 1:5]. And to the Galatians Paul prescribes a faith active in love [Gal. 5:6]. Thus it can be said in the matter of a vow and its works that the works are still necessary, even after the vow has been set aside, for these works are still commandments, just as the fruits of righteousness, even though they are not necessary for the attainment of the righteousness which is of faith alone, are still righteousness. Nor can the freedom of the gospel dispense with the commandments of God. The commandment of God is, "Make your vow and keep it" [Ps. 76:11]. For we do not destroy the law by faith, we establish it, as Paul says in Romans 3 [:31].

Now that the question is raised, we must have a look at the nature of Christian freedom. Christian or evangelical freedom, then, is a freedom of conscience which liberates the conscience from works. Not that no works are done, but no faith is put in them. For conscience is not the power to do works, but to judge them. The proper work of conscience (as Paul says in Romans 2 [:15]), is to accuse or excuse, to make guilty or guiltless, uncertain or certain. Its purpose is not to do, but to pass judgment on what has been done and what should be done, and this judgment makes us stand accused or saved in God's sight. Christ has freed this conscience from works through the gospel and teaches this conscience not to trust in works, but to rely only on his mercy.

And so, the conscience of a man of faith depends solely and entirely on the works of Christ. The conscience may be likened to the dove resting in safety in the clefts of the rock and in the secret places [Song of Sol. 2:14]. Such a soul knows with absolute cer-

[60] Jas. 2:20; I Cor. 13:2.

tainty that it can have neither confidence nor peace except in Christ alone, and that in its own works nothing but guilt, fear, and condemnation can abide. It is in this way that conscience discerns and judges between Christ's works and its own. It embraces the works of Christ and speaks in this way: Through these works shall I be justified, through them be saved, through them set free from all sin and evil. I have no doubt about all this because it is for this very purpose these things were done by him, and in baptism all these blessings were poured over me. Without these there is no salvation, no peace for my bones [Ps. 38:3], no satisfaction for sins. In fact, such a conscience sees that its own works are evil and condemns them. It is by the works of Christ that conscience is victorious and despises its own works, lest they destroy it. The works of Christ are more powerful to save us and to give us peace than are our works to capture and terrify. If only you could believe this! Of course, conscience lays hold of its own good works too, but declares these works are to be done freely and only for the good of one's neighbor, and to give the body something to do, but in no case to acquire righteousness and peace and the satisfaction and remission of sins. For conscience seeks these things only in the works of Christ and finds them in a firm faith, just as it sees that Christ did all his works freely for our good and submitted his life to the will of God.

It is this knowledge of freedom and this health of conscience that is assailed by every device of human and ungodly doctrines. It is here that the craftiness of the serpent seeks to corrupt the simplicity which is in Christ. Here you see how ungodly are the laws about satisfactions by which we are taught to wipe out our sins by our own works. These are the jaws of ravening wolves, which tear consciences from Christ and, when they are torn away, pitifully cast the consciences on the resources of their own works. These are the people who are always learning and always performing works, but who never come to the knowledge of truth and peace [II Tim. 3:1-7]. Paul in Acts 20 [:29-30] calls such people grievous wolves who have broken in, not sparing the sheep, men who arise and teach perverse doctrine to draw disciples after them. What does it mean to draw the disciples after them if not to take them away from Christ? This is what happens when consciences are taught to effect their own salvation by their own efforts and works, to wipe away their sins and earn grace by merit, when this should be sought only in the works of Christ through faith.

Here you see the entire canon law as well as the dominion of the pope condemned as being against Christ, because they do nothing else but ensnare consciences in their own works and take them away from Christ, after having first destroyed their freedom as well as any teaching or knowledge of freedom. But in particular it is the Parisian school[61] that is condemned in this connection, that impure and foul whore which has declared that Aristotle's teachings on morals are not in conflict with the teachings of Christ,[62] since he teaches nothing other than that virtue is acquired by works, saying, "By doing good we become good." The Christian conscience curses this statement as bilge water of hell and says, "By believing in a Christ who is good, I, even I, am made good: his goodness is mine also, for it is a gift from him and is not my work." To sum up, in this you see the theology of all the schools condemned, speculative as well as practical, because they teach not Christ but human wisdom, which on their own admission they allege even creates the faith they call acquired faith.[63] Woe to these lost and dreadful men of Sodom and Gomorrah! You see now why Paul condemned the works of the divine law (or the righteousness by the law)—and also why he considered his own pharisaic righteousness as dung and loss, even though he boasts in Colossians 2 [Phil. 3:6-7] that his righteousness was blameless—because it is opposed to the righteousness which is from Christ and in Christ. Pharisaic righteousness tears the conscience away and will not let it cling to the righteousness of Christ, but presumes upon

[61] Cf. p. 259, n. 8.

[62] Cf. *Disputation Against Scholastic Theology* (1517) (*LW* 31, 9-16) and *Against Latomus* (1521) (*LW* 32, 137-260), where Luther deals with this same matter. He discusses these issues further in *Opinion of the Parisian Theologians on Doctor Luther's Doctrine. Doctor Luther's Dissenting Opinion. (Eyn Urteyl der Theologen tzu Parisz uber die lere Doctor Luthers. Eyn gegen Urteyl Doctor Luthers)* (*WA* 8, 289-312); *Theses on Vows* (*WA* 8, 323-335); *Lectures on Galatians* (1519) (*LW* 27, 224-225), and *Disputation on Infused and Acquired Faith* (*Disputatio de fide infusa et acquisita*) (*WA* 6, 85 ff.).

[63] Cf. p. 275, n. 27.

its own righteousness and upon the works performed by itself. Romans 9 [:30-32] says, "The heathen who do not pursue righteousness have taken hold of righteousness, but a righteousness which is of faith. Israel, however, in pursuing the law of righteousness has not attained the law of righteousness. Why? Because they sought it not by faith, but, as it were, by works."

Do you now understand why I have said so often that neither our vows nor our works are necessary for righteousness and salvation? A good conscience declares this of the works of Christ alone, works which were poured out over us and freely given to us in baptism. Thus a good conscience is free from all works, not only from those that ought to be done, but from those that accuse us as well as those that shield us from condemnation. To those who believe in Christ there are no works so bad as to accuse and condemn us, but again, there are no works so good that they could save and defend us. But all our works accuse and condemn us. Christ's works alone protect and save us. You yourself see how the works of the Ten Commandments these days are either set aside or performed, and these works are chastity, obedience, meekness, generosity, and the like. They ought not be dispensed with, but observed (if I may so express it) according to their inner meaning, but not according to our conscience. This means that they are not works that shield us from condemnation, nor are they works that justify us. For this would be to bruise the conscience and seduce it from Christ the groom, with whom the conscience is of one flesh and with whom it shares all his riches. But these works should be done freely and for no reward, to the benefit and advantage of our neighbor, just as the works of Christ were done freely for us and for no reward. Actually, then, our works are no longer works of the law but of Christ working in us through faith and living in us in everything we do. For that reason these works can no more be omitted than can faith itself, nor are they less necessary than faith. Otherwise, works that are only the works of the law are fancied and false. Apart from Christ no one at heart is gentle, chaste, generous, obedient, good, God-fearing, and so on; a man acts not from a free conscience but for gain, desire for glory, or fear of punishment. And since a simulated holiness is a double iniquity, it is clear that works of this kind not only are not necessary, but should be dispensed with altogether and avoided like the plague.

But here you will perhaps say, "Then your idea of Christian freedom teaches whoredom, murder, robbery, falsehood, rebellion, and idolatry. Don't be a fool! As if I would tell you to commit a far worse evil by teaching you to set aside a lesser evil! I tell you not to get angry and do you then set off to commit a murder to prevent your getting angry? I want these imaginary works to be set aside and the true works done, so that you will cease being kind in an ungodly way, but will become kind in a godly way. For the works, too, will have to undergo a change (although they look the same outwardly) when you yourself have been changed inwardly, so that no longer are they your own works, but they become the works of Christ in you. Of course, it is not the task of human judgment to decide whether an ungodly spouse is worse than an adulterer, or the other way around. It is God who searches the heart. An adulterer abuses the flesh for illicit pleasure. An ungodly spouse abuses the flesh for an illicit glory. So, then, we command that judgment be reserved in this matter. In the gospel we see that the publicans are closer to Christ than the Pharisees, so that even though they are worse in man's eyes, the gospel certainly commends them as being more fortunate; for it seems better to have fallen openly than to have held one's ground in secret godlessness. But we do not recommend that people go and sin on this account. We leave to God the judgments that are his own, judgments that are hidden and to be feared.

It follows from this that when the divine law is taught and observed through works, it results in human teaching. For the law itself is spiritual and given to humble a man and to compel him to seek Christ. The office of the law is not to demand works of us, but to show us our sin and our inability [to keep the law]. "Through the law comes the recognition of sin" [Rom. 3:20]. Therefore, just as the works of the law ought to be given up, so the teaching of the law ought to be given up. Here again you will say, "Are we therefore to live free of the law?" Another silly question! As if I would want to teach you less when I am telling you to know more! Although even in this context Paul in Romans 2 and 3 is bold enough to make the Jews who know and the Gentiles who do not equal to one another, making no distinction between those who are without the law and those who are under it.

But let us come now to their vows and works. Just as we have compared vows to the works of the divine law in the other objection[64] (for these days they seem to be regarded as a matter of law on the basis of the text, "Make your vow and keep it" [Ps. 76:11]), let us now compare them in the answer.

We have learned that the works of the law are done in two different frames of mind. Sometimes they are done simply by our own efforts and are our own works. Sometimes they are done by Christ who is in us; they are then Christ's work in us and Christ's gift. For the same reason that vows are included under the term law (more about this later), they must of necessity be performed in the double way in which the law is fulfilled. In some instances vows are undertaken by us and are our own efforts. Without any doubt they ought to be given up in these cases and condemned as things which draw the pious conscience away from Christ and turn that conscience to reliance on works, for they teach that righteousness and remission of sins can be achieved apart from Christ. But there is nothing in that except the kind of righteousness which Paul discarded as dung and dead loss [Phil. 3:8]. And moreover, it is not in our power to state whether he who keeps a vow is a better man than he who breaks a vow, which we gave an example of earlier to illustrate the works of the law.[65] Sometimes vows are made through Christ working in us in the spirit of freedom, provided that they are taken and kept voluntarily, when neither satisfaction for sins is claimed by them, nor righteousness and salvation sought through them. For a Christian man may observe all the laws, rites, and customs of all men everywhere and accommodate himself to them, to the extent that they are not contrary to the laws of God, and not put the confidence of his conscience in them. The conscience be-

[64] Cf. p. 298.
[65] Cf. p. 302.

longs to Christ and Christ to the conscience, and no one intrudes into the secret bedchamber of this spouse and his bride.[66] Whether you abstain from wine with the Turks or drink wine with Christians makes no difference at all, as long as you drink it with a good conscience. Paul accommodated himself to both gentiles and Jews with a perfectly free conscience in this way: with the one he used to fast and allow circumcision; with the other he used to eat without restriction and circumcise no one.[67] And so, if you vow to take up the religious life, and if you live with men of like mind, with a clear conscience that in monasticism you seek nothing to your advantage in your relationship with God, but because either your situation has brought you to embrace this kind of life, or it appeared to be the best way of life for you, without your thinking thereby that you are better than he who takes a wife or takes up farming, then in that case you are neither wrong to take vows nor wrong to live in this way, insofar as the propriety of the vow is concerned. But if love should demand that the vow be broken and you were to hold fast to your vow, you would be sinning, as we shall explain.

It is impossible to make vows with a conscience of this kind unless you are led inwardly and wondrously by the Spirit of Christ and are already saved. In other words, vows can be taken only by the elect. Otherwise, the whole rationale for taking and living under vows is entirely opposed to this kind of conscience. The whole idea of vows has been devised to ensnare the conscience and hold it captive to the bondage of the law. It actually takes pride in so doing. For who among the religious would allow himself to be put in the same class as a married man, a farmer, or a workman in the sight of God? Do not the religious in fact take their vows for the express purpose of appearing to serve God with a more devoted obedience than anybody else? Why do they despise as they do all other ways of living and esteem this one only? These people do not say with the prophet, "Thy mercy is better than all the ways of life" [Ps. 63:3]. The opinion that "one life is better than all

[66] Cf. pp. 223-224.

[67] Cf. Rom. 14:2-3; I Cor. 7:18-19.

others" may be true as far as men are concerned, but it is not true as far as God is concerned. So let us reveal here the thoughts of their hearts. What would the nuns and monks do if they heard that in the sight of God they are not a bit better than married people and mud-stained farmers? Will they not murmur against the householder that they are being treated the same as those who worked for but one hour while they alone have borne the burden and heat of the day? [Matt. 20:11-12]. Show me, I beg you, a nun or a monk who is content with the penny common to us all.[68] They say, "Why then have I persevered? Why have I not married? Why have I denied myself everything?" Do you see the thoughts of their hearts against the householder? First, they demand that God respect persons, that he regard works and not faith, that he prefer men to Christ. They are not concerned about what precious things others have received from Christ, but only with how many more wonderful things they have offered than anyone else. They confess by this murmuring that they have continued as monks not gladly and freely, that is, with a Christian and godly will, but with a will that is in bondage and which seeks its own advantage, in other words, a Jewish and godless will.[69] This is why their virginity is like that of the foolish virgins whose lamps went out because they had no oil in their flasks [Matt. 25:8] (which means they did not have a faith that was free and had a good conscience). What then do those magnificent bulls amount to which vaunt virginity, celibacy, vows, prerogatives, halos, and all the rest of the rot they preach whereby Christians are under oath to profess celibacy? What are they but satanic lies which stir up pride and lead to the corruption of the innocent conscience? They are all of one opinion. They would have all preferred to have married, had it not meant that they would be regarded as inferior in the sight of God, or so they thought. Since, therefore, the very nature of the institution is such that it calls to works not faith, how could a Christian vow ever be left intact unless it were kept by a divine miracle?

Indeed, just as one disputation gives rise to another, these

[68] I.e., with what all have in common in the mercy of God.
[69] Cf. p. 288, n. 49.

ungodly people will shout that I am a Jovinian and they will bring Jerome's[70] argument against Jovinian, in which he defended celibacy, to bear against me.[71] They will think that I have never read Jerome. They think that it is enough just to have read him; they never think it necessary to form some opinion about what they have read. Whatever they read is an article of faith. I myself do not know what Jovinian really meant.[72] Perhaps he did not handle the argument properly. What I do know, however, is that Jerome has not handled it properly. He treats virginity as a thing existing in its own right. He neither relates it to faith nor uses it to build up faith. If this kind of teaching goes on—it is only human teaching—no good work or virtue can be taught without disaster and danger. No one can deny that the holy man was brought to this view by human impetuosity and zeal and by too great a desire to please his friends, especially his dear Eustochium,[73] so that he overpowers Jovinian more by the weight of his authority than by the weight of learning. Jerome shows great indiscretion in raking together all sorts of scriptural proofs, appropriate and inappropriate alike. He would have made himself a great laughingstock had he had an opponent of the same authority as himself. For those very texts which Jerome holds out as the most important and which he thinks are the cardi-

---

[70] Cf. p. 346, n. 117.

[71] Jovinian, an unorthodox monk who died *ca.* 405, denied that virginity was a higher state than matrimony and that abstinence was better than eating with thankfulness. He opposed the idea that merit could be earned by virginity and fasting. As a result of his teaching monks and nuns left their monasteries to marry. He was condemned by synods of Rome and Milan, and both Jerome and Augustine wrote against him; Jerome in his *Adversus Jovinianum* (English translation in *PNF*² 6, 346 ff.), to which Luther refers, and Augustine in *On the Good of Marriage* (*PNF*¹ 3, 397 ff.), *Of Holy Virginity* (*PNF*¹ 3, 417 ff.), and *De haeresibus* (*MPL* 42, 45-46).

[72] Jovinian's works are not extant.

[73] St. Julia Eustochium (370-*ca.* 419) was a Roman virgin of aristocratic descent. She, her two sisters Blessila and Paulina, and their mother Paula, came under the strong ascetic influence of Jerome, who advised them on how to live a holy life in the midst of the city. Cf. Jerome's letter to Julia in *PNF*² 4, 22-41. When Blessila died as a result of austerities, there was a riot at the funeral. The crowds threatened to throw Jerome into the Tiber River. The women joined Jerome, who left the city. Jerome and the three women traveled in Egypt and Palestine, founding four monasteries in Bethlehem. Upon the death of her mother in 404, Julia assumed direction of these institutions. Cf. F. J. Foakes-Jackson, *The History of the Christian Church from the Earliest Times to A.D. 461* (6th ed.; Cambridge: J. Hall and Son, 1914), pp. 482-485.

nal points of his victory he manipulates—no, I would even go further and say he perverts them. For when Paul says, "He who takes a virgin does well, but he who does not does better" [I Cor. 7:38], he clearly reads into it the idea that this doing well and doing better is related to the idea of merits in the sight of God. He makes divisions among the people of God, while it is abundantly clear that Paul is talking about what is good and better in this life, saying that a young woman not encumbered by any responsibilities is more free to serve God. Every thought of merit Paul leaves to the faith common to us all.[74] And who knows, Jerome might be one of those of whom Ezekiel says, "If the prophet has erred and told a lie, I the Lord have deceived that prophet [Ezek. 14:9]. And what is still more to the point, why do we not pay attention only to the words of God? Why do we go on disregarding the counsel of the Holy Spirit and not prove all things before we accept them [I John 4:1]?

I too admit that when compared with everything else, virginity is no light matter; but at the same time I say this: If a virgin makes herself superior to others or even equal to others before God because of her virginity, she is a virgin of Satan. The gospel teaches us to sit in the lowest place [Luke 14:10] and to think more highly of others than of ourselves [Phil. 2:3]. It is in this way that virginity is to be handled and taught, so that it is retained not on account of any law, necessity, or hope of reward, but with a selfless and willing mind. The virgin would then think like this, "Although I could marry, I am content to remain unmarried, not because it is commanded, not because it is advised, not because it is greater and more sacrificial than all other virtues, but because this seems to me to be the right way to live, just as marriage or farming may seem right to somebody else. I do not want the responsibilities of married life, I want to be free of responsibilities and have time for God." See here, this is what it means to be a virgin in Christian simplicity, for she glories not in her virginity, but in Christ. Every one of us ought to serve God freely with the gift he has, but we must all glory in what is common to us all, a simple virgin faith in the one

[74] Cf. Jerome's argument in *PNF*² 6, 22-41.

and only Christ, in whom there is neither male nor female, and consequently neither married nor unmarried, neither widow nor spinster, but all are one in Christ [Gal. 3.28].

Most appropriate in this connection are those wonderful stories in the *Lives of the Fathers*[75] where, by authority of divine oracle, that Alexandrian tanner was regarded as equal, indeed, superior to Anthony, where the married were regarded more highly than the virgin or celibate, the citizen than the monk, the common man than the father of monks. Or again, that story where two married women and a certain piper who had at one time been a robber were made equal to Paphnutius, an abbot of Thebes.[76] And there are others. What did God want with these stories except to use the examples of these saintly men to get rid to some extent of the blasphemous teachings and institutions of the sects, which even by that time were beginning to rise with the greatest speciousness against the way of faith. Now there are diverse gifts of God, some great and some small, I Corinthians 12 [:4-11], 7 [:7]. The rich have more than the poor, but no one should introduce divisions for that reason and disburse merits and rewards before God according to gifts. Nor shall they prefer themselves to others. Rather, all shall serve freely, abounding in the same faith in Christ common to us all. He is the same in everyone, but does different works in us all. If you take it as an indignity that you, a virgin, should be treated the same as a married woman, then get married. It is far better for you to be a godly and free married woman than a godless virgin seeking rewards. The saying holds true, "God regards neither works nor person, but the heart and faith." Jeremiah 5 [:3], "O Lord, thine eyes regard faith."

You can see, therefore, that what is proved by these examples is this: even if you can find some instance of a vow that is godly by virtue of a miracle, still the very institution of the vow and the reason for teaching such a life are condemned as ungodly. Even the

[75] *Vitae patrum. MPL* 73, 1038. Luther used these stories quite often. Just before his death he persuaded Georg Major to edit these legends and stories for the use of preachers and teachers in giving sound examples from the history of the church and the words and deeds of the fathers. Luther actually wrote a brief preface for the book. Cf. *WA* 54, 109-111.

[76] Cf. p. 316, n. 85; cf. also *MPL* 73, 1170.

law when it is taught according to the letter can contain a good example, as in Paul, who never interpreted the law according to the letter. Yet the method of teaching the letter of the law and its works is blasphemous. Bernard took his vows in the same way, and he lived up to them, not because the vows compelled him to do so, but from a free choice of spirit, although I grant you his vow did not teach this freedom; rather it taught the necessity of the absolute opposite of freedom. These things are said in answer to the aforementioned objection so that we may know that if a vow were a precept (in accordance with Psalm 76 [:11], "Make your vows and keep them"), its works would have to be done in a spirit of freedom just like the works of the Ten Commandments, not because they are vows, but because they are done freely and gladly. Although, as I have just said, no one keeps them except by miraculous guidance; for the very nature of these vows, together with the way of life that goes with them, is repugnant. Men are torn away from freedom and are taken off into bondage.

But we now go further and deny that a vow is or ever could be a precept, just as the works of the law are not and never could be precepts. For God is not a God who wants ungodliness (Psalm 5 [:4]). In fact, we are proving that evangelical freedom forbids vows. Paul is asserting evangelical freedom when he says in Galatians 1 [:8], "But if an angel or someone else from heaven were to teach anything other than what you have heard, let him be anathema." And later, "You, brethren, are called to freedom" [Gal. 5:13]. And again, "He that is unsettling your minds, whoever he be, will bear his judgment" [Gal. 5:10]. You can take it from this that no man may teach or permit anything that is against evangelical freedom. This freedom comes from divine authority. God ordained it. He will never revoke it. He can neither accept anything that runs counter to it, nor allow anyone to violate it even by the most insignificant ordinance. It is, however, not only that freedom which reigns in the spirit and conscience (about which we spoke earlier and by which we are neither accused nor defended by any works we do); it is also that freedom under which all the commandments of men are summed up, as well as what may be regarded as outward ceremonies, which include such matters as food, clothing, persons, gestures, places, vessels, and days, things a man may observe or not observe, for as long as, where, how, when, and as often as he likes or the occasion demands. Everything not specifically commanded by God is abrogated and made a matter of free choice. Paul says in Colossians 2 [:20-23], "If therefore you have died with Christ and have passed beyond the rudimentary notions of this world, why behave as though you were still living in the world, held fast by human ordinances? Do not touch that, Do not touch the other, Do not handle this. . . . All of these are things which perish in the use. They are human injunctions and precepts. True, they have about them an air of wisdom with their religiosity, and humility, and disciplining of the body, but they are not an honorable way of coping with the flesh." In this passage the Apostle plainly prohibits the holding of human ordinances. And in Matthew 15 [:9] Christ says, "They worship me in vain who teach the commandments of men." And Titus 1 [:14] says, "Do not heed the commandments of men who are opposed to truth."

Quite certainly these are divine commandments prohibiting the teaching and hearing of the doctrines of men. Is the taking of vows not a human institution, pure and simple? Is it not based on tonsure, garb, food, drink, days, places, postures, and other ceremonies? Where did God command any of them? Where did he command this poverty, this obedience, this chastity? Well then, so what? Are you still in any doubt that it is wrong to make such vows, or that it always was? By divine decree these things are optional, but by human decree you make them obligatory. Do you think God would rather accept what you are wrong about than what he himself has ordained? God cannot permit a sin to be made out of matters of clothing, food, drink, and certain days, because he never willed it to be possible for a man to commit sin with respect to these matters. Yet you maintain that sin can be committed. By the same argument he never wanted celibacy to be made obligatory, but left it a matter of free choice. God did not want it to take on the nature of sin if someone chose to marry. Yet by your vow you make celibacy lifelong, as well as obligatory under the law.[77] Since it can no longer be denied that they are simply doctrines of men,

[77] The law referred to here is the tradition of the monks.

what else is there to do then, but to demonstrate here that the vows of the religious as well as the whole idea of monasticism are against the freedom of the gospel, and are forbidden by divine commands? It is no less sinful to violate the freedom established by divine providence than to sin against any other commandment of God. Indeed, you may take and keep all the vows you like,[78] as long as you do no violence to the freedom commanded by God. You have no right at all either to take away that freedom or to set up sin where God has not willed sin to be. God has not willed that it be possible to sin in the practice of chastity, but made chastity a matter of option, so that the man who marries does not sin. This was Paul's teaching in I Corinthians 7 [:36-38], when he counseled virginity. He added this: the man who had decided to keep his virgin[79] was under no compulsion. In this statement Paul forbade that chastity be demanded of anyone, or forced on anyone, or made a matter of necessity. Therefore, as soon as it began to be forced on people and demanded of them, it was immediately refuted and made a matter of free choice by Paul.

Let us go back then to what was said earlier. The vow to chastity and the whole of monasticism, if godly, ought necessarily to include the freedom to retract the vow. The vow should be interpreted something like this: "I vow to thee obedience, chastity, and poverty, together with the whole rule of St. Augustine until death. I do it of my own free will, which means that I would be free to change my mind if it seemed good." If you interpret the vow otherwise, or take a different view of it, you sin against the divine freedom God ordained for us, as you can see from the earlier arguments. Under no circumstances can God accept anything else without revoking his own freedom, that is, without denying himself. What is it to me if the holy fathers (or anyone else) never took vows in this way or understood them in this way? What if they were all wrong, or were strangely misled? What the gospel has to say is clear and irrefutable: the doctrines of men are condemned, vows are a matter of free choice, and we are their masters. Therefore, we cannot become slaves to vows even on the authority of

[78] Cf. Ps. 76:11.

[79] I.e., to preserve her virginity.

angels, not to mention our own foolish religiosity and humility, as Paul says [Col. 2:23]. Likewise, the truth is clear that the institution of vows is a slavish doctrine of men. Why then do we go on letting the slaves ride and the masters walk, as Solomon expressed it?[80] Why do we not rather give thanks to Christ, who has honored us by this gift of freedom and kept it inviolate, while we have striven to violate it with our ungodly vows, to Christ who has decreed that our vows are void, a matter of free choice, and of no matter? While we raved on, he kindly watched over us.

At this point someone will perhaps laugh, and deride a vow of this kind as ridiculous. They will say it is some sort of sham vow. They will ask, "What else is it but delusion to say, 'Of my own free will I vow to thee to do whatever seems good to me'?" Let him laugh who wants to laugh. Only let him bear this in mind at the same time: there is nothing remarkable or new in men behaving foolishly and ridiculously when they conduct their affairs in the light of their own wisdom, apart from and beyond the word of God. "Thy word is truth," Christ says [John 17:17]. What then do you think the word of man is in contrast, if not a lie? This is ridiculous—except to those who hear and understand the true gospel of freedom. What is more, the error of their absurd teaching only stirs up the wrath of God in its severest and worst form for so many thousands of souls which are utterly lost and desperately caught up in these snares. The vow is and remains a human invention. Yet it is not altogether ridiculous. Voluntarily to vow subjection of this kind for only a given time is not without worth. We know this kind of voluntary vow was an institution of the primitive church and was a wholesome practice whereby for a time the elders instructed the young people who had been handed over to them in faith and in discipline.[81] The epistles of the apostles Peter and Paul declare that youth should be subject to its elders [I Pet. 5:5]. The first Christian schools arose from this practice. Even girls were educated in them, as the story of St. Agnes shows.[82] Colleges and monasteries even-

[80] Cf. Eccles. 10:7.
[81] Cf. *MPL* 17, 735. Luther often expressed the view that monasteries had developed from these early schools of discipline and learning and that it would be better were they to return to this function. Cf. *Theses on Vows,* Thesis 99 (*WA* 8, 333), and also Theses 90 and 91 (*WA* 8, 327).
[82] Cf. p. 174.

tually developed from these early beginnings for the benefit of those who of their own volition wanted to remain in these schools for life. When, however, wealth and leisure increased, those who had taken on the education of the young began to grow lazy and to look after their own interests, and when the young people had grown more rebellious, they invented the snares of vows. By means of vows they bound the consciences of youth so that each held himself in check by the dread of sin, and those responsible for them secured peace and quiet for themselves. These days the mad custom of the schools is to ensnare the youths by vows and to tear their consciences to shreds, so that it is no longer necessary to look after these young people and take care of them—that way the teachers can peacefully catch another forty winks. And so free Christian schools have been made into servile Jewish monasteries, which are actually nothing but synagogues of ungodliness. If then the present-day vow were related to the ancient custom, and kept in the same spirit, there would be no harm in it. Without any doubt God would regard it as nothing but the temporary continuation of an old tradition whereby immature, unlettered souls may absorb a Christian education, and eventually be allowed to go out again as free men. We shall prove this later on, and even bring in works of God in support of our case.

At this point some simpleton or quarrelsome person might object and say: If God wanted to make celibacy so free as to be interchangeable with marriage, then on the basis of the same freedom it is permissible to desert one's wife and exchange marriage for celibacy. Or, if God's law compels a man not to forsake his wife, then God's law would compel a celibate not to forsake his vows. Either procedure is sinful and prohibited by God's law. Or, alternatively, it would not be permissible to contract a marriage lest, when the freedom of choice is taken away, celibacy would be disallowed. Or, it will be obligatory to keep the vow, since marriage will have become an impossibility because vows had been taken.

This is my answer to these objections. The freedom of the gospel is valid only in matters relating to the relationship between you and God, and not in matters between you and your neighbors. For God does not want robbery with sacrifice [Isa. 61:8]. Neither does he want anything to take place or anyone to do anything that is harmful to one's neighbor. In fact he wants everything to be done for the benefit of one's neighbor. He ordained freedom for you so that you could marry or live before him as a celibate in perfect freedom. Nor was it his wish that this freedom would be altered between him and you. Neither does he allow you to bind yourself and put yourself under obligations for his sake. He gave you freedom in all things and makes you free. What else is a vow except your making something obligatory that he declares is a matter of choice. But in granting you this freedom God does not prevent you from putting yourself under obligation or binding yourself to your neighbor, because your neighbor has not, like God, commanded you to be free. Otherwise, it would even be permissible to make and break all contracts, agreements, and treaties at will. Therefore, in matrimony you are already given over to the claim and authority of another [I Cor. 7:4]. God does not want his law thrust aside to enable you to serve him. Yet, if marital claims should cease owing to the wife's death or to her having given consent to separate, then perfect freedom to marry or not to marry exists between you and God, as existed in the first place before marriage. The vow of celibacy may be likened to a marriage bond made either with a husband who has since died or with a husband where the marriage has been dissolved by mutual consent. In the case of a deceased husband, or in the case of separation, where you have the power to withhold access to your person, the husband will no longer exercise his rights to sexual intercourse. (We are assuming, of course, that the agreement between you had been properly attested in writing, under seal and before witnesses.) In this situation it is as if you, foolish creature that you were, in your desire to do something really big, were solemnly to vow to have sexual intercourse with your husband for the first time, seeking by this very proposal not only to corroborate the earlier right of remaining chaste, but to top it and go one better! Wouldn't everybody say you were mad!

In a similar way God has made a pact of freedom with you in baptism. Consequently, it is always a matter of free choice whether you marry or do not. He will never accept anything that runs counter to this freedom. And yet you, by taking vows to keep this freedom better and more perfectly, turn this freedom into bondage and obligation. Could anything more insane be done? Therefore, properly speaking, monks are devotees of Baal who want to make God, who made them free by the freedom of the gospel, into some sort of spouse for themselves through the bondage of their vows. For the word Baal means a husband who has a wife. And so, not content with the freedom common to us all, the monks presume to make God into some sort of Baal who uniquely and especially belongs to them above all other others. They think that by this kind of worship they are acting in a more than evangelical manner, when they are really raging like madmen against the gospel. [I say this] because it is their practice to leap around the altar[83] and boast of their works over and above the faith common to us all, and devise cultic practices, and torture themselves with the petty little rules and teachings they have devised for themselves. Yet they never mortify the old man, etc.[84]

Let us bring this discussion to an end now by reaching the conclusion that lifelong poverty, obedience, and chastity may be observed, but cannot be vowed, taught, or imposed. The freedom of the gospel may still be retained by observing these things (poverty, obedience, and chastity), but as soon as you teach them, vow them, and demand them, then evangelical freedom is lost. By the same argument, the saints who observed these things did so freely. They would have observed them even if they had never made vows, even if vows had never been taught or demanded of them. For that very reason their vows, though foolish, did no harm to their faith and their freedom of spirit. It is one thing for something to happen when it has neither been taught nor demanded, but quite a different thing altogether for the same thing to be taught, demanded, and made compulsory. This makes a law out of a single instance, a precept out of a work, a rule from one example, an essential out of the nonessential. What could be more absurd and what could be more harmful? The former is of God; the latter, of man. Therefore, we must abide by the first and let the other go. We do not there-

[83] Cf. I Kings 18:26.
[84] Cf. Rom. 8:13 and Col. 3:5.

fore condemn vows in themselves if anyone should choose to follow them; it is the teaching and the prescribing of vows that we condemn. What has happened with these vows is what began to happen at the Council of Nicaea on the subject of continence. For some years priests and bishops had lived as celibates of their own volition; then certain persons began to try to turn this example into a commandment and thereafter to compel celibacy as a matter of conscience. By this time faith and the gospel had already grown weak to this extent, even in this holy synod, and the traditions of men were growing strong. But a certain Paphnutius[85] resisted the whole council and prevented any legislation on the matter of celibacy. It remained for the Roman Antichrist to bring this idolatry to pass. And so, while in former times the monks were celibates and lived in poverty and obedience of their own free will, their successors eventually turned their voluntary and evangelical example into a compulsory vow. This time there was no Paphnutius to resist, since by now sin was in control and the wrath of God had brought to a head the fruits of their error, as Paul had prophesied [II Thess. 2:11]. Consequently, St. Bernard and others kept vows of chastity, obedience, and poverty, but not because of the vows. Instead, they observed the ancient example of the fathers and of the gospel. Having fallen because of natural human failing, they justified this reprobate tradition and taught this damnable business of vows, though they themselves had long followed another, very different way. But the result of their error had to be upheld, even by a wrong understanding of the examples of the fathers, for the sake of those who had never made the love of truth their own that they might be saved [II Thess. 2:10].

---

[85] Paphnutius (d. *ca.* 360), bishop of a city in Upper Thebaid, was an Egyptian monk who had been a disciple of St. Anthony. He had suffered such persecution that his scarred and mutilated body was a marvel to the bishops assembled at Nicaea. A proposal at Nicaea to follow the Spanish custom and prohibit marital relations to married bishops, priests, and deacons after ordination was effectively resisted by Paphnutius on the ground that it would lay too heavy a yoke on the clergy.

IV

Vows Are Contrary to the Commandments of God

We see then that the monastic institution not only has no divine authority, but that it is actually contrary to the Christian faith and evangelical freedom. Proof that it has no divine authority lies in the fact that monasticism has no testimony from Scripture. Nor is there any sign or wonder whereby its divine authority may be proved. In fact, it is actually prohibited and condemned along with all other traditions of men. Now let us consider our fourth point, namely, how monastic vows can be reconciled to the divine commandments. They cannot be anything else but contrary to all divine commandments when they are contrary to the One from whom and through whom and in whom all things exist. For he is holy with the holy and perverse with the perverse [Ps. 18:26]. And so, just as nothing is clean to the unclean, but everything is unclean [Titus 1:15], so with the perverse, everything is perverse and nothing right. And here again I want the saints exonerated once for all, so that we do not always have to make excuses for them. I do not dispute that the saints lived under this very vow; I am disputing the institution itself. [I am not disputing] whether the three youths survived the furnace in Babylon,[86] but whether everyone everywhere should be allowed to rush into the same furnace or worship the golden image of the king. I am not arguing whether Paul lived a life of celibacy, but whether his example should be made into a law or a matter of doctrine. This same Paul used to keep the Mosaic law in its entirety, but he never wanted that law to be taught or learned for the purpose of keeping it. In the same way Bernard used to live under the vow, yet without the vow, just as the Apostle lived under the law, yet without the law. But it does not necessarily follow that a vow or a rule has to be made into a matter of doctrine or a way of life. In fact, it should rather be abolished.

[86] Cf. Dan 3:8-30.

And earlier, when we considered faith,[87] we showed quite clearly that this institution of monasticism was contrary to the First Table of the commandments, that is, the first three. Faith is commanded in the first commandment; praise and confession of the name [of God] in the second; and the works of God in us are commanded in the third. In these three commandments the true and legitimate worship of God is fulfilled. But the institution of vows, when it teaches works, makes faith devoid of content (as we have said). And then when people have cast aside the name of God, they establish their own. They are no longer called Christians, or children of God, but rather Benedictines, Dominicans, Franciscans, Augustinians. They boast of these names and of their father-founders more than they do of Christ. They do not believe that it is by this name that they are saved, and that they are justified because they are baptized and because they are Christians. [They believe they are saved] simply because they bear the name of their order. Therefore, they trust in their own name and glory in it as if baptism and faith had perished long ago in a shipwreck. Consequently they bear and invoke the name of God in vain. They bear only their own name, for they have built on works. You can see that they are in absolute despair when they realize they have broken the rules of their order. That is because they think that the keeping of these rules is essential for righteousness and salvation. But when they see that they have kept the rule or repent because they have not observed it, then they confidently expect to receive the crown of glory in the name of their order far and away more certainly than because they are baptized in Christ. In fact, by trusting in these things, pursuing their own interests, and expecting to be crowned before God because they were monks, they have forgotten that they have been baptized into the works of Christ. They are quite satisfied that they have emulated their fathers when they have kept their statutes and followed their examples, or when they are penitent for not having attained them. They make nothing of the fact that they have Christ and his works in faith. O what perdition! And how we ought to dread it!

So you see, faith and the first commandment cannot stand alongside the teaching of the monastic vow (save by a miracle of

[87] Cf. pp. 273-295.

God's grace). Neither can the second commandment [stand alongside] their self-glory and their love of titles. For since Christ alone ascended into heaven, who also descended[88] and is now in heaven, it is impossible for a Benedictine, an Augustinian, a Dominican, a Carthusian, and their like to ascend into heaven. The whole lot of them are seeking heaven with lamps that have no oil [Matt. 25:1-13]. In other words, they seek heaven by means of their own works. Without their own works they expect nothing of God, for this is what their way of life and their vows teach them. But a Christian man ascends to heaven by virtue of the works of another, and that other is Christ, in whom he has been baptized and with whom he has been raised.[89] It is no longer he himself who lives, but Christ who lives in him [Gal. 2:20] and grants him a perfect sabbath rest from all his own works. What a dreadful thing it is, therefore, to be held bound by such a conscience! You cannot be saved unless you keep the rules of your order, and you can only be saved if you do! Is not Christ in all his power made silent and ineffective by this? Yet this kind of conscience would never have existed if vows had never been instituted. But now this conscience is everywhere. Nowhere is there a holy sabbath.[90] The word of the psalmist, Psalm 74 [:8] is fulfilled, "Let us abolish all the festival days of God from the land." See if this is not what Paul says in Romans 2 [:22, 24], "You who abhor idols are committing sacrilege: the name of the Lord is blasphemed through you among nations." Who of all men boasts as much of the worship of God as the monastic? No one curses idolatry more, yet they are sacrilegious. What sacred thing do they rob? The very thing which sanctifies everything else, the holy name of God! They blot out the name Christian and set up their own in its place. They want to be saved in the name of their own order when a man can be saved and ought to be saved only in Christ's name. As Peter says in Acts 15 [4:12], "Neither is any other name given to us under heaven in which we can be saved."

Just as it is impossible for a man who depends on faith in Christ to seek salvation in his own name (for he knows the works

[88] Cf. John. 3:13.

[89] Cf. Rom. 6:3-5.

[90] I.e., a rest from works.

and merits of no person save Christ alone and therefore does not have any name by which he may be saved and sanctified except that of Christ alone), so is it impossible for him who relies on works and vows not to seek salvation in his own name. Such a man has works and merits over and above the works and merits of Christ; therefore, he also has a name other than the name of Christ. What else is this then but stealing the name of Christ and appropriating it to oneself, saying, "I am Christ," as we have shown earlier in Matthew 24 [:5].[91] What could be a greater sacrilege than that? The man who says, "I shall be saved by my own works" says nothing else than "I shall be Christ," since the works of Christ alone save as many as are saved. That blasphemy of the name of the Lord among the nations is when holiness and sanctification are everywhere attributed to a name other than that of God. They all say that their orders are holy, as if orders made those who observed them holy, or as if it were something holy to live under their order, when only the name of the Lord sanctifies and when holiness consists in walking in him alone. They themselves are the authors of this widespread blasphemy in their sacrilegious acts by which they lay hold of the name of the Lord and the work of the Lord's name. They seduce and ensnare the whole world by this blasphemy.

Since Christians, however, ought to keep as far away as possible from such sacrilegious acts, blasphemous opinions, and consciences, why do you remain in doubt any longer that you ought to abstain from monastic vows, flee from them and avoid them, and change them altogether, as well as the whole way of life that goes with them? It is further shown that this kind of life produces this kind of conscience. By its very nature it cannot do otherwise, and you may see as a matter of everyday experience that consciences of this kind are produced the world over. Or, if you were to see Korah swallowed up with his tents and his goods, would you remain in the midst of the pit or would you not rather follow the prudence of the rest of Israel and flee, saying, "Lest the earth swallow us up also" [Num. 16:31-34]? Or would you remain because you saw that the children of Korah, who remained there, were saved [Num. 26:11]?

---

[91] Cf. pp. 286-287.

You must realize that this happened (as Moses records) through a great miracle. You cannot deny that the monastic institution is a seditious movement directed against Christ, and is exactly the same kind as Korah's rebellion. For monasticism encourages divisions among the people of Christ, and, as you see, its teaching is contrary to faith and causes men to have faith in their own works and to hold them in esteem. You cannot point out a single monk (apart from a miracle) who is not bound fast by this sacrilege and by a blasphemous conscience, and who does not believe that he will be saved by keeping the rules of his order and actually damned if he does not. How else would he take his vows and keep them, if his conscience were not of such a kind? What help will it be to you if the children of this Korah are preserved in these sacrilegious and blasphemous tents? It is a miracle of divine power, not a general rule for life.

Monkery, however, is well named Korah. The word Korah means "bald," or "shorn." The Apostle says that a man is the glory of God and ought not to cover his head [I Cor. 11:7] so that you may understand that that rebellious Korah set himself up as head without Christ as Head and without the glory of God, and that Korah gloried in his own name against Christ. How rightly Peter described such people when he said in II Peter 2 [:1-2] that they are lying teachers who shall bring in their own ideas and damnable sects, denying even the Lord who bought them, through whom the way of truth will be blasphemed. What else are these opinions of theirs and the damnable sects to which Peter refers but matters we have just discussed—their ideas of conscience, their teachings and division into sects, their sacrileges and blasphemies? By these things Christ is denied, along with all his works as well as his name. The works and names of men are set up in Christ's stead, and all that is of Christ—righteousness, salvation, and sanctification—is attributed to the works and names of men.

But when at this point these blasphemers, since they are incorrigible and without faith, see they are caught in such patent blasphemy, they devise distinctions, of which they have an abundance. They say that they had never taught anything but that Christ and the grace of God are the main points in their orders and are regarded as the holiest of all things. In other respects the orders are holy in a lesser way[92] by virtue of belonging to what is holy,[93] etc. Or will they produce another figment out of their head to prevent their appearing to be trapped or confused. My reply is: Why were these things not taught from the start? Who has yet shown those souls already lost, as well as those on their way to perdition, this distinction, which had to be thought out at a later time? These people simply took the word "holy" at its face value and knew nothing of this dark and ambiguous illusion. So far, so good! Let them stand up and teach the distinctions they are now making. Let them cry out to the people in words to this effect, "Understand this: it is far better to be a Christian than a monk." Then you will see how many will enter the monastery, or, what is more to the point, how many will remain inside. Yet they still teach that monks are far better and much holier than the ordinary believers. This is that voice of perdition by which the faithful separate themselves from Christ in the hope of a greater piety than they found in Christ. This is sacrilege. This is blasphemy. Christ cannot abide with this. If they had not been so proud of their monasticism, they, too, could not have remained as monks.

There is nothing to their claim that the important, principal notion is enhanced when its lesser and secondary notion is strengthened. Even if this were true, who will guide the uninstructed masses to prevent their laying hold of the lesser for the greater, as they are actually doing now? It is a miracle not to go astray here. This is why the stumbling-block[94] must be removed entirely, and only the greater One put in its place. Why then do they not persuade men to the utmost of their strength to leave the lesser and lay hold of the greater? And why do they not teach the monks to leave their monasteries with the same energy they expend in leading them from something greater to something less and in ensnaring people into entering religious orders?

Now this is false on two counts. First, they actually hold that their own monastic institution is greater and more significant, and

[92] *Minus principaliter.*

[93] *Participative.*

[94] I.e., the state of affairs which permits men to choose the lesser (monasticism) for the greater (Christ).

that the simple Christian life is the lesser and is to be held in disdain. Their sacrilegious and blasphemous talk proves this when they call men to the monastic life rather than to Christianity. Second, a totally different idea of holiness is depicted. Now only Christ is holy, and he will not tolerate our being sanctified and saved in any other name, as we earlier quoted Peter.[95] So, whichever way you turn you will find an institution which in its very nature is ungodly, sacrilegious, blasphemous, and against Christ, an effective cause of perdition to all who are not miraculously saved like the children of Korah.

And so, the true worship of God established in the first three commandments lies dead. The streets of Zion mourn because there is none that comes to the solemn assembly [Lam. 1:4]. In place of this true worship they have substituted another which is most becoming to them. It is a great pomp of ceremonies distinguished by vestments and postures, by canticles and lections. In the whole lot there is nothing about faith, the divine name, or about the work of God. Everything about it is utterly and completely human. A trace of this kind of worship can be detected in the institution of Paul in I Corinthians 14 [:1-19] where he teaches that three things should take place in the assembly of the church. First, speaking with tongues or singing psalms; second, prophesying or interpretation; third, prayer. In the first place, that means that something used to be recited from the Scriptures or the psalms. Then the prophets would interpret and teach. Third, they prayed together. That was a divine and most Christian institution ordained for teaching and exhortation. The first one is emulated today by the readings at Matins, by the Epistles, by the Gospels, and by the selected canticles; the second by the homilies; the third by responses, antiphons, graduals, and all the rest of the things generally read or sung. But none of it is done properly! All these things are done not with the intention of teaching or instructing, but simply with the desire of performing so many works. They are quite satisfied just to have read them, sung them, or bellowed them.

This work is seriously sought after, and it is called the worship of God. What is actually read and sung, however, or why it is read

[95] Cf. p. 321.

and sung, never even enters their mind, and there is no prophet to interpret or teach. Therefore, to prevent their being entirely inactive in this wonderful worship of God, they devote great care and solicitude to the reading and the singing. They painstakingly distinguish one part from another, they make proper pauses and phrases, giving the closest attention to these details. They have regard for just one thing, and that is how well, how devotedly, and how commendably the office has been read or sung. This is the ultimate end of divine worship. In their idea of worship disciplines, penances, clauses, statutes, sins, and merits are given the place of honor. It might even be said that this very demanding worship of God is performed so that during their lifetime these important and serious-minded men might learn at least a little bit about grammar and music. What else can they be judged as seeking?

If now (as Paul says) some unbeliever were to enter into the midst of these men and heard them braying, mumbling, and bellowing, and saw that they were neither preaching nor praying, but rather, as their custom is, were sounding forth like those pipe organs (with which they have so brilliantly associated themselves, each one set in a row just like his neighbor), would this unbeliever not be perfectly justified in asking, "Have you gone mad?" [I Cor. 14:23]. What else are these monks but the tubes and pipes Paul referred to as giving no distinct note but rather blasting out into the air [I Cor. 14:7]? Is it any different from a man who seeking to lecture mounts the platform and talks for a whole hour in a language which is foreign to the people and which nobody understands? Is not this talking into the air [I Cor. 14:9]? Would we not think this man mad? I grant that divine worship of this kind suits sacrilegious and blasphemous enemies of Christ, since they are not one whit better than those dumb, wooden pipes, sounding forth with much effort, teaching nothing, learning nothing, and praying nothing. And yet they boast that this senseless work is the highest worship, and draw to themselves the world's wealth on the merits of this work. Such an idea of holiness is becoming to a household like this.

I am not talking about those saints who lived a godly life in the midst of these follies. I am talking about the idea of divine worship involved in these practices. If other factors had not operated toward the disruption and dissolution of monastic vows, this in itself is a more than sufficient cause. For what else is it but a pure laughingstock, or, as the Apostle puts it, madness. But this is exactly what does happen, because those who become monks earnestly seek what they have vowed above all else. This is the way they propose to serve God. Because of this they forsake the world, its affairs, and their parents. Because of this they deny themselves to follow Christ. In this way audacious and blasphemous men adapt the divine oracles of Christ to fit in with this childish, ridiculous, and foolish performance, in which they actually stand in rows to worship God like rows of tubes, pipes, and trumpets, mute and insensate. In so doing they at the same time deny all true worship of God. If you knew that you had taken your vows earnestly, and afterward understood that those vows were both ludicrous and ridiculous, would you not repent of your vow? Would you not change? Would you not excuse it as a mistake if you had taken a vow in ignorance? Quite certainly you see that this applies in the case of monastic vows today. Or do you think that vows of this kind are acceptable to God and praiseworthy in his sight? Or do you think God wants a lot of dumb pipes to assemble themselves and delight him by blowing off into thin air?

I know perfectly well that Bernard and many men like him were upheld by God, so with all godly seriousness they might hold this nonsense in check. The sermons which he preached and taught are extant in the community of brothers. By this one work he restored the old institution of Paul,[96] and saved himself and his brethren with him, as Paul said of Timothy [I Tim. 4:16]. If there were men of Bernard's caliber in the monasteries they could be tolerated, because they would in part be observing the institution of Paul in all seriousness. But where they are just dead pipes and dumb tubes which sound in the air, they are, as Paul says, to be criticized by the unbeliever and charged with insanity. How much more then ought the faithful to give up vows completely and get away from them! Unless we wanted to be worse than heathen and infidels and call wholesome and holy that which the heathen, in agreement with Paul, quite properly deem mad. Do not believe,

[96] Cf. pp. 288-293.

then, that your vow has been demanded by God or that it is justified by these mad practices, but confidently believe that it is rejected and condemned, since you not only tempt God, but you even mock him by these ridiculous performances. These few observations on the first three commandments must suffice for the time being.

Vows Are Against Love

Let us pass on to the Second Table of the commandments and sum up its contents under two headings: obedience to parents and love of neighbor. After faith in God there is nothing greater than obedience to parents, about which Paul spoke magnificently when he discussed widows in I Timothy 5 [:4], "Let them first learn to rule their own house and make a return of duty to their parents, for that is acceptable to God." Here Paul expressly prohibits the acceptance of a widow[97] if she has a house she ought to look after and parents she ought to obey. He even goes further and says, "If anybody does not provide for his own, and especially those of his own household, he has denied the faith and is worse than an infidel" [vs. 8]. It is quite unnecessary to record how Paul prefers love above everything else (I Corinthians 13), making everything nothing if it is done without love. What Paul says in the case of a widow, however, must be taken to apply in the same way to all children. Again, I am not talking here about the examples of the saints or of a miraculous event. I am talking of the very institution of making vows, and I pronounce and declare by divine authority that no vow, if it is to be godly and gracious in the sight of God, can be absolute. All vows are conditional, except those of obedience to parents and love of neighbor. Let the man be anathema who has taken a vow or will have kept a vow in conflict with his responsibility toward his parents and toward his neighbor. Or put differently, he has denied his faith and is worse than an infidel, as the Apostle expresses it. For we can do nothing against God, but only for God [II Cor. 13:8]. Since the monastic institution impiously, impudently, and openly teaches that it is not permissible to obey par-

[97] I.e., as a responsibility of the congregation.

ents or to care for the affairs of others (for they say that a monk is dead to the world, dedicated to God, and must do so much in the monastery that parents, neighbors, indeed, the whole world, can suffer distress, collapse, and perish), then let it be absolutely anathema either to take vows or keep them. They quote here an example from the *Lives of the Fathers,* an example as godless as it is horrible, where a mother was trying to visit her two sons who were hermits and wanted with all a mother's natural desire to see the fruit of her womb. But the two sons shut the gates and refused to let their mother see them. They promised that she would see them in future glory if she put up with never seeing them in this life.[98] When I hear this example praised (and there are many of the same kind in the *Lives of the Fathers*) I seem to be listening to people who praise Lucretia[99] or Saul[100] because they killed themselves nobly, or to certain other strange tales of the heathen. But these men call this virtue, even Christian virtue. In this way they corrupt those words of Christ which are both saving words and applicable to all, "Whoever loves father and mother more than me is not worthy of me" [Matt. 10:37]. And again, "Everyone who has forsaken home, or brethren, etc., shall receive a hundredfold, and shall inherit everlasting life [Matt. 19:29]. And Psalm 45 [:10], "Hearken, O daughter, and consider, and incline your ear; forget your own people and your father's house," etc. These and like words, which are spirit and life, are crying aloud the doctrine of faith in Christ. It is on account of faith in Christ that everything should be forsaken. But these sacrilegious and blasphemous men make these words suit their own death and deceit, their own flesh and blood.[101]

This is where my indignation is sorest, and I am burning to put these lies right for this foolishness is far worse than sacrilege or blasphemy. But words and thoughts with which I could decently attack these monstrosities fail me. On account of them—perhaps on

[98] *MPL* 73, 792.

[99] After she had been outraged by Sextus Tarquinius (545-510 B.C.), the seventh and last Roman king, Lucretia summoned her husband and friends, and, after making them take an oath to drive out the tyrannical ruler, she plunged a knife into her heart.

[100] I Sam. 31:3-4.

[101] I.e., their own ideas of self-sacrifice and discipleship.

account of this abomination alone—I want the whole idea of the monastery rooted out, wiped out, and abolished, as indeed it ought to be. Would that the Lord, as he did in the case of Sodom and Gomorrah when Lot and his daughters were snatched out of the midst of it all [Gen. 19:15-29], would sink them into the depths with fire and brimstone from heaven, so that not even their memory should be left and there would then be no need to invoke anathema on them.

Just take a look at your holy and wonderful vow! In former times you took vows not because you wanted to be better Christians, but because you had a sublime faith: the simple mistake [of taking vows] excused your audacity. But now you take your vows to a brazen godlessness which will not accept you unless you first forswear obedience to parents as well as service to neighbors. It greatly disturbs me that such audacity and impudence, glaringly mad though it is, rages furiously against the clear commandments of God, until now it promises esteem as well as eternal life. Even if all the monks radiated the sanctity of angels, nevertheless, the whole institution is still mad and contrary to the commandments of God. Not only should no vows be taken, they ought not to be kept. Vows should be avoided and damned as the height of godlessness. If you were to take a vow of murder or adultery, the vow would be considered null and void; it would be condemned. Why is it not nullified and condemned if you vow disobedience to parents and cruelty to neighbors? Or if you were to confess that you were going to associate with thieves and throw in your lot with adulterers [Ps. 50:18], would you not be allowed to follow the advice of Solomon and withdraw from the sinners who lure you to evil [Prov. 1:10]?

But let us hear their excuses for their impiety. First of all, they quote, "Obedience is better than sacrifice" [I Sam. 15:22]. From this they argue that serving our neighbors and doing them good is not allowed, except by permission of the superior. Second, they argue that spiritual fathers take precedence over natural fathers, and so obedience to the former must take priority over obedience to the latter. Third, they argue that love is exercised no less among the brothers within the monastery than it is in the outside world.

So they say! You see then that obedience and love are drawn from the public arena by these men and forced into their small corner of the world. Let us look then at these three arguments in turn. That first passage, "Obedience is better than sacrifice," refers first and only to the divine commands; in reality it is an attack on monasticism. They say that the man who vows to enter monastic life is actually offering himself as a sacrifice to God, but the Lord says that he abhors such sacrifice if it contravenes obedience to his commandment. Yet it is God's command to obey parents and to serve neighbors. Is this not perversity of the highest order, then, to call their obedience greater than sacrifice, when God calls it a sacrifice contrary to obedience? The monks teach that Scripture is to be understood in such a way that the things which are said about the commandments of God apply to the commandments of men, and the things which are said against the commandments of men apply to the commandments of God. Obstinately applying this kind of obedience, then, the Minorite[102] does not give his neighbor a helping hand or offer him a red cent even if he is dying and in dire need. As far as he is concerned, his brother can perish in hunger, nakedness, and need. And afterward he boasts to God that obedience was better than sacrifice. In plain words it means that in his baptism he vowed obedience to God, but in the monastery he nullified this by a novel obedience to men.

Under the pretext of this kind of obedience they exonerate themselves very nicely from those works of mercy which Christ warns will be expected of them in the day of judgment, Matthew 25 [:34-40]. If a monk sees anybody who is hungry, thirsty, naked, homeless, captive, and all the rest, he is warned that he cannot leave the monastery to visit the sick and comfort the sad. He just lets perish what is going to perish. He shuts his heart to compassion, even if he can help. Afterward he is likely to say that he did not do the charitable thing because he did not want to offer sacrifice before obedience. He would do the same if his father and mother needed his help to look after them and care for them. What an unheard-of madness! As a monk, I myself, although I am an ordinary, simple sort of man, found this harshness and blasphemy of denying

[102] I.e., the Franciscan.

love the hardest thing to bear. Nor could I ever persuade myself to believe with any peace of mind that this monastic obedience, which was against love and so offensively harsh, was right and proper. To this they will reply, "If freedom to wander around were given to monks, the whole monastic system would collapse. Monasteries would be deserted and the worship of God would cease if individuals went around looking after parents and neighbors in need." Good! The command of God has to be overthrown to let sticks and stones remain standing that the wailing of pipes and mumbling in the choir might go on, that the tonsure and the habit not be laid aside. Even blood has to be shed, life and everything sacrificed for monasticism. How wisely and impartially these men judge the commandments of God! Is this not exactly what I said, that the monastic system and the divine command are diametrically opposed to one another?[103] If you want to keep the divine commandment, you cannot keep the lifelong vow. Choose the one you want. I ask you, what harm can the monastic system suffer if a monk were to leave the monastery when the need arises to look after his parents, visit the sick, and give himself to divine obedience and divine love? Does that make it necessary to lay aside charity, poverty, and obedience? He could always return to the monastery when he had fulfilled his call to obey God and his obligations of love. And what if obedience and charity do not permit his return? How will he have sinned? Will he have sinned against wood and stone?[104] Will he have sinned because he had not stood in the choir, not donned the cowl, not been tonsured, not slept in a common dormitory, not eaten in a common refectory, not mumbled in the general buzz of unintelligible voices? If so, then, that means that these things are so important and that salvation is so bound up with them that the divine commandments have to be trodden underfoot for the sake of just these things. Does this mean that the man who has given himself to these things has dedicated himself to God, and that the man who in baptism vowed obedience to parents and love of neighbor has not dedicated himself to God? What can we say to these crazy ideas except what is said in Mark 7 [:9], "You have a fine way of

[103] Cf. pp. 317-326.

[104] I.e., the monastery buildings.

rejecting the commandment of God to keep your tradition."

Therefore, let every Christian be quite certain that just as you cannot take vows to deny God and his commandments, so you cannot take vows which deny obedience to parents and service to neighbor; for God has commanded obedience to parents and service to neighbor. Therefore with absolute confidence you should so interpret your vow that when your parent or neighbor has need of you, you may be absolutely certain on divine authority that you need keep your vow no longer. Are these points not clear enough? Who could grumble against this in any way? If you could break but one of God's commandments on account of a vow, you could break them all and deny God completely. If, however, you cannot deny God or any of his commandments, you cannot deny or break a single one, not even the least. The monastic vow ought to be efficacious for the commandments of God, not against them, and ought always to give way to them, even if it means that in the long run the vows have to be given up and eventually abolished. Have no doubt about it, God himself cannot demand a vow of you or recognize a deed that is contrary to a single iota of his commandment. He is faithful and true; he cannot deny himself [II Tim. 2:13].

If they suggest that obedience to parents ought to give way to the worship of God as more meritorious, because the worship of God is enjoined as the first commandment, but obedience to parents as the fourth, then my reply is this: You have just heard earlier in this argument that the monastic worship of God is mockery.[105] The true worship of God, however, cannot be hindered by obedience to parents and service to neighbor. In fact, this very obedience to parents and service to neighbor is the real and true worship of God, which they empty of all content by their mockery of worship. For what else is the worship and service of God than the keeping of his commandments? Yet obedience to parents is commanded as well as love of neighbor. To bellow at God and mumble in the choir is not commanded. In fact, because this is to tempt God and mock him, it is prohibited. Nor is prayer, which is the best thing in their worship —but not that bellowing, impeded by obedience to parents and service to neighbor. You could live in chastity and poverty in the midst

[105] Cf. pp. 323-326.

of your obedience and service, and pray and bellow as much as you wanted. You are prevented from doing one thing only, and that is treading the sacred stones and boards of the monastery with your fellow-monks, and standing alongside them in the flesh. On the other hand, were your parents or neighbor to command you to deny the faith, the name and the work of God, which we said are commanded in the First Table, that would be the occasion, of which they now boast, when obedience to parents and all else ought to give way to the worship of God. But worship understood in this way is quite common among the faithful, and nowhere is it worse understood than in the monasteries and among those seditious sects,[106] which can very easily be understood from what we have just said.

Their second point, that they are spiritual fathers, pertains exactly to what St. Peter said when he prophesied that they would exploit us with feigned words [II Pet. 2:3], as well as to the text about obedience and sacrifice,[107] which they change and pervert. Spiritual fathers are those who teach us to obey the commandments of God before all else, to be subject to parents and to serve one's neighbors, as the apostles did. Since, however, they teach contrary to these principles and purvey the commandments of men along with their own ideas, they are indeed spiritual fathers—spiritual in the sense that their spirit is the spirit of error about which Paul prophesied in I Timothy 4 [:1] when he said that men would fall from faith and "give heed to the spirits of error." For men ought not to obey even apostles, nor for that matter angels, if their teaching is contrary to obedience to parents and love of neighbor. How much less, then, ought men obey these godless, blasphemous men who are worse than nonbelievers and who deny the faith. If these men taught pure faith, and your parents or your neighbors were not willing for you to learn from them, that would be a clear case where your parents and neighbors could be disregarded. Even so, you cannot permanently swear away by any vow the obedience and service you owe them. It is not necessary to subject oneself to parents and neighbors and be under others all the time to learn the faith. Paul proudly claimed that while lying in chains he had be-

[106] I.e., religious orders.
[107] Cf. I Sam. 15:22.

gotten a spiritual son, although Onesimus was not Philemon's son, but slave.[108] And although Paul had rights over Philemon himself, whom he had also begotten as a spiritual son, he did not compel Philemon to obey, but sent Onesimus back to his master to seek his master's approval. What do you think he would have done had Onesimus been Philemon's son? And yet our present-day monks, although they teach neither faith nor sound doctrine, but rather everything blasphemous, dare to snatch sons away from their parents into a permanent bondage.

It follows, then, that just as a wife has the power of withdrawing her husband from a monastery if he has donned the cowl, or if he has been anointed into the priesthood, or been duly purified without her consent, so a father or mother has a right to withdraw his son or daughter from the monastery. And the son or daughter is bound to obey his parents under the necessity of salvation and the wrath of God, to lay aside the cowl without ado, and to regard it as invalid, even though he had vowed a thousand vows and had as many indelible characters as he had hairs on his head. And now they completely absolve sons from being obedient to their parents, and at the same time babble away that everybody is free in spiritual matters. By the same argument, then, why do they not separate married couples as well? Or why do they not snatch the children from their mothers' breasts, if this argument that there is freedom in spiritual matters were sufficient? By this kind of reasoning we could free all sons from their parents, all servants from their masters, all people from their magistrates. We could annul all treaties, all pacts, all agreements, by saying that all men were free in spiritual matters and were judges in their own cause, and that no man in fact was subject to the authority of another. But these men are blind, sacrilegious, and blasphemous. They are authors of new-fangled notions and call their own human traditions spiritual.

If love could be exercised among the monks themselves so that they could actually serve one another, then it would be all right. But this is not the case. Love is free; it is directed to no person in particular. But these people limit love only to their own kind and

[108] Cf. Philemon 10.

to themselves. They completely neglect everyone else. This kind of love is just make-believe. It foments division and hatred, for we see monastery frantically raging against monastery, and one religious order against another. But that real and universal love described by the Apostle in I Corinthians 13, which is offered to everyone, friend and foe alike, for the purpose of helping them, is forbidden to them and is not allowed. For, as we explained above, a religious is not allowed to leave the monastery, visit the sick, and devote himself to other Christian service, even if it was necessary as well as possible. In fact, they turn everything the other way around. Because manual labor is prohibited, they do no work. They are supported by the rest of the world, devouring everyone else's substance although they are perfectly hale and hearty. This is to the great detriment of the genuinely poor. They repay their benefactors by spiritual works of mercy, that is, by the worship of God which we described earlier, a lot of mumbling and bellowing, of sighing and reading, and so on. Above all, the masses are among the most execrable of abominations in God's sight.

These high sounding words blot out those true works of mercy demanded by Christ and bring solace to them when they have abolished the works Christ demanded, lest they recognize their ungodliness, repent, and become worthy recipients of mercy. If it had been in the interests of the young people that they kept the tradition of not being allowed to wander about at will, so that youth, while at a gentler and more amenable stage, might be the more easily restrained and learn in the monasteries a love for their own which they might later extend to everyone quite openly, then monasticism would be a tolerable institution, even a good one. But as things are they are boys their whole life long, and what is more, they learn love for their own which they think is the highest and only love. Nevertheless, we can see the divine work in Bernard and men like him. Bernard, lest he leave his monks in this state of puerile and narrow love, wrenched them away and thrust them into the midst of all the real concerns of life. He did this so that in these activities love might show its real power, a love poured out and shed on all men, shown to everyone, ready [to serve anyone]. Moreover, it was by this secret miracle that he saved them so that they did not perish in that damnable institution of a narrow and artificial love in which others perish because they do not understand this work of God. Nevertheless, I do not deny that some have been saved by this very same kind of love by which they served only their own kind, because the opportunity of serving others as well did not arise in their case. They were saved because they were quite prepared to serve everyone. I condemn this institution because it prevents service to any but fellow-monks.

In this matter of obedience to parents and love of neighbor, we see most clearly that this institution of vows is by its very nature contrary to the commandments of God and that therefore vows ought not and cannot be made or kept, even though it is true that some have been saved who, though living under vows, did not sin in this matter. And it is certain that those who were saved never vowed vows of this kind, or, if they did take vows of this kind, God overlooked their error and did not accept the vow in the way they offered it. Therefore, to be found in this kind of life is something worthy of condemnation. You can see by its very nature that it is contrary to the commandments of God. It makes for nothing but idlers, who, like locusts, caterpillars, and beetles devour everyone else's substance, or, as Peter says, they use our alms for their luxury [II Pet. 2:13]. But they in their turn neither serve nor show charity or do good to anyone. To be men of this kind they take vows and bind themselves with oaths; they make the commandments of God ineffectual for God's sake, and they distort the word of God and twist it to mean what they want it to mean. In short, they turn everything upside down. And further, to complete their evil work, their execrable masses are by an abhorrent perversity turned into sacrifices and good works to repay their benefactors with spiritual gifts. In other words, these people make young men put their confidence in falsities and drag them into the pit with them. They are just blind leaders of the blind. I say that these masses are so abhorrent that if anyone has taken vows imprudently and changed his mind, he should leave their company[109] to return to the purity of the simple Christian life. For on the basis of what has been said—that no one can make a devout vow or one

[109] I.e., the company of the monks.

that is pleasing to God in this kind of life, or if he does make such a vow, it is a mistake, because what he finds is something other than what he hoped for—a man in the monastery must make either a godless or a false vow, and in God's sight he can keep neither. Thus a vow must always remain a matter of free choice. In fact, we have to change all this, revoke this kind of vow, and return once again to Christian freedom and to the commandments of God. Perhaps this is all we need say about the fourth point. Let us turn to other things.

V

Monasticism Is Contrary to Common Sense and Reason

Fifth, let us go one step further and compare the monastic system with natural reason; that is, let us look at it in the plain light of nature. Even if natural reason in itself is not concerned with spiritual truth or divine activity, nevertheless, when it asserts affirmative statements (to use their jargon) its judgment is wrong, but when it asserts negative statements its judgment is right. Reason does not comprehend what God is, but it most certainly comprehends what God is not. Granted, reason cannot see what is right and good in God's sight (faith, for instance), but it sees quite clearly that infidelity, murder, and disobedience are wrong. Christ also applies reason in the same way when he declares that every kingdom divided against itself is brought to desolation [Luke 11:17]. Paul, too, when he said it was contrary to nature for a woman to prophesy with her head uncovered [I Cor. 11:5]. If anything is really contrary to reason, it is certainly very much more against God also. For how can anything not be in conflict with heavenly truth when it is in conflict with earthly truth? In the same way, Christ, in John 3 [:12], distinguished truth and argued from the standpoint of both heavenly and earthly truth, "If I have told you earthly things and you do not believe, how will you believe if I tell you heavenly things?" Would then that we saw that the institution of monasticism is contrary not only to the law and the gospel and the whole of Scripture, that is, to all that God said or did, but also that it is actually contrary to the common sense of all mankind.

In the first place, let us understand this: a vow, even though it was once godly and right in every respect, ceases to be a vow and is no longer binding even in the sight of God if circumstances or events have made it impossible to keep. For example, let us assume you have vowed a pilgrimage to St. James of Compostella,[110] but you are prevented from going either by death or insufficient means or illness or imprisonment. In such a case, the vow is set aside without further ado. This proves that every vow is made conditionally. The impossibility of keeping it is always conceded. Are these arguments not clear and definite enough?

Now what is asserted of one vow must be true of all. For all vows, whether great or small, temporary or permanent, are equally comprehended in this command, "Make your vow and keep it" [Ps. 76:11], as we shall see. If, therefore, the impossibility of fulfilling a vow is admitted in one instance, even in the least of vows, it has been admitted in any other, even the greatest. If, therefore, you vow celibacy and afterward think that it is an impossibility for you, are you then not free to marry, having interpreted your vow conditionally? What then is to prevent you from doing so in such a case, or from being able to do so? Is infirmity of the flesh not an impediment to celibacy as much as need or illness are to a pilgrim? We all know without argument that the commandments of God are immutable. Yet external works are excepted where what is commanded cannot be done. You will not condemn St. Peter for not preaching when he was chained up by Herod [Acts 12:6], or for not serving his neighbor according to the rule of love. The blessed impossibility excused him. You will not make Paul guilty of a lapse of love because he always wanted to go to Rome but was always hindered [Rom. 1:13]. And in Acts 16 [:7] he wanted to go to Bithynia, but either the wind or the Spirit did not permit it. We will be calling the martyrs in prison ungodly, unless they are released from the demands of the commandments because it is impossible for them to keep them.

[110] Cf. p. 12, n. 9.

But at this point you will say, "God takes the will for the deed. This is why the devotee of St. James fulfils his vow in intention even if he is not actually in a position to fulfil it. This is how the saints fulfil the commandments of God." My reply to that is twofold. Either this objection does not meet the case, or else it confirms my argument. It does not meet the case because a vow as much as a commandment is concerned not only with the will or intention but also with the actual deed done. This man vowed to make a pilgrimage, not a willingness to do so. What would be the point of vowing, "I vow to thee my willingness to undertake a pilgrimage to St. James"? In the same way, a commandment of God necessarily demands its execution. What is the use of saying, "I command you to have the intention of keeping my commandments"? Thus, I conclude from these examples that vows always allow for the impossibility of keeping them. And the same also applies to the actual performance of the commandments of God. By the same argument, if it is found impossible to observe celibacy after it has once been vowed, it is not comprehended within the vow, at least as far as the actual deed is concerned. Nor do you have any argument that you could bring to the contrary. I have already made my view known, however, about when the intention is there but the opportunity to implement it is not. I am discussing the case only of the man who wants to keep his vow of celibacy, but owing to infirmity of the flesh cannot, the man who has tried time and again and still cannot control the instincts of the flesh either by fasting or personal effort, the man who against his will is driven at one time or another to be overcome by burning lust, and experiences impure seminal emissions sleeping or waking, and yet who in all other respects lives a blameless life.

But here you might say, as some obtuse people who are not concerned with the cure of souls are wont to say, "You must pray to God for grace. He denies no one." True enough. Why then did you not counsel St. Peter to pray to God so that Herod would not bind him in chains? Why did Paul not pray that he would not be hindered from going to Rome? Why did the martyrs not pray that they not be prevented from doing works of love on account of imprisonment? And why do you not teach the devotee of St. James to pray that he does not become poor, that he is not taken ill, that he does not die, that he is not imprisoned? Is that not playing with things that are otherwise very serious? What if God does not want to be entreated? Or if he is prayed to, what if he is not willing to listen? By this kind of reasoning you will teach us all first to vow celibacy and then afterward pray that it prove not to be impossible. Moreover, by the same reasoning, you are trying to compel God to revoke his word, that divine commandment of nature by which he created all things, "Increase and multiply" [Gen. 1:28]. All this is absurd and puerile. Each one is left to see from his own experience whether this law, or rather, the privilege of increasing and multiplying, is quite settled and established, or whether he has the power to change things.

But again you will say, "It is one thing to discuss the impossible in the case of a saint, but quite another to discuss the impossible in the case of a celibate. In the case of saints, their will is effective and mature and goes on to do the works to which it has set itself. No intrinsic impediment is allowed to stand in the way if they can help it. There is an extrinsic impediment, however, which stands in their way, but which is not under their control, and that is despotic power. But in the case of a celibate the will is neither effective nor mature, nor is it impeded by an extrinsic impediment, but by an intrinsic one, namely, his flesh and his own nature, which he has in his own power at any rate. If the will were whole and entire it would be impossible for him not to keep his vow of celibacy. Therefore, your case is not admissible, that someone may be a celibate as far as intention goes, but does not have the strength to be celibate." To this I reply: In normal health our body of flesh is in our own power. We can put out its eyes and cut off its hands, its feet, its tongue. We can strangle it with a rope, or drown it in water. We could do the same with a tyrant, if he were weaker than we and were in our power. What has that to do with what we are investigating and discussing here? If you poked your eyes out, would you be any more pure on that account? Moreover, as far as celibacy is concerned, who does not know that that inward and intrinsic tyrant in our members is no more within our power than is the ill will of an external tyrant? To some extent you can mitigate an external tyrant with soft words and bring him over to your own way of thinking, but you cannot bring the inward tyrant into subjection by any amount of effort, much less by words. What do you say to Paul, Romans 7 [:19]? Was his will not complete and effective when he said, "The good that I would, I do not; the evil I would not, that I do." Why then does he not do what he admits he wants with all his heart to do? What about what you were saying earlier when you said that an intrinsic impediment is no impediment and does not render the vow impossible to fulfil when the whole and entire will has determined it? "The flesh wars against the spirit and the spirit against the flesh. These things war against each other, so that you cannot do the things you want to do" [Gal. 5:17]. So then, I want a celibate released from his vow if in his heart he would rather be celibate than married, but because this is not possible for the flesh, he is compelled to do the opposite and to lay aside his vow. [He is] like a man impeded by a severe illness or an indomitable tyrant. Would not that person who had vowed a pilgrimage to St. James also be hindered by a similar intrinsic impediment if he were ill? Yet how much more violent and harsh an illness is the tyrant of the flesh than any other illness of the body! In this situation may God accept the will when he does not find the power, as long as no sin has been committed in deed or in intent against any one of his commandments. If the will be present, however, the vow is fulfilled over and above the commandment. Only the external expression of the vow is foregone because of the compulsion of an insuperable weakness.

But again you will object, "By this kind of argument you allow the possibility of violating even the commandments of God in an external work if the will is weak. Therefore, the man who wants to live a chaste life will be excused if he associates with harlots, since the commandments of God are impossible for us, as you yourself have so often taught." My reply is: At this juncture you ought to bring in the difference which you tried to make earlier between saints who were prevented [from fulfilling the commandments] and the celibate who succumbs [to temptation]. Although it is true that it is impossible for us to keep the commandments of God, yet it is not true that anyone wanting to live chastely keeps company with harlots. For the man whose will is set upon the law of God, it is not only possible to keep the law, but it is made easy. If he cannot be continent, this impossibility does not compel him to act contrary to the law of God and to consort with harlots. He does not consort with harlots because he has no other alternative. Marriage offers a middle course. Let him take a wife, and the law of chastity will be easier for him. But the celibate I am discussing is not of this kind.[111] As far as it lies in his power he wants to be continent with all his heart, and satisfy the law of God in every detail. He is content when he has taken a wife, but he would rather be without a wife and be celibate. Nevertheless, he cannot master the nature of his sexuality so as to be able to do without sexual intercourse naturally, and he commits fornication because he cannot do anything else. There is no similarity between a vow and a commandment. For it is the will which makes it possible to keep the commandments of God, but the will is not adequate to keep a vow. Now if the will can keep the commandments of God but not a vow, the vow ought to be put aside and the commandments remain, lest a man break both the vow and the commandment at the same time by commiting fornication. There is left to the celibate, therefore, if celibacy is too much for him, the right to marry and lay aside his vow, although I must confess that where the Spirit abounds, the Spirit effects the will's power to remain continent. In this event continence is an inevitable consequence, as we are certain happened in the case of the saints. But the rest of these celibates can only desire that kind of will; they cannot produce it. Yet sinners do not wish to keep the commandments of God as St. Paul wished in Romans 7 [:15-19], though he could not wish it with his whole being. In fact, sinners do not want the law of God in all sincerity because the ungodly will can only hate the law of God. This ungodly will only simulates the will to do the commandments as well as the works of the commandments. But I have spoken elsewhere about this,[112] and it lies outside the scope of our argument. It seems then that the proper form of the vow to be made to God should be on this order, "I take a vow of chastity for as long as it is possible to

[111] Luther still has in mind that celibate who is bound to celibacy by oath.
[112] Cf. *Against Latomus*. *LW* 32, 133-260.

keep it; if however I am unable to keep it, may I be permitted to marry."

Well now, if there is any one who is not convinced by this argument about the impossibility of keeping all vows, we shall have to compel him by sheer weight of examples, and prove the truth of the argument by facts. Now look! In my own case I have taken vows to keep the entire rule of Augustine, in which he commanded that wherever I go, another, or even two others, shall accompany me.[113] In other words, I may go nowhere alone. This I have vowed to keep to my life's end, as the vow expressly puts it. Yet at the moment I am a prisoner.[114] I am forced to live alone. Now, I ask you, does my vow still hold good? I ought to allow myself to be killed rather than to be left alone if the vow does not make an exception of the impossible. But what if I am so held that I cannot be killed? What do I do then? In a situation like this the vow is broken. Or else it must have been previously understood that where the vow cannot be kept an exception is made. In exactly the same way I vow under this rule to pray the prescribed offices, to wear prescribed clothes, eat prescribed foods, live in prescribed places. Yet if ever I fall ill so that I cannot read the hours, the vow is no longer kept. Illness, however, will not excuse me, because the commandments of God must be kept in life, in death, in all circumstances. The commandment of God is, "Make your vows and keep them" [Ps. 76:11]. In the same way I could adduce examples from all the other statutes of the rule. Therefore, as I said earlier in the case of a vow to make a pilgrimage to St. James of Compostella, if in all other rules it is necessary to make impossibilities exceptions, what reasonable ground can there be for allowing no exception in the case of chastity? If both serious danger and grave necessity cause a state of affairs in which impossibility has a place in every part of the rule, then it must also have a place in chastity before all else. If it has no place in the matter of chastity, how much less a place ought it to have in the other vows! Now I ask you, what harm is there if you compel a prisoner to take a companion, or a sick man to pray? Actually, there is no harm at all in such an event,

[113] Cf. *Second Rule* (*Regula Secunda*). *MPL* 32, 1451.

[114] Luther was in the Wartburg.

since he can do what you are trying to make him do. But on the other hand, if you compel an incontinent person to be continent, how many uncleannesses, how many fornications, how many adulteries and other evils will you provoke? And as I have said earlier, what you say is not valid, that in the case of a prisoner or a man who is sick it is sufficient if he displays the will, for in that case there is no difference between the man under vows and the man not under vows. For what layman would not wish to have a companion or to pray according to the rule? You cannot trifle in this way with matters concerning the conscience or with matters pertaining to salvation. You have to make judgments firmly and with intelligence. It is quite clearly laid down in the rule that actions are prescribed and vowed, not intentions. It is also clearly laid down that where necessary a vow may be dispensed with in the case of a sick man or a prisoner,[115] which would not be lawful if a vow precludes the impossibility of keeping it. The text stands, "Make your vows and keep them." Not one jot or tittle of that law will pass away till all be fulfilled [Matt. 5:18]. Therefore, either the vow is binding only up to the point where it becomes impossible, or you are compelled to admit that there have never been any real monks. There never was a monk who at one time or another was not ill or who was not prevented from keeping some part of his rule for one reason or another. And that is absolutely contrary to his vow.

There is a further objection. When there is the will to persevere in the vows, even where external circumstances make them impossible, that will is persistently set aside. We simply dispose of it. It is everywhere agreed that Bernard, in his book *Concerning Commandment and Dispensation*[116] argues that every part of the rule is in the hands of the superior, who may grant dispensation to those set under him, not only if it is impossible or if a danger arises, but even if in his judgment it seems appropriate or convenient. This means that these particular rules sometimes hold good and sometimes do not hold good. And all this in the mere judgment of the father superior! As a consequence, popes constantly claim

[115] Cf. *Rules for the Servants of God (Regula ad Servos Dei). MPL* 32, 1380.
[116] *MPL* 182, 859 ff.

full authority to make or change all of the rules, and to grant dispensation. In fact, whatever this seat of Satan does is suspect. I do not want his authority to protect me in matters of conscience. Let us stand by the deeds of the saints and the ordinary usage accepted by everybody else.

It is therefore certain that in these dispensations the will to keep the vow is set aside and the freedom to abrogate it conceded. The man who acts according to a dispensation is not thereby compelled to act against his will, nor does he think or want to do anything to the contrary. I reply, therefore, if a dispensation of that kind is permissible, I shall confidently conclude that the meaning of a monastic vow is as follows, "I vow to keep this rule according to the judgment of my father superior." If in fact such is not the real meaning I will go on to argue that all monks and all monasteries are condemned, and that until now no true monk has ever existed. For no monk has ever thought or believed other than I have just described.

They believe all the other parts of the rule are in the hands of the father superior, not only with respect to the actual deed but even to the intent. That means he may absolve those in his charge from the entire vow and give them their freedom, even when no impossibility and no danger demand such a course. Tell me, if you can, why if this is the case he cannot by the same authority give his brother the opportunity to marry, which he ought to do for his brother who is struggling with the storms of passion and is in grave peril, and give him at least the freedom that an external impediment grants—even if it was a vow of chastity and even if the will was not there? Why is only the vow of chastity as hard as flint, while all the others are straw and stubble? Could it not be fairly argued that monasticism is both iniquitous and cruel, and on this ground alone is highly suspect as Satan's charade, for it is so merciful in matters of no moment, but so severe in matters which are of moment? What can anybody say to such perversity, except the words of the gospel, "You strain at a gnat and swallow a camel" [Matt. 23:24]? Or again, "You tithe your cummin and mint, but neglect the weightier matters of the law" [Matt. 23:23]. Or again, "You lay on men's backs heavy burdens they cannot even bear" [Matt. 23:4]. What will the man in the street think about it all except that Satan's wickedness is its inspiration? Only chastity is indispensable, and by this vow Satan ensnares their souls in a net from which there is no escape. Yet other things are dispensable. Satan is simply ridiculing their artificial religion.

What then will the monks say to the following argument? Either no parts of the vow may be subject to dispensation, or every part can, because there is no weightier reason for one than for another. If anything, there are more compelling and demanding reasons for dispensation in the case of chastity. Yet on this very issue they deny dispensation and refuse more stubbornly than in all other cases to grant it. Pause for a moment, dear reader, and think it over. I am saying nothing of the iniquity and harshness of such a system of dispensation, but how uncertain and dangerous everything is concerning this wretched institution. If this way of granting dispensation is wrong and displeasing to God, who would dare to enter the religious life or even remain in it? Who would remain in the monastery, or who would take and keep vows to a way of life in which the authorities teach by their own admission and example that what has been vowed need not be kept? Is this not to mock God as some kind of fool? Yet, if that practice were not wrong, who could make us certain, especially since God says, "Make your vows and keep them"? Then, as has been said above, we cannot be certain either by the examples of the saints or from the testimony of the majority, since all are capable of sin and error. Yet, here a certain and clear word of God says, "Make your vows and keep them."

If, however, there is any uncertainty in this erroneous custom, I say again, who would dare to enter or remain in religious orders? And everything I have inferred in relation to the error I will infer here also. For it is just as great an impiety to pursue what is to your certain knowledge an error as it is to embrace as truth something about which you are uncertain. O what dangerous times, times about which St. Paul prophesied [II Tim. 3:1-7]! Now that they base their vow and its institution on the word of God, "Make your vows and keep them," I declare that this custom of making dispensation is blasphemous and is a damnable error of works. At any rate, I want to convince you that all vows are ruled out and are a matter of free choice. So that I may do this more adequately, let us look in the first place at the grounds of their all too easily obtained dispensations, which are available in all other points of the rule, and also at their harsh rigor in retaining the vow of chastity.

They argue that chastity is a thing of incomparable worth and that its equal is nowhere to be found. They quote the text from Wisdom, "There is nothing to compare with a chaste soul" [Ecclus. 26:15]. To this kind of talk they add high sounding sayings in praise of virginity, of which this one from Jerome is one of the choicest, "I confidently declare that though God can do all things, he cannot restore a virgin after a fall."[117] There are other things, however, that can be made the subject of dispensation and commuted, because they are less important. O what total blindness we have here, a blindness so complete that in Christian and divine matters it judges commandments according to works, and faith according to persons, something not even the heathen do in their human affairs, which drives them to clutch at a word of man as the highest article of faith! Jerome says that he will confidently declare that God cannot restore a virgin after a fall. What is that to me, what you confidently declare? What I have to consider is not how confidently you speak, but how truly you speak. For it is not your confidence in which I believe, but in God's truth. Where is your proof that a virgin cannot be restored after a fall, not even by God? From talk of this kind the uneducated reader learns to esteem nothing as more precious than virginity; in other words, to put works before faith. Can God restore a virgin spiritually corrupted in faith, but not one corrupted in the flesh? How I wish that this praise of virginity had never been spoken, especially by such an authoritative person, for it puffs up the idea and glory of works. It is not even true. No less a person than Hugo of St. Victor[118] refuted Jerome long ago. For God can even restore the flesh whole. He can, in fact, raise a virgin who has died, and utterly replace the

[117] *Epistola* 22, *ad Eustochium. MPL* 22, 397.

[118] Hugo of St. Victor (1097-1141) was a famed mystic and member of the Augustinian Order.

flesh in its entirety and give it a new life. This same virgin would never know a man. "For we are his clay, and he is the potter" [Isa. 64:8]. If a man believes that a virgin cannot be restored because God lacks the power to do so, that, in other words, what has been done cannot be undone, he will have the same audacity to declare that no virtue and no grace which has once been corrupted can ever again be restored by God.

But let us get back to the subject and take a look at a new impiety of this monastic system and see how odious its iniquity is. They assert that a vow is in all respects a precept of God, for Scripture says, "Make your vows and keep them." But the real way to keep a vow is not to be sought in the form of the precept; it has to be sought in the importance or the insignificance, in the worth or the worthlessness, of the works or things commanded. This means that you offer the virginity you have vowed because that is a great thing. It is not necessary to keep the other works of the rule; they may be the subject of a dispensation because they are unimportant matters. What else is this but to say, "I keep chastity, not because it is commanded by the vow, but because it is a great thing"? And what is this except to say, "What a vow commands lies not in the will of God but in my own will, to what extent it is or is not a precept, to what extent it ought or ought not be fulfilled"? Does it not occur to you that God might be angry with all this gall, these provocations and temptations, this mockery of his majesty? They are a perfect example of Saul's conduct.[119] They arrogate to themselves the right of interpreting obedience to the Lord after they have reserved the fat beasts for sacrifice to God. These are the people who boast that obedience is better than sacrifice. They boast that they keep the precept of the vow to the letter, yet they deny it by their works.

With this attitude you will look at a woman with lust, yet you will say that it is no sin because it is a small matter in relation to the actual deed. You will take your neighbor's cloak and will say that this is not prohibited because it is a small thing. You will say "Raca!" to your brother and yet do no sin because you have not killed your brother. And you will apply this rule of monastic

[119] Cf. I Sam. 15:15, 22.

theology to all the precepts of God. You will teach that in the case of important matters and important works these commandments are to be kept, but in the case of unimportant matters they can be dispensed with and abolished. Then, to leave nothing to the authority of God, you allot to yourself the right to judge what things are unimportant and what things are important, just as in this instance the monks, on their own authority, prefer celibacy to all other works. There is monastic piety for you—the maddest, the most sacrilegious and blasphemous godlessness! They learned this madness from their king and chief, the pope, who arrogates to himself the right to grant dispensations in all vows except vows of chastity and of making a pilgrimage to Jerusalem or Compostella. In his view the meaning of the commandment under discussion will be, "Make your vows and keep chastity and pilgrimages to Jerusalem or Compostella; but in the other things make a vow, of course, but do not bother to keep it!" Why? Because these three things are important, the others are not. The monks say, "Make your vows and keep chastity according to the rule. The rest of the rule, however, vow but do not bother to keep." O what insanities, fit only for the last days of wrath! Christ says in Matthew 5 [:19], "Whoever shall relax one of the least of these my commandments and teach men [to do the same] shall be called least in the kingdom of heaven." And again, "Not one jot or tittle of the law shall pass away till all things are accomplished" [Matt. 5:18]. Yet the pope and the monks take away not only the jot or the tittle, but the plain meaning of the very words and the entire precept when they say, "Keep the precept in the important points; we absolve you of the less important." But we ourselves curse and hate these abominations and know that they ought to be abhorred.

In the first place, we make no distinction between one work and another. They are all equal in the sight of God. It is only as we see them, or in relation one to another, that some seem important and others unimportant. Everything is given according to the measure of faith, as Paul says in Romans 12 [:3]. It is not the man who has done many great things who is approved, but the man who has acted in greater faith and love. The conjugal chastity of Abraham and Sarah is to be preferred to the virginity of many. And the marriage of the Apostle Peter will without the slightest doubt prove superior to the virginity of St. Agatha.[120] It is by the standard of faith, I say, that everything should be measured. It is not the man who has performed works who will be saved, but he who has believed [Mark 16:16]. It is the way of the heathen to judge according to works, yet even they judge with regard to the intention of the doer. But it is the way of Christians to judge according to faith. Therefore, in obeying commandments nothing else should be regarded than the form of the precept and the intention of him who commands. No regard should be paid to whether the works are trivial or important, worthless or worthwhile, many or few, of a short or a long duration, or of whatever form they take or whatever name they bear. For it is not the work as such which God demands, but obedience in the work, or, as Scripture expresses it, "Obedience not sacrifice." God does not need our good works. That is why Samuel said to Saul, "Does the Lord want burnt offerings? Would he not prefer us to obey his voice?" [I Sam. 15:22].

Now let us address ourselves to the monks. They cannot deny that they vow their rule in its entirety and not just chastity alone, because in any case the entire rule is comprehended under the word, "Make your vows. . . ." So it necessarily follows that the entire rule is also comprehended under the word, "Keep. . . ." It does not say, "Vow the lot and keep part," but, "Whatever you vow, keep it." If, therefore, they interpret their vow as a precept, they are compelled to admit that in God's sight obedience to the whole rule down to the smallest detail is demanded without any dispensations. In this case no help at all is derived from the painstaking way in which some have tried to console themselves by subdividing their rules into precepts, counsels, and interpretations. The divine voice still says, "Make your vows and keep them." If this word begins to plague the conscience at the hour of death, these straws of human ingenuity will profit nothing. The conscience will quake with fear at the voice of God and no longer hear the voices of men.

What will the monks do then? They will eventually open their

[120] This early virgin and martyr is particularly venerated in southern Italy and Sicily.

eyes and see that their vows are foolish and impossible. And who will not rue that he is a monk? And which of them can be saved? For you will never find a man who has been a monk who completely fulfilled the demands of his rule by his work. But even they themselves have seen this and have been aware of it for a long time now; so they have invented yet a further evasion of the divine precept. Acute regret and desolation troubled the hearts of these wretched men once they had started to wander from the royal road of faith. They have seen rules and ordinances tied up with so many statutes and precepts which are vowed but never kept that they were overwhelmed that as many as had violated their vows were to be damned. Then and there they understood that it was absolutely foolish and impossible to assume that all those vows could be kept. Then these wretched people began to reflect on these things and started to divide this chaos of vows into two parts: one part was called essential (*substantialia*), the other nonessential (*accidentalia*). They made three of the vows essential: poverty, chastity, and obedience. They preferred the rest to be nonessential. And so they decreed that only those who had broken the vow in the matter of the three essentials were violators of the vow. They all hold this view. But it is no use. It is just a human fiction. It is absolutely useless for strengthening the conscience, although it is very useful for leading the conscience astray. Who can convince us that this division is pleasing to God? Will you edify my conscience on the basis of your dreams? What can I say to God when he holds up his precept to me, "Make your vows and keep them," and decrees that all his commands are essential? (As, of course, they are.) For it has been said that in his eyes there is no difference in works. All are essential because they are done in obedience to the same precept. They are all equally binding and are all vowed in the same way. They are all vows, and a vow is a vow, as you yourselves call them. God knows nothing about nonessential vows. He simply says, "They are vows, therefore you will keep them. If you make them, then they are essential." And so whichever way they turned they were caught in difficulties and could not escape. The word of God and his commandment stand fast for ever and ever. He does not allow its evasion or perversion.

Therefore these two adversaries, conscience and law, meet and dash themselves against each other. My Moses also led his Israelites out of their camp to meet with God. What else was there to see except the smoking and terrible mountain [Exod. 19:17-18]? That means the wrath from heaven shown on earth, and extended from the earth to the farthest point of heaven. Whither will they go from the sight of this fiery law? But these people make dispensations of the commandments of God and subdivide his works and detract from them. Yet a precept demands total obedience. If you have vowed to kill a fly or lift a straw you ought to keep the vow without any qualification. You ought to obey the vow not because of what you vowed but because you made the vow, especially if the vow does not conflict with any other commandment of God. How much more ought you to keep what you have vowed according to the rule of your order? You see, therefore, dear reader, that in itself the monastic institution is nothing but a Babylon of error and ignorance, disobedience and perfidy, sacrilege and blasphemy, it is new-fangled ungodliness and sin. Or do you doubt that this is the case? Do you not see that they not only do not fulfil their vow, but even teach a doctrine in which vows may be professed but not fulfilled? This one thing they do: when taking vows they appear not to have vowed, and in not fulfilling them, they appear to have fulfilled them. Is there a pig or donkey that would allow itself to be made sport of and ridiculed in the way these people with their inanities presume to make sport of and ridicule the true and living God?

Now see if any man can be saved in this furnace of Babylon [Dan. 3:21], except by the power of a divine miracle, by which the elect have been saved—provided that while under their vows they erred, humanly speaking, yet at the same time adhered to the pure gospel of God in the spirit of freedom. In this way the judgment of God is fulfilled by which he confounded the tongues of those who were building the tower [Gen. 11:7]. They make a reputation for themselves while they do and say things which are not befitting, things they themselves do not understand because their understanding is darkened. They say that a vow is not a vow; they make the impermissible permissible, a precept no precept, what is impious pious, the sacrilegious sacred, blasphemy, something to be venerated, and many other things of this kind, which is like the night in which Christ was mocked, forsaken, and spat upon, when the servants of the High Priest said to him, "Prophesy to us, O Christ, and tell us who it was who struck you" [Matt. 26:68]. Perhaps some do not believe these monstrous charges against the monastic system on the ground that they are much too horrible. These people I let go their own way, and leave them to luxuriate in their own ideas. It is not they whom I serve by this writing. I am serving only those who want to save their souls, who, I think, are satisfied with what has been said already and believe that what I say is true. True indeed is the commandment of God, "Make your vows and keep them," for he fails no one save him who does not believe that it is either a commandment or that it is true. It is also true—and unbroken usage and experience show it to be the case—that they take vows which they not only do not keep, but which they also teach ought not to be kept. There is no better way to recognize lies than in the disagreement and contradiction they produce. It is a divine decree that godlessness always brings its own confusion, and lies never agree with one another, but always testify against each other.

What then shall I do, you will say, to save myself from this Zoar into which I fled to escape Sodom? What will you do? Now that you have heard the kind of life to which you have dedicated yourself—a way of life contrary not only to the word of God, the gospel, faith, Christian freedom, and the precepts of God, but shockingly at odds with itself and utterly self-contradictory—do you still think that it is debatable whether you should make haste to the mountain of liberty?[121] Granted then that this kingdom will be brought to desolation because it is divided against itself [Luke 11:17]—do you think that this vow is required by God? Do you think you should take a vow in a matter so revolting when God himself neither wills it nor wants it? He who never wanted you to take your vows does not even want the vows kept. He would much rather they were given up and abolished altogether.

But I complain about the monks themselves, and I repeat my

[121] Cf. Gen. 19:15-23.

question. Let them tell us, therefore, why they grant dispensations in all other parts of the vow but grant none in the case of chastity? Or, why do they teach that all the other parts are nonessential and only these three essential? Let them declare by what authority they assert that a vow is a commandment in some things yet not in all things? Clearly the mouth of those who speak iniquity is stopped [Ps. 63:11], and they are forced to admit that if any one part of the vow can be set aside or made a matter of dispensation, then the whole vow can be set aside and made a matter of dispensation; or, if the whole vow cannot be set aside and made a subject of dispensation, then no part of it can be laid aside and made a subject of dispensation. If then the superior can grant a dispensation to a brother to eat meat, drink wine, suspend his offices, lay aside his habit—all of which the rule of his order forbids—he can even grant indulgence for him to own property, go free, and take a wife, especially if it is necessary for him.

Therefore, I demand an answer from them. Yet I do not want their defense, because this is what they give or, rather, are compelled to give. For because of their shocking godlessness they cannot possibly have any faith or any authority. What if they—men whose lives and vows are nothing but error—err in their answers, too? Consciences are made strong by a sounder and safer authority. That means by a divine authority and that only. Peter says, "If any man speaks, let him speak as the oracle of God" [I Pet. 4:11]. That means let him be certain it is the word of God he is speaking. Paul makes the same recommendation to Timothy when he says, "Abide in those things you have learned, knowing from whom you have learned them" [II Tim. 3:14]. He had learned nothing but the word of God, however. Therefore, we have to abide by the word of God alone.

I now pursue only this: to show that they rage against common sense and that they contradict themselves and to conclude on the strength of their own arguments that chastity is impossible and is optional and that the vow of chastity is by its very nature conditional and temporal. This is so because I have proved that they conceded this for some parts of the vow, so there is no good reason why it ought not to obtain in all parts of the vow, particularly when more powerful reasons press for chastity to be a matter of free choice than for any other part in which they grant dispensations. It is the mere caprice of their own will to make some essential and others nonessential, to except only chastity from dispensation, while granting it to the others. All this happens to the ruination and ensnaring of souls.

Furthermore, our consciences are fortified by the following reflection. We have proved by clear and certain proofs of Scripture that the monastic vow is by its very nature contrary to the word of God, the gospel, faith, Christian freedom, and the commandments of God, not to mention common sense and its own inner contradiction. I say "by its very nature" because I would not want to deny that saintly men have used this perversity quite happily and been saved by a divine miracle, just as I say that death, the cross, and the evils of the world by their very nature work against faith, yet Christ and those that are his have used these adversities to their gain and found honor in them. But in making vows nobody follows the example of the saints, who used evil for good. They all vow the evil itself. Nobody vows to live in the spirit in which Bernard lived. They ought, but this cannot be brought under the control of a vow. This is already vowed at the start of life and begun in baptism. But they vow the law of deeds or the works of the law, the righteousness of the flesh and those other things that are nothing but human inventions and decrees. These God prohibited in the New Testament, as we have proved. Further, by their very nature they lead to destruction because of the specious reasoning of their own wisdom.

Therefore, although I may find saints who held this very same opinion (namely, that vows are subdivided into what is essential and what is nonessential), and who even made and accepted dispensations in many parts of the rule as well, yet because it is not certain whether they did what they did with God's approval or in ignorance of their error, it is not a safe or reliable enough plea for consciences to assert anything on the basis of their example or their actions. He who presumes to do this stands in opposition to Christ, who prophesied that even the elect may be led into error [Matt. 24:24]. Otherwise, if their sanctity were to prove that what they did was approved by God, then we could prove quite convincingly by these same deeds of the saints (in other words, by the proof of their godly works) that all vows are a matter of free choice. We would also prove that in God's sight the manner in which to take vows is nothing but what we described earlier, "I vow the rule for the time being and at the discretion of the prior." And monasteries would then have the character God intended them to have and nothing else. They would simply be Christian schools for youth, designed to establish ardent young people in the faith by means of a godly upbringing, till they reached the years of maturity.[122] But now, since the authority of holiness is not sufficiently weighty to establish a model to follow, it must be reinforced by another authority, that is, by divine authority. Although the deeds of the saints were pleasing to God, the institution of the monastic vow displeased him, and he therefore not only permitted his saints to make dispensations and to act against the vow, he even wanted them to do so. He did this for the faithful admonition of all, lest they be led away from the royal road of the gospel by the deceitful appearance of this institution of perpetual vows. When Bernard left his monastery and went hither and yon on papal missions, he did not sin, neither did he keep his vow in all respects. God wanted Bernard to do that lest the monks believe that God approves the institution of vows. For exactly the same reason Christ allowed his disciples to eat with unwashed hands, contrary to the tradition of the elders [Matt. 15:2].

To sum up, when we measure the examples and deeds of the saints against the words of God, it is adequately proven that monastic vows are contrary to the word of God. But these men measure the word of God by the deeds and words of the saints, and as long as they do they will be reluctant to appear to have been wrong.

The Last Part

Let us now make our final assault on them. Let us suppose for

[122] Luther maintained that monasteries should be schools. Cf. pp. 312-313.

the sake of argument that these three vows are essential, that they are approved by God, and that they are not open to dispensation. If I prove that two of the vows are matters of free choice even among you yourselves, will you not then admit that the third ought also to be a matter of free choice? I am referring to chastity. Let us then attempt just that, although we have already said enough about these from the outset.

First, let us look at poverty, which is of two kinds. There is a spiritual poverty of which Christ said, "Blessed are the poor in spirit, for theirs is the kingdom of heaven" [Matt. 5:3]. This kind of poverty cannot be vowed, for it is common to all Christians. This kind of poverty means to employ one's possessions with a free spirit, using them and being a master over them, not a slave to them, not setting one's heart on them, not trusting and glorying in riches, and not being men of wealth. But the monks do not sin in this simply by first making a counsel out of this idea of poverty; they claim this poverty for themselves alone, and they boast that only they are dedicated to it by vow. That this is not a counsel at all is proved when Christ calls these poor in spirit "blessed," and so he is willing for those who are not poor in spirit to be condemned. He was wont to attribute blessedness to those who observe those things which are necessary, as on the occasion when he reproved the woman and said, "Indeed, blessed are those who hear the word of God and keep it" [Luke 11:28]. And Christ said, "Blessed art thou Simon Bar-Jona" [Matt. 16:17]. And again, "If you do these things you are blessed" [John 13:17]. Similarly, his words, "for theirs is the kingdom of heaven," mean that he reserves the slavery of hell for those who are not poor.

Now when the monks take this vow, they sin in two ways. First, they give way to a godless doctrine, believing that what is really a precept is a counsel. In so doing they abolish a divine precept by denying that it is a precept. Second, they sin when they pretend that they are vowing something other than what they vowed in baptism. By this hypocrisy they abrogate and despise the baptismal vow as if it were not enough or even nothing compared with this vow. But this is to blaspheme baptism, which is everything to all Christians. If then a vow ought not to be an impious, sacrilegious, and blasphemous thing in God's sight, they ought not to vow this kind of poverty.

The other kind of poverty is material poverty. This can be of three kinds (if I may be permitted to play the fool with fools!). Either you need nothing at all, which is quite impossible, for you have to have food and clothing to keep alive; or, you take no responsibility for any concerns or cares. This is how babies have to live, small boys, the sick, the insane, and people of that sort who are under the control or care of somebody else. Or, you possess nothing of your own but manage goods held in common. It is these last two kinds of poverty monks must vow if they take the vow of poverty, especially the second. Otherwise, material poverty is, properly speaking, a want of food and clothing, where a man needs outside help and is unable to help himself from his own resources.

Now you see what a satanic game this is. In the book of Acts Luke praises the work of the apostles because they held all things in common and because of this all had enough [Acts 2:44]. He did not call this poverty nor [the people] paupers. What is more, where companions pool all they have in common and live on this common stock it is not poverty, nor ought it to be described as such. Rather it is the greatest abundance for all. For as Luke records it, it was the glory of the primitive church that while they were in spiritual and evangelical poverty they all thrived, and even had more than enough of this world's goods for each others' needs. Later, however, when their substance was used up and famine prevailed, they began to be in need even of material goods and were reduced to actual material poverty. Because of this Paul and Barnabas made collections for them among the faithful everywhere. But the apostles did not institute this kind of poverty when they held everything in common; they suffered because of a general dearth. Therefore, our monks vow neither spiritual poverty nor material poverty; they take vows to a general abundance which is liberally meted out to them. As I have already said, you can only bluntly describe this poverty as the poverty enjoyed by children and the mentally defective, since this is nothing less than poverty. They enter their orders not to live in want but in plenty. They are moved to do so because they know that there are full granaries in the monasteries which afford enough from generation to generation. As soon as poverty prevails in the monasteries, they either do not enter them or regret they ever did.

Is this not a brazen mockery of God and men to pretend the vow of poverty, and yet by so doing to seek in idleness sure plenty and excess, produced and provided by others, when nothing less is meant than to be in real need, to be in real poverty? Or do they not want us to know what poverty is or what it means? Or do they want to empty words of their proper meaning? By general assent, by common usage, and in everyday language material poverty means to be in want, in need of food and clothing. Who ever heard tell of a poverty which possessed nothing of its own but everything of everyone else? O fools and deceivers, who through covetousness will exploit the people with feigned words, as Peter prophesied [II Pet. 2:3]. Therefore, when these monks take their vow they lie even with regard to material poverty, and consequently they are godless with regard to spiritual poverty as well as liars with regard to material poverty. Do you think that this feigned and lying vow is pleasing to God? The saints certainly must have seen something different in this vow. As we have said, the nature of the vow is lying, ungodly, sacrilegious, and blasphemous.

But further. Let us say for the sake of argument that these godless vows were godly and gracious and that their unassailable security and affluence could be called poverty. What then would they say of those who are taken out of the monasteries and set in the papacy, the cardinalate, the episcopacy, and other ecclesiastical offices, when quite certainly they are moved out of the sphere of their vows into a state of having their own possessions? You cannot say in cases like these, unless you wanted to play with feigned words again, that the pope, the bishop, the cardinals, and the like do not possess property of their own which they use exactly as they wish. Granted that those in charge of monks care for things which are not their own, yet these men certainly look after their own possessions, although these possessions are accepted from the church. Consequently, it means nothing when they say that these things are not their own but belong to the church. This is what is meant by speaking with feigned words. The pope gives them these things as if he were lord of them. In fact, the pope makes himself the lord of both, even when saintly men like Anastasius,[123] Bernard's disciple, are set in office. Where is the vow of monastic poverty in a case like this? Further, you will have to condemn the status of bishop, cardinal, and pope, or else say that a monk cannot aspire so high. Their answer to this objection is that a monk's duty to obey this vow lapses and that he has entered a state of perfection. How superbly you deceive yourself! Why did you say earlier that monasticism is a state of perfection? I ask, how many states of perfection do you have? If a bishop lays aside his mitre and enters a monastery (as has sometimes happened), he enters a state of perfection from a state of imperfection. Likewise, when a monk leaves his monastery because he has been made a bishop, he enters a state of perfection. Here you see how the states change and make each other perfect and imperfect in turn. Lies rush at each other, attacking and destroying one another. What do you think these insolent, crazy people will say next? They could even go so far as to make it a state of perfection to abandon married life for a brothel! O merciful Christ! There is nothing in this sacrilegious kind of life except the most confused muddle of lies.

Further, if the vow of poverty is broken in deference to the vow of obedience and for the sake of the state of perfection, why not the vow of chastity, too? Where are those essential vows now? Is poverty now a nonessential vow? These people who have forsaken the solid rock of truth, presumed to invent new paths, an authority of their own, and a rarefied paradise for themselves are bound to be tossed about and chased by the winds of [their own] lies. The Bible says, "I gave them up to the lust of their own heart, and they will walk in their own counsels" [Ps. 81:12]. And Peter says, "Mockers and deceivers shall come in the last days who will walk after their own lusts" [II Pet. 3:3]. What will they say to this? Is the vow not a divine command? Especially if (as you say) it is essential. A commandment that is of God cannot be transgressed, not even on the authority of angels, not to mention the pope's authority or any other human authority. The statement still holds true, "We must

[123] Pope Anastasius IV (1153-1154).

obey God rather than men" [Acts 5:29]. Otherwise, by the same argument, theft, murder, adultery, and disobedience to parents would be permissible on the strength of a human authority and a human obedience. In short, you could deny God by means of his own commandments. If it is permissible to transgress one commandment, then it must be permissible to transgress all of them. The result of all this is that either it is impossible for a vow of this kind to be a divine precept, or, alternatively, all monks who have been created bishops are necessarily guilty [of breaking] this vow and stand condemned. Now in this context it is nonsense to allege that they remain in poverty. We are dealing with a serious matter. When we discuss matters of conscience we have to teach sound doctrine. We know perfectly well that a monk cannot be compared with a pope when it comes to a discussion of the vow of poverty. The monk vows to live in poverty in a monastery, and he intends to keep this vow his whole life long, because the vow is a commandment of God. And it does no good to bring in the state of perfection, not only on account of the lie just discussed, by which they even contradict themselves, but also on account of that other lie, namely, that the state of perfection cannot exist apart from and contrary to the commandment of God; this state is much rather a state to be condemned. No commandment of God is opposed to perfection. In fact, perfection consists only in the commandments of God. That man is perfect who keeps all of God's commands. What is it but brazen impudence to assert that a vow is both a commandment of God and a state of perfection? Or further, to assert that the state of perfection must be abandoned for the sake of a state of perfection? You see, dear reader, how overwhelmed I am by the size and number of their lies, so that I am not able to follow them up with arguments! A forest, a sea, a wilderness of lies—this is their famous monkery! I ask you, what a glorious lie is this one, to call the pontificate a state of perfection, a state which belongs only to faith and love, when it is much rather the state of pomp, luxury, and wealth! At its best, when everything about it is well ordered, it is only the greatest superstition and hypocrisy. And on account of this lie they teach that a vow may be dissolved, even though they want a vow to be regarded as a divine precept.

The miserable and insubstantial nature of this vow of monastic poverty has vanished before our eyes into thin air. It has been found that it can neither be called poverty, nor can it consequently be regarded even by themselves as an essential vow or a commandment, as they teach it is. Why therefore does that wretched chastity have such a firm place in a monk's vow, even ahead of poverty? Must you not admit one of two things? Either chastity is not essential, or you are hopelessly mixed up about the vow of poverty and are throwing away your life in keeping it as well as teaching it. I therefore conclude: inasmuch as a religious or a layman can proceed to the episcopate in exactly the same way, either the vow of the religious amounts to nothing, or, when he becomes a bishop, the religious is damned. For he rises to the same position as he who is restricted by no vows, which would be impossible if the vows of the religious were different from those of the layman. A bishop does not take the vows of a religious, nor is he bound to take vows. But nobody would want to take vows of this kind because they would be far too harsh and unattainable.

And so to sum up, I would say this: it appears that the vow of poverty has been devised by Satan to provide a pretext for freeing the religious from the responsibility of helping [to relieve] the poverty of others and from the works of mercy and love expected of them, a matter we touched upon earlier. For the vow keeps them closed up in their monasteries so that they cannot help anyone at all. It keeps them absolutely free from the necessity of working with their hands with the consequence that they allow themselves to be served by others. Under this arrangement the common people turn aside from helping those who are really poor—married couples, widows, orphans, and beggars—to pour their substance on these self-styled poor, who in fact are wealthy, fat, lazy, self-satisfied hypocrites.

Let us see whether obedience stands up to the test any better than poverty. We said earlier that there are two kinds of obedience.[124] First, there is evangelical obedience, whereby we are all subject one to another. This we vowed in baptism and it cannot be vowed anew unless we are just pretending and playing. The second

[124] Cf. pp. 328-336.

kind of obedience is a physical or corporal kind of obedience. If this sort of obedience does not run counter to the first, then I know nothing. It may be defined as the obedience which is offered by wives, children, sons, slaves, prisoners, and by all who for some reason or another are subject to somebody else. For evangelical obedience is a free and spontaneous obedience directed toward someone who has no claims upon us, except of course that God has willed that we be subject to those who have no real claims upon us at all. It is at this point that monks go wrong and make the same foolish mistake they do in the vow of poverty. First, they make it into a counsel. [And] they arrogate it to themselves alone. Therefore, by making obedience a vow they godlessly deny the commandment of God and blasphemously condemn their own baptismal vow. They pretend they are vowing something different and better than what they had vowed in baptism. If, indeed, some of them were to take vows in a truly godly fashion, they would certainly vow nothing but a physical or corporal obedience. But unless the Spirit is in them and eventually subjects them to the needs of others also,[125] nothing will be vowed at all save what is contrary to evangelical obedience, as we said before. The man who vows obedience vows it to one superior, not to all men, and he vows an obedience that is prescribed by a rule, which makes it impossible to render evangelical obedience. Indeed, it is forbidden to submit to equals, inferiors, other superiors, and to all other men and to be pleasing to them, yet evangelical obedience commands us to be well-disposed even toward our enemy and always to yield to him in everything.

I grant that in their hearts they intend an evangelical obedience. I am not denying this. I likewise grant that in their hearts they intend an evangelical poverty, as was certainly the case of the saints. Yet the institution itself, the very reason for taking vows, runs contrary to the gospel. For, as I said earlier, I am not arguing about the example the saints left or the spirit of their lives. Even a married couple needs that spirit. What I am discussing is the rightness and validity of a vow, for it is not right to establish, teach,

[125] Cf. pp. 325-336.

or take a vow, because to do so is contrary to the gospel. The vow does not allow you to be subject to everyone, but the gospel wants you to be subject to everyone. These two are diametrically opposed to one another, even though the spirit of the gospel is present in some of those who are under vows which are contrary to the gospel.

Much holier and much more excellent than the obedience of monks is that of a wife, of children, servants, prisoners, and such people, although even they cannot always discharge the corporal obedience, for they are bound hand and foot and are under the authority of another. And then we said earlier that evangelical freedom is such that it deprives no one of his legal rights or his property. Yet those who stand in an evangelical freedom go beyond [corporal obedience] and are ready and willing to serve and obey all men. They obey their superiors implicitly and without a prescribed rule covering all points. In actual fact the monks render obedience only to their own superiors, and even these not implicitly, but according to the exact standard of a prescribed rule, as no less a person than Bernard teaches.[126] In this they are utterly different from the early monks and hermits. Consequently, they arrive at this limited and false idea of obedience not as the need or situation demands (as applies in the life of a wife, of children, servants, prisoners, and others like them), but of their own volition. Quite certainly there is not a worse or more impoverished idea of obedience under heaven than that which the monks exhibit, an idea of obedience, moreover, which contradicts the gospel.

In addition to all this, there is a further felicity attached to the obedience a son, a wife, a servant, a citizen shows, which is far removed from impiety and blasphemy. For none of these believes that he distinguishes himself before God with this kind of obedience by rendering a service more remarkable than that of anyone else and beyond the demands of the gospel. None of these calls this kind of obedience a counsel. Yet if this impious and blasphemous opinion did not exist in monastic obedience, it could be neither taught, nor vowed, nor held. The monks want to exceed all others in their obedience, far and away beyond what the gospel teaches.

[126] Cf. p. 343, n. 116.

They alone want to be the spouses and brides of the Divine Majesty. They make their own Baal out of all this, in other words, a husband who especially belongs to them and to whom they very especially belong, one flesh and one spirit with him.[127] They regard the others as if they were servants, hirelings, and concubines in the household. It is quite certain, nevertheless, that the saints were not infected with this opinion. Possessed by the spirit of humility, they never extolled themselves above anyone. So you see, monastic obedience, no less than monastic poverty, is a novel and imaginary idea beyond and other than the normal usage of all language. To this fiction they add both impiety and blasphemy. For they call that obedience which both in a spiritual sense as well as in an actual sense is disobedience as far as the gospel goes, just as they call that poverty which, properly speaking, is plenty. So then, they vow this same fictitious obedience in a godless frame of mind in the belief that this is a more excellent and worthier obedience than the evangelical and true obedience, thereby sacrilegiously blaspheming the obedience of both baptism and the gospel. Therefore, the obedience accorded by a son, a wife, a servant, or a prisoner is a better and more perfect obedience than that of the monk, even at its best. That is, it is without impiety and sacrilege. It is the kind the saints possessed. Where it is impious and sacrilegious, however, it should not be compared with unchastity and murder, and still less with good obedience.

Therefore, I would venture to suggest with some confidence that unless monastic obedience is vowed and kept for a limited time as a kind of first step toward a Christian and evangelical obedience, so that young people in practicing it might learn to submit to everyone in everything, just as the monk by his vow submits to his superior in the monastery in certain things, just as certain examples in the lives of the fathers also prove—unless, as I was saying, monastic obedience is regarded in this way, then clearly it is ungodly and should be abandoned at once. This is akin to the poverty under which children live. They may not administer affairs until they learn to be careful, for because of their youth they would become wasteful and reckless if at that age affairs were put in

[127] Cf. p. 315.

their hands. What sort of madness is it which condemns the general obedience demanded of everyone to extol a particular kind of obedience observed by a particular class of people? Or will monastic obedience teach us that it is better to do a few good things for the few than many good things for the many? Therefore, if we have to advance from the imperfect to the perfect, we must move from monastic obedience to the obedience shown to parents, masters, husbands, tyrants, enemies, and everyone. Moreover, while they make the vow of obedience almost the greatest and most important in their order, we on the contrary see it as the smallest and the least important, even in those circumstances where it is pious and righteous, that is, when it is vowed as a first step in evangelical obedience. Where it is vowed for purposes of perfection, it is neither the smallest nor the least, but is perversity and sacrilege. And so it comes to pass, as we said of poverty, that just as poverty is never less present than when men boast of it, so obedience is never less present than when men boast of it. Here the word of Paul is fulfilled, "They have the appearance of piety but deny its power" [II Tim. 3:5]. Thus either monastic obedience is to be regarded as rudimentary and as obligatory for only a limited time, or it must be abandoned at once. Either we must return to the lawful obedience shown to parents and masters, or to an evangelical obedience shown to everyone. We must not hesitate here even if it has been buttressed by a thousand vows, for this vow runs counter to the gospel and can neither be approved by God nor demanded by him.

These things may be said of obedience in accordance with truth, but let us now speak on the same subject following the monastic lies so that we can see how no lie exists by itself in isolation. They say the vow of obedience is an essential vow and is now a divine precept. Here I repeat those arguments I introduced earlier with regard to the vow of poverty. What will they say of bishops who have been taken out of monasteries?[128] Where is their essential vow in that situation? They will say at this point that they move to a state of perfection and are offering obedience. I introduce again the arguments I made earlier, that is, a bishop is not allowed to become a monk and move over to a state of perfection

[128] Cf. p. 359.

in this way. Further, the states of perfection conflict with one another in their argument. To each state they attribute first perfection and then imperfection. And then in turn they deprive each of both. And so these most charming men measure the states of perfection not in relation to faith and love, not even, in the last resort, by the very outward hypocrisy of their works, but by the sheer whim of wanting to move. If a bishop becomes a monk he rises to the state of perfection because it is convenient for them to call this a state of perfection. On the other hand, when a monk is made a bishop, he, too, rises to the state of perfection. According to their scale of reckoning whichever way you move, you move to a state of perfection. A member of the secular clergy (as they call him) is already more perfect without vows than a member of the monastic order, since the secular clergyman can become a bishop without having taken vows. No monk can aspire to this unless he ascends beyond his vows to the state of perfection. Therefore, the monks as monks are at once both equal and inferior to the secular clergy. This is absurd and childish. Yet the logic of their position eventually compels us to understand their view in this way.

This is a serious matter. If a vow is a precept, it is not permissible under the pretext of any kind of obedience whatsoever for a monk to become a bishop, since it would not be permissible to abandon a commandment of God under any authority at all, or to alter it with a great good in view, no matter how great a good it may be. God wants us to obey his voice. Moreover, this is the remarkable thing about a vow of obedience: when a man forsakes monastic obedience he retains that obedience which is common to us all. For just as the bishop is obliged to obey the pope, so every Christian is bound to obedience, although they themselves teach that he took the vow to fulfil a greater and more perfect obedience than that common to us all. Therefore, when he yields to a lower kind of obedience and abandons the more perfect, he is in the position of any man who owes ordinary, common obedience. He who had first vowed a perfect obedience superior to the common obedience now assumes the obedience common to all. Has he not broken his vows? Has he not returned to the world? Has he not broken the yoke of obedience? What will they say to this? Quite certainly they either will allow the vow of obedience to be effective for an early disciplinary stage and for a limited duration, or they will condemn everybody who leaves the monastery to become a bishop as a sinner who has broken his vow. But yet, some regard this kind of person as a saint, as they did Bonaventure[129] and others.

How great a lie and a blasphemy it is to say that the breaking of an essential vow and the abandonment of a precept of God constitute a move to the state of perfection! As if a commandment of God could be inconsistent with perfection or that any beginning of salvation (not to mention perfection) could be outside the scope of God's commandment! If, therefore, a monk wants to be perfect he will abide by his vow and keep the divine precept, although, as I have said, all these things are false deceptions. It belongs to the state of a bishop to preach the word of God. That is not a state to which the religious climb, since no one is more able to preach the word than monks, as St. Bernard did and those like him. Thus when a monk, like those who have held episcopal office for more than four hundred years, becomes a bishop, he moves from the real state of a bishop to that of a mere figurehead, an episcopal caricature.

And now to make an end of all these lies and fictions. Among all the monastic vows none is less essential than the vow of obedience, and none argues more convincingly that the institution of monasticism is merely an introductory period for Christian youth—which, like the old custom of the fathers,[130] ought to be observed only for a time—for the purposes of learning faith and growing in the gospel. I can prove this in the following way. It is quite impossible for monasteries not to have their superiors who are in charge and who govern and have pastoral care of the monks. Is this not true? Indeed, what confusion there would be if the flock had no shepherd! If this is true then, it is quite impossible for such an order of government not to please God, because it is a power ordained by God, Romans 13 [:1]. But to be in charge and at one and the same time to obey and be subject is equally impossible. I am now speaking of corporal obedience or subjection, which is

[129] Bonaventure (1221-1274) entered the Order of Friars Minor in *ca.* 1238. In 1273 Gregory X named him cardinal-bishop of Albano. Cf. *The Catholic Encyclopedia*, II, 648 ff.

[130] Cf. pp. 312-313.

all that is vowed, as we said earlier. But even the rule says, "The head of the monastery must be obeyed, and the maintenance of discipline is in his hand." And at this point they drag in the word of the Apostle, "Obey those set over you, and be subject to them" [Heb. 13:17]. He who is appointed to govern cannot, in this corporal sense, be subject either to a congregation or to one who is subject to him. It follows, therefore, that in God's sight everybody who has been set over others is absolved from the vow of obedience as long as he is in this position of authority. He can, however, occupy this position permanently, either he or someone else. It follows, therefore, that in God's sight either no one is bound permanently and necessarily even by the vow of obedience, or else no one can be set over the others in the monasteries. For the superior of the monastery does not obey, but is obeyed; and, moreover, the rule declares that he has to be obeyed, as does the provision of his profession or vow.

In my opinion it makes hardly a scrap of difference to the argument when they say that the superior is subject to superiors of his own and that he governs according to the rule. I know all this. But what has that to do with the vow of obedience, which you have already said is a divine precept that cannot be altered? You are not at liberty to cast away one precept of God in favor of any other precept of God, much less in favor of a human consideration. It is one thing to govern and quite another to obey all one's superiors. For in the last resort this obedience refers back to the pope, who obeys no one. No one takes a vow to preside over or to obey the pope and those set over the superior, but he does vow within the monastery obedience to the prior himself. Obedience, I said. He vows corporal obedience and subjection, which cannot be the same for the superior's office. Do not play with words. Yet how unfitting it would be if a simple layman were to command the monks according to the rule while obeying no one and taking no vows himself! For what is the difference between a layman in this position and a superior under vows? Therefore, the conclusion holds good: monastic obedience is an elementary and infantile obedience; it is instituted for a limited duration for the instruction of the young. It is not otherwise acceptable to God or otherwise permissible, unless you want to create an impious, sacrilegious obedience. Thus since the evangelical way of living is the more perfect way, we must eventually proceed to this evangelical obedience from this corporal obedience, as from the part to the whole. For when that which is perfect is come, then that which was imperfect must pass away, and when the time comes that we are men, childhood must be put behind us [I Cor. 13:10-11].

Therefore, all vows are valid only for a limited time and are subject to change. Only chastity abides untouched in solitary splendor. Who can show why this vow is not valid for a limited time, since more than all the other vows it is subject to time? Sadly, this is no feigned concern but a real one, even if the vow of chastity is godless and sacrilegious in itself. Their vow does not invent a chastity which is a figment of the imagination, as it does in the case of obedience and poverty by coining new words. Their vow means real chastity in every sense of the word. Yet this vow is totally deceiving. There is never less chastity than in those who vow to be chaste. Almost everything about it is befouled, if not by unclean seminal emissions, then by the continual searing of lust which never dies out. But further, it would be most desirable that if anything fictitious has to be vowed in the monastery, it should be a fictitious chastity. This would be a salutary fiction. If only someone would make it possible to exchange that vow of fictitious poverty and obedience for a fictitious chastity, so that just as under poverty plenty was preserved, and under obedience disobedience was preserved, in the same way under chastity the bed of matrimony would be preserved, they would be driven into a true poverty and a true obedience. A fiction of this sort could be accepted and would be a happy exchange! But as far as the vow of chastity is concerned there is no semblance to which Satan can turn. The difference between chastity and marriage is all too clear. Therefore, he has never made chastity a sphere of operation for his deception. But poverty was most beautifully simulated simply by not having property of one's own, and obedience was made most plausible by selecting a particular aspect of it. For nothing is more like evangelical and general obedience than the selective monastic obedience. The flesh of the finger is like the flesh of the rest of the body. At this point, then, the devil had a lot of room in which to work; he taught them to live in opulence for poverty and in disobedience for obedience, since he could teach neither marriage nor lust in the place of chastity.

Yet even this served to further the devil's teaching. Although he failed to teach lust, he proved all the more active in furthering lust. Since chastity is a rare thing, even impossible with most of those who take vows, the intentions of Satan were realized. That fiction would have been much too apparent if the monks had been married men while under the vow of chastity! Nor would such an observance of the vow have cost them their souls! For that reason Satan turned his thoughts to another really worthy fiction. Not content with defiling the vow of chastity with prostitution, debauchery, and adultery, he hit upon the lust that besets the monk, the nun, the hermit: he devised the lust of the solitary. This was Satan's device. Let others see for themselves whether he brought it to perfection. My intention is just to uncover his devices, by which he has always striven to do his very worst against Christians. Beware you do not assume these monks are living in chastity when it is generally known that they live an ungodly life. They are fattened by the labors of other men's hands. They live securely in idleness, luxury, and plenty. As Ezekiel says, "Behold, this was the guilt of your sister Sodom: she and her daughters had pride, surfeit of food, and prosperous ease, but did not aid the poor and needy. They were haughty and did abominable things before me; therefore I removed them when I saw it" [Ezek. 16:49-50]. Chastity is scarcely preserved by great effort, striving, privation, and the cross, even in the case of the most godly people, that is, those who "gird their waists with the spirit of faith." As Isaiah says, "And righteousness shall be the girdle of his loins, and faith the girdle of his waist" [Isa. 11:5]. And also in Zechariah 9 [:17], "The grain of the elect and wine which bears virgins," which means the goodness and beauty of the people of Christ. What is more, Paul is emboldened to declare about the widow who lives in self-indulgence, "She is dead while she lives" [I Tim. 5:6]. How can these men persist, therefore, when they do no work as other men do and when we see that everything Ezekiel says of Sodom—pride, idleness, excess, and plenty—holds sway in them? No one is more negligent of the poor. They even persecute faith and the Holy Spirit. We shall say nothing about their possessing neither! In the meantime they solace one another. Each one presumes chastity in the other, though he knows that he himself cannot remain chaste. On the strength of this presumption their order is nonetheless holy! O what times! What leadership! What goings-on! Everything is in Satan's clutches!

What more shall I say then on the subject of the vow of chastity, since it is not my intention to speak about keeping it, and I have spoken at great length on the non-keeping of it? I have clearly proved that the whole institution of the vow is fictitious both in its first principles and in its most important essentials, namely, obedience and poverty. Even though it is vowed and kept by most holy and godly men, it is really a lie, and to those who are not holy and godly it is by its very nature impious, sacrilegious, and blasphemous. What more do you want? What is most eagerly sought after by those who take vows, namely, divine worship itself, is by far and away more detestable and abominable. By its very nature it is nothing else but playing a part. It is mocking God, with its tonsure, unction, garb, bellowing and muttering, standing up, sitting down, bowing and scraping, genuflecting, burning of incense, and sprinkling of holy water. In fact, the crowning point of this very worship, namely, the mass, exceeds all other impiety and abomination because they always resort to it as a sacrifice and a work. Consequently, if nothing else moved them to lay aside the cowl, leave the monastery, and hate the vow, the abomination of the masses alone would be more than enough to prevent their joining in all good conscience with men who are misguided—especially when you cannot be under the vow and inside a monastery without being involved in their masses and taking part in them. For there is not one of them who has taken vows whose first and last thought is not about the masses and the worship of God. That is the reason they become monks, so that they can worship God. No one takes to the monastic life to be chaste. Everyone knows that one can be chaste without the cowl no less happily than with the cowl. But this abominable worship of God attracts us through the wiles of Satan, and by the subtlest deceptions the devil entices us into the inescapable snare of chastity (or rather lust). It is at this fantastic price that he sells us the glossy deceit of this abomination, so that if you are not willing to open yourself to the continual danger of an unmentionable lust, he does not admit you to his delights.

Since the very reason for taking vows is in itself an abomination, its conditions sacrilegious, and its intention a deception, it follows that in its main essentials the vow is feigned and false. Why then do you continue to doubt that a vow of this kind is utterly worthless and not valid in a single part? Not philosophy, but nature, law, and common sense alike teach that any agreement is null and void when its conditions are evil, its reason sacrilegious, and its intention deceptive, even though a simple soul keeps such an agreement. Yet these are the very factors which completely dominate the monastic vow. The reason lies in this grotesque worship of God and in the abomination of all those masses. Its conditions depend on regarding obedience and poverty as evangelical counsels from which they deduce that corporal[131] obedience and poverty are essential vows. The intention of the vow is to accept all these things as other than what they really are. The monk does not keep the vow in terms of its plain meaning. In fact, he cannot but break it. I grant that the saints were saved by a miracle of the Holy Spirit in the midst of these abominations. They kept this very vow over and above what it required and even against what is required. Imagine that you had promised to kill your father and violate your mother, and that this could be completed only when certain fasts and prayers and other good works had been done. Would you feel bound to fulfil your promise because the prayers and works you had vowed were good, when you see that the whole idea of the vow in conception and intention is thoroughly revolting? In fact, you would forego the good along with the bad. You would promise something else that did not include anything evil, or nothing at all, as you wished. Thus even in the case of the monastic vow you see how the matter stands with all those who because of the Spirit have not despised their monastic vows nor regarded them as worthless.

In all truth chastity has a godlessness of its own, just like the other parts of the vows. Its godlessness exists in that it boasts of a

---

[131] Cf. pp. 361–363.

faith over and above the common general faith. And this is a direct disservice to Christ. But we have said enough about that already. It is not the virgin or the chaste who will be saved, but the Christian. In Christ there is neither male nor female [Gal. 3:28], neither virgin nor wife, or any similar distinctions. But there is one faith, one baptism, one Lord [Eph. 4:5]. And where the Spirit is not present, chastity can be neither vowed nor kept in any but a godless fashion, for he who takes this vow believes that he is pleasing God by this work of chastity, but it is written, "Without faith it is impossible to please him" [Heb. 11:6]. It follows then that he who takes the vow of chastity in this frame of mind is actually vowing nothing at all and is free not to fulfil the vow. Moreover, there are those who took their vows while holding these views. It is not possible to settle the matter with so many words, but it is left to their own conscience. They cannot be restrained because of the perilous times. Paul foretold all this [II Tim. 3:1-6]. Right in the forefront of their lives they set the scandals and perils of an exalted virginity and the vaunted continence of their vow. They emphasize the examples of the saints. The unthinking crowd seizes these ideas. As long as they silence the gospel and faith, they embrace whatever is commended and set before them. And so they rely upon works and perish. On the other hand, it can happen that some understand these ideas in the spirit of faith, and keep their vows in joy and gladness without a breath of scandal, as we believe the saints did. And since we can neither condemn the saints nor praise these others, everything is highly dangerous and it is difficult to be precise about them. If the gospel really reigned alone and supreme, and vows were no longer there to ensnare people, there would no longer be any danger, neither would there be any need for a work to be defined in this way beforehand. Everyone would know that he should be chaste not because of a vow but on his own volition. Everyone would know that a Christian must set his hope on Christ and not on works. Let him who now believes in vows go on believing, let him who does not, believe no longer. What more can we say until the scandals and perils are removed once more from the kingdom of Christ?

But perhaps they will raise an objection by quoting that passage in Isaiah 56 [:3-5] against me, where the Lord promises to the eunuchs a place and a name in his house better than that of sons or daughters, for it seems from this that greater merit is attributed to virginity and chastity than to the rest of the faithful, and that the merits are not attributed to faith alone. My answer: this text is seeking to say the same thing as Paul said in I Corinthians 7 [:26], "It is good for a man to be thus [unmarried]," as well as when he said it would be better if a virgin were not given in marriage than if she were [I Cor. 7:38]. We know, too, that in our Father's house are many mansions [John 14:2], and that one star differs from another in brightness [I Cor. 15:41], and that every man will receive the reward of his labor [I Cor. 3:8]. Indeed, Paul made the presbyters who labored in the word worthy of double honor [I Tim. 5:17]. And now let us come to the passage in Isaiah. The Lord comforts eunuchs of the gospel lest they think they are nothing because they are childless, on the grounds that chastity was cursed in the law.[132] So he abrogates this curse and says, "Let not the eunuch say, I am a dry tree . . ." [Isa. 56:3]. Now the Lord is not praising chastity for its own sake, nor does he praise it above all else, as our monks are trying to do. Isaiah says, "For the Lord says this to the eunuchs who keep my sabbaths and choose the things that please me, and keep my covenant, I will give them a place in my house and within my walls and a name better than I give to sons and daughters. I will give them an everlasting name, a name that shall never die" [Isa. 56:4-5].

You see, in this instance chastity is praised in such a way that the keeping of the sabbaths of God, the choosing to do the will of God, and the keeping of the covenant of the Lord are far preferred to it. Now these things are the common duty of us all. It necessarily follows that without these chastity is worth nothing. And so this place and this name which is better than that given to sons and daughters can be understood in no other way than that there is a diversity of gifts, and that in the household of God some gifts are greater than others. Just as Paul labored more abundantly than the others [I Cor. 15:10], so then virginity and chastity are greater

[132] Luther means that obligatory chastity violates the divine command of Gen. 1:28.

works and greater gifts than marriage. And in actual fact there are names and places among the sons and daughters which in relation to one another in the house are better and greater. But in relation to the true God and the eunuchs there is no name other than the one we all enjoy, and that name is Christ. This is the name that keeps the sabbaths, chooses the things that please God, and keeps the covenant of the Lord. The name enunch, on the other hand, does none of these, but rather derives its existence from them. This is the way all those passages are to be understood which seem to boast of works and to distinguish between them. Even Paul describes differences in graces, gifts, and works in I Corinthians 12 [:4-6], but he always adds that there is one God, one Lord, one Spirit. Peter also speaks of many kinds of graces, but says that they are to be ministered to one another [I Pet. 4:10]. And in Romans 12 [:4-5] and I Corinthians [:12-31] Paul discusses the one body and the many functions of the various members in one and the same healthy body of faith.

But to strengthen consciences we want to discuss the chastity which is godly and which has been vowed for good reasons, although it must be said that either it is no chastity at all, or else it is a possibility for everybody, because the Spirit who began it is faithful and will perfect that which has been begun [Phil. 1:6], even though he allows it to be buffeted and tempted. Nevertheless, we will discuss it at some length.

In Romans 7 [:18-23] Paul confesses that there is in his flesh sin of such a kind that he could never be free of it in this life. Without a shadow of doubt this sin is against the law of God, but for the sake of faith, which fights in the Spirit, this sin is overlooked and not imputed, even though the law demands there be no sin in us. The law of the Spirit of life in Christ Jesus, on the other hand, succors us, so that our not being able to keep the law in no sense works condemnation in us as long as we walk according to the Spirit and not according to the flesh [Gal. 5:16].

Therefore, I argue from the greater to the lesser. God, in the law he himself gave, is forbearing and pardons our inability to keep it. The inability to keep his law remains in us, but it constitutes no danger even though real sin is there. If, then, God deals with us in this way, how much more ought we to have confidence in his goodness and believe that the vow of chastity will not be counted against us if it proves impossible to keep and if the danger of lust threatens. We need only abide within the limits of the humbler chastity of marriage and not walk according to the flesh. After all, it was not God who commanded chastity, nor did he counsel or recommend it. It was introduced by human temerity and ignorance. Will he be more severe in his demands in the case of a vow invented by our own foolishness than he is in the case of his law laid down in all his wisdom?

In Acts 15 [:3-21] the Apostle Paul demonstrated evangelical freedom by the miracles and wonders God had wrought, for the Spirit was given to the gentiles apart from circumcision and the law of Moses. Although almost the entire primitive church, erring in conscience, was of a different opinion, Peter, Paul, and Barnabas brought in this view of freedom, on the authority of the miracles and wonders God had wrought, and established their view against all opposition. We learn from this case that where testimonies of Scripture give no precedent, we must rely on the works of God and be guided by them in the absence of scriptural testimonies. This is exactly what we have to do in the case under discussion. When we see that his goodness is merciful in his most holy law because no man can keep that law, we may presume that he is equally merciful with regard to the impossibility of the vow we impose upon ourselves. It is quite unbelievable that he who is so benign in his righteousness should be so unbending in demanding something that derives from our foolishness. And it is my belief that if anyone is unable to keep his vow of chastity and takes a wife, confident of God's mercy, as he grows in this faith he will discover a merciful and understanding Father. After all, he is doing this to avoid sinning more grievously against God's law.

That is what God's mercy is like.[133] In no sense does God attribute sin to the conjugal rights of married people, which is due solely to his mercy, although Psalm 51 [:5] refers to it as sin and iniquity in no way differing from adultery and whoredom, because

[133] *WA* reads, "*Tale est el illud opus, quod debitum coniugale [vocant]. . . .*" The Wittenberg, Jena, and Erlangen editions omit *vocant.*

it springs from passion and impure lust. It is impossible to avoid this emotion, since we are restrained to forego it. Why then should it not also be supposed in the case of a monk who is unable to keep his vow of chastity, and who would otherwise sin, that this impossible vow may be relaxed, and that once the vow is nullified, he be permitted to marry? Or, if it is done in sin while still under the vow, why may it not be mercifully pardoned as is a conjugal right? Consider the immensity of the law God gave us, and then compare the following points carefully. Consider the impossibility of keeping the law, our sin which is forgiven, and the boundlessness of his mercy and goodness. And then, compare all that with the foolishness and stupidity of our vow, a mere tradition and invention of men. The reasonableness of this argument will most certainly compel you to consider it a small thing for the marriage of a stumbling celibate who is unable to keep his vow of chastity to be excused, compared with the forgiveness of sin in the law of God, because no man can keep that law. This law is valid for us all. Consequently, from this work of God's mercy we may conclude with absolute confidence that an impossible vow is not binding as far as the goodness of God is concerned, even though it may be binding in some way within its own limitations.

For my part I do not say these things because I seek to concede that it is impossible for such a vow to be made within the framework of the monastic institution, or because I consider them necessary for those who have piously taken their vows under the institution of monasticism as it is. These men, as I have already said, are guided by the Spirit and will continue to be so guided. These men would have taken vows and lived like monks under the institution of monasticism even if there had been no institution of monasticism. They neither take nor keep their vows because the form and law of the institution dictate and demand them. They gladly and voluntarily do the things prescribed by the institution. Otherwise, they would want to do the works of the law and effect a righteousness of good works, which is utterly contrary to the gospel. Because these people take their vows and live their lives according to the pattern of the institution and for the sake of the institution they are in all truth Jews. They both take their vows and live them in godlessness and contrary to the gospel. Therefore, their vow cannot be a kind that needs this advice. It must be revoked and given up immediately because in the New Testament—the testament of freedom, where the ministry of the spirit, not of the letter, reigns—it is not permissible to establish and teach the letter [II Cor. 3:6]. If, moreover, both the institution and its teaching lead into temptation, it is not right to accept them. We must turn and flee from them. Even Paul says in Romans 16 [:17-18], "I beseech you brethren that you keep an eye on those who cause divisions and offenses contrary to the doctrine you have learned, and turn from them. Such men do not serve our Lord Jesus Christ, but their belly, and by good words and fair speeches they deceive the hearts of the innocent." These words can only be understood as referring to those who, contrary to the Christian way, teach something different as if it were something better. Paul does not say they deny our teaching, but that they teach another kind along with and other than ours. This is exactly what the monastic institutions do. We never see divisions and sects except among monks. Among them we find servitude to the belly. Still more, we meet the good words and boasting speeches, the praises and privileges, and the other benedictions of orders and works. Among them [we find] the deceiving of the hearts of the innocent. Since Paul commands us to look out for these things and to turn away from them, there is not a shadow of doubt that such vows are null and void, and have never been worth anything. So we too must turn from them, either in the Spirit as the saints did, or in both Spirit and letter at one and the same time. We must turn away from them as from the very worst kind of deception, defined and condemned here by the Apostle. He seeks the same thing when in both epistles he wants Timothy to abide in the doctrines he had taught him and to permit nothing to be added.[134] "In doing this (he says) you shall both save yourself and those who heed you" [I Tim. 4:16]. Without a doubt this means that were he not to abide in those doctrines he would be lost along with those who heeded him. On this very point Peter, in II Peter 2 [:1], calls them sects of perdition, and with a grim and terrible statement he warns us against sects and opinions which have nothing

[134] Cf. I Tim. 4:16; II Tim. 3:14-15.

to do with Christ. And in I Peter 4 [:10-12] he ordered that nothing other than the word of God was to be taught, and nothing other than the work of God to be laid down, that God alone may be glorified in us in all things through Christ Jesus, adding, "lest we go astray in our fiery trial." Let us hear the sound words of the Apostle himself, "As every one has received the gift, let him minister it among you as good stewards of the manifold grace of God. If any man speak, let him speak as the oracles of God. If any man minister, as one who ministers by the strength which God gives; that in all things God may be glorified through Jesus Christ, to whom is the glory and the dominion for ever and ever. Dearly beloved, do not be led astray in the fiery trial in your midst, as if some alien experience had befallen you. It has come to try you. Rather, be partakers of the sufferings of Christ."

In the first place, he wants nothing to be offered but the gift which was received; nothing is to be taught except the word of God; nothing is to be done except what God works in us. He wants this so that nothing human but everything divine be spoken and worked in us, because we are stewards not of our own riches, but of the manifold grace of God. This must be done for God to be glorified through Jesus Christ, whose is the glory and the dominion for ever and ever. For since we are his kingdom and it is his right to reign and rule in us, no word or work is to be permitted which he does not utter or effect in us. If, on the other hand, we permit it, we, along with the Jews, reject him and prevent his reigning over us [Luke 19:14]. In the midst of God's kingdom we set up an alien. And so the kingdom of God is laid waste and the abomination sits in the holy place [Matt. 24:15]. The church is the kingdom of God, and is so described because God alone reigns in her: God alone rules, speaks, works, and is glorified in her. If, therefore, a man teaches and works something in us which God does not teach and work, then in that case God is not glorified in us through Jesus Christ. It is the man whose word and work it is who is glorified. God is not glorified by an alien word and work. And so it necessarily follows that if an alien word and work rules in us, God loses the glory and the kingdom in us: for the man whose word and work it is will have the glory and the kingdom. What harder thing could be said against the papacy, the episcopacy, monasticism, and the priesthood as they now exist? Is anyone so ignorant or so bold as to assert that the teachings and works of the pope and the monks are God's, handed down by Jesus Christ? For where did Jesus Christ teach these things? And yet, what was not said to us or worked in us by Jesus Christ cannot be returned by us to the glory of the Father by this same Jesus Christ! Whose, then, is the glory and the dominion among the monks? Without a doubt it is Satan's! This he achieves through St. Benedict[135] and other holy men who earn praise and fame for what is only a blasphemous hypocrisy and a perverse emulation of works. Therefore, just as Christ does not teach monastic vows, neither does he effect them, although I do grant that Christ worked and spoke in a wonderful way, without vows, through those saints in the grip of the monastic vow.

In the second place, Peter says with a gentle insistence, "Dearly beloved, do not be led astray in the fiery trial in your midst, as if some alien experience had befallen you." The fact that he says this shows concern for us lest we forsake the way laid down by him when we are in the grip of some temptation or another. He uses the word *peregrinari,* which in Greek is *me xenizesthai,* which means not to wander abroad, not to become sojourners.[136] In using this word Peter has in mind many examples of the Old Testament. He wants exactly what Paul wants in Ephesians 4 [:14] when he says that we should not be tossed to and fro and carried about with every wind of doctrine, or permit ourselves to be invited to the sacrifices of the Moabites,[137] or to become sojourners among all the races round about, but to hold fast to our own and proper doctrine. By the fiery trial in your midst Peter means one's own spirit which he depicts under the imagery of fire. When it is said in the Old Testament that idols are forged and became molten images, it means that godless doctrines of works are being devised.[138] He prophesies that this spirit both within us and among us will never

[135] St. Benedict of Nursia (*ca.* 480-543) was the founder of the celebrated Monte Cassino Monastery and author of the Benedictine rule.

[136] Cf. the Greek text of I Pet. 4:12.

[137] Cf. Num. 25:2.

[138] Deut. 27:15. Note Luther's choice of words, *conflare* ("fire"), *conflari* ("forged"), and *conflatilia* ("molten images").

be lacking, but he warns us beforehand so that we do not wander astray as sojourners into temptation and scandal on account of this same spirit. There have been and always will be people trying to effect these things in us. But, he adds, you must not turn away from your own tradition as if, to use his expression, something strange and alien were to happen to you. This means, you may be quite certain, that nothing new will be taught by God. What you have heard is the eternal word, and this abides for ever. If anything new or strange comes to pass, be assured that it comes from some place other than from God, and that it is calling you away and making you into this sojourner. In this text, and before it actually happened, Peter clearly concerned himself with the lie of the papists that was yet to be told, by which they allege that Christ and the apostles did not command and institute everything, but that the church had to command and institute many more things. This is what is meant by alien and new, which Peter tells us ought not and must not happen in our case. Peter, therefore, is condemning here all things which are not the words and works of God. In other words, he is abolishing monastic vows.

Christ speaks most clearly against monastic vows in Matthew 24 [:23-26], "Then if any man shall say to you: Behold, here is Christ, or there, do not believe it. For false Christs and false prophets shall arise and they shall show great signs and wonders, so that if it were possible even the elect would be led into error. Behold, I have told you beforehand. If therefore they shall say to you: Behold, he is in the desert, do not go there; Behold, he is in the secret chambers, do not believe it." These words can be understood of no heretics except those who teach (to use their own expression) the ways and means of living which lead to righteousness and salvation. No one except the papists and monks has ever had the effrontery to teach these ways and means. These are the people who vaunt their hermits. In other words, they are the ones who call people to the wilderness and secret chambers, that is, to the cloister or the monastery. They teach that Christ is to be found in these places, in other words, that righteousness and salvation are to be found there. They teach this so brazenly that they call all other ways of living secular, as if salvation were to be found only in their brotherhood. Yet in so doing they are the false Christs who draw people away from the faith in which we all stand to a faith founded on works. They drag people away from Christ to follow them instead. It is related in the *Lives of the Fathers* that St. Silvanus[139] had a vision in which he saw hell filled with monks. For the rest of his life he refused to be comforted after he had seen such men, who by all appearances were holy, perishing in great numbers.[140] This story and its vision fit in very well with the gospel. It seems that God revealed this vision to show the working of the error just beginning at that time and to put an end to it. God wanted to do this by many other signs, too, as in the case of St. Anthony,[141] Paphnutius,[142] and others. There are many other very dangerous examples in that book of those who rail madly against the doctrine of faith in favor of works. If the monastic life was undertaken in error and was even then bringing the monks to perdition at that early stage, I ask you, what do you imagine it is these days, when faith and the gospel have been extinct for so long?

At this point the argument of these asses from Paris[143] and these pigs of the papist sect falls to the ground. They base their argument on two grounds: the argument from the many and the argument from sanctity.[144] Christ exploded the argument from the many when he said, "And they shall deceive many, so that even the elect could be led into error" [Matt. 24:24]. In fact, he demolishes the argument from holiness by the same text when he prophesied that even the elect would be led astray. These ignorant asses accomplish nothing by saying that the church had not been forsaken for so long and was not unaware of the things Luther shows them he knows. These people call their sects the church, but these sects are

---

139 St. Silvanus, an early Egyptian monk, is mentioned frequently in the *Lives of the Fathers (Vitae Patrum)*. The story of which Luther speaks is in *LCC* 12, 46.

140 Cf. *MPL* 73, 806.

141 St. Anthony is traditionally regarded as the first hermit. Cf. p. 253, n. 4.

142 Cf. p. 316, n. 85.

143 Cf. p. 259, n. 8.

144 The argument from the many holds that because the majority hold to the papacy, truth is on the papal side. The argument from sanctity holds that he who denies what all others believe and what the church fathers and councils teach is a self-confessed atheist and unbeliever. Cf. Luther's *On the Opinion of the Parisian Theologians (Ein Urteil der Theologen tzu Pariss)*. *WA* 8, 269-270.

no more the church than the prophets, priests, elders, kings, princes, Pharisees, and Sadducees were the synagogue. All have erred and lived in ignorance even as in the days of Elijah when only seven thousand were left [I Kings 19:18]. These seven thousand had been in utter obscurity until that time, and therefore they were not regarded as being the synagogue, for they were not even seen. Even Elijah did not know a single one of them! What a terrible state of affairs! Therefore, you now have it on the authority of Christ that if you have gone out into your desert or entered one of those secret chambers, you may turn back. In fact, you ought to turn back. What else does this mean except that your vow must be revoked and annulled because it was made in accordance with a teaching other than Christ's and is therefore erroneous and impious? For as I have already said, St. Bernard was saved when, of his vows and his whole life, he sincerely said, "I have wasted my life!"[145] Does he not nullify his vows with these words and by this confession, and return to Christ? By the same token, other saints under vows were saved apart from those vows, but they have lived under vows in the error of the elect [Matt. 24:24] and thereby lead those who are perishing and do not believe the gospel into a snare and religion of works. Since then these words of Christ apply so perfectly to monasticism, and at the same time demolish their arguments, one has to rely on them with confidence and hold that the vows are null and void. For you know full well that these vows are made and relied upon [on the authority] of men, not of God. This is something which is forbidden. By their very nature these vows sin against the glory of God and against his kingdom.

The impression gathered from all these examples is of the foolishness of the vow, especially the vow of chastity. If other things were not destroying this vow, in the end its very folly would not allow it to last. In vowing chastity what does the monk vow but something which is not and cannot be in his hands, since chastity is a gift from God alone, which a man can accept, but never proffer. He is mocking God, therefore, when he takes such a vow. It is no different from vowing to become a bishop or an apostle, a prince or a king, since he knows perfectly well that none of these things lies

[145] *MPL* 183, 867. Cf. *WA* 8, 601, ll. 20 ff., and in this volume, p. 290.

within the power of the man making the vow, but rather within the will and authority of another who has the power to confer such appointment. Imagine, I beg you, a madman who vowed something like this to God, "I vow to thee, O Lord, to make new stars or to move mountains." What would you think of such a vow? Yet the vow of chastity is no different from a vow like that, for chastity is no less wonderful a work of God than creating stars and moving mountains. The Lord commands that he who makes a vow or an offering should make it of his own substance and from the gifts given him by a gracious Lord, as every word in the law of Moses on the subject of vows maintains.[146] Since this is so, it is evident that the vow of chastity can neither please God nor be demanded by him, for it issues from something not yet given and does not even lie within our power. If a single vow is valid in matters which do not lie within our power, but in God's, then we could quite legitimately and piously vow everything that lies only in God's power and which only he can do. If all these foolish vows are not valid, then neither is that single vow of chastity. You might just as well vow that you will most certainly be saved, that you will be equal to Peter, that you will lay waste the kingdoms of the Turks, live as long as Methuselah—and all else that God works in man or has the power to work. If it is not lawful to vow these things which are not in your power to do, why then do you vow chastity, which is not within your power? Why do you vow something which lies within God's power alone, not within yours, in just this single instance? Why do you not vow these things in all other instances? If not in all, why just in one? You will say, can I not attain chastity by prayer? I am listening. But then what are you not able to obtain by prayer? Did Christ not promise, "Whatever you shall ask in my name, believe and it shall come to pass for you" [Matt. 21:22]. Why do you not vow everything else as well and obtain them?

But perhaps you will object [and say], "If this opinion were accepted, then it would not be permissible to make a vow to God in baptism, since both faith and the fulfilment of the commandments of God are not in our hands but God's alone." I reply: That is beautifully and well said if the case were at all the same in the mat-

[146] Deut. 16:17; cf. II Cor. 8:12.

ter of baptismal vows as it is with your vows. In baptism it is God who makes the promise and the offer; we vow nothing else but to accept Christ who is offered us. It is a happy vow indeed which does not promise to give anything, but which only accepts good things and holds on to what has been accepted. Here it is quite clear that nothing is vowed by us either of our own possessions or of the gifts which are in the hand of God. In fact, if you consider the matter properly, God makes the vow for us, and the vow comes from God, who makes the promises and at the same time gives the grace and all that his commandments demand. We on our part make vows to accept his vow and his promise freely and gladly, and to heed them. But when you vow virginity or chastity, do you think that God is at your side and taking the vow on your behalf? Do you think he is promising anything? Do you think he is offering anything? When, then, did he promise to give chastity to you? What makes you so certain what he will give? Do you not come along as a suppliant, and without that which you are promising? Are you not absolutely alone when you make this promise? Is anyone there to answer you and to accept your promise? And why should he accept your promise, if you are brainless and stupid enough to promise something you do not have? You see, therefore, that the vow of baptism and the vow of continence are two utterly contrary things: the vow of continence offers to give what it does not possess; the vow of baptism accepts what it does not possess. In the case of a vow of continence a man is offering with empty hands what he does not even possess; while in the case of the vow of baptism God out of his abundance promises what is his own. Therefore, as long as you cannot prove that the promise of God is given in the vow of continence, you cannot excuse the foolishness and vanity of such a vow. God cannot accept or demand what is foolish and vain. On the other hand, the vow of baptism is true and perfect, because it is based on God, who makes the promise and offers the gift. What if some do not accept? He who makes the offer is nevertheless true.

To this foolishness they add yet another. To extol the rigor and indissoluble character of the vow, these merciful and kindly men liberally grant a full year of probation, as they call it. Further, I could give them some credit for this if the novices would use this year of probation to enter the monastery and see their customs, their mode of living, their manner of dressing, and other things which pertain to the body. But these days it is a year of probation only to the extent that he who is about to take his vows is tested to see whether he is able to live in chastity for that year. I ask you, if you examine the real nature of the institution what foolishness can be equal to this? (In this discussion I always make an exception of the saints and of the wonderful things they did.) What all this amounts to is that the test of chastity is not measured by the power of the Spirit, but by a certain number of days, and a man who has lived chaste for one year is judged capable of living chaste all his life. When, therefore, chastity has to be measured by external things, why not measure it in terms of places and people? Then that man would be deemed worthy who had visited many places and seen many people. In this way we would make monks of travelers and merchants! Or, if a spiritual matter could be proved by a simple consideration of time, why could that person not become capable even of patience, gentleness, faith, and love if he had tested himself in them during that one year? Then there would be no need of God's grace to attain these virtues. It is sufficient for time to have passed, and as soon as the time has elapsed, he is capable of becoming a new man. Or, if time is not sufficient, why does it suffice only in the matter of chastity? I say these things so that you will see that there is nothing in the whole business of monasticism that is not singularly stupid and godless, clearly worthy of nothing but the papist kingdom.

But further, since Peter wants nothing to be done in the church unless it is quite certain that it springs from that power which God himself richly supplies [I Pet. 4:11], who will make them absolutely certain that this year of probation is sufficient in the sight of God? Who says that such a period of probation is approved by God? On the contrary, Peter says it is not approved by God because it is based on human resources. Yet when based on divine resources, there is no such thing as a year of probation, for the whole of life is the year of probation. It could happen that you lived in chastity not for one, but for two or even three years, but at the end of that time when the flesh burned and the blood was at fever heat, Satan blew his fiery breath and made the coals burn (as Job said [41:21]), and immediately you were no longer able to be continent. The real test of chastity, however, cannot take place when lust is dormant, but only when it is raging. But no one can tell the hour when lust is aroused and begins to rage, and that is the hour of testing. Why then do you figure this on a basis of time? Why do you call that probation which is no probation at all? I myself, along with many others, have experienced how peaceful and quiet Satan was wont to be in the first year of being a priest and monk. Nothing seemed more delightful than chastity. But this most insidious enemy did this to lead us into temptation and into his trap. These mad monks are working on his side! It is not only that they do not measure the year of probation by the Spirit, but they do not even measure it by its own principles. They measure it with a calendar by counting the days! They only prove that there is neither rhyme nor reason in them; they rush into spiritual and momentous considerations like brute beasts born to be slaughtered (as Peter puts it [II Pet. 2:12]). The year of probation depends just on foolish men who senselessly count off the days. It is not certain whether it pleases God, in fact, it is quite certain it displeases him. Since this is the case, by the very nature of the thing as well as by the authority of God, no precise period of probation can be indicated or laid down. On the contrary, the whole of life is of necessity a year of probation. You see, then, that the vow of chastity based on this year of probation amounts to nothing. There can never be any certainty about the vow because they themselves think that the vow must be subjected to a prior test which can never be certain and conclusive. Since their year of probation has been established by men, arbitrarily and of their own accord, the result is that the fulfilment of the vow must also be arbitrary. If they revoked and did away with the probationary year on which the vow depends, then they ought to revoke and do away with the vow.

But the most foolish thing of all was when they began to prescribe the age for the taking of vows. Some orders designated the age of fourteen; others, eighteen. I ask you, where do men get the right to prescribe in such matters? Some of these orders please me in at least one respect: they provide ample opportunity for monks who took vows before the age of eighteen to leave the monastery. This is the only thing I have noticed in monasticism which in my opinion is praiseworthy and evangelical, though this is not the case in all of the monasteries. It is regrettable that they do not do this in the case of those who took vows before they were sixty! To a certain extent they might then emulate Paul, who rejected widows of less than sixty years [I Tim. 5:9]. These were not to be enrolled and supported by the resources of the churches. In the case of men, since they have a more robust and stronger constitution than women and die later, they ought to be supported by the church only when they are seventy or eighty. On this point I regard the monks as completely fettered by their own legislation. If they absolve a young man who had taken vows before he was eighteen, and if there is no reason for prescribing this age except that of human opinion (for by the same token they could just as well set the age of thirty, forty, fifty, or sixty), then they ought to absolve anyone who has taken vows whatever his age. For it is not a commandment of God or a vow of God for which they have regard, but the frailty of a man under vows. They modify the rigor of a monastic vow with a sound and godly mercy to meet that very frailty. Now it can happen, and no man can prevent it, that a young man, or even a man of sixty, could be just as weak or even weaker in remaining continent and could be more thoroughly consumed by lust than an adolescent. If, therefore, lust and weakness are to be the determining factors in the vow and mercy the guide in interpreting a commandment (as indeed is the case, and always has been from the start), then all vows should henceforth be optional and subject to a time limit. If they do not do this, then clearly they are the most horrible and cruel murderers of souls. If, however, they think that it is not permissible to do this, then neither will it be permissible for them to absolve [anyone from the vow] before the eighteenth year, even if the candidate was a boy or child when he took his vows. A young man cannot be certain and does not know what it is to live in chastity, or indeed whether he is able to live in chastity at all, for he is only a boy or a child, as the case may be. Who knows what he may be able to do in the future? In baptism and the sacraments of God we are always quite certain what to expect or suffer, and that is things from God. Therefore, God's vows to us are good and faithful. Moreover, to vow things which do not lie within our power to vow is one and the same foolishness, and it is one and the same reason for making it null and void, whether it is the case of a child, a boy, a man, an old man, even all men.[147]

Let us then add a corollary to the matters we have settled, namely, the text from Mark 3 [2:25-28] where Christ hands down a faithful rule of mercy applicable to all laws when he says, "Have you not read what David did when he was in need and those who were with him, how he went into the house of God under the high priesthood of Abiathar and ate the shewbread which only the priests might lawfully eat, and he gave [some] to those who were with him? And he said to them: The sabbath was made for man, not man for the sabbath. And so the son of man is lord even of the sabbath." Christ said this. I beg you, let us not pass over these majestic words full of comfort and spiritual refreshment. Let us not heed them carelessly or treat them with coolness. In the first place, it is certain that the sabbath was divinely appointed. It was not invented [by man] but expressly commanded by God. With no less inflexible rigor the shewbread was prohibited to the laity. It was a law of God which applied to everyone. And yet David broke it without a pang of conscience because of his need. And when Ahimelech the priest was afraid and said, "I have only hallowed bread, which only the priests may eat," he was afraid because of the law. But David interpreted the law with confidence and said, "It is a common journey but their vessels are pure" [I Sam. 21:4-5]. This is exactly what Paul meant when he said, "To the pure all things are pure, but to the impure nothing is pure" [Titus 1:15].

Christ, in fact, makes this example into a general principle when he argued similarly and said David broke the law which prohibited the eating of hallowed bread. It therefore follows that it is permissible to break both the sabbath and all other laws. Unless this general deduction holds good, Christ is arguing a foolish case

[147] The following section, up to the Appendix, did not appear in the Wittenberg and Basel editions. *WA* 8, 662, n. 1.

by showing that the law concerning the sabbath may be broken on the basis of a very different law about not eating hallowed bread. Therefore, it is evident in this case that there is always an exception to divine laws in cases of need, not only in the interest of our souls, but even in consideration of our bodies as well as our material possessions. Any other law may be modified by the same argument which permits one law to be broken. This means that the law is to be interpreted and understood in the light of common sense as to what extent it is binding or not binding. In fact, the Scripture cannot be broken, John 10 [:35]. Further, "Not one jot or tittle of the law shall pass away till all be fulfilled" [Matt. 5:18]. So then, when we speak of breaking and violating the law, we must be understood not as speaking of rejecting a false interpretation, but of actually keeping the law in its true sense. In Matthew 12 [:5] Christ added that the sabbath was profaned by the priests in the Temple, but they were not blamed. It can even be broken to pull an ox out of a ditch or to lead it to water [Luke 13:15]. This means it can be broken not only in the interests of souls and of bodily welfare, but even for the sake of animals and of material things. This is only to say that God did not lay down his precepts that soul or body or substance might perish, but that they should be kept safe and sound in exercising his commandments. For this reason his commandments are always to be understood in such a way that in keeping them you do not forget that God created the body, the soul, and all their material belongings, and that he wants you to take care of them, so that if any of them is endangered, you may know at once that his precepts are precepts no longer.

Let us now turn to the matter we have been discussing. The vow of chastity is a purely bodily affair that concerns absolutely nothing but the flesh. Therefore, it can be abolished with absolute confidence. In fact, it was never binding, or could it ever be binding where it imperiled soul or body. A vow never demanded that you lose your soul and body. According to Christ's own interpretation the vow of chastity means this, "I vow chastity insofar as it is possible to do so without danger to the body or soul." If afterward you feel the surge of passion, then the vow is void and you may safely follow Paul's advice, "If they cannot be continent, let them marry," and again, "It is better to marry than burn" [I Cor. 7:9]. Did the Jews not vow the law of the sabbath and law of hallowed bread just as rigidly as you vow chastity? There is absolutely no difference. You may safely argue on the basis of Christ's principle that these men did break the law about the sabbath and about the shewbread because necessity demanded they do so and necessity interpreted the law's true meaning. I will break the law of the vow of chastity on the ground of a greater necessity as well as a greater danger to the soul. Fear not; Christ will not fail you. You are not really breaking the vow; you are laying hold of a sound interpretation of what the vow really means.

At this point some stupid fellow will say, "By the same argument adultery will be allowed, if necessity demands. Or, for that matter, murder or theft. All the precepts of God could be broken!" I reply: Such a necessity does not come about in practice. There are women, and there are men: marry, take a wife. There is danger neither to body nor possessions if you are gentle and control your temper. "But can you make out such a case for stealing?" I reply: If necessity demands, stealing is permissible.[148] Then the proverb is shown to be true, namely, "In necessity all things are common."[149] How foolish it would be, even godless, if you were to kill yourself by hunger for fear of the law when you could steal food from the abundance of another and thereby save your life. You are just as foolish if you do not take a wife when passion stirs and you remain continent to the danger of your soul. Under the stress of a consuming passion you must interpret the law of the vow as though the vow of chastity were not required, just as under the stress of hunger you would regard the law about stealing as if it did not exist. It seems that this was laid down even by Solomon in Proverbs 6 [:30-32], where the Hebrew literally says, "Men do not condemn a thief if he steals to feed himself because he is hungry. But if he be found, he shall restore sevenfold and shall give all the substance of his house. But whoever commits adultery with a woman is lacking in understanding and will destroy his soul." This means that a thief will not be condemned even if he is caught and punished

[148] Thomas Aquinas makes the same point. *Summa Theologica,* II, 2, ques. 32, art. 7. *WA* 8, 663, n. 1.
[149] Wander (ed.), *Deutsches Sprichwörter Lexicon,* III, 97.

before the law by someone determined to be without mercy, provided that he steals under the necessity of hunger.

What more shall we say? What do we read in Judges 21 [:19-23], where, with the approval of all Israel, the sons of Benjamin carried off the daughters of Shiloh for wives? Be that as it may. The sons of Israel sinned by taking a vow not to give their daughters in marriage, or at least by keeping their vow [Judg. 21:1]. But the sons of Benjamin did not sin in seizing the women since there were no other women at all for them to take in marriage, for both the Israelites and the Shilohnites had denied them their daughters. Yet how much less a thing is the theft of goods compared with the theft of daughters! This conduct was a violation and theft if you interpret the law strictly to the letter, that is, if you interpret it too scrupulously and stupidly. Therefore, the children of Israel make a sound spiritual interpretation of the affair when they say to the Shilohnites, "The sin is yours because you did not give your daughters when you were asked" [Judg. 21:22].

Indeed, relying on the authority of Christ, I for my part would venture to assert that if there are any sons or daughters who had taken the vow of chastity and were able to care for their parents in no other way except by marriage to a wealthy person who could support them, they ought to give up their vow and the life that goes with the vow. Those who chatter away with their nonsense about chastity being an incomparable treasure do absolutely nothing to meet this situation. Take the law of God concerning the sabbath, as well as the shewbread. Is obedience to these laws not an equally incomparable treasure? What is more precious than obedience? And yet God demands this obedience only in such a way that the body he created should not be destroyed by you or your possessions go up in flames. He demands these things to train the body in obedience. Otherwise, why has he not simply commanded us to kill ourselves, to crucify ourselves with illnesses and hunger? For what is the difference between commanding death, or at any rate bringing ourselves to death's door, and demanding the observance of a law which cannot be kept unless we bring ourselves to illness or death? Let such thinking about God be put out of our minds altogether. How much more ought a precept or a vow exacted to the danger of the soul be regarded as absolutely worthless!

To sum up the whole argument, when it comes to the mitigation of laws and their right interpretation the only safe guide is love. Whatever is contrary to love can in no circumstances be imposed, nor can any law be interpreted to work against love, for no case of hardship or necessity works against love. To put it another way, whatever is not against love is a matter of free choice, permissible and sanctioned, especially in cases of necessity. Paul stands on solid ground when he says boldly, "Owe no man anything but to love one another" [Rom. 13:8]. Who, I ask you, can set up another law as necessary which is over and above this law of Paul? And if it were to be established, vowed, and demanded, how can it take precedence, or how should it take precedence, since we are obliged to owe no man anything except to love one another? Therefore, we may keep the vow, but we are not bound to keep it, since nothing is binding on us except to love one another. Christ says in Matthew 7 [:12], "This is the law and the prophets." And in Matthew 22 [:40] he says, "On these two commandments depend all the law and the prophets." Therefore, nothing that is contrary to love, and nothing more than love, is or can be binding. It is now easy to see why there is no dispensation in cases of adultery, murder, unnecessary theft, and similar things. It is easy to see why dispensations can and ought to be made with respect to the vow of chastity and, in fact, in all vows, for love suffers in cases of adultery, murder, and theft. But in relaxing the vow of chastity, love suffers no harm and its interest is served. No one is harmed if you marry. In fact, just as you want to be permitted to marry if you so choose because passion consumes you, so you ought to want the same for someone else, as well. You should not only want this permission, you should help bring it about.

Christ confirms this view in Matthew 12 [:7] when he prefers mercy to all laws. He says to those sabbatarian Pharisees, "If you had known what the saying, 'I will have mercy and not sacrifice,' means, you would not have condemned the innocent." He says this because where necessity befalls a person or his property, a man must be merciful, and a law must not be interpreted as being against this kind of necessity. By the same principle he defended the disciples when they plucked ears of corn because they were hungry. In other words, they needed sympathy and kindness in that situation of need. By the same argument, if a strong sexual impulse demands the need for marriage, then the vow of chastity must give way to the dictates of mercy for even stronger reasons. God wants mercy much more than that horrid, constrained sacrifice of chastity. Therefore, our David may eat the forbidden bread with confidence and say, "The vow of chastity was made for man, not man for the vow of chastity. And so, the son of man is Lord of the vow as well as of chastity." It is not the same, however, in the matter of faith, because God does not exist on account of man; man exists on account of God. But I shall write at another time and place on the subject of that spiritual law.

Then let him give thanks who understands this truth, this sweet freedom of the faithful in Christ. Let him enter marriage with certainty and confidence if he cannot be continent. Let him despise these mad puppets and pawns, with their wicked, blasphemous laws at one moment and their threats at another. These men dare to commit blasphemy in that well-known sacrilegious decretal of theirs. *Clementis I de vita ac honestate clericorum,*[150] where they allege that a man cannot serve God in marriage. What is this but to argue that marriage is perfidy, impiety, and universal apostasy? Does this mean, O pope, you servant of Satan, that Abraham and all the patriarchs, Zachariah and Elizabeth did not serve God? What have I to do with such monstrous ideas which are even more monstrous than those who hold them? The decision is already made. We must avoid these people like the plague and put them to rout because of their excessive and blasphemous frenzy.

Consequently, when many argue that marriage is harmful and on that ground advise men to be continent, they understand the matter humanly enough, but also most foolishly. Does this mean

[150] *Clementis Papae V, Constitutiones,* lib. iii, tit. I, *de vita et honestate clericorum. CIC* 2, 1199. These decretals, promulgated by Clement V (1264-1314) in Vienne in 1311, were the last to be embodied in canon law. It is expressly stated therein that clergy who marry do so illegally and are to be deposed.

that you would teach men to avoid trouble by inviting them to martyr their conscience? We do not advocate marriage as an easy way out, nor do we hold out any promises that it will be such. We want it to be permitted, to be a matter of option, so that the man who is able may be continent for as long as he wants. We want the conscience to be free from offense, not from marriage. How much happier a state of affairs it is to tolerate a marriage irksome twice over than to be tortured by the constant pangs of conscience! This kind of trouble has been laid on us by God, and all the holy patriarchs have borne it.

Paul warned those about to marry of the same difficulty, but he did not dissuade them or condemn them. He said, "Such people will have tribulation of the flesh" [I Cor. 7:28]. But he does not say, "Do not take on this tribulation of the flesh." Nor does he say, "It is evil and to be condemned." In fact, marriage is beneficial if you enter it in a proper and God-fearing manner. The harmful thing is to be bound in chains for Christ's sake. But you would never turn a man from Christ for that reason, would you? Would you not rather encourage him to endure his chains steadfastly? As far as we are concerned, we are not writing for those who marry at leisure and for their own pleasure. They deserve hardship because of their pursuit of pleasure. We are writing for those who want to exchange the peril of salvation—man's proneness to sin and his inability to stay continent—together with the whole hell of their conscience, for any hardship or labor, for those who want to live nobly, not for pleasure. Let these people spend their days in the midst of good things. We for our part say to married people, "In the sweat of your brow you shall eat bread" [Gen. 3:19]. As far as you are concerned, do not ever believe that those who abstain from marriage to avoid harm are happy in their continence. Experience teaches how continent these distinguished despisers of marriage and boasters of chastity really are. The only people who are continent are not those who flee harm, but those to whom continence is given for the sake of the kingdom of heaven.

What concern of ours is it any longer what the papal bulls will say? Let us do good in good repute and in evil repute [II Cor. 6:8], for the Lord judges his people and all the earth with righteousness [Ps. 96:13]. All men are liars. God alone is true [Rom. 3:4]. Amen.

[Appendix]

Concerning Widows in Paul's First Epistle to Timothy, Chapter 5

One place is left which perhaps someone will think is in favor of vows. That is Paul's first letter to Timothy, chapter 5, where he speaks of apostate widows, in this fashion, "When they have begun to grow wanton against Christ they will want to marry, incurring condemnation because they have made their first pledge void" [vss. 11-12]. It is apparent that this is the text which that famous statement of Augustine came, in which he said that condemnation was incurred by nuns not only for marrying but even for wanting to marry.[151] But first, let us take a look at Paul. If Paul does not hold such a view, neither may Augustine. First of all it is certain that Paul was not talking about the institution of vows at all, for the early church never knew anything about this kind of vow. He is talking about widows who are supported by the church and cared for by the ministry of deacons, an example of which we read in Acts 4 [6:1-6]. This passage has nothing to do with monks and nuns. It deals with the matter of poor widows whose care the law of Moses stringently enjoins. In the very same chapter Paul insists that widows whose own relatives are able to support them ought not to be supported from the resources of the church. He says, "If any man who is a believer has widows [among his relatives] let him aid them and let not the church be burdened, so that the church may aid those who are widows in the full sense of the word" [vs. 16]. He follows this up by saying the same thing about widows who have parents or children. He says, "If any widow has children or grandchildren, let her first learn to rule her own house, and let these children serve their parents in their turn. This is acceptable to God" [vs. 4]. Paul regards as a widow in the full sense of the word a woman who has neither parents nor children nor anyone else to look after her. This is how he expresses it, "She is a real widow who

[151] Augustine, *De bono viduitatis*, IX. *MPL* 40, 437.

is left alone, who has set her hope in God, and who continues steadfastly in prayer and supplication day and night" [vs. 5].

Among widows Paul finds two kinds whom he condemns. The one kind are those who live for pleasure, that is, those who have inherited wealth and are rich, and therefore care only for their own interests. Of these he says, "She who lives for pleasure is dead while she lives" [vs. 6]. The other kind are those who have been accepted by the church because of their poverty. But because they were younger and were supported by the resources of others, they grew wanton. No one sought after these widows because they were poor. But now that they had grown fat on other people's resources, they were wantonly seeking to marry. But it is not because they wanted to marry that Paul condemns them, but rather because they had made their earlier pledge null and void. Paul says this expressly, "They have incurred condemnation because they have made their first pledge void." Otherwise, he would contradict himself when he goes on to say, "I would prefer that the younger widows marry and bear children" [vs. 14]. Pledge certainly cannot mean a vow in this context. First, they had not vowed to be widows. Second, nowhere in all of Scripture does faith mean a vow. Actually, it is faith in Christ which they have denied in order to marry and be more secure. They reverted to Judaism or heathenism, as both the circumstances as well as what follows prove. This is what follows, "For some are already turned aside after Satan" [vs. 15]. And again, "At the same time they learn to speak what they ought not" [vs. 13]. These things are quite certainly spoken of as apostasy from faith and doctrine, as is sufficiently well known.

Paul also expresses the same view in II Timothy when he writes, "Demas has forsaken me because he loves this present world" [II Tim. 4:10]. And again, "You know that all those who are in Asia have turned away from me." If they had not sinned in the matter of faith he would not have spoken of them in this way, but would have commanded them to concern themselves with these matters as he had commanded the Corinthians in the matter of fornication [I Cor. 5:1-5]. So we conclude that "first faith" means the Christian faith from which many in the early church were apostacizing, for the faith was as yet new. And the apostles censured this apostasy severely. The author of the Epistle to the Hebrews also inveighs against this apostasy when he asserts that those who have once lapsed cannot renew their salvation because they were of the opinion that they could be saved equally well by a different faith, either their old heathen faith or Jewish faith, which ever the case may be.[152] This passage has nothing whatever to do with vows, much less with the vows of religious orders. Further, it is strong evidence that Paul is speaking of faith in Christ when he says, "They grew wanton against Christ." To "grow wanton against Christ" means not just to go mad with the lust of the flesh, but to presume to strive against faith in Christ on account of our wantonness—and when faith in him has been denied, to start looking elsewhere.

But just suppose the Apostle were talking about vows and not widows. Then this text immediately supports our argument most effectively. No passage in all Scripture condemns vows and monks so powerfully and clearly. So much so that it is thoroughly to be wished that it referred to, or could be interpreted as referring to, vows. If he has vows in mind, it is clear that in the future vows are to be reproved and condemned in the same way as were those widows who sinned in the past. He says, "Refuse to support young widows" [vs. 9], and again, "I prefer that the younger widows marry." Well then, after this explanation of the Apostle it is no longer permissible for anyone to take vows before he is sixty years old. So choose whichever you wish. Either the Apostle is talking about vows, or he is not talking about vows. If he is not talking about vows, then this passage proves nothing. If he is talking about vows, then every person under vows prior to the age of sixty is reproved and condemned by none other than the Apostle. This supremely reliable authority will plead our cause so that the conscience will be absolutely at ease if a man annuls his vows.

To sum up, since more than enough has been said about this kind of life being contrary to the gospel because it finds sin in matters of food, clothing, drink, places, persons, works, acts, where Christ finds no sin but commands that there be freedom in everything; and since vows cannot exist unless they make sins of these

[152] Cf. Heb. 6:1-6.

things and ensnare consciences, as is absolutely clear to everybody (for vows would disappear at once if [people] thought that these things were optional and not binding on consciences); so it is at once absolutely clear that vows of this kind are null, unlawful, blasphemous, and contrary to the gospel. Therefore, it is not a matter of debating whether you take a vow with a godly or ungodly intent. The fact is that what you vowed is blasphemous. Therefore, it is the gospel in which you have to put your trust, and these vows, whatever the circumstances, whatever the intent, whatever the time they were uttered, are to be abandoned in complete confidence and a return made to the freedom of the Christian faith. This is my firm, undoubted conviction, for which I praise and give thanks to my most merciful Redeemer, our Lord Jesus Christ, who is blessed forever and ever. Amen.

This is all I wanted to say on monasticism for the time being. I shall say more if anyone attacks what I have said, although I am of the opinion that it is all supported by the Scriptures and sound reason in such a way that not only can it stop the mouths of enemies (to which I have given little consideration), but can even raise up consciences to stand before God with confidence and make them safe and sure (to which I have given the greatest consideration). It is certainly extremely difficult to cure those who are enmeshed in their daily regulations and customs, their anxieties and scruples, people who are overshadowed by the authority of holiness and the amount and weight of human authority, but above all, blinded by an abysmally wrong interpretation of divine Scriptures, and to convince them of so joyful a freedom, which they, sitting in their hell, have so long despaired. It gives me no pleasure that these ideas oppose and triumph over the pope and his synagogues, that vast herd of academies, monasteries, and colleges. What do we care what inspires this lost kingdom of the pope and his infinitely worse henchmen who behave like Turks, when I have long despised this kingdom? Our concern is to strengthen consciences against Satan in the hour of death and to restore them safe and sound to face the Son of man. Let men rave as they want. At least they will leave us alone when we die, whether they are vanquished or victors. But who can stand in the presence of Satan and before the judgment seat of God except the man who can stand firmly on solid ground made strong by the most certain warrant of the word of God, a man ready to hear whatever may be brought against him, able to say to God without hesitation or trembling of heart, "You, who cannot lie, have said these things"?

So, then, for Christ's sake, I beg all who want to follow my advice, who want to leave the monastery and regain freedom for themselves, that above all they examine their conscience, lest perhaps they attempt this either because they are led astray by the novelty of the thing or just out of contempt or hatred of their fellowmen. Such people will not stand in the hour of death when their conscience has been aroused and harassed by Satan because of their apostasy, their broken vow, and all the rest. They will direct their gaze to sacrilegious penance, and the last state will be worse than the first [Matt. 12:45]. The task at this point is to sustain oneself by depending mightily on the pure word of God alone, and not for a moment to shrink back from the judgment seat of God, since we know that he is true and cannot deny himself. The words that prevail here are those we laid down earlier, words in which Christ and Christ alone was set before us as our light and our leader, and in which whatever man has invented is condemned. Therefore, may he himself, our gentle leader and light, Jesus Christ, lighten our way and strengthen our heart with his own strength and his saving word unto eternal life. His is the glory and the dominion unto all ages. Amen.

Peter

"As free, but not as making liberty a cloak for malice,
but as servants of God" [I Pet. 2:16].

Paul

"You have been called to freedom: but do not make freedom an occasion for the flesh" [Gal. 5:13].

INDEXES

INDEX OF NAMES AND SUBJECTS

INDEX TO SCRIPTURE PASSAGES